IN THE DARKROOM

IN THE

DARKROOM

SUSAN FALUDI

WILLIAM
COLLINS

William Collins
An imprint of HarperCollins*Publishers*
1 London Bridge Street
London SE1 9GF
WilliamCollinsBooks.com

First published in Great Britain by William Collins in 2016
First published in the United States by Metropolitan Books,
Henry Holt and Company, LLC in 2016

This is a work of nonfiction. The names and identifying characteristics of
three individuals have been changed to protect their privacy.

A catalogue record for this book
is available from the British Library

ISBN (HB) 978-0-00-819349-2
ISBN (TPB) 978-0-00-819350-8

Designed by Kelly S. Too

Printed and bound in Great Britain by
Clays Ltd, St Ives plc

MIX
Paper from
responsible sources
FSC
www.fsc.org   FSC® C007454

For the Grünbergers of Spišské Podhradie and the Friedmans of Košice, and their children and their children's children, the family I found, and who found me

He thought about how he had been despised and scorned, and he heard everybody saying now that he was the most beautiful of all the beautiful birds. And the lilacs bowed their branches toward him, right down into the water. The sun shone so warm and so bright. Then he ruffled his feathers, raised his slender neck, and rejoiced from the depths of his heart. "I never dreamed of such happiness when I was an ugly duckling!"

Hans Christian Andersen, "The Ugly Duckling"

The identifying of ourselves with the visual image of ourselves has become an instinct; the habit is already old. The picture of me, the me that is *seen*, is me.

D. H. Lawrence, "Art and Morality"

Long ago
there was a strange deception:
a wolf dressed in frills,
a kind of transvestite.
But I get ahead of my story.

Anne Sexton, "Red Riding Hood"

CONTENTS

Preface: In Pursuit   1

PART I

1. Returns and Departures   5
2. Rear Window   17
3. The Original from the Copy   29
4. Home Insecurity   37
5. The Person You Were Meant to Be   47
6. It's Not Me Anymore   59
7. His Body into Pieces. Hers.   71
8. On the Altar of the Homeland   81
9. Ráday 9   103

PART II

10. Something More and Something Other   129
11. A Lady Is a Lady Whatever the Case May Be   147

12. The Mind Is a Black Box   165

13. Learn to Forget   179

14. Some Kind of Psychic Disturbance   203

15. The Grand Hotel Royal   221

16. Smitten in the Hinder Parts   235

17. The Subtle Poison of Adjustment   251

18. You're Out of the Woods   271

19. The Transformation of the Patient Is Without a Doubt   299

PART III

20. Pity, O God, the Hungarian   325

21. All the Female Steps   345

22. Paid Up   359

23. Getting Away with It   371

24. The Pregnancy of the World   389

25. Escape   407

IN THE DARKROOM

In Pursuit

In the summer of 2004 I set out to investigate someone I scarcely knew, my father. The project began with a grievance, the grievance of a daughter whose parent had absconded from her life. I was in pursuit of a scofflaw, an artful dodger who had skipped out on so many things—obligation, affection, culpability, contrition. I was preparing an indictment, amassing discovery for a trial. But somewhere along the line, the prosecutor became a witness.

What I was witness to would remain elusive. In the course of a lifetime, my father had pulled off so many reinventions, laid claim to so many identities. "I'm a Hungaaaarian," my father boasted, in the accent that survived all the shape shifts. "I know how to faaaake things." If only it were that simple.

"Write my story," my father asked me in 2004—or rather, dared me. The intent of the invitation was murky. "It could be like Hans Christian Andersen," my father said to me once, later, of our biographical undertaking. "When Andersen wrote a fairy tale, everything he put in it was real, but he surrounded it with fantasy."

Not my style. Nevertheless, I took up the dare with a vengeance, and with my own purposes in mind.

Despite the overture, my father remained a refractory subject. Most of the time our collaboration resembled a game of cat and mouse, a game the mouse generally won. My father, like that other Hungarian, Houdini, was a master of the breakout. For my part, I kept up the chase. I had cast myself as a posse of one, tracking my father's many selves to their secret recesses. I was intent on writing a book *about* my father. It wasn't until the summer of 2015, after I'd worked my way through many drafts and submitted the manuscript, and after my father had died, that I realized how much I'd also been writing it *for* my father, who, in my mind at least, had become my primary, imagined, and intended reader—with all the generosity and hostility that implies. It wasn't an uncomplicated gift.

"There are things in here that will be hard for you to take," I warned in the fall of 2014, when I called to announce that I had a completed draft. I braced myself for the response. My father, who had made a career in commercial photography out of altering images and devoted a lifetime to self-alteration, would hate, I assumed, being depicted warts and all.

"Waaall," I heard after a silence. "I'm glad. You know more about my life than I do." For once my father seemed pleased to be captured, if only on the page.

PART I

Returns and Departures

One afternoon I was working in my study at home in Portland, Oregon, boxing up notes from a previous writing endeavor, a book about masculinity. On the wall in front of me hung a framed black-and-white photograph I'd recently purchased, of an ex-GI named Malcolm Hartwell. The photo had been part of an exhibit on the theme "What Is It to Be a Man?" The subjects were invited to compose visual answers and write an accompanying statement. Hartwell, a burly man in construction boots and sweat pants, had stretched out in front of his Dodge Aspen in a cheesecake pose, a gloved hand on a bulky hip, his legs crossed, one ankle over the other. His handwritten caption, appended with charming misspellings intact, read, "Men can't get in touch with there feminity." I took a break from the boxes to check my e-mail, and found a new message:

To: Susan C. Faludi
Date: 7/7/2004
Subject: Changes.

The e-mail was from my father.

"Dear Susan," it began, "I've got some interesting news for you. I have decided that I have had enough of impersonating a macho aggressive man that I have never been inside."

The announcement wasn't entirely a surprise; I wasn't the only person my father had contacted with news of a rebirth. Another family member, who hadn't seen my father in years, had recently gotten a call filled with ramblings about a hospital stay, a visit to Thailand. The call was preceded by an out-of-the-blue e-mail with an attachment, a photograph of my father framed in the fork of a tree, wearing a pale blue short-sleeved shirt that looked more like a blouse. It had a discreet flounce at the neckline. The photo was captioned "Stefánie." My father's follow-up phone message was succinct: "Stefánie is real now."

The e-mail notifying me was similarly terse. One thing hadn't changed: my photographer father still preferred the image to the written word. Attached to the message was a series of snapshots.

In the first, my father is standing in a hospital lobby in a sheer sleeveless blouse and red skirt, beside (as her annotation put it) "the other post-op girls," two patients who were also making what she called "The Change." A uniformed Thai nurse holds my father's elbow. The caption read, "I look tired after the surgery." The other shots were taken before the "op." In one, my father is perched amid a copse of trees, modeling a henna wig with bangs and that same pale blue blouse with the ruffled neckline. The caption read, "Stefánie in Vienna garden." It is the garden of the imperial villa of an Austro-Hungarian empress. My father was long a fan of Mitteleuropean royals, in particular Empress Elisabeth—or "Sisi"—Emperor Franz Josef's wife, who was known as the "guardian angel of Hungary." In a third image, my father wears a platinum blond wig— shoulder length with a '50s flip—a white ruffled blouse, another red skirt with a pattern of white lilies, and white heeled sandals that display polished toenails. In the final shot, titled "On hike in

Austria," my father stands before her VW camper in mountaineering boots, denim skirt, and a pageboy wig, a polka-dotted scarf knotted at the neck. The pose: a hand on a jutted hip, panty-hosed legs crossed, one ankle over the other. I looked up at the photo on my wall. "*Men can't get in touch with there feminity.*"

The e-mail was signed, "Love from your parent, Stefánie." It was the first communication I'd received from my "parent" in years.

My father and I had barely spoken in a quarter century. As a child I had resented and, later, feared him, and when I was a teenager he had left the family—or rather been forced to leave, by my mother and by the police, after a season of escalating violence. Despite our long alienation, I thought I understood enough of my father's character to have had some inkling of an inclination this profound. I had none.

As a child, when we had lived together in a "Colonial" tract house in the suburban town of Yorktown Heights, an hour's drive north of Manhattan, I'd always known my father to assert the male prerogative. He had seemed invested—insistently, inflexibly, and, in the last year of our family life, bloodily—in being the household despot. We ate what he wanted to eat, traveled where he wanted to go, wore what he wanted us to wear. Domestic decisions, large and small, had first to meet his approval. One evening, when my mother proposed taking a part-time job at the local newspaper, he'd made his phallocratic views especially clear: he'd swept the dinner dishes to the floor. "No!" he shouted, slamming his fists on the table. "No job!" For as far back as I could remember, he had presided as imperious patriarch, overbearing and autocratic, even as he remained a cipher, cryptic to everyone around him.

I also knew him as the rugged outdoorsman, despite his slender build: mountaineer, rock climber, ice climber, sailor, horseback rider, long-distance cyclist. With the costumes to match: Alpenstock, Bavarian hiking knickers, Alpine balaclava, climber's harness, yachter's cap, English riding chaps. In so many of these pursuits, I was his accompanist, an increasingly begrudging one as I approached adolescence—second mate to his captain on the Klepper sailboat he built from a kit, belaying partner on his weekend assays of the Shawangunk cliffs, second cyclist on his cross-the-Alps biking tours, tent-pitching assistant on his Adirondack bivouacs.

All of which required vast numbers of hours of training, traveling, sharing close quarters. Yet my memory of these ventures is nearly a blank. What did we talk about on the long winter evenings, once the tent was raised, the firewood collected, the tinned provisions pried open with the Swiss Army knife my father always carried in his pocket? Was I suppressing all those father-daughter tête-à-têtes, or did they just not happen? Year after year, from Lake Mohonk to Lake Lugano, from the Appalachians to Zermatt, we tacked and backpacked, rappelled and pedaled. Yet in all that time I can't say he ever showed himself to me. He seemed to be permanently undercover, behind a wall of his own construction, watching from behind that one-way mirror in his head. It was not, at least to a teenager craving privacy, a friendly surveillance. I sometimes regarded him as a spy, intent on blending into our domestic circle, prepared to do whatever it took to evade detection. For all of his aggressive domination, he remained somehow invisible. "It's like he never lived here," my mother said to me on the day after the night he left our house for good, twenty years into their marriage.

When I was fourteen, two years before my parents' separation, I joined the junior varsity track team. Girls' sports in 1973 was a faintly ridiculous notion, and the high school track coach, who was first and foremost the coach of the boys' team, mostly ignored his distaff charges. I designed my own training regimen, leaving the house before dawn and loping the side streets to Mohansic State Park, a manicured recreation area that used to be the grounds for a state insane asylum, where I ran a long circuit around the landscaped terrain, alone. By then, I had developed a preference for solo sports.

Early one August morning I was lacing my sneakers in the front hall when I sensed a subtle atmospheric change, like the drop in barometric pressure as a cold front approaches or the prodromal thrumming before a migraine, which signaled to my aggrieved adolescent mind the arrival of my father. I reluctantly turned and made out his pale, thin frame emerging from the gloom at the bend of the stairs. He was wearing jogging shorts and tennis sneakers.

He paused on the last step and inspected the situation with his peculiar remove, as if peering through a keyhole. After a while, he said, "I am running also," his thick Hungarian accent stretching out the first syllable, "aaaalso." It was an insistence, not an offer. I didn't want company. A bit of doggerel, picked up who knows where, spooled in my head.

> Yesterday, upon the stair,
> I met a man who wasn't there
> He wasn't there again today
> I wish, I wish he'd go away . . .

I pushed through the screen door, my father shadowing my heels. The air was fat with humidity. Tar bubbles blistered the blacktop. I poked them with the toe of one sneaker while my father deliberated, turning first to his old VW camper, then to the lime-green Fiat convertible he had recently purchased, used, "for your mother." My mother didn't drive. "Waaall," he said after a while. "We'll take the Fiat."

We drove the five-minute route in silence. He wheeled into the lot of the IBM Research Center, a block from our destination. Prominent signs made clear that parking was for employees only. My father paid them no mind. He took a certain pride in pulling off small scams, which he called "getting awaaay with things," a predilection that led him to swap price tags on items at the local shopping center. He acquired a camping cooker in this manner, at a savings of $25.

"Did you lock your door?" my father asked as we headed across the lot, and, when I said I had, he looked at me doubtfully, then turned and went back to check. The flip side of my father's petty transgressions was an obsession with security.

We hoofed it down the treeless corporate drive to Route 202, the thoroughfare that runs along the north edge of the park. We dodged between speeding cars to the far side, and climbed over the metal divider, jumping down into the depression beyond it. My father paused. "It happened there," he said. He often talked this way, without antecedents, as if mid-conversation, a conversation with himself. I understood what "it" was: some months earlier, after midnight, teenagers returning from a party had run the stop sign on Strang Boulevard and collided with another car. Both vehicles had hurtled over the divider and landed on their roofs. No one survived. A passenger was decapitated. My father had been witness not to the accident itself but to its immediate aftermath. He was on call that night with the Yorktown Heights Ambulance Corps.

My father's eagerness to volunteer for the local emergency medical service had seemed out of character, at least the character I thought I knew. He shrank from community affairs, from social encounters in general. On the occasions when my parents had guests, my father would either sit mum in his armchair or take cover behind his slide projector, working his way through tray after tray of Kodachrome transparencies of our hiking expeditions, naming each and every mountain peak in each and every frame, recounting every twist and turn in the trail, until our visitors, wild with boredom, fled into the night.

He referred to his service with the ambulance corps as "my job saaaaving people." Which I also didn't understand. Our town was a place of non-events, the 911 summons a suburban emergency: a treed cat, a housewife having an anxiety attack, an occasional kitchen-stove fire. The crash in Mohansic State Park was an exception, although again there was no one to save. When my father arrived, the police were covering the bodies. The ambulance driver grabbed his arm. "Steve, don't look," my father recalled him saying. "You don't want that in your memory." The driver had no way of knowing the wreckage already lodged in my father's memory, and of how hard he had worked to erase it.

Leaving the old accident site behind, the two of us took off running along the paved road and into the picnic area, past rows of empty parking lots. The route began on a dull flat stretch of baseball diamonds and basketball courts, then looped around the giant public pool (where I worked summers at the snack stand) and along Mohansic Lake, finishing up a long hill. By the lake, we picked up a narrow footpath. We ran without speaking, single file.

At the final climb, the path gave way to wider pavement, and we began jogging side by side. Minutes into the ascent, he picked up his pace. I sped up. He ran faster. So did I. He pulled ahead again, then I did. We both gasped for breath. I looked over at him, but he didn't return my gaze. His skin was scarlet, shiny with sweat. He stared straight ahead, intent on an invisible finish line. All the way up the hill, the fierce mute maneuvering maintained. When the pavement flattened, I ached to ease the pace. My stomach was heaving and my vision had blurred. My father broke into a furious stride. I tried to match it. It was, after all, the early '70s; "I Am Woman (Hear Me Roar)" played on the mental sound track of my morning jogs. But neither my ardor for women's lib nor my youth nor all my training could compete with his determination.

Something about my father became palpable in that moment, but what? Was I witnessing raw aggression or a performance of it? Was he competing with his daughter or outracing someone, or something, else? These weren't questions I'd have formulated that morning. At the time, I was trying not to retch. But I remember the thought, troubling to my budding feminism, that flickered through my mind in the final minutes of the run: *It's easier to be a woman.* And with it, I let my legs slow. My father's back receded down the road.

At home in those years, my father was a paragon of the *Popular Mechanics* weekend man, always laboring on his latest home craft project: a stereo and entertainment cabinet, a floor-to-ceiling shelving system, a dog house and pen (for Jání, our Hungarian vizsla), a shortwave radio, a jungle gym, a "Japanese" goldfish pond with recycling fountain. After dinner he would absent himself from our living quarters—our suburban tract home had one of those living-dining open-floor plans, designed for minimal privacy—and descend the steps to his Black & Decker workshop in the basement. I did my homework in the room directly above, feeling through the floorboards the vibration of his DeWalt radial arm saw slicing through lumber. On occasion, he'd invite me to assist in his efforts. Together we assembled an educational anatomy model that was popular at the time: "The Visible Woman." Her clear plastic body came with removable parts, a complete skeleton, "all vital organs," and a plastic display stand. For much of my childhood she stood in my bedroom—on the vanity dresser that my father also built, a metal base with a wood-planked top, over which he'd staple-gunned a frilled fabric with a rosebud pattern.

From his domain in the basement, my father designed the stage sets he desired for his family. There was the sewing-machine table with a retractable top he built for my mother (who didn't like to sew). There was the to-scale train set that filled most of a room (its Nordic landscape elaborately detailed with half-timbered cottages, shops, churches, inns, and villagers toting groceries and hanging laundry on a filament clothesline) and the fully accessorized Mobil filling station (hand-painted Pegasus sign, auto repair lift, working garage doors, tiny Coke machine). His two children played with them with caution; a broken part could be grounds for a tirade. And then there was one of my father's more extravagant creations, a marionette theater—a triptych construction with red curtains that opened and closed with pulleys and ropes, two built-in marquees to announce the latest production, and a backstage elevated bridge upon which the puppeteer paced the boards and pulled the strings, unseen. This was for me. My father and I painted the storybook backdrops on large sheets of canvas. He chose the scenes: a dark forest, a cottage in a clearing surrounded by a crumbling stone wall, the shadowy interior of a bedroom. And he chose the cast (wooden Pelham marionettes from FAO Schwarz): Hunter, Wolf, Grandmother, Little Red Riding Hood. I put on shows for my brother and, for a penny a ticket, neighborhood children. If my father ever attended a performance, I don't remember it.

"Visiting family?" my seatmate asked. We were in an airplane crossing the Alps. He was a florid midwestern retiree on his way with his wife to a cruise on the Danube. My assent prompted the inevitable follow-up. While I deliberated how to answer, I studied the overhead monitor, where the Malév Air entertainment system was playing animated shorts for the brief second leg of the flight, from Frankfurt to Budapest. Bugs Bunny sashayed across the screen in a bikini and heels, befuddling a slack-jawed Elmer Fudd.

"A relative," I said. With a pronoun to be determined, I thought.

In September 2004, I boarded a plane to Hungary. It was my first visit since my father had moved there a decade and a half earlier. After the fall of Communism in 1989, Steven Faludi had declared his repatriation and returned to the country of his birth, abandoning the life he had built in the United States since the mid-'50s.

"How nice," the retiree in 16B said after a while. "How nice to know someone in the country."

Know? The person I was going to see was a phantom out of a remote past. I was largely ignorant of the life my father had led since my parents' divorce in 1977, when he'd moved to a loft in Manhattan that doubled as his commercial photo studio. In the subsequent two and a half decades, I'd seen him only occasionally, once at a graduation, again at a family wedding, and once when my father was passing through the West Coast, where I was living at the time. The encounters were brief, and in each instance he was behind a viewfinder, a camera affixed to his eye. A frustrated filmmaker who had spent most of his professional life working in darkrooms, my father was intent on capturing what he called "family pictures," of the family he no longer had. When my husband had asked him to put the camcorder down while we were eating dinner, my father blew up, then retreated into smoldering silence. It seemed to me that was how he'd always been, a simultaneously inscrutable and volatile presence, a black box and a detonator, distant and intrusive by turns.

Could his psychological tempests have been protests against a miscast existence, a life led severely out of alignment with her inner being, with the very fundaments of her identity? "This could be a breakthrough," a friend suggested, a few weeks before I boarded the plane. "Finally you get to see the *real* Steven." Whatever that meant: I'd never been clear what it meant to have an "identity," real or otherwise.

In Malév's economy cabin, the TV monitors had moved on to a Looney Tunes twist on Little Red Riding Hood. The wolf had disguised himself as the Good Fairy, in pink tutu, toe shoes, and chiffon wings. Suspended from a wire hanging off a treetop, he flapped his angel wings and pretended to fly, luring Red Riding Hood out on a limb to take a closer look. Her branch began to crack, and then the entire top half of the tree came crashing down, hurtling the wolf in drag into a heap of chiffon on the ground. I watched with a nameless unease. Was I afraid of how changed I'd find my father? Or of the possibility that she wouldn't have changed at all, that *he* would still be there, skulking beneath the dress.

> *Grandmother, what big arms you have! All the better to hug you with, my dear.*
> *Grandmother, what big ears you have! All the better to hear you with, my dear.*
> *Grandmother, what big teeth you have! All the better to eat you with, my dear!*
> *And the Wicked Wolf ate Little Red Riding Hood all up. . . .*

Malév Air #521 landed right on time at Budapest Ferihegy International Airport. As I dawdled by the baggage carousel, listening to the impenetrable language (my father had never spoken Hungarian at home, and I had never learned it), I considered whether my father's recent life represented a return or a departure. He had come back here, after more than four decades, to his birthplace—only to have an irreversible surgery that denied a basic fact of that birth. In the first instance, he seemed to be heeding the call of an old identity that, no matter how hard he'd run, he'd failed to leave behind. In the second, she'd devised a new one, of her own choice or discovery.

I rolled my suitcase through the nothing-to-declare exit and toward the arrivals hall where "a relative," of uncertain relation to me, and maybe to herself, was waiting.

2

Rear Window

In my luggage were a tape recorder, a jumbo pack of AA batteries, two dozen microcassettes, a stack of reporter's notebooks, and a single-spaced ten-page list of questions. I had begun the list the day I'd received the "Changes" e-mail with its picture gallery of Stefánie. If my photographer father favored the image, her journalist daughter preferred the word. I'd typed up my questions and, after much stalling, picked up the phone. I had to look up my father's number in an old address book.

A taped voice said, in Hungarian and then in English, "You have reached the answering machine of Steven Faludi . . ." By then, more than a month had passed since she'd returned from Thailand. I added another to my list of questions: *Why haven't you changed your greeting?* I left a message, asking her to call. I sat by a silent phone all that day and evening.

That night, in a dream, I found myself in a dark house with narrow, crooked corridors. I walked into the kitchen. Crouched against the side of the oven was my father, very much a man. He looked frightened. "Don't tell your mother," he said. I saw he was missing an arm. The phone rang. Jolted awake, I lay in bed, ignoring the summons. It was half past five in the morning. An hour later, I forced down a cup of coffee and returned the call. It wasn't just the early hour that had stayed my hand. I didn't want to answer the bedside extension. My list of questions was down the hall in my office.

"Haaallo?" my father said, with the protracted enunciation I'd heard so infrequently in recent years, that Magyar cadence that seemed to border on camp. *Hallo.* As my father liked to note, the telephone salutation was the coinage of Thomas Edison's assistant, Tivadar Puskás, the inventor of the phone exchange, who, as it happened, was Hungarian. "*Hallom!*" Puskás had shouted when he first picked up the receiver in 1877, Magyar for "I hear you!" Would she?

I asked about her health, my pen poised above my reporter's notebook, seeking safety in a familiar role. A deluge commenced. The notepad's first many pages are a scribbled stutter-fest of unfinished sentences. "Had to pick up the papers for the name change, but you have to go to the office of birth records in the Seventh District for—, no, wait a minute, it's the Eighth because the hospital I was born in—, waaall, no, let me see now, it maaay be . . ." "I'm so busy every day, I don't have time for dilation, and they tell you to dilate three times a day, four times at first, waaall, you can do it two times probably, but—, there are six of these rods, and I'm only on the number 3. . . ."

The operation, I noted, had not altered certain tendencies— among them, my father's proclivity for the one-sided rambling monologue on highly technical matters. When I was young, he had always operated on two modes: either he said nothing, or he was a wall of words, a sudden torrent of verbiage, flash floods of data points on the most impersonally procedural of topics. To his family, these dissertations felt like a steel curtain coming down, a screech of static jamming the airwaves. "Laying down covering fire," we had called it. My father could hold forth for hours, and did, on the proper method for wiring an air conditioner, the ninety-nine steps for the preparation of authentic Hungarian goose pâté, the fine print in the regulatory practices of the Federal Reserve, the alternative routes to the first warming hut on the Matterhorn, the compositional revisions to Wagner's score of *Tannhäuser*. My father had mastered the art of the filibuster. By the time he was finished, you'd forgotten whatever it was you'd asked that had triggered the oral counteroffensive—and were as desperate to flee his verbal bombardment as he was to retreat to his cone of silence.

"I could have gone to Germany, they cover everything," my father rattled on, "but they make you jump through so many hoops, and, waaall, in the U.S., the surgery is vaaary expensive and it's not in the front line, but, now, in Thailand, they have the latest in surgical techniques, the hospital has an excellent website where they go into all the procedures, starting with . . ." "I have to change the estrogen patch twice a week, it was fifty micrograms before the operation, but after the operation it gave me hot flashes, now it's twenty-five micrograms and . . ." "I got the first hair implant in Hungary, five hundred thousand forints, it came out pretty good, but it's still short in front, but maybe my hairdresser can do something, waaall, I could get another one, but it might be better in Vienna, yaaas but to go just for—, I'm taking hair growth medication, so—"

I quit trying to get it down verbatim.

"Long speech abt VW cmpr stolen," I wrote. "Thieves evywhre. Groc store delivry this wk., many probs." "Great trans sites online, evrythng on Internet, many pix dwnloaded."

My attempts to cut through his verbal eruption—"Why have you done this?"—only inspired new ones.

"Waaall, but you couldn't do it for a long time, waaall, you could, but it was risky. In Thailand, the hospital has greaaat facilities, faaantastic. In every room, bidets with special sprayheads, a unique nozzle that . . ."

I asked if she'd been dressing as a woman before.

"No. Waaall . . . Maybe a little. . . . I have to pick up the papers to get my passport changed, and I need to get my name changed with the Land Registry, but first you have to go to the municipality office and get a certificate to bring to the Ministry of . . ."

"Why didn't you tell us before you had the operation?"

"Waaall . . . I didn't talk until everything was all right, *successful*. Dr. Sanguan Kunaporn, he was faaantastic, trained with one of the leading surgeons of vaginoplas—, his name was—, it's—, no, wait—waaall, he is well-known as the best of—"

I lost my patience.

"You never talk to me. You aren't talking to me now."

Silence.

"Hello?" I ventured. *Hallom?*

"Waaall, but it's not my fault. You never came here. Every year, you never came."

"But you—"

"I have a whole dossier. They stole our property." My father was referring to the two luxury apartment buildings that my grandfather once owned in Budapest. They had been commandeered by the Nazi-allied state during the Second World War, nationalized under the Communist regime, and then sold off to private owners after 1989. "You showed no interest whatsoever."

"What am I supposed to do?"

"You're a journalist. You should at least somewhere mention it. They're consorting with thieves. Your country of birth, you know."

"Mention to whom?" I asked, thinking: *the country of* my *birth?*

"A family should work together to get back their stolen property. A normal family stays together. I'm still your father."

"You're the one who—"

"I sent you the notice about my school reunion, and you never came," my father said. The surviving members of my father's high school class in Budapest had gathered in Toronto three years ago. Guilty as charged: I didn't attend. "I sent you a copy of the movie I made of the reunion, and you never said anything." She wasn't finished. "One of my classmates lives near you, right in Portland, and I e-mailed you the Google map with his address, and you never contacted him. You never . . ."

I wasn't sure how to respond to this writ of attainder.

After a while, I said, "I'm sorry."

Then: "You said you were going to write my life story, and you never did."

Had I said that?

"Is that what you want?"

We both went mute. I scanned my list of questions. What I wanted to ask wasn't on the page.

"Can I come see you?"

I could hear her breathing in the silence.

In the arrivals hall at Ferihegy Airport, a line of people waited to greet passengers. I reluctantly scanned the faces. Maybe I wouldn't recognize him as her. Maybe she wouldn't be here. Maybe I could turn around and fly home. Salutations in two genders were gridlocked on my tongue. I wasn't sure I was ready to release him to a new identity; she hadn't explained the old one. Did she think sex reassignment surgery was a get-out-of-jail-free card, a quick fix to a life of regret and recrimination? I can manage a change in pronoun, I thought, but paternity? Whoever she was now, she was, as she herself had said to me on the phone, "*still your father*."

I spotted a familiar profile with a high forehead and narrow shoulders at the far end of the queue, leaning against an empty luggage cart. Her hair looked thicker than I remembered his, and lighter in color, a henna-red. She was wearing a red cabled sweater, gray flannel skirt, white heels, and a pair of pearl stud earrings. She had taken her white pocketbook off her shoulder and hung it from a hook on the cart. My first thought, and it shames me, was: no woman would do that.

"Waaall," my father said, as I came to a stop in front of her. She hesitated, then patted me on the shoulder. We exchanged an awkward hug. Her breasts—48C, she would later inform me—poked into mine. Rigid, they seemed to me less bosom than battlement, and I wondered at my own inflexibility. Barely off the plane, I was already rendering censorious judgment. As if how one carried a purse was a biological trait. As if there weren't plenty of "real" women walking around with silicone in their breasts. Since when had I become the essentialist?

"Waaall," she said again. "There you are." After a pause: "I parked the camper in the underground lot, it's a new camper, a Volkswagen Caaalifornia Exclusive, much bigger than my last one, the biggest one they make, the next-to-the-fastest engine, I got it from the insurance for the old one, it was one year on the market because the German economy is bad, the first one I bought was six years old, eighty thousand marks—forty-six thousand euros—fifty thousand dollars, the new one they sold to me for forty thousand euros, the insurance paid twenty thousand euros, it's parked by the guard booth, it's safer there, waaall, nothing's safe, thieves stole my old camper right out of the drive, I had the alarm on, they must've disabled it, climbed the fence, thieves were probably watching the house, they saw no one was home for weeks and—"

"Dad, Stefánie, how are you? I want—" My desire got lost in my own incoherence.

"—and they came right into my yard, and the neighbors did aaabsolutely nothing, no one saw anything, waaall, that's what they said. But they were great at Rosenheim, the man there was vaaary nice, he said to me, 'Oh, *meine gnädige Frau*, it's not safe for a woman to travel alone!' "

"Rosenheim?" I asked. I put my luggage on the cart, and she led the way to the parking garage. I trailed behind, watching uncomfortably the people watching us. The dissonance between white heels and male-pattern baldness was apparently drawing notice. Some double-chinned matrons gave my father the up-and-down. One stopped in her tracks and muttered something. I didn't understand the words, but I got the intent. When her gaze shifted to me, I glared back. *Fuck off, you old biddy*, I thought.

"Rosenheim VW," my father said, "in Germany, where I bought the new camper, aaand my old one, they do all my servicing and maintenance, aaand I register the camper there, you can't trust anyone else to work on it, waaall, they're German, they're very good, and the man was very courteous. Now that I'm a lady, everyone treats me very nicely."

We had no trouble finding the van. It was, as advertised in the brochure my father still had at home, VW's biggest model (eight and a half feet high), "Der California Exclusive." It looked like a cruise ship beached in a parking lot, a ziggurat on wheels. A heavily defended ziggurat: my father had installed a wrap-around security system, which she set off twice while trying to unlock the driver's door. Right there in the airport lot, she gave me the tour: the doll-sized kitchenette (two-burner gas cooker, fridge, sink, fold-out dining table, and pantry with pots and pans and well-stocked spice rack), a backseat bench that opened into a double bed (an overhead stowaway held duvet, linens, and pillows), a wardrobe with a telescopic clothesrail, and, in the very rear, a tiny bathroom and closet (with towels, toiletries, wall-mounted mirror). She opened up the cabinets to show me the dishware she'd just purchased, a tea service in a rosebud pattern.

I couldn't quite put the disparities into focus: *Motor Trend* meets *Marie Claire*. Was this why I'd flown fifty-six hundred miles?

Here we were, meeting after twenty-seven years, a high-stakes reunion after a historic Glasnost, and she was acting like she'd just returned from Williams-Sonoma by way of NAPA Auto Parts.

"Ilonka helped me pick it out," my father said, handing me a saucer to admire.

Ilonka—I had met her; for some years after my father returned to Hungary she'd been what he called his "lady friend." She had accompanied my father to a family wedding in California, but I hadn't gleaned much from our encounter: she spoke no English. I wasn't clear on their relationship—though Ilonka would tell me later that it was platonic. She was married and very Catholic. For years she seemed to function as an unpaid housekeeper for my father, cleaning, cooking, sewing. She helped him pick out the furnishings for his house, from the lace curtains to the vintage Hungarian Zsolnay porcelain (purchased to impress a snooty couple, distant kin of Ilonka's, who had come to dinner at my father's house one night; the husband had claimed to be a "count"). My father had taken Ilonka on trips around Europe and loaned money to her family. When one of her grandchildren was born, my father assumed the duties of godfather, now godmother.

"How is Ilonka?" I asked.

My father made a face. "I don't see her so much." She took the saucer from me and placed it carefully on the cabinet shelf with its mates. The problem evidently was Ilonka's husband. "It was fine with him when I was the man buying things for his wife and giving money to his family. But now that I'm a woman, I've been banished."

She shut and secured the cupboard doors. We went around to the front. It took some effort to hoist ourselves into the elevated cockpit. My father disengaged the clutch and shifted into reverse and we lurched backward, nearly plowing into a parked car. I noted with dismay that the makers of the well-appointed Exclusive had excluded one feature: a usable rear window. The tiny transom above the commode showed only empty sky.

At the pay booth, she fished through her purse for her wallet. The ticket taker, another Magyar babushka, stuck her head out the window and gave my father the once-over. As the bills were counted, I studied my father, too. I could see the source of her thickening hair (a row of implant plugs) and the lightened color (a dye job). Her skin had a glossy sheen. Foundation powder? Estrogen? What struck me most forcefully, though, wasn't what was new. I'd spotted it in the airport—that old nervous half-smile, that same faraway gaze.

On the road, she steered the lumbering Gigantor into the fast lane. It was rush hour. A motorist trailing us in a rusted subcompact blasted his horn. My father leaned out the window and swore at him. The honking stopped. "When they see I'm a laaady, they pipe right down," she said.

We merged onto a highway, and I gazed out the window at the dilapidated industrial back lots flying by, a few smokestacks belching brown haze, boarded-up warehouses with greasy windows, concrete highway dividers slathered in graffiti. We passed through a long stretch of half-finished construction, grasses growing high over oxidizing rebar. Along the shoulder, billboards proliferated, shiny fresh faces flashing perfect teeth, celebrating the arrival of post-Communist consumption: Citibank, Media Markt, T-Mobile, McDonald's. Big balls of old mistletoe parched in the branches of trees. Along the horizon, I could make out the red-roofed gables of a distant hamlet.

Half an hour later, we entered the capital. My father threaded the monster vehicle through the tight streets of downtown Pest, shadowed by Art Nouveau manses nouveau no longer, facades grimy and pockmarked by a war sixty years gone. A canary-yellow trolley rattled by, right out of a children's book. We drove past the back end of the Hungarian Parliament, a supersized gingerbread tribute to the Palace of Westminster. In the adjacent plaza, a mob of young men in black garb and black boots were chanting, waving signs and Hungarian flags.

"What's that about?" I asked.

No answer.

"A demonstration?"

Silence.

"What—"

"It's *nothing*. A stupid thing."

Then we were through the maze and hugging an embankment. The Royal Palace, a thousand-foot-long Neo-Baroque complex perched on the commanding heights of Castle Hill, swung into view on the far bank of the Danube, the Buda side. My father swerved the camper onto a ramp and we ascended the fabled Chain Bridge, its cast-iron suspension an engineering wonder of the world when it opened in 1849, the first permanent bridge in Hungary to span the Danube. We passed the first of the two pairs of stone lions that guard the bridgeheads, their gaze stoical, their mouths agape in perpetual, benevolent roar. A faint memory stirred.

The camper crested the bridge and descended to the Buda side. We followed the tram tracks along the river for a while, then began the trek into the hills. The thoroughfares became leafier, the houses larger, gated, many surrounded by high walls.

"When I was a teenager, I used to ride my bicycle around here," my father volunteered. "The Swabian kids would say, 'Hey, you dirty little Jew.'" She lifted a hand from the wheel and swatted at the memory, brushing away an annoying gnat. "Yaaas but," she answered, as if in dialogue with herself, "that was just a stupid thing."

"It doesn't sound—" I began.

"I look to the future, never the past," my father said. A fitting maxim, I thought, for the captain of a vehicle without a rear window.

Growing up, I'd heard almost nothing about the paternal side of my family. My father rarely spoke of his parents, and never to them. I learned my paternal grandfather's first name in 1967, when a letter arrived from Tel Aviv, informing us of his death. My mother recalled aerogrammes with an Israeli postmark arriving in the early years of their marriage, addressed to István. They were from my father's mother. My mother couldn't read them—they were in Hungarian—and my father wouldn't. My mother wrote back a few times in English, bland little notes about life as an American housewife: "Between taking care of Susan, cooking, and house-keeping, I'm very busy at home. . . . Steven works a lot, plus many evenings doing 'overtime.' " An excuse for his silence? By the early '60s, the aerogrammes had stopped.

I knew a few fundamentals. I knew my father's birth name: István Friedman, or rather, Friedman István; Hungarians put the surname first. He'd adopted Faludi after World War II ("a good authentic Hungarian name," my father had explained to me), then Steven—or Steve, as he preferred—after he'd moved to the United States in 1953. I knew he was born and raised Jewish in Budapest. I knew he was a teenager during the Nazi occupation. But in all the years we lived under the same roof, and no matter how many times I asked and wheedled and sometimes pleaded for details, he spoke of only a few instances from wartime Hungary. They were more snapshots than stories, visual shrapnel that rattled around in my childish imagination, devoid of narrative.

In one, it is winter and dead bodies litter the street. My father sees the frozen carcass of a horse in a gutter and hacks off pieces to eat. In another, my father is on a boulevard in Pest when a man in uniform orders him into the Grand Hotel Royal. Jews are being shot in the basement. My father survives by hiding in the stairwell. In the third, my father "saves" his parents. *How?* I'd ask, hungry for details, for once inviting a filibuster. Shrug. "Waaall. I had an arm-band." *And?* "And . . . I saaaved them."

As the camper climbed the switchbacks, I gazed out at the terra-cotta rooftops of the hidden estates, trying to divine the outlines of my father's youth. As a child and until the war broke out, he'd spent every summer in these hills. The Friedmans' primary address was on the other side of the Danube, in a capacious flat in one of the two large residential buildings my grandfather owned in fashionable districts of Pest. My father referred to the family quarters at Ráday utca 9 as "the royal apartment." But every May of my father's childhood, the Friedmans would decamp, along with their maid and cook, to my grandfather's other property in the hills, the family villa. There, an only child called Pista—diminutive for István—would play on the sloping lawn with its orchards and outbuildings (including a cottage for the resident gardener), paddle in the sunken swimming pool, and, the year he contracted rheumatic fever, lie on a chaise longue in the sun, tended by a retinue of hired help. As we ascended into the hills of Buda I thought, here I am in the city that was the forge of my father's youth, the anvil on which his character was struck. Now it was the stage set of her prodigal return. This proximity gave me a strange sensation. All my life I'd had the man without the context. Now I had the context, but with a hitch. The man was gone.

3

The Original from the Copy

I'd met the lions on the Chain Bridge before, when I was eleven. We were on a family vacation in the summer of 1970: my mother, my father, my three-year-old brother, and me. It was, all and all, a vexed journey. One evening we drove across the river to attend an outdoor performance of *Aida*. I remember the crossing for its rare good cheer; family trips were always fraught affairs. The car seemed to float over the Danube, the cable lights winking at us from above, the leonine sentries heralding our arrival to the city. My father reminisced about how his nurse used to push his pram past the lions and over the bridge to the base of the Sikló, a charming apple-red funicular that chugged up the Castle Hill palisade. He told us the story about the sculptor who had forgotten to carve tongues for the lions: a child had pointed out their absence at the opening ceremonies, and the humiliated artist leaped off the bridge into the Danube. It was a popular tale in Hungary, he'd said, but "probably not true."

Castle Hill, my father informed us, was honeycombed with subterranean caverns, carved out of the limestone millennia ago by thermal springs coming up "from the deep." The occupying Turks had turned them into a giant labyrinth. "They say Vlad the Impaler—the real-life Dracula!—was locked up down there." During World War II, the caves were retrofitted to accommodate air raid shelters and a military hospital. Thousands of the city's inhabitants took refuge here for the fifty days of the Siege of Budapest. "It's said that some people even had their mail delivered here," my father reported. "But that's probably a made-up story, too."

Some days earlier, we had driven to Lake Balaton, south of Budapest. I remember walking a long way out into the shallow lake, the water only reaching my thighs. No matter how far I fled from shore, I could still hear my parents, their voices raised in acrid argument. The sour climate extended beyond our domestic circle. A scrim of sullenness seemed to hang over every encounter: the long waits in queues to receive a stamp so that we could proceed to other long queues to be issued other certifications of approval from scowling apparatchiks; the pitiful settee spitting yellowed foam in the guest room my father had rented; our aged landlady's resentful eyes, sunk deep in a walnut-gnarled face, as she gave us each morning a serving of boiled raw milk, a thick curdled rind floating on its surface; the murky intentions of the "priest" in vestments who approached us one day after we'd toured the Benedictine monastery of Pannonhalma, asking my father if he'd deliver a letter to "friends" in the States—a government agent, my father said. The day we crossed the border into Hungary from Austria, customs officers combed through every inch of our luggage. My father stood to the side, uncomplaining, eager to please, a strange servility in his voice.

Throughout that visit, my father was in search of "authentic" Magyar folk culture. Driving through the countryside, we stopped to watch "traditional village dances" that were, in fact, staged tourist attractions: the government paid locals to whirl in what was billed as the national dress, the women in ornamental aprons and floral wreaths, the men in black vests and high leather boots. (As I'd learn later, the outfits and dances were only marginally traditional: they had been enshrined by urban nationalists in the mid-nineteenth century, and again in the interwar years, to create the impression of an ancient Magyar heritage.) In a village shop, my father insisted I try on folk dresses. As I modeled elaborately embroidered frocks, while cradling an elaborately clad Hungarian doll in my arms, my father took what felt like far too many rolls of film. The shop owner played stylist. Eventually my father purchased a lace-up bodice-and-dirndl number with a puffy-sleeved embroidered chemise, bell-shaped blue skirt, and a starched white apron with a tulip and rosebud motif. He thought I could wear it to school. His American daughter thought there was no way in hell she was going to junior high dressed as the Hungarian Heidi.

That fall, there ensued a series of tense standoffs over The Dress. My father would demand I put it on in the morning before school. I'd wait until he left for work, then run upstairs and change. He caught me once in suburban mufti. I was ordered to wear the costume to school the next day, which I did in a state of high mortification. Eventually he lost interest, and I banished the dress to the back of my closet. A year or so later, with hippie garb in vogue, I dug the offending garment out from its purgatory, detached the embroidered chemise from the rest of the outfit, and paired it with acid-washed jeans. It was my attempt at an au courant peasant look. Which was about as "authentic" as my father's Hungarian folk fashions.

The visual chronicle of this vacation resides in a stack of Kodak carousels that my father kept for the rest of her life in an attic closet, slide after slide of my mother and me and my brother in the shadow of Gothic cathedrals and castle ruins, leaning against the rails of a Danube cruise boat, waving from a train at a saluting Pioneer scout in starched uniform and red neckerchief, or staring up at the mammoth Hungarian Parliament topped by a red star. We often face away from the camera. Many of the shots are taken from a distance, as if my father were on safari, tracking a fleeing herd.

On that long-ago trip we took a break from sightseeing one day to visit two apartment buildings in Pest, fin de siècle Vienna-Secession edifices once grandly appointed, now derelict and coated in soot. Tatty shutters hung catawampus over the graceful arched windows of Váci út 28; the ceremonial balconies of Ráday utca 9 were visibly rotting. At Ráday 9, we climbed a set of dimly lit stairs to knock on a door. And toured a series of high-ceilinged rooms, partitioned now with plywood boards, shabbily furnished and overflowing with tenants, several families jammed into living quarters meant for one. I remember especially my father's distress. This building, like the other one, once belonged to my grandfather. The flat was my father's childhood domicile, the "royal apartment." On the sidewalk again, my father looked back up at the dingy facade of Ráday 9, where a blond girl in a white hair ribbon peered down from a crumbling double balcony, the one attached to the opulent rooms where a boy named Pista had grown up. He took a photograph. It was the last frame on the roll.

In 1940, when Pista turned thirteen, he'd received a Pathé 9.5mm movie camera. It was a bar mitzvah gift from his father. From then on—in Hungary where he joined an amateur film society during the war and a youth film club right after, in Denmark where he started a movie-distribution business, in Brazil where he made documentaries in the rain forests and on the pampas—my father would continue to prefer the moving picture over the still one. "With photography, you get one chance," my father told me once. "You're stuck with that shot. With film, you can cut it up and change it all around. You can make the story come out the way you want it."

For a brief time in my infancy, my father's filmmaking enterprises were domestic. In a box in my cellar, I possess the results, salvaged from a trash can, where my mother had relegated them after the divorce. A set of metal canisters holds the reels of the 16mm home movies my father had made from 1959 to 1961, the two years following my birth. My parents and I were living then in Jackson Heights, Queens, in a tiny upstairs rental in a brick duplex, and the films record the banal milestones of newlywed life: my mother large with child and eating pizza in her third trimester, my mother pushing a baby stroller and washing diapers in a plastic bucket, my first birthday, my first day at the beach, my first Easter Parade and Christmas. The "director," as my father listed himself in the credits, makes an occasional appearance. In a shot filmed with the aid of a tripod, my father poses just inside the front door of our apartment, impersonating the man he aspired to be. He is wearing a suit and tie, a herringbone coat, leather gloves, a fedora. His gaze is trained on the camera. He leans over to give my mother an awkward peck on the cheek. Then he gives a stagy wave and mimes something in the direction of my mother, his eyes still fixed on the lens, and heads out the door. It's a silent film, but I can script the "Father Knows Best" voice-over.

The longest reel is dedicated to Christmas. The camera lingers on the tree—reverential close-ups of frosted ornaments, tinsel strands, a large electric nativity star. Then a slow pan over the three red-and-white-striped stockings tacked to the wall in descending order. Poppa Bear, Mama Bear, Baby Bear. And finally the ceremonial unwrapping of the gifts: my father holds up each of his to the camera—tie, striped pajamas, Champion Dart Board. He mugs a forced grin and mouths, "Just what I wanted for Christmaaas!" My mother sits cross-legged on the floor in a ruffled blouse and pleated skirt, staring at her gifts with a wan expression: apron, bedroom slippers, baby-doll nightie.

In the final minutes of "Susie's First Christmas," the camera shifts to an eight-month-old me, wobbling to a precarious standing position before the full-length hall mirror, baby-fat fingers scrabbling along the slick surface for a purchase. I press my nose and then crush my whole face against the mirror, as if searching for something behind the reflection. What the film hid, I thought as I watched it decades later, was my father. Who was nowhere more absent than in the brief moments when he appeared on-screen, surrounded by the props of his American family, parading an out-of-the-box identity before the camera, splicing himself, frame by frame, into a man whose story had been replaced by an image, an image of anyone and no one.

By then, he was working in a darkroom in the city, commuting to a windowless chamber that would become as thoroughly his domain as our suburban basement. He became a master of photographic development and manipulative techniques: color conversions, montages, composites, and other transmutations of the pre-Photoshop trade. "Trick photography," he called it. He always smelled of fixer.

My father was particularly skilled at "dodging," making dark areas look light, and "masking," concealing unwanted parts of the picture. "The key is control," he liked to say. "You don't expose what you don't want exposed." In the aquarium murk where he spent his daytime hours, hands plunged in chemical baths, a single red safelight for navigation, he would shade and lighten and manipulate, he would make body parts, buildings, whole landscapes disappear. He had achieved in still photography what he had thought possible only in film. He made the story come out the way he wanted it to.

His talent made him indispensable in certain quarters—most notably in Condé Nast's art production department. From the '60s to the '80s, Condé Nast relied on my father to perform many of the most difficult darkroom alterations for the photography that appeared in its premier magazines, *Vogue, Glamour, House & Garden, Vanity Fair, Brides*. For years a note that one magazine art director had sent to another hung in my father's studio: "Send it to

Steve Faludi—don't send it to anyone else!" My father performed his "tricks" on the work of some of the most celebrated fashion photographers of the time—Richard Avedon, Francesco Scavullo, Irving Penn, Bert Stern—at several commercial photo agencies and, later, on his own at his one-man business, Lenscraft Studios, in a garment-district loft previously occupied by fashion photographer Hank Londoner. He also worked his magic on many vintage photographs whose negatives had been lost; he could create a perfect copy from a print. Among the classic images he worked on were those by the preeminent Hungarian photographer (and World War II Jewish refugee), André Kertész. My father's handiwork "was so precise and close and meticulous, there would be no bleeding of color or light," Dick Cole, the director of Condé Nast's art production department in that period, told me many years later, as we sat in his living room in Southern California, leafing through glossy coffee-table books that featured my father's artifice. "It was amazing. You could never tell what had been changed. You couldn't tell the original from the copy."

Occasionally as a small child I would take the commuter train to the city with my father and visit one of the series of Manhattan photo agencies where he worked. He'd lead me to the other side of the partitioned studio, where men perched on high stools before light tables, effacing with fine-tipped brushes the facial imperfections of fashion models. He regarded retouching as the crowning glory of the photographic arts. He would hold up the before-and-after shots of ad copy for me to appreciate. See, she no longer has that unsightly mole! Look, no more wrinkles! He admired the men bent over those light tables, obliterating blemishes. My father rarely involved himself with my educational or professional prospects. But he did, several times, advise me to become a retoucher. Which was peculiar counsel for a daughter who was consumed, from the day she first joined the staff of her grade school newspaper, with exposing flaws, not concealing them. At the heart of our relationship, in the years we didn't speak and, even more, in the years when we would again, a contest raged between erasure and exposure, between the airbrush and the reporter's pad, between the master of masking and the apprentice who would unmask him.

4

Home Insecurity

Hegyvidék (literally, "mountain-land"), the XIIth district of Budapest, is high in the Buda Hills. Always an exclusive enclave—home to embassies, villas, the residences of the nouveaux riches—its palatial properties were hot investments in post-Communist, new-millennial Budapest. As the broken-English text from one online real estate pitch I read put it, Hegyvidék is "the place where the luxury villas and modern detached houses—as blueblood estates—are ruling their large gardens in the silent milieu." To reach my father's address required negotiating several steep inclines and then a series of hair-raising tight turns on increasingly potholed and narrow roads.

"Damn Communists," my father said, as the Exclusive plunged in and out of craters in the macadam. "They never fix the streets."

"Weren't they fifteen years ago?" I said.

"Waaall, they call themselves the 'Socialists' now"—she was speaking of the party in power at the time—"but it's the same thing. A bunch of thieves."

The camper wheezed up the final precipice and around a tight curve. A house loomed into view, a three-story concrete chalet. It had a peaked roof and stuccoed walls. A security fence ringed the perimeter, with a locked and alarmed gate. A large warning sign featured a snarling, and thankfully nonexistent, German shepherd.

I wasn't sure whether the bunkered fortress was an expression of my father's hypervigilance or that of the culture she'd returned to. Later, I read Colin Swatridge's *A Country Full of Aliens*, a reminiscence of the British author's residence in Budapest in the '90s, and was struck by his remarks on the Hungarian fetish for home protection:

> You may peer at the grandiosity of it all—at the grey-brick drive and the cypress trees, and the flight of steps, and the juttings, and the recesses, and the columns and the quoins—but you may do this only through the ironwork of the front gates, under the watchful eyes of a security camera, and of movement-sensitive security lights. It is fascinating, this need to reconcile security and self-display. The house must show its feminine lacy mouldings, its leggy balusters, its delicate attention to detail, its sinuous sweep of steps; yet it must also show its teeth, and muscular locks, and unyielding ironwork. It must be at once coy and assertive, like a hissing peacock—a thing beautiful and ridiculous. . . .
>
> What is, perhaps, characteristically Hungarian about these green-belt houses, these kitsch castles in the Buda Hills and the Pilis Hills, by Lake Balaton and the Bükk, is the conflation of exhibitionism with high security. It is akin to the confusion of the feminine and the masculine that is a feature of the language.

I knew all about that linguistic confusion. It was a staple of my childhood. "Tell your mother I'm waiting for him," my father would say. Or "Your brother needs to clean up her room." Hungarians are notorious for mixing up the sexes in English. Magyar has no gendered pronouns.

My father steered the camper to the far shoulder and yanked on the parking brake. She teetered perilously across the road in her white heels and keyed in the code in a box installed on the defending wall, and the gate creaked open—and shut again as soon as we'd pulled through. The camper labored up the steep driveway and came to a halt in a grassy patch—it was too tall to fit in the house's two-car garage. A twenty-five-foot flagpole presided over the front lawn. It had three ropes, "so I can show all my flags," my father told me. "I put up the Hungarian flag on March 15"— National Day, commemorating Hungary's failed 1848 revolution against the Austrian Empire—"and the U.S. flag on July 4." The third rope periodically hoisted the banners of my father's other past residences, Denmark and Brazil.

My father scrambled down from the pilot's seat and swung her purse over one shoulder. We stood in the drive for what felt to me like a good quarter hour while she fussed with various security measures. First she had to reengage the VW's internal burglar alarm. Then she had to reset an outdoor surveillance system that "protected" the driveway. Once it was armed, we had sixty seconds to hurry to the front door, the one on the right. The house was a duplex; the other side-by-side identical unit, a doppelgänger residence, stood empty.

Before we entered, my father disarmed a third alarm system— and reactivated it as soon as we got inside. While she punched in numbers, I tried to find my bearings in the gloom. We were standing in a dark hallway. To the right was a stairwell, shrouded in shadow. Wooden steps ascended two levels. At the far end of the hall, through an open door, I caught a glimpse of yellow kitchen cabinets, the same cabinets that had adorned his Manhattan loft. (My father had shipped them, along with the refrigerator, dishwasher, oven, and everything else he owned at the time, including a giant stash of lumber and his VW van, in a forty-foot crate.) She led me down the hall and through another door on the left, which led to a large tiled living room and, off it, a dining room with a chandelier and a display case full of Zsolnay china.

A wall of glass with French doors overlooked the front terrace, but they, too, were dark, the thick drapes closed. "Someone could look in and want to steal my electronic equipment," she said. She had a lot of it to steal. A wall-mounted cabinet system in the living room was filled, floor to ceiling, with monitors, receivers, amplifiers, speakers, woofers, CD, DVD, VHS, and Betamax players, a turntable, even a reel-to-reel tape machine. The last served to play her old opera recordings, the same ones my father used to blast every weekend in our suburban living room in Yorktown Heights. A half dozen cabinets contained a thousand or more operas on CDs, tapes, videos, and record albums.

Bookshelves lined the opposite wall. On one end were all my father's old manuals on rock climbing, ice climbing, sailboat building, canoeing, woodworking, shortwave-radio and model-airplane construction. The My-Life-as-a-Man collection, I thought. Not that there was a corresponding woman's section. Other shelves were populated with works devoted to all things Magyar: *Hungarian Ancient History*, *Hungarian Fine Song*, *Hungarian Dog Breeds*, and thick biographies of various Hungarian luminaries, including a two-volume set of memoirs by Countess Ilona Edelsheim Gyulai, the daughter-in-law of Admiral Miklós Horthy, the Regent who ruled Hungary during all but the final months of World War II.

Another section of books belonged to a genre that was as lifelong a preoccupation of my father's as opera: fairy tales. Even as a girl, I understood that the puppet theater and the toy-train landscapes my father constructed were only ostensibly for his children. They gratified his craving for storybook fantasy. And the more extravagant the fantasy, the better. Likewise with opera. He hated a production that wasn't lavishly costumed and staged. The two obsessions were, in fact, conjoined. One of my father's most treasured childhood memories is of the night when his parents first took him to the Hungarian Royal Opera House. He was nine, and the opera was *Hansel and Gretel*.

"I wish I still had that book," my father said, gazing over my shoulder at her impressive assortment of fairy tales. She was referring to a children's anthology that the first of several nannies had read to Pista in his infancy. The nursemaid was German, and her mother tongue would become her young charge's first language. "Leather binding, thick pages, gorgeous illustrations," my father reminisced. "A gem. Whenever I go to a bookstore, I look for it." Over the years she'd amassed many similar volumes, most featuring the tales of her most beloved storyteller, Hans Christian Andersen. She owned editions of his works in Danish, German, English, and Hungarian. (And could read them all. Like so many educated Hungarians, my father was a polyglot, fluent in five languages, plus Switzerdeutsch.) In 1972, when we took a family vacation to Denmark, my father made repeated pilgrimages to the Little Mermaid statue in Copenhagen's harbor. I remember him standing for a long time by the seawall, pondering the sculpture of the sea nymph who cut out her tongue and split her tail to become human. I had studied him as he studied the statue, a girl in bronze on a surf-swept rock, her pain-racked limbs tucked beneath a nubile body, her mournful eyes turned longingly toward shore. My father had taken many pictures.

In idle moments on my first visit to Hegyvidék, and on the visits to come, I would take down from the shelf the English version of Hans Christian Andersen's collected stories and leaf through its pages, repelled and riveted by the stories of mutilation and metamorphosis, dismemberment and resurrection: The vain dancing girl who has her feet amputated to reclaim her virtue. The one-legged tin soldier who falls in love with a ballerina paper cutout and, hurled into a stove, melts into a tiny metal heart. The lonely Jewish servant girl who dreams her whole life of being a Christian—and gets her wish at the resurrection. And most famously, the despised runt of the litter who grows into a regal cygnet. "I shall fly over to them, those royal birds!" says the Ugly Duckling. "It does not matter that one has been born in the hen yard as long as one has lain in a swan's egg." And I'd wonder: if the duckling only becomes a swan because he is born one, if the Little Mermaid cleaves her tail only to return to the sea, what kind of transformation were these stories promising?

On still more shelves on the living-room wall kitty-corner to the electronic equipment, stacks of photo albums contained snapshots from my father's multiple trips to Odense, Andersen's birthplace. "I took Ilonka there once," my father said. "I think she was a little bored." Flipping through them, I was startled to find a familiar townscape: the distinctive step-gabled roof of Vor Frue Kirke (the Church of Our Lady), a GASA produce shop (a Danish market cooperative), and the half-timbered inn of Den Gamle Kro (there's an inn by that name a block from the Hans Christian Andersen Museum). Had my father reproduced the city of Odense in the train set he'd installed in our playroom? Later, when I inspected the two photos I still had of our childhood model railroad, I admired all the more the particularity of my father's verisimilitude. The maroon snout of the toy locomotive bore the winged insignia and royal crown of the Danish State Railway.

Above the Odense photo albums, on two upper shelves, a set of figurines paraded: characters from *The Wizard of Oz*. My father had found them in a store in Manhattan, after my parents divorced and he'd moved back to the city. They were ornately accessorized. Dorothy sported ruby-red shoes and a woven basket, with a detachable Toto peeking out from under a red-and-white-checked cloth. The Tin Man wore a red heart on a chain and clutched a tiny oil can. The Scarecrow spewed tufts of straw, and the Lion displayed a silver-plated medal that read COURAGE. My father had strung wires to the head and limbs of the green-faced Wicked Witch of the West, turning her into a marionette. I paused

before the dangling form and gave it a furtive push. The witch bob-
bled unsteadily on her broom.

My father pulled the drapes aside a few inches so we could slip
through a glass door onto the terrace. I'd asked to see the view. The
deck ran the length of the house and was lined with concrete flower
boxes. Nothing was growing in them, except weeds. "You have to
plant geraniums in May," my father said, by way of explanation.
In May, she had been lying in a hospital room in Thailand.

The lawn sloped steeply to the street. Down the center, a path
of paving stones was shaded by huge and gnarled chestnut trees,
an arboreal specter that put me in mind of Oz's Haunted Forest
("I'd Turn Back If I Were You . . ."). Smashed shells and shriveled
bits of nut meat littered the steps. From our aerie, you could see
down a series of hills to a thickly wooded valley. To the right of the
deck was a small orchard my father had planted when she first
moved in. She enumerated the varieties: sour cherry, peach, apri-
cot, apple, walnut. "Strange, though," she said, "this year they bore
no fruit." Her horticultural inventory reminded her of the long-ago
resident gardener who had tended the grounds of the Friedman villa
in the Buda Hills, the villa where my father had spent every summer
as a boy. "The gardener's family lived in the cottage on our property," she recalled.

She leaned over the far edge of the deck and pointed to a bunga-
low a half block below us, the only small structure on the street. "He
lives there," my father said.

"Who?"

"Bader."

"*Bader?*"

"*Baaader,*" my father enunciated, correcting both my pronun-
ciation and my failure to recognize the name. "Laci Baaader." Laci,
diminutive for László. "The gardener's son."

"You were playmates?"

"Haaardly. I was one of those." Jews, she meant.

"That's weird," I said.

"What?"

"The coincidence. His living on your street now."

My father didn't think so. "He lives in his father's house." The gardener's cottage that sat on my grandfather's property. She pointed to one of the residential McMansions a stone's throw from the Bader cottage. I could just see over the high concrete wall that moated it. It was, she said, the old Friedman villa. "There!"

The news rattled me. I had suspected that my father had purchased Buda Hills real estate as a way of recovering all that the Friedmans had lost. I hadn't understood that my father had bought a house directly overlooking the scene of the crime.

"Waaall, it *waaas* there," she amended. "They remodeled it, into that atrocity." Nonetheless, some weeks after my father had arrived in Budapest on an exploratory visit in 1989, he'd tried to buy the atrocity. "It wasn't for sale." When a house nearby came on the market that fall, he'd paid the asking price at once, $131,250, in cash.

The house proved to be a disaster zone of shoddy and half-finished construction. My father summoned Laci Bader. "He took one look and he said, 'This is no good!' " The roof was a sieve, the pipes broken, the insulation missing, the aluminum wiring a crazy-quilt death trap. "If you drilled into the wall, you'd get electrocuted." It took most of a year, and tens of thousands of dollars more, to make the place habitable.

The house still needed significant maintenance, for which my father often enlisted Bader. "Now that I'm a lady, Bader fixes everything," she said. "Men *have* to help me. I don't lift a finger." My father gave me a pointed look. "It's one of the great advantages of being a woman," she said. "You write about the disadvantages of being a woman, but I've *only* found advantages!" I wondered at the way my father's new identity was in a dance with the old, her break from the past enlisted in an ongoing renegotiation with his history. She hadn't regained the family property, but by her change in gender, she'd brought the Friedmans' former gardener's son back into service.

We went back inside, my father pulling the drapes shut again. She said she'd show me to my quarters. I followed her up the dark stairwell to the second floor, and into one of the three bedrooms.

"I sleep here sometimes, but I'm giving it to you because it's got the view," she said. She gestured toward the far wall of windows, which was shrouded in thick blackout liners covered by lace curtains. I inched the layers aside to see what lay behind them: closed casement windows that looked out over a concrete balcony, covered in dead leaves. A fraying hammock hung from rusted hooks. The walls were painted a pale pink and the room was blandly, impersonally furnished: a double bed in a white-painted wood frame, a white wooden wardrobe, a straight-back chair (an extra from the dining-room set downstairs), and an old television on a metal stand on wheels. A generic oil painting of a flower bouquet seemed to belong, like the rest of the decor, to a '60s Howard Johnson's.

"I had Ilonka sew this," my father said, gesturing toward the matching fuschia duvet cover and pillowcases. "I built the bed frame. And the wardrobe."

"You're still doing carpentry?"

She said her workbench was in the basement. "Like in Yorktown." She rapped her knuckles on the side of the wardrobe to demonstrate its solid craftsmanship. "You can hang your things in here," she said.

I opened the wardrobe doors. My father followed my gaze into its shadowy innards and grimaced. Stuffed inside her hand-built armoire was a full armament of male clothing: three-piece business suits, double-breasted blazers, pin-striped shirts, khaki trousers, ski sweaters, rock-climbing knickers, plaid flannel jackets, hiking boots, oxfords, loafers, boat shoes, silk ties, wool socks, undershirts, BVDs, and the tuxedo my father wore to a family wedding.

"I need to get rid of all of this," she said. "Someone will want these."

"Who?"

"Talk to your husband."

"He's not my—" My boyfriend and I wouldn't get married for a few more years. I could hear an old anxious hesitancy rising in my voice, which had suddenly lofted into helium registers. "He's not your size," I said, willing my voice to a lower pitch.

"These are quality clothes!" The hangars rattled as she slammed the closet door.

She left me to unpack. Ten minutes later, a summons from the adjoining bedroom. "Susaaan, come here!"

She was standing before a dressing table with a mirror framed in vanity lights. I recognized it: the makeup table for fashion models that used to sit in my father's photo studio in Manhattan. She held an outfit in each hand, a yellow sundress with flounces and a navy-blue frock with a sailor-suit collar. "Which should I wear?"

I said I didn't know. And thought, petulantly: change your clothes all you want, you're still the same person.

"It's hot out—I'll wear the sundress." She started peeling off her top. I backed toward the door.

"Where are you going?"

"To unpack."

"Oh, come now," she said, half in, half out of her blouse. "We're all women here."

She pulled the top over her head and gestured toward the closet. "Help me pick out the shoes to go with the dress."

I stood in the threshold, one foot in, one foot out.

My father gave me a familiar half-grin. "Come closer, I won't bite!"

5

The Person You Were Meant to Be

One evening in the early winter of 1976, an event occurred that would mark my childhood and forever after stand as a hinge moment in my life. The episode lay bare to my seventeen-year-old mind the threat undergirding the "traditional" arrangement of the sexes. Not just in principle and theory, but in brutal fact.

I was in my room, nodding over a book, when I was jolted awake by a loud crash. Someone was breaking into the house, and then pounding up the stairs with blood-curdling howls. It was my father, violating a restraining order. Six months earlier he had been barred from the premises. I heard wood splintering, a door giving way before a baseball bat. Then screams, a thudding noise. "Call the police," my mother cried as she fled past my room. When I dialed 911, the dispatcher told me a squad car was on its way.

"Already?"

Yes, the dispatcher said. Some minutes earlier, an anonymous caller had reported "an intruder" at the same address.

The police arrived and an ambulance. The paramedics carried out on a stretcher the man my mother had recently begun seeing.

He had been visiting that evening. His shirt was soaked in blood, and he had gone into shock. My father had attacked him with the baseball bat, then with the Swiss Army knife he always carried in his pocket. The stabbings, in the stomach, were multiple. It took the Peekskill Hospital's ER doctors the better part of the night to stanch the bleeding. Getting the blood out of the house took longer. It was everywhere: on floors, walls, the landing, the stairs, the kitchen, the front hall. The living room looked like a scene out of *Carrie*, which, as it happened, had just come out that fall. When the house went on the market a year later, my mother and I were still trying to scrub stains from the carpet.

The night of his break-in, my father was treated for a superficial cut on the forehead and delivered to the county jail. He was released before morning. The next afternoon, he rang the bell of our next-door neighbor, wearing a slightly soiled head bandage, trussed up, as my mother put it later, "like the Spirit of '76." He was intent on purveying his side of the story: he'd entered the house to "save" his family from a trespasser. My father's side prevailed, at least in the public forum. Two local newspapers (including one that my mother had begun writing for) ran items characterizing the night's drama as a husband's attempt to expel an intruder. The court reduced the charges to a misdemeanor and levied a small fine.

In the subsequent divorce trial, my father claimed to be the "wronged" husband. The judge acceded to my father's request to pay no alimony and a mere $50 a week for the support of two children. My father also succeeded in having a paragraph inserted into the divorce decree that presented him as the injured party: by withdrawing her affections in the last months of their marriage, my mother had "endangered the defendant's physical well being" and "caused the defendant to receive medical treatment and become ill."

"*I have had enough of impersonating a macho aggressive man that I have never been inside,*" my father had written me. As I confronted, nearly four decades and nine time zones away, my father's new self, it was hard for me to purge that image of the violent man from her new persona. Was I supposed to believe the one had been erased by the other, as handily as the divorce decree recast my father as the "endangered" victim? Could a new identity not only redeem but expunge its predecessor?

As I came of age in postwar America, the search for identity was assuming Holy Grail status, particularly for middle-class Americans seeking purchase in the new suburban sprawl. By the '70s, "finding yourself" was the vaunted magic key, the portal to psychic well-being. In my own suburban town in Westchester County, it sometimes felt as if everyone I knew, myself included, was seeking guidance from books with titles like *Quest for Identity*, *Self-Actualization*, *Be the Person You Were Meant to Be*. Our teen center sponsored "encounter groups" where high schoolers could uncover their inner selfhood; local counseling services offered therapy sessions to "get in touch" with "the real you"; mothers in our neighborhood held consciousness-raising meetings to locate the "true" woman trapped inside the housedress. Liberating the repressed self was the ne plus ultra of the newly hatched women's movement, as it was the clarion call for so many identity movements to follow. To fail in that quest was to suffer an "identity crisis," the term of art minted by the reigning psychologist of the era, Erik Erikson.

But who is the person you "were meant to be"? Is *who you are* what you make of yourself, the self you fashion into being, or is it determined by your inheritance and all its fateful forces, genetic, familial, ethnic, religious, cultural, historical? In other words: is identity what you choose, or what you can't escape?

If someone were to ask me to declare my identity, I'd say that, along with such ordinaries as nationality and profession, I am a woman and I am a Jew. Yet when I look deeper into either of these labels, I begin to doubt the grounds on which I can make the claim. I am a woman who has managed to bypass most of the rituals of traditional femininity. I didn't have children. I didn't yearn for maternity; my "biological clock" never alarmed me. I didn't marry until well into middle age—and the wedding, to my boyfriend of twenty years, was a spur-of-the-moment affair at City Hall. I lack most domestic habits—I am an indifferent cook, rarely garden, never sew. I took up knitting for a while, though only after reading a feminist crafts book called *Stitch 'n Bitch*.

I am a Jew who knows next to nothing of Jewish law, ritual, prayers. At Passover seders, I mouth the first few words of the kiddush—with furtive peeks at the Haggadah's phonetic rendition and only the dimmest sense of the meaning. I never attended Hebrew school; I wasn't bat mitzvahed. We never belonged to the one synagogue in Yorktown Heights, which, anyway, was so loosey-goosey Reform it might as well have been Unitarian. I'm not, technically speaking, even Jewish. My mother is Jewish only on her father's side, a lack of matrilineage that renders me gentile to all but the most liberal wing of the rabbinate.

So if my allegiance to these identities isn't fused in observance and ritual, what is its source?

I am a Jew who grew up in a neighborhood populated with anti-Semites. I am a woman whose girlhood was steeped in the sexist stereotypes of early '60s America. My sense of *who I am*, to the degree that I can locate its coordinates, seems to derive from a quality of resistance, a refusal to back down. If it's threatened, I'll assert it. My "identity" has quickened in those very places where it has been most under siege.

My neighborhood in Yorktown Heights was staunchly Catholic, mostly second-generation Irish and Italian, families who were one step out of the Bronx and eager to pull up the drawbridge against any other ethnicities or religions—in particular, blacks and

Jews. In the mid-'60s, when a petition circulated to block a black family from buying a home on the street, my mother squared off against the petitioners. The family eventually bought the house; my mother remained the neighborhood pariah. Soon after we arrived, a boy down the street welcomed me by hurling rocks while yelling, "You're a kike!" How he knew was a mystery: we'd shown no signs, and wouldn't. My father made sure we aggressively celebrated Christmas and Easter and sent out holiday cards with Christian images (The Little Drummer Boy, Little Jesus in the Manger ...). His eagerness to pass only reinforced my sense of grievance and, perversely, my commitment to an identity I barely understood. You could say that my Jewishness was bred by my father's silence.

And my womanhood bred by my mother's despair. When she gave up her job in the city (as an editor of a life-insurance period-ical) and moved to the suburbs, my father awarded her the various accessories to go with her newly domesticated state: a dust mop, a housedress, hot rollers, a bouffant wig (with Styrofoam head stand, on which the hairpiece was left to languish), and a box of stationery printed with a new name that heralded the erasure of hers, "Mrs. Steven C. Faludi." No doubt I learned some of my anti-nesting tendencies from my mother in this time. My father, for his part, was eager to present himself as a model of postwar American manhood, with wife and children as supporting cast, along with the convertible sports car (and before that, a Lincoln Continental), the saws and drills in the basement, the barbeque grill, the cigar boxes and pipe on the mantel, and the oversized armchair with a headrest in the living room that we all under-stood to be "his." The chair was his throne, proof of his dominion and dominance over his quarter-acre crabgrass demesne. We were careful not to sit in it.

When I was in grade school, my father bought me a tabletop weaving loom. After a halfhearted effort that produced a couple of uneven fabric coasters and one miniature scarf, I took the loom off my desk and stashed it in the closet—to make room for my writing pads. Journalism was my calling from an early age. I perceived it, specifically, as something I did as a *woman*, an assertion of my female independence. I worked my way through stacks of library books on intrepid "girl reporters" and imagined myself in the role of various crusading female journalists, fictional and real, Harriet the Spy and *His Girl Friday*'s Hildy Johnson, Ida B. Wells and Ida Tarbell. In my schoolgirl fantasies, the incarnation of heroic womanhood was Nellie Bly exposing the horrors of Blackwell Island's asylum for women, Martha Gellhorn infiltrating D-Day's all-male press corps (and one-upping her war-correspondent husband, Ernest Hemingway). On the Little Red Riding Hood stage that my father had built, I turned the girl in the red cape into an investigative reporter uncovering the crimes of a wolf who was now the Big Bad Warmonger (it was the Nixon years). By fifth grade, I was championing my causes in my elementary school newspaper—for the Equal Rights Amendment and legal abortion—incurring the wrath of the John Birch Society, whose members denounced me before the school board as a propagator of loose morals and a "pinko Commie fascist." The denunciations made me all the more a journalist, my sense of selfhood affirmed as that-in-my-makeup-that-someone-else-opposed. And all the more a defender of my gender. I asserted my fealty to women through my reportorial diatribes against the canon of womanly convention. I renounced the standards of femininity not to renounce my sex but to declare it. In short, I became a feminist.

That identity became explicit the day my teenaged self consumed Marilyn French's *The Women's Room*. I read that overwrought fulmination against suburban marriage in one sitting, shortly after my now-divorced mother had fled suburbia with her two children, resettling in a cramped two-bedroom apartment in the East Village in New York. But more accurately, my feminist consciousness emerged a season earlier, following a bloody night in a suburban house in 1976, seeing my mother unjustly demoted to "fallen" woman and my father falsely elevated to defender of home and hearth. I would spend the next many decades writing about the politics of women's rights, always at that one remove of journalistic observer. My subject was feminism on the public stage, in the media and popular culture, legislative halls and corporate offices. But I never forgot its provenance: this was personal for me.

Feminism, according to the insistent mantra, is all about "choice." Did I choose to be a feminist? Wasn't it also what I inherited, what I made out of a childhood history I couldn't control? I became an agitator for women's equality in response to my father's fury over his own crumbling sense of himself as a man in command of his wife and children. My identity as a feminist sprang from the wreckage of my father's "identity crisis," from his desperation to assert the masculine persona he had chosen. Feminism, as an avocation and a refuge, became the part of my life that I chose. The part I couldn't escape was my father.

The term "identity" is a hall of mirrors, "as unfathomable as it is all-pervasive," Erik Erikson asserted in 1968. He had coined the term (shortly before he coined the phrase "identity crisis"). But on the first page of his weighty tome on the subject, *Identity: Youth and Crisis*, he confessed he couldn't define it. The best he could hazard was that "a sense" of identity felt like a "subjective sense of an invigorating sameness and continuity."

A crisis seemed inevitable, given the murkiness of personal identity evident in subsequent definitions, like the one in the Oxford English Dictionary: "The fact that a person or thing is itself and not something else." Over the years, attempts to come up with "identity theory" have foundered. In 1967, sociologist Nathan Leites bemoaned (as recounted by UCLA colleague and transsexual-treatment pioneer Robert Stoller), "The term identity has little use other than as fancy dress in which to disguise vagueness, ambiguity, tautologies, lack of clinical data, and poverty of explanation." Mass popularization didn't help. In a 1983 essay titled "Identifying Identity," historian Philip Gleason observed: "As identity became more and more a cliché, its meaning grew progressively more diffuse, thereby encouraging increasingly loose and irresponsible usage. The depressing result is that a good deal of what passes for discussion of identity is little more than portentous incoherence." And yet, for all its ambiguity, the question of identity would define and transfix Erikson's age, and ours.

Identity as a concept didn't enter psychological theory until after World War II. When Erikson searched for antecedents in the utterances of his professional forebears, he found that Sigmund Freud invoked the term seriously only once, in an address to the Society of B'nai B'rith in Vienna in 1926. The founding father of psychoanalysis was describing what made him Jewish: "neither faith nor national pride," Freud confessed, but "many obscure emotional forces, which were the more powerful the less they could be expressed in words, as well as a clear consciousness of inner identity." In short, he felt like a Jew but couldn't say why.

Early on, Erikson counseled against the urge to define individual identity as something you acquire and display all by yourself. "Mere 'roles' played interchangeably, mere self-conscious 'appearances,' or mere strenuous 'postures,' " he wrote, are not "the real thing," although they are some of the prominent elements of "the 'search for identity.' " A sturdier selfhood, he maintained, emerges from the interplay between self-development and a collective inheritance. "We cannot separate personal growth and communal change," he wrote, "nor can we separate . . . the identity crisis in individual life and contemporary crises in historical development because the two help to define each other and are truly relative to each other."

Just as it is impossible to separate your individual identity from your social identity, Erikson held, so is it necessary to synthesize your past with your present, to incorporate all aspects of your

experience, even (or especially) the parts you prefer not to acknowl-
edge. When someone tries to deny unwanted history, "the diverse
and conflicting stages and aspects of life," and insists instead on a
"category-to-be-made-absolute," Erikson cautioned, "he restructures
himself and the world by taking recourse to what we may call *totalism*," an inner tyranny in which an internal despot patrols "an
absolute boundary," maintaining it regardless of whether the new
identity is organic or its components coherent.

Erikson famously failed to heed his own warning. In a 1975
article titled "Erik Erikson, the Man Who Invented Himself," philosopher Marshall Berman, Erikson's former graduate student,
detected a disturbing absence in his mentor's autobiographical
writings: Erikson had scrubbed his past. The erasure began with
the family name, Homburger, which he had first reduced to a middle
initial, "H.," then eliminated altogether. The deletion suggested to
Berman a more disturbing equivocation:

> As we unravel [Erikson's] story, we discover something else he
> cannot bear to say: that he is a Jew. We infer that his mother, "nee
> Karla Abrahamsen," was Jewish, and we read that his stepfather,
> Dr. Theodor Homburger, was not only a Jew, but a member of a
> synagogue. However, Erikson says of himself that as a child he
> didn't look Jewish: blond and blue-eyed and "flagrantly tall," he
> was jokingly "referred to as 'goy' in my stepfather's temple."

As an adult, Erikson reinforced that goyishness (along with
marrying an Episcopalian minister's daughter and displaying a
crucifix on the wall of his Harvard study) by adopting a new and
invented last name, one that implied not only gentile origins but
self-genesis. "I made myself Erik's son," he told a friend. "It is better
to be your own originator."

Better, that is, if you succeeded in shucking your provenance.
Had he? In a long letter to a social worker who had asked him to

describe his religious faith, Erikson wrote, "I know that nobody who has grown up in a Jewish environment can ever be not-a-Jew, whether the Jewishness he experienced was defined by his family's sense of history, by its religious observances, or, indeed, by the environment's attitudes toward Jews."

In *Identity: Youth and Crisis*, Erikson described a patient, a "tall, intelligent ranch owner" who had concealed his religious origins from everyone but his wife. Despite an outwardly successful life, he was plagued by "a network of compulsions and phobias" that derived from his childhood as an urban Jew. "His friends and adversaries, his elders and his inferiors all unknowingly played the roles of the German boys or the Irish gangs who had made the little Jewish boy miserable on his daily walk to school," Erikson wrote. "This man's analysis provided a sad commentary on the fact that [Nazi publisher Julius] Streicher's presentation of an evil Jewish identity is no worse than that harbored by many a Jew," even a Jew living as far from his collective past as the American West. "The patient in question sincerely felt that the only true savior for the Jews would be a plastic surgeon."

Whenever as a child I'd press my father on his Jewish heritage, and its banishment from our suburban home, he would dismiss my questions with a vaguely regal wave of the hand and a look of withering condescension. "That's not interesting," he'd say. Or, one of his trademark conversation-enders, "A *stupid thing*." Later, on my first visit to my father in Hungary, I'd ask why she'd changed the family name. In 1946, the Friedmans became the Faludis. It was eighteen-year-old István's idea. My father chose Faludi, she told me, for two reasons: it was an old Magyar name, meaning "of the village" (true Magyars hail from the countryside), and she'd seen it roll by on the credits of so many Hungarian films she'd adored as a boy ("Processed by Kovács & Faludi").

Had she also shed the name Friedman, I asked, because it sounded Jewish? My question prompted her usual gesture.

"I changed it because I was a Hungarian." She corrected herself, "Because I *am* a Hungarian. *One hundred percent Hungarian.*"

I was someone with only the vaguest idea of what it meant to be a Jew who was nevertheless adamant that I was one. My father was someone reminded at every turn that she was a Jew, who was nevertheless adamant that her identity lay elsewhere.

6

It's Not Me Anymore

My father stood in the doorway in her favorite crimson bathrobe; she wore it every morning of my first visit. It had a monkish cowl and angel-wing sleeves. She called it "my Little Red Riding Hood outfit." It wasn't entirely closed. "What are you doing?"

"I'm"—my voice squeaked; I looked down at the receiver in my hand—"phoning someone."

"Who?" She eyed me, suspicious.

"Just a friend of a friend," I said guiltily, though I was telling the truth. "She lives in Pest. She wanted to meet me."

"There's no time," my father said.

"I just—"

"You're only here another week."

I set down the receiver. *No time?* I thought. I'd been here four days, and we'd only left the house once—to pick up her new Web camera at Media Markt. My confinement had me wondering whether my father's elaborate home security system was meant to keep burglars from invading or guests from escaping. She kept the gate in the security fence locked on both sides. Merely to step

outside, I had to ask her for the key. Stefánie's Schloss was starting to
feel more like Dracula's Castle, and as the days passed, I was acting more and more like the passive captive, a character in one of
my father's treasured fairy tales, Rapunzel in the tower. Why didn't
I finish dialing the phone number? When my father refused to visit
her family's old summer villa a half-block away—a place I was
eager to see, having heard about it all my life—why didn't I just go
knock on the door? If she didn't want to venture out, why didn't I
hike down the hill and catch the bus into town? Instead, I retreated
to my room, made resentful cracks under my breath, and attempted
furtive phone calls when my father was out of earshot. I was slipping back into that twelve-year-old self, timid and sullen, fearful
of Daddy. Who was no longer Daddy.

Yet inside the ramparts my reclusive father seemed determined,
even desperate, to come out of hiding, or to bring at least one aspect
of herself out for inspection. That first week she'd led me up and
down the stairs, unlocking closets and cabinets, modeling outfits,
donning makeup, and reciting labels ("Max Factor English Rose
Lip Gloss," "Wet n Wild Cover-All Stick," "Vogue Self-Adhesive
100%-European-Hair Lashes, Trimmed and Feathered"). She was
introducing me to "Stefi," as she preferred to style herself, displaying the evidence of what she called "my new identity."

Including and especially the evidence of her new physique. The
robe seemed always to be falling open. Or the blouse. Or the nightgown. Every morning, she'd summon me to her room for wardrobe counsel. "Do these shoes go with this purse?" she'd ask, more
often than not standing in her underwear. *What does it matter*, I'd
mutter to myself, *we're not going anywhere.* Or she would barge
into my room on some pretext—"I think I left my stockings in
here"—to present her new body in a negligee. Her exhibitions felt
more like invasions. She said she was "showing" herself. But as the
shows piled up, so did my distrust. What lay behind the curtain of
her new transparency?

"This is where I put the things I wore when I first started 'dressing,' " my father said on the second morning of my visit. We were standing on the third-floor landing, before a large, gray-metal locker. She extracted from her apron pocket a key ring worthy of a prison warden. After a half dozen failed attempts and a lot of rattling, she found the one that opened the creaking door. The locker's contents might have outfitted a Vegas burlesque show: a sequin-and-beaded magenta evening gown with sweep train, a princess party frock with wedding-cake layers of crinoline, a polka-dotted schoolgirl's pinafore with matching apron, a pink tulle tutu, a diaphanous cape, a pink feather boa, a peek-a-boo baby-doll nightie with matching ruffled panties, a pair of white lace-up stiletto boots, a Bavarian dirndl, and wigs of various styles and shades—from Brunhilde braids to bleach-blond pageboy to Shirley Temple mop of curls. "Why do you keep this locked?" I asked.

"Waaall. . . . These clothes are more"—she considered—"flamboyant. They are from before the operation. Before I became a laaady. Now I dress sedate."

Another morning, my father summoned me to the two computers in her attic office. Under the eaves was her image palace. On one wall were two locked doors. The first led to her reconstructed photographic darkroom, which she had had crated and shipped from New York in the summer of 1990. And then never used. The digital age had made my father's talent for "trick photography" with film and print obsolete. Behind the second door was more photo equipment, including her old and giant photo-print drum dryer. The main room contained still more photographic supplies, several studio lights and jumbo rolls of paper for the advertising shoots she no longer conducted. An aluminum frame to hold backdrops was bolted into the floor.

The floor-to-ceiling shelves that wrapped around the central room held a video library: more than two thousand DVD, VHS, and Beta tapes of Hollywood epics, romantic comedies, Disney animations, TV sitcoms, mountaineering documentaries, and, to my dismay, a full set of Leni Riefenstahl films. ("Okay, she was a Nazi," my father conceded, "but a greaaat filmmaker!") She also possessed a vast array of digitized NASA footage—she subscribed to the space agency's daily e-mailed download—and a cache of flight-simulator games. At her request, I'd arrived with the latest edition of Microsoft's "takeoffs and landings" video, an unnerving item to be carrying in my hand luggage so soon after 9/11. My father wanted me to buy it in the States to avoid the import tax.

Tucked into the far alcove was my father's electronic command station. Here she trolled the blogosphere, Photoshopped her images, visited the lunar landscape, and piloted her virtual fighter jets. We fell into a routine the first week, sitting for hours every day in front of a computer monitor, my father at the keyboard, me in a folding chair by her side, reporter's notebook and tape recorder at the ready. Some mornings she wanted me to see all the cross-dressing Web links she had bookmarked to "My Favorites" in the years leading up to her operation: "Costume Wigs," "Fantasy Femmes," "Gender Bender," "Gender Heaven," "Just Between Us Special Girls," "Maid Service," "Miss Elaine Transformations," "Mrs. Silks," "Paper Dolls," "Petticoated.com," "Pink Gladiolas," "Sweet Chastity Online," "T-Girl Shopping," "Top Sissy Sites" . . .

"You can find everything on the Internet!" my father exulted.

The longer we spent in the third-floor garret viewing virtual non-reality, the more frantic I became to escape into the world beyond the perimeter. If I stood at the attic window and stretched on tiptoe, I could just make out, over the chestnut and fruit trees and down the sloping hills and across the river, Pest, that fabled cosmopolis, the historic venue of so much creative and cultural ferment. At the turn of the century, Pest had been host to a spec-tacular upwelling of artists and writers and musicians whose works had packed the museums and bookstalls and concert halls, who'd painted and scribbled and composed in the six hundred coffeehouses, published in the twenty-two daily newspapers and more than a dozen literary journals, filled the more than sixteen thousand seats of the city's fast-proliferating theaters and opera and operetta houses, and transformed the identity of the long backward capital into the "Paris of Eastern Europe." The city in my mind was the one I'd read about in John Lukács's *Budapest 1900*, the one the *London Times* correspondent Henri de Blowitz described in the late 1890s: "Buda-Pest! The very word names an idea which is big with the future. It is synonymous with restored liberty, unfolding now at each forward step; it is the future opening up before a growing people." Blowitz's city, I knew, belonged to a time long past. Still, my mind somehow wanted to hitch the city's old aspiration to my father's current one. Even when I was growing up, I'd felt that a key to my father's enigma must lie in that Emerald City of István Friedman's birth. I still couldn't dispel the notion that to understand Stefi, I had to see *her* in the world where *he* was from, visit the streets and landmarks and "royal apartment" that little Pista had inhabited. But Pest was down the hill, visible only on tiptoe.

On those mornings when we weren't lost in NASA rocket launches or Gender Heaven beauty tips, we were inspecting the images she'd assembled under "My Pictures." Few of them were actually *her* pictures; most had been lifted from the Web. An exception was her Screen Saver image, a photo of a servant girl in a French maid's outfit, a pink bow in her platinum blond curls. She had one white stiletto heel thrust out and was reaching down to adjust a stocking. The chambermaid was my father, who'd taken a selfie standing in front of a mirror.

Then there were the montages: images she'd pulled from various Internet pages, into which she'd inserted herself. All that long experience doctoring fashion spreads for *Vogue* and *Brides* had found its final form: Stefi's face atop a chiffon slip originally worn by a headless mannequin. Stefi implanted on the long legs of a woman ironing lingerie in a polka-dot apron. ("I added the apron," she said.) Stefi transported into an online Christmas card of a girl wearing a red ruffle around her neck and not much else. Stefi in a pink tutu and ballet slippers, captured in mid plié. Stefi in another maid's outfit, this one belonging to a little girl, who was being disciplined by a stern schoolmarm in tweeds and lace-up boots. The girl held the skirt up in back to reveal her frilly underwear.

"I did these before I had the operation," my father said, "but it was too extreme. Transvestite pretension."

The theme of "before" and "after" was a recurrent one in these viewing sessions. My father seemed intent on drawing a thick line between her pre- and post-op self, as though the matron respectability she'd now achieved renounced her earlier sex-kitten incarnations, made them into a "flamboyance" that she no longer needed or recognized.

"What's that?" I asked, pointing to a link she'd bookmarked called FictionMania. I was hoping for narrative relief from the onslaught of images. "Oh, people make up these stories about themselves and post them on this site," she said. "We don't need to look at that."

"Stories?" I pressed. I'd look it up later: FictionMania was one of the largest transgender fantasy sites on the Internet, a repository for more than twenty thousand trans-authored tales, the vast majority of them sexual. A popular story line involved a dominatrix (often a female relative) forcing a cowed man into feminine undergarments, dresses, and makeup. The genre had a name: "Forced Feminization Fiction."

"You know, stories," my father answered, "like they're little boys and their mothers make them dress up as a girl as punishment and then their mothers spank them. And they have illustrations." I reached for the mouse to click on the link. My father pushed my hand aside. "I wouldn't even share that with a psychiatrist." Not that she had one; she regarded psychiatry as one of those "stupid things" best given a wide berth. I asked if she had ever posted a story on the site.

"No, I just used some of the pictures they have on here. For my montages," pasting her face onto one or another costumed playmate. She'd done more than that, though. Her upstairs hall closet contained stacks and stacks of file folders of forced feminization dramas she'd downloaded from FictionMania and similar sites, in which she'd montaged her names into the text (Steven "before," Stefánie "after"). Her stash showed a predilection for subjugation and domestic service, often set in Victorian times: "Baroness Gloria, the Amazing Story of a Boy Turned Girl" (in which Aunt Margaret in Gay Nineties Berlin disciplines her nephew into becoming a corseted "real lady") or "She Male Academy" (in which Mom sends her misbehaving son to the Lacy Academy for Young Ladies, a "vast mansion designed in the Victorian Gothic manner," where whip-wielding mistresses exact a transformation: "Steven will become Stefánie; his bold, brash and arrogant male self will be destroyed and replaced with the dainty, mincing and helplessly ultra-feminine personality of a sissy slave girl"). Along with the altered downloads were a few stories my father had written herself. Her character stayed true to form, submitting to the directives of a chief housekeeper while an all-female crew of iron-handed maids order "Steven" into baby-doll nighties, Mary Jane shoes, and a French chambermaid's uniform.

At the computer, my father had moved on to another page of links. "I haven't looked at that website for two years at least," she said of FictionMania. "It was just a—, like a hobby. Like I used to smoke cigars, but I gave it up. This was all *before*."

"And now?"

"Now I'm a real woman," she said. "But I keep these pictures as souvenirs. I put a lot of work into them; I don't want to throw them out."

She hadn't stopped montaging; she'd only shifted genres. She showed me a few of her more recent constructions. Now she was the lady of the house: Stefánie in a long pleated skirt and high-necked bodice. Stefánie with hair swept up into a prim bun and holding the sort of large sensible pocketbook favored by Her Majesty the Queen of England. This was certainly a persona shift from the "sissy slave girl" in Mary Janes, or at least an age adjustment. And yet, it seemed less a repudiation of her erotica collection than a culmination of it.

The sex fantasies and lingerie catalogs in my father's file folders in the hall closet were commingled with printouts of downloaded how-to manuals on gender metamorphosis ("The Art of Walking in Extreme Heels"), many of them narrated by virtual domina-trixes: "This is your first step on your journey into femininity, a journey that will change your life," read the introduction to "Sissy Station," a twenty-three-step electronic instructional on "finding your true self" by becoming a woman. "You will be humiliated and embarrassed. Most of all, you will be feminized." The journey required, in different stages, applying multiple coats of red toenail polish every four days, beribboning testicles, and practicing sub-mission with sex toys before a mirror.

"There isn't any one way to be a trans," a trans friend cau-tioned me some years later. "I think of transsexuality as one big room with many doors leading into it." My father's chosen door was distinct. But the big room, like any condo, had its covenants and restrictions. A reigning tenet of modern transgenderism holds that gender identity and sexuality are two separate realms, not to be confused. "Being transgender has nothing to do with sexual orientation, sex, or genitalia," an online informational site instructs typically. "Transgender is strictly about gender identity." Yet, here in my father's file folders was a record of her earliest steps toward gender parthenogenesis, expressed in vividly sexual terms. And here in FictionMania and Sissy Station and the vast electronic literature of forced feminization fiction was a transgender id in which becoming a woman was thoroughly sexualized, in which femininity was related in terms of bondage and humiliation and orgasm, and the transformation from one gender to another was eroticized at every step. How to tease the two apart?

My father clicked the mouse and a greeting card popped up: Stefi's visage pasted onto a frilled lace gown, hands clutching a bouquet, above the card's preprinted message, "Wish I could be a bridesmaid on your Wedding Day!"

"You sent this card?"

"Not this one. I've sent others."

"To?" Who, I wondered, was the bride she wished she "could be a bridesmaid" for?

"Other trans friends," my father said.

"People you know?"

"People who have websites. You know, 'Internet friends.'"

My father had bookmarked some of these "friends'" websites: Annaliese from Austria who, according to her page, "dresses sexy," is "a size 12," and "loves to go shopping." Margit from Sweden, who "loves" bustiers, plush teddy bears, and "the color pink." Genevieve of Germany, whose blog featured shots of herself topless on a nude beach and a timeline of "my second birth."

"These pictures aren't retouched," my father said, unimpressed. "They aren't as good as mine."

"Where are your family photographs?" I asked. Suddenly, I'd had all I could handle of bustiers and second births. "From your childhood."

My father gave her dismissive wave. "I don't look at those."

"But where are they?"

Silence. Then, airily: "Oh, somewhere."

"Somewhere *where*?"

She shrugged, kept clicking through her images. Finally: "I keep all the old stuff, the important documents, in the basement. In a lockbox."

"Could I see them?"

"It's irrelevant," she said. "It's not me anymore."

I looked at the clock; the day was half over. Day Five in the fortress.

"Dad, Stefi, please," I said. "Let's go out. You can show me the places you love in the city. Show me where you used to go in Pest as a child."

"It doesn't pay to live in the past," my father said. "'Get rid of old friends, make the new!'"

"I don't think that's how it goes," I said. At any rate, I was here to see if I could make a new sort of friend: her. If only she could drop her age-old obstinance long enough to allow it. But our interactions were persistently one way: instead of mutual exchange, a force-fed guided tour of frou-frou fashions and hard-drive fantasies. When was she going to let in the daughter she wouldn't let out?

"I don't want to go to old places," my father said. "It's not interesting."

"It interests *me*," I said, hating my whininess, my own age-old obstinance.

"You are off the subject," she said, tapping an insistent pink-polished nail on my notepad. "I'm Stefi now."

One late afternoon, we stood in the kitchen, my father peeling an apple with her latest Swiss Army pocket knife. It was the "ladies'" version, she noted, with an emery board and cuticle scissors.

"Can I ask *you* a question?" my father said.

I nodded, hopeful. She was never the one who asked the questions. Maybe this was the start of an actual conversation.

"Can you leave your door open?" she said. "You close it every night when you go to bed."

I drew back, speechless.

"Can you leave it open?"

"Why?"

"Because I want to be treated as a woman. I want to be able to walk around without clothes and for you to treat it normally."

"Women don't 'normally' walk around naked," I said.

The blade snapped shut, and the conversational opportunity, if that's what it had been, shut with it. She returned her ladies' knife to an apron pocket.

That night, I closed the bedroom door. Then I reconsidered, and opened it a crack. As much as her intrusions disturbed me, I sensed that she wasn't really targeting me. Or, if she was, it was only me as a mirror. After a while, a hesitant knock.

"Can you help me with something?"

My father was standing with her back to the door. She was in her bedroom slippers but still wearing her dress.

"I can't get the zipper. . . . Will you do it?"

I stood there for a moment, then reached for the zipper pull. I stopped when it was halfway down her back.

"You can get it from there," I said.

"Thanks," she said.

"You're welcome."

I watched her pad back down the hall. And wondered: how could someone so hidden be so intent on being unzipped? If, indeed, that's what she wanted. All these exposures and disclosures seemed, literally, skin deep.

In the days to follow, my father continued her guided tour of surface ephemerality, leading me through the dresses in her closets, the lingerie in her bureau drawers, the cosmetics in her vanity table, the estrogen patches and dilation rods in her medicine chest, all the secret curiosities in her many Cabinets of Wonder. I couldn't tell if she thought she was dispensing revelations or distracting me from the real secrets. Look at me, but don't look at me. As the daughter of a photographer, I knew that letting light into a darkroom can illuminate the evidence or destroy it, depending on your timing. My father and I were in a battle over time, past and present. She wanted me to admire the decorations in Stefi's new display windows. I wanted to know the contents of another sealed chamber: the lock-box in the basement.

7

His Body into Pieces. Hers.

On the sixth day of the visit, my father decided to lift the house arrest. "If you want to see something authentically Hungarian," she said, "we could go to the Castle District."

The Castle District, the former domicile of nobility, sits atop the two-hundred-foot-high limestone escarpment of Castle Hill, over-looking the Danube on the Buda side. It is now a high-toned tourist trap, home to the Royal Palace and, perched above that, the colon-naded Fisherman's Bastion, a viewing terrace and promenade of turrets and parapets from which seemingly every panoramic pic-ture postcard of Budapest is taken. It is as removed as my father's own redoubt from the city I wanted to see. Still, it was out of the house.

We rode over in Der California Exclusive in the early afternoon. My father dressed for the excursion in a polka-dotted skirt, white-heeled sandals, and her usual pearl earrings. "Before I decided on Stefánie," my father told me, "I was thinking of naming myself Pearl."

"Why?" I asked.

"I like how it sounds," she said. "Pearl" in Hungarian, which also serves as a female name, is Gyöngy. I flashed on one of my father's attempts at forced feminization fiction, titled *Gyöngyike Becomes a Maid: Confession of Sissy Gyöngyike—Let the Party Start.* "Anyway," my father said, "I love pearls."

"And Stefánie?" I pressed. I knew that it was also the name of one of my paternal grandmother's three sisters. "Did you pick it for your aunt Steffy?"

My father shrugged. No more divulgences were forthcoming.

There was no place to park and we made many circles in the camper before my father backed into a space of questionable legality. "It doesn't matter if I get a ticket," she said. "The camper's registered in Rosenheim. They can't get me." She reached for the two cameras she'd brought, strapping one to each shoulder. I put my notebook in my back pocket. I was wearing blue jeans.

We descended the cobblestoned steps to the broad forecourt of the Royal Palace, a magisterial muddle of Neo-Medieval and Neo-Baroque architecture, topped off by a gigantic dome in the shape of a studded helmet. Presiding over the parade grounds was a heroic equestrian statue of Prince Eugene of Savoy, whose armies beat back the Turks from Hungarian territory in 1717, and a giant bronze of the Turul, the mythical bird that, according to legend, engendered the country's thousand-year Magyar rule, the fabled "Hungarian Millennium." The Royal Palace was now showcase to the National Library, the National Gallery, and the Budapest History Museum, a diadem set atop the city, containing the glittering artifacts of Hungarian antiquity and culture. I was pleased. Not only had I convinced my father to leave her own castle on the hill, I'd managed to get her to visit a palace that housed her past—or at least her nation's past. Or at least the past her nation claimed to have, for its history was as shrouded in fancy as my father's.

The Hungarian Millennium is said to have begun when Árpád and six other Magyar chieftains rode over the mountains from somewhere in the East and conquered the great Carpathian Basin sometime in the ninth century, setting the stage for their heirs to establish a Christian monarchy, the Hungarian Kingdom, sometime around the year 1000. What actually happened is hard to say. The story of the "Magyar Conquest" is derived from the *Gesta Hungarorum*, an account written three hundred years later by a royal notary identified as P. dictus magister ("P. who is called master"), who drew on folk ballads, medieval romances, and the Bible to create a cast of Magyar heroes and the enemies that they allegedly vanquished. The Árpád dynasty, in any event, was extinct by 1301. Kings drafted from foreign dynasties (but generally claiming a drop of Árpád blood) occupied the throne for the next two centuries. And for even more centuries the country was ravaged by invasions, defeats, and occupations from foreign forces—Mongols, Turks, Russians, Habsburg Austrians, Germans, and Russians again. With few exceptions, Hungary's liberators, like so many of the country's most celebrated figures, were "foreign," too. As Paul Lendvai observed in *The Hungarians: A Thousand Years of Victory in Defeat*:

> One of the most astounding traits of Hungarian history, subsequently suppressed or flatly denied by nationalistic chroniclers, is that the makers of the national myths, the widely acclaimed heroes of the Ottoman wars, the political and military leaders of the War of Independence against the Habsburgs, the outstanding figures of literature and science, were totally or partly of German, Croat, Slovak, Romanian or Serb origin.

In other words, not Magyar.

Hungary achieved its cultural zenith in Europe's Belle Époque—under the rule of the Austrian Habsburgs. In 1867, Habsburg emperor Franz Josef loosened the reins by creating the Austrian-Hungarian Monarchy—usually called the Dual Monarchy—a compromise that granted Hungary a large measure of self-determination and ushered in a cultural and economic revival. The country's long sense of itself as an autonomous kingdom seemed validated, though the Dual Monarchy's sole monarch was still Franz Josef. The fall of the Austro-Hungarian Empire at the end of World War I finally brought full independence, albeit with destruction hot on its heels.

The Treaty of Trianon, the 1920 peace agreement reached at the Grand Trianon Palace in Versailles, forced Hungary to relinquish a whopping three-fifths of its population and two-thirds of its landmass to the successor states of Romania, Czechoslovakia, Yugoslavia, and Austria. If the nation was thus constricted, its self-image as sacrificial lamb was confirmed. "We are the most forsaken of all peoples on this earth," Hungary's national poet Sándor Petőfi had written in the mid-nineteenth century. After Trianon, Hungary became all the more a martyr among nations, a people identified by its stigmata. "The realm held together by the Holy Crown has been dismembered, and the lopped off limbs of the Holy Crown's body are faint with the loss of blood," jurist Kálmán Molnár pronounced at the time, in language as typical as it was overheated. "In a swoon, they await death or resurrection." To Hungary's more recent irredentists, Trianon remains the unholy desecration, a devastating wound, an appalling act of national identity theft undimmed by the passage of more than eighty years.

My father and I headed for the Hungarian National Gallery, which was offering a retrospective of Mihály Munkácsy. The celebrated Hungarian painter had been born and buried in Hungary, but little else. Born Michael von Lieb to German parents, he was trained in Munich and Düsseldorf, spent most of his career in Paris, and died in a sanitarium in Germany. Nonetheless, he was one of Hungary's most venerated artists—venerated especially for having been celebrated as a "great Hungarian" in the world beyond Hungary. After Munkácsy's death in 1900, the authorities gave him a state funeral in the city's sacred Heroes' Square, his body displayed, beside the plaza's galloping statuary of the seven Magyar chieftains, on a forty-five-foot-high catafalque surrounded by flaming bronze torches.

The museum's ticket taker, another crabby granny, scowled at my father as she handed us our passes. I couldn't tell if the disapproval registered; my father gave no sign. In the exhibition hall, I gravitated to Munkácsy's earliest efforts, bleakly realistic renderings of impoverished peasant life. (The desperate conditions of the rural Magyar populace, deep in semifeudal penury well into the twentieth century, earned Hungary the moniker "The Country of Three Million Beggars.") My father frowned; this period didn't put Hungary in a "positive" light. "You're making too much of that," she said, pulling my sleeve as I lingered before paintings of careworn women gathering firewood and tending to hungry children. My father was eager to move on to Munkácsy's later and more famous creations: the salon portraits of fashionable Austro-Hungarian aristocracy and the epic extravaganzas of biblical dramas and victorious scenes from the Magyar Conquest. "This is *authentic* Munkácsy," my father said, directing me to the walls that displayed the artist's final blast of bombastry.

When we'd exhausted the Technicolor lollapaloozas, she led the way to the permanent collection, a labyrinth of galleries dominated by lugubrious melodramas of Magyar affliction displayed in heavy gilt-edged frames. I sped through the next dozen halls showcasing scenes from Hungary's genesis—from the heralded arrival of Prince Árpád to the nineteenth-century revolution led by Lajos Kossuth, "The Father of Hungarian Democracy"—and sank onto a bench in a corridor to wait for my father. The room was hushed and dark; light filtered weakly through a set of high grated windows. I thought of catacombs, and that endless trip we took as a family to Hungary in 1970, when my father was so insistent that we tour the nation's cathedrals and monasteries. Endless, that is, from the perspective of an eleven-year-old who experienced the sepulchral quarters, the cloying smell of candle wax, and the echo of heels

clattering on yet another cold marble ambulatory as her own private purgatory. Why, I wondered, did we never visit a synagogue?

There was no sign of my father. A stout matron in a guard uniform inspected me darkly from her wooden chair in the corner.
Maybe it was me. Maybe these battle-axes weren't staring at my
father in a dress, after all. Maybe they disapproved of a girl wearing jeans. Or maybe they just didn't like foreign women. After a
while, I got tired of the evil eye and retraced my steps. I found my
father many rooms back, transfixed before Gyula Benczúr's *The
Baptism of Vajk*, an operatic depiction of the tenth-century chris-
tening of Hungary's first king. The Magyar tribesman Vajk kneels
bare-shouldered before the holy font and gilded chalice, about
to shed his pagan name and receive his new Christian one: István,
Stephen. My father's namesake.

I studied the baptism of the former Vajk over the former István's
shoulder.

"Isn't it a bit"—I searched for the proper word—"histrionic?"

"It's a work of true greatness," she said with a flourish of matching grandiosity, her polka-dot skirt billowing with her enthusiasm.
"It's characteristically Hungarian."

In an eggheaded attempt to prepare for my visit, I'd read István
Bibó's scathing inspection of "Hungarianism," in an essay published
at the end of World War II. The political scientist saw his country's
identity as Potemkin, a society "deceiving itself" and held together
by little more than "wishful" thinking and "frills and veneers."
"Today's Hungarians are among Europe's least well-defined groups,"
Bibó wrote—and Hungarianism a "grand illusion." As I recalled
Bibó now, the afternoon's displays threatened to turn hallucino-
genic. Everything we were looking at seemed oddly, fatally confectionary, the face of a nation montaged onto one fantasia after
another: The anointed Saint Stephen was the "patriarch" whose patrimony had no heirs; Prince Eugene was the (French-born) Austrian
Imperial Army general who freed Hungary from the Ottoman

Empire only to hand it over to the Habsburgs; Lajos Kossuth was the Father of Hungarian Democracy whose 1848 bid for Hungarian independence (celebrated every March 15 on National Day) was stillborn; the Turul was mythical herald to a thousand-year Magyar reign that never hatched.

I considered the illusions hanging from these walls. As we worked our way back through the echoing galleries, I looked at my father in her polka dots and the image that flashed momentarily through my brain was of a tour guide in theme-park costume, leading me through a tarted-up history that concealed a darker past, a Tinker Bell guide to a storybook culture, neither person nor place what they really were. What the Magyars were was humiliated. Just about every power that had ever dealt with Hungary—whether the Mongols in 1241 or the Turks in 1526 or the Austrians in 1711 and 1848 or the Soviets in 1956—had seen fit to kick it in the teeth.

In the next station of our Castle Hill cultural tour (the Budapest History Museum), my father lingered admiringly before another hagiographic painting of another lionized Hungarian. This one was at least more modern than Vajk. He was dressed in a naval uniform, pinned with rows of medals: the Hungarian Regent, Admiral Miklós Horthy, whose governance of the country from 1920 to 1944 encompassed the arc of my father's youth. Her reverence for the man who presided over the deportation of nearly a half-million Jews galled me.

A make-believe royal, I pointed out. (Horthy was elected Regent by the Hungarian National Assembly in 1920, intended as a placeholder for the exiled Habsburg king, who never reclaimed the throne.) And what's with the "Admiral"? A navy in a landlocked state?

"You don't know anything," my father said. "Trianon took away the Hungarian coast. A tragedy. A *catastrophe*."

She was right about the coast. The treaty at the end of World War I, which dealt Hungary the harshest penalties of any warring state (including Germany), had stripped the nation of its seaports, along with 65 percent of its waterways, 88 percent of its forests, and all of its coal, salt, and silver mines. In the Second World War, Horthy's Hungary would ally itself with the Axis in hopes of resurrecting "the lost territories" (and Hitler, indeed, returned two land parcels that Trianon had lopped off). When my father and I would finally make it down into the city, I'd notice the ubiquitous image—plastered on walls, affixed to bumpers, appliquéd onto backpacks—of the map of pre-Trianon "Greater Hungary," also known as "the mutilated motherland." The map featured the nation as a butchered torso, surrounded by its four severed appendages. The defenders of Hungarian honor call Trianon "the amputation."

"It destroyed the motherland!" my father said now, her voice rising. "It cut his body into pieces."

"Hers," I corrected.

My father hiked up her purse on a camera-burdened shoulder and headed for the exit.

We left the museum and, instead of descending to the streets of the city I so wished to visit, we climbed even higher to Fisherman's Bastion. My father wanted to take some "panoramic" pictures.

A turnstile blocked the entrance. You had to buy a token if you wanted to see the view. My father forked over some forints, and we were admitted to the Neo-Romanesque stone arcade punctuated by viewing turrets, viewing balconies, and seven viewing lookout towers (in honor of the seven Magyar tribes). Despite the name, the bastion wasn't built for fishermen; it was designed in the 1890s *as* a viewing terrace. "It was meant to be like a fairy tale," as one chronicler put it, to "*feel like history* rather than *be history*." *Follow the Yellow Brick Road*, I thought, as I morosely trailed my father's footsteps.

She stopped at one of the designated lookout towers to take

some shots of the city across the river. "A good thing I brought the telephoto," she said, wrestling the lens out of her purse. While she clicked away, I leaned through a vaulted arch to bask in the fading autumn sun and, despite my cynicism, admire the view. The Danube was a broad dusky ribbon under the city's seven bridges. To my left, I could see the enchanted greensward of Margaret Island and, beyond it, the approaching river's long bend to the south.

On the far shore, Pest was a hazy blur. The Hungarian Parliament, a Neo-Gothic wedding cake encrusted with half a million precious stones and nearly a hundred pounds of gold, took up nine hundred feet of prime waterfront real estate. This temple to democracy, the largest parliament building in Europe and the third largest in the world, was built in the late nineteenth century, when Franz Josef reigned and less than 10 percent of the Hungarian population could vote.

On this side of the river, the red incline train, the Siklò ("the Little Snake"), was inching down the cliff. Directly below, the Chain Bridge arced across the water toward the Neo-Renaissance splendor of the Hungarian Academy of Sciences. The learned society was inaugurated by the same man who spearheaded the construction of the Chain Bridge, Count István Széchenyi, a preeminent Hungarian statesman of the nineteenth century. Széchenyi's quest for an authentic national culture would end in personal despair. "We have no national habits," Széchenyi lamented once. "Our existence and knowledge depend on imitation." Subsequent seekers of Hungarianism have been equally riddled with doubt. They have generated two centuries of literature, journalism, and oratory devoted to the question that doubles as the title for many of their angst-ridden jeremiads: "Who Is a Hungarian?" Long before Erik Erikson coined the phrase, Hungarians were having an identity crisis.

My father traced the descent of the shiny red funicular with her camera lens. "I was so happy when they reopened the Siklò," she said. "The first time I saw it, I cried."

I asked why and she said, "Because the Russians had destroyed it." The Sikló was bombed, along with pretty much everything else along this stretch of the Danube, during the Siege of Budapest, the fifty-day Soviet campaign in the winter of 1944–45 to evict the die-hard Waffen-SS and Hungarian troops bunkered along Castle Hill.

"Would you have preferred the other side won?" I asked.

"You have a very stupid American concept of this."

"Enlighten me."

"The Russians destroyed everything that was Hungarian."

Later I would pick up a brochure on the history of the Sikló and take a perverse pleasure in finding that it was put back in service in 1986, under Soviet rule. I didn't bring it up with my father. By then I knew better than to stick a pin in Hungarian "grand illusion."

8

On the Altar of the Homeland

I learned to time my more probing questions to my father's golden hour. She was at her most expansive over late-afternoon coffee, which she took with a slice of Linzer torte or Sacher torte or Dobos torte or some other confection evoking the Austro-Hungarian era. Cake was always served with a hefty dollop of freshly whipped cream, because that's "the correct *Viennese* way to do it." The Habsburg Empire lived on in my father's prandial habits.

The ritual was lifelong, though in Yorktown Heights confined to the weekends and the selection from American bakeries, which my father found contemptible. Even in his guise as suburban dad, my father had asserted his Old European taste. Weekends, he'd sit in his armchair in his beret and cravat, a demitasse balanced on one knee and classical music thundering on the hi-fi, and heap scorn on Reddi-wip, Cheez Whiz, and ice cubes in drinking water, along with his American children's proclivity for pop tunes with drum tracks and sitcoms with laugh tracks. He went into a swivet once when it became clear I had never heard of one of his treasured European authors, the Austrian (and Jewish) writer Stefan Zweig.

"You have *no culture*," he yelled, ripping out of my hand whatever "tacky" novel I'd been reading. On a series of weekend afternoons, my father attempted to get me to master the basic waltz steps in our burnt-orange-carpeted living room, Johann Strauss on the turntable. The lessons ended badly. "You are *leading* again!" he would shout as I stepped on his foot, not always entirely by accident. "How many times do I have to tell you? The woman does not lead."

In the years after my father moved back to Hungary, he made regular pilgrimages to Vienna, often with his friend Ilonka in tow, to shop for the "correct" Viennese comestibles and tour the faded palaces and hunting lodges and architectural glories of Emperor Franz Josef's nearly seventy-year reign, photographing the last vestiges of the empire that collapsed with the assassination of Archduke Franz Ferdinand in Sarajevo in 1914. Or he'd take Ilonka to Switzerland, where they paid homage to the ancient Habsburg Castle, the dynasty's original seat. Or to Germany, where he made a long detour so they could cruise past the Bavarian villa of the then still living Archduke Otto of Austria, last crown prince to the Austro-Hungarian throne. "The best time was under the Habsburgs," my father told me. "Even as a young child, I could still feel its good influence. If only we could bring the monarchy back—all of Hungary would welcome it."

My father's latest transition, from man to woman, debuted in the Habsburg emperor's former guesthouse. Over coffee and Esterhazy cake one afternoon, she waxed nostalgic about the scene at what was now the Parkhotel Schönbrunn, where she attended the LGBT Rainbow Ball the year before her operation.

"Everybody was beautifully dressed, very elegant," she said.

"Yes, I know," I said. She had shown me the video she'd made of the ball, formal dancers in white satin gowns and black tie, white gloves, and cummerbunds, stepping in stately minuet formation across a polished parquet floor while an all-female orchestra played "Eine Kleine Nachtmusik." At the end of the evening, each performer received a single rose.

"They always have good taste in Vienna," my father sighed, licking the last speck of whipped cream from her demitasse spoon. "Even Ilonka enjoyed it." In my father's image gallery in the attic, she kept a photograph of the two of them at the ball. In the picture, he (still pre-op) is wearing a bleach-blond wig and a midnight-blue velour evening gown with spaghetti straps; Ilonka is in a plain navy sheath. They are holding hands. My father stares straight into the camera, with a pasted-on smile. Ilonka is looking away from my father, her mouth downturned. Her eyes are sorrowful.

"She didn't want you to have the operation," I said, a question.

"Ilonka thought it was a game. She never thought I'd go all the way with it. Ilonka wants nothing to change. Everything has to be the same way it was in the past. She even has to sit in the same pew in the church. I'm not like that. I get used to new things in five minutes!"

She grinned and took another forkful of cake. It seemed like a good moment to press my inquiry.

"Are you *used to* being a woman?" I asked.

"Waaall, that was easy."

"How so?"

She held up her arms, as if for surrender. "Look at this," she said, waggling her arms up and down, a fledgling out of the nest. "Does this look like a man's body? I never developed. There's hardly any hairs on my body." Did this mean the Ugly Duckling had been a swan all along? "Waaall, I had the organs, I did my job, as a man. But I didn't fit the role. They didn't approve of me."

"Who didn't approve of you?"

"Women didn't approve of me. I didn't know how to fight and get dirty. I'm not muscular, I'm not athletic, I had a miserable life as a man. And it became more miserable when I wasn't accepted for the umpteenth time. By *your mother*." My father liked to characterize

her that way, *your mother.* "She didn't accept me and she threw
me away."

"She didn't—"

"I wasn't in the proper role. They can sense that. Now, as a
woman, women like me more. I fit my role now better as a woman
than when I was miscast in the wrong role."

I flashed on hostile Magyar babushkas. "Why do you have to
cast yourself in any role? Why can't—?"

"Before, I was like other men, I didn't talk to people. Now I can
communicate better, because I'm a woman. It's that lack of com-
municating that causes the worst things."

"Like what?"

"They see you as some sort of monster. Because you are not
doing the things others are doing. They don't know what you do.
You're vermin. They gas you. They—"

We had fallen through one of my father's verbal trapdoors.

"—don't want you around. It's like once when I was flying to
Hungary, and the stewardess heard this man sitting across from me
talking and she said, 'Oh, you're Hungarian!' And this man said
very angrily, 'I am *not* Hungarian! I'm Israeli!' This is a provocative
attitude we don't need. It helps that I'm a woman. Because women
don't provoke."

"Some women do," I provoked.

"You can't switch back and forth," my father said. "You have to
develop a habit and stick to it. Otherwise, you're going to be a for-
lorn something, not a whole person. The best way is not to change
someone into someone else, but to put the person back as the person he was *born* to be. The surgery is a complete solution. Now I am
completely like a woman."

Completely, I thought, or completely like?

"You have to get rid of the old habits. If you don't, you're going
to be like a stranger all the time, with this"—she fished around for
the right words—"this anxiety of non-belonging."

She repeated the phrase. *This anxiety of non-belonging.* She polished off the remains of her cake. "That would make a good title for your book," she said.

She got up and started collecting the dishes. "Back to the kitchen!" she trilled as she left the room. "A woman's place!"

I didn't budge from my chair as she washed the cups and saucers.

"Susaaan!" My father was standing at the foot of the stairs. It was early morning, and I'd hoped to sleep in. My father had other plans. "Susaaan, come down here! You'll be interested in this." I threw on some clothes and stumbled into the dining room. She had set out on the table the contents of a file folder marked "Stefi."

"These are my media appearances," she said, pointing to a fanned-out collection of articles, a cassette tape, and a book. She'd given interviews about "The Change" to a Hungarian LGBT magazine (the only one at the time), an alternative radio station called Tilos Rádió (Forbidden Radio), an academic social-sciences journal called *Replika*, and a freelance photojournalist who was putting together a coffee-table book titled *Women in Hungary: A Portrait Gallery*, in which my father was featured, described as a *"feminista."* I studied the stash with some astonishment. All of Steven's life, he'd been behind the camera; Stefi, it seemed, had decided she'd be in front.

The Stefánie who appeared in these pages and recordings was a bit of a coquette. She told her interlocutors that she was a "typical woman" who "loved gossip." When they asked how old she was, my father answered coyly, "Now, it's not appropriate to ask a lady her age!" In the photo spread for *Mások*, the Hungarian LGBT magazine, my father perches on the edge of a planter on her deck, in a floor-length floral dress with a ribbon at the waist. She is clutching two daisies. As she made clear in the accompanying article, she was 100 percent female, "a woman in complete harmony with her wishes." She was taking dance lessons, she told the magazine, and could waltz "all the female steps," and had attended a ball "in an elegant full dress."

The longest account appeared in the academic journal *Replika*. A young PhD student studying social anthropology had come to my father's house to interview her for two days. The resulting Q & A was nearly twenty-five thousand words. That morning and for several mornings to follow, my father translated the text for me, altering the parts she didn't like. ("Don't write that down! It sounds better if you have me say it this way. . . .") While the purpose of the interview was to discuss her change in sex, my father had been eager to expound on life in Hungary before the "catastrophe"— the catastrophe, that is, of 1920.

"The Austro-Hungarian Empire was a very peaceful world," my father said, reading (and revising) her words from the opening pages of the interview. "Hungary grew very fast. Railroads came in, economies were growing. It was a world of plenty. One minority, the Jews, dealt especially with commerce. Many were managers of noble estates. I had an uncle who was managing a noble's estate and also my great-grandfather was the director of some estates of the wealthy. . . . Then came the tragedy. Trianon. The country lost its thousand-year-old borders. And the era when minorities still lived nicely together came to an end. Whatever they say, there was no persecution of minorities in that time."

"No persecution?" I sputtered.

My father gave me one of her you-know-nothing looks. "It was the best time," she said. "The best time for the Jews."

Her history wasn't so Pollyanna. From the 1867 passage of the Jewish Emancipation Act, granting Jews civic and political equality, until the 1920 signing of the Treaty of Trianon, an extraordinary set of circumstances led to the "Golden Age" of Hungarian Jewry. The era yielded a spectacular opportunity for the bourgeois Jewish population. And unprecedented acceptance. For a significant subset of the country's Jews in that period, it seemed possible to be "100 percent Hungarian." Our family was among them. A century before my father changed gender, her forebears had crossed another seemingly unbreachable border.

My father's parents, Jenő and Rozália Friedman, came to Budapest out of the hinterlands of what was then northeastern Hungary (and after Trianon, part of Czechoslovakia, and now Slovakia). The members of my grandmother's side of the family, the Grünbergers, were among the most prominent Jews in the town known in Hungarian as Szepesváralja and later, in Slovak, as Spišské Podhradie—both of which translate roughly as "The Place under the Beautiful Castle." Overlooking the town atop a limestone cliff is a hulking twelfth-century ruin, the largest castle in central Europe and erstwhile home to Magyar nobles. (It is a UNESCO World Heritage site and perennial location for Hollywood movies, among them *Dragonheart* and *Kull the Conqueror*.)

As I later learned from my Grünberger relatives, the baron of the town's commercial age was Rozália's father, my great-grandfather, Leopold Grünberger, who owned the biggest lumber enterprise in the region. The train tracks into town terminated in front of his mill. He had risen from poverty in a nearby village, served in the Habsburg cavalry in World War I, and was a Hungarian patriot and avid believer in Central European culture; he reportedly abhorred Zionism. He sat on the town council and was head of the Jewish community, the latter position due less to his piety, which was pro forma Orthodox, than to his wealth and philanthropy, both of which were substantial.

The Grünbergers vacationed at spas in Baden-Baden, skied in the Tatra Mountains, and ordered their clothes, bespoke, from boutique tailors in Bratislava and Budapest. The four sons were sent to universities in Paris and Prague, the four daughters to music lessons and finishing schools. Among the family's many emblems of privilege (along with the first running water, gaslight, refrigeration, and electricity) was the town's first telephone—phone number "1." The Grünberger home was a showpiece of gentility, from its fountain-adorned courtyard and gardens to its chandeliered salon with a grand piano draped in a Shiraz rug and an extensive Rosenthal and Limoges porcelain collection, from its full retinue of maids, cooks, and governesses to its stable of groomed horses. Persian rugs hushed footsteps in every room. The linens were from Paris and monogrammed.

The region's lumber trade had become a lucrative industry, thanks to the invention of steam-powered electricity and railway construction in the late nineteenth century, which turned the virgin Slovak forests into a commercial honeypot. More than 90 percent of the lumber mill owners and wholesale suppliers in the region were Jewish. The area's artisans, merchants, and professionals were, likewise, predominantly Jews, and had been ever since the ban on Jews in towns and cities was lifted by government edict in the mid-nineteenth century. By the 1920s, the Jews of Spišské Podhradie owned thirteen of the nineteen grocery and general stores, six of the seven taverns and restaurants, all of the liquor stores, all of the tool and iron shops and small factories, the saw mill and flour mill. They were the doctors, the lawyers, the pharmacist, and the veteri-narian.

The Jews in the Hungarian countryside no longer had to live in remote primitive villages or skulk around the edges of towns, ped-dling their wares. They no longer had to pay a "tolerance tax" to the nobles for the privilege of renting a hovel on their estates. Some of them even owned agricultural land. My great-grandfather's property included a working farm with cornfields and livestock. Spišské Podhradie also became a flourishing rabbinical center for Orthodox Jewry, with its own synagogue, cheder, yeshiva, beit midrash, mikveh, and charitable and community associations, and (on a patch of hillside two miles out of town, granted because it was too steep to be arable) a walled cemetery. In 1905, after the town's first synagogue burned down, my great-grandfather marshaled the funds to build a new temple, with a Neo-Classical façade and a Moorish interior. It was installed a few doors down from the Grünberger family home—on Stefánikova Street.

When I visited Spišské Podhradie in 2015, the synagogue (which became a furniture warehouse in Communist times) had recently been restored but sat unused: the town's last postwar Jewish resident, a dentist named Ferdinand Glück, either left or died (no one seemed to know) in the 1970s. The Grünberger manse, now shabby and painted in Day-Glo colors (with a satellite dish on the roof and curtains for doors), was subdivided and occupied by several generations of a poor and devout Christian family. The old carriage entrance displayed a dozen Madonna icons. In the courtyard, a giant plaster Jesus hung on a four-foot cross. On the outskirts of town, weeds flourished in the Jewish cemetery. Many tombstones were missing, looted over the years, or fallen. The lone Grünberger headstone, marking the grave of Moritz Grünberger, firstborn son of Leopold and Sidonia, who died at sixteen, lay on its back in the grass.

Leopold bestowed a lavish dowry upon each of his four daughters. So endowed, the eldest daughter, my grandmother Rozália, or Rozi as she was usually called, merited the attentions of my grandfather Jenő Friedman, who belonged to one of the wealthiest Jewish families in the largest city of the region, Kassa (later renamed, in Slovak, Košice). Jenő's father, Sámuel Friedman, owned Kassa's biggest wholesale goods business. Like Leopold Grünberger, Sámuel was head of his city's Jewish community and held the post for his affluence, not his religiousness. Unlike Leopold, he fancied himself something of a silk-stocking socialite. "My grandfather Sámuel was a man of leisure," my father said. "I remember my grandmother saying all the time, 'Go get your grandfather from the casino!' He was always in there with the other rich men, playing cards and smoking cigars."

By the time of Jenő and Rozi's engagement, the groom was a man of leisure, too. He had begun purchasing luxury apartment buildings in Pest—with a bonanza payout from the Friedmans' real estate investments in Hamburg. The origins of that bonanza were hardly savory, according to accounts from my few surviving Friedman relatives. My father's cousin Viktor Schwarcz told me the Friedmans intentionally torched their company warehouse in Kassa and used the fire insurance money to buy properties in Hamburg. "The legend from the Jews in town," Viktor said, "is that Samu and his sons burned the shop to get the money. No one told the police because they didn't want to turn in fellow Jews. The Friedmans got rich from it—they bought whole streets of houses in Hamburg and sold them during the great inflation. And from that came your grandfather's buildings in Budapest."

However ill-gotten her fiancé's gains, Rozi had landed, at twenty, the richest catch of the four sisters. She didn't have much to do with the landing: the marriage was arranged—based on a desire of the patriarchs of both families to meld their wealth. The bride and groom barely knew each other when they were wed in an extravagant ceremony in the Grünberger home and headed off, first by horse-drawn carriage and then by first-class coach, to a fairy-tale honeymoon in Venice. They returned to a sumptuously appointed apartment in one of Jenő's buildings in Pest, where they spent their days at cards in the casino, their nights at the opera. Their only child was raised by a succession of nursemaids, governesses, and tutors. Rozi's one other pregnancy, my father told me, ended in miscarriage.

Once in a while when I was young, my father would allow me a glimpse into the vanished world of his childhood, a pinprick or two of light in a landscape otherwise dark. "The parents," he would say, opening the pasteboard family album my mother had created and pointing to a creased and curling-at-the-edges tinted picture of his progenitors, the lone representative in the album of my father's side of the family. The photo is a formal studio portrait, vintage '20s with its soft-focus lighting and pretensions to motion-picture glamour. A halo of light wreathes the heads of two newlyweds, a vignette effect fading into shadow at the edges. Bride and groom stare straight at the camera, not smiling. My grandmother Rozi has the severe dark beauty and hooded eyes of a silent-movie star. Her eyebrows are tweezed to pencil-thin crescents and she sports a Joan Crawford hairdo, cropped and set in a tight wave, dark lipstick, and a double-stranded choker of pearls with matching pearl earrings. My grandfather Jenő looks older—which he was, by nine years—and wears an expensively tailored suit; his thinning black hair is oiled and slicked back.

As for the post-wedding life of Rozi and Jenő, their bitter separation when my father was twelve, their forced wartime reconciliation, and their miserable last years in Israel, my father had little to say. But it was clear to me whom she held responsible for her parents' troubled marriage. Rozi, my father told me, was a "spoiled diva" and a "phony" who "put on airs," read "lowbrow" books, and was either at the hairdresser or out chasing "rich men." "She wasn't interested in a relationship with her child." Jenő, on the other hand, was "very cultured," a "true gentleman" who delivered occasional poems at dinner parties and wrote letters in "pearly handwriting," a man who knew how to mingle in "educated circles." Jenő was a prominent figure in the Jewish community, an observant but modern Jew who enrolled his son in the most prestigious Jewish educational institutions for boys in Budapest: the elementary school run by the Rabbinical Seminary of Hungary and then the Zsidó Gimnázium, the elite Jewish high school in Pest celebrated for its world-class teachers. "But my father was *not* Orthodox," my father stressed, a statement that perplexed me; the Friedmans belonged to the Kazinczy Street Synagogue, which was Orthodox. What she meant was that Jenő didn't *look* like an Orthodox Jew, whose appearance might, as she put it, "provoke."

My father liked to parse out the same several set pieces of this early domesticity, more interior design than life experience, decorative backdrops to a privileged and assimilated bourgeois lifestyle. "My father had all his suits tailored in London." Or: "We were the first on our street to own a car," a Renault with leather seats, wood paneling, "a lace curtain on the back window," and a dashboard vase that "held one rose." Or she'd recall their "wind-up record player, spring driven," and the first tune young Pista had played on it, "The Fox and Goose Song":

> Fox, you have stolen the goose.
> Give it back to me.
> If not, the hunter will get you
> With his gun.   —

More than anything, my father talked about the family real estate: the summer villa in the Buda Hills with its swimming pool and gardening staff, the two apartment houses in posh sections of Pest, and, most of all, the "royal apartment" at Ráday utca 9. The Friedmans' majestic domicile featured a double balcony, soaring ceilings, French doors between every room, a "salon" to receive guests, and maid's quarters. My grandfather's study, which contained "first-edition collectibles" in a locked bookcase, featured heavy carved-wood furnishings with red and brown upholstery in what my father called a "Napoleonic Empire style." The salon boasted emerald-velvet love seats and chaise longues, a vitrine stocked with Rosenthal porcelain, and a writing table in a "Louis the XVI theme." One wall displayed three near-life-sized family portraits commissioned from the then noteworthy Hungarian artist Jakab Ödön. The paintings depicted the Friedmans in aristocratic poses: my grandfather in a smoking jacket, my grandmother in a floor-length evening gown, and my ten-year-old father in velvet cutaway coat and matching knee pants. Until, that is, my father "came of age," at which point the artist was recalled—at the insistence of the adolescent subject—to paint on a pair of long trousers. Young István was already Photoshopping. "It wasn't manly to be in short pants," she explained.

In the salon presided over by these imposing regal portraits, my grandparents hosted "balls," the name my father gave to their dinner and dance evenings. Sent to bed early, Pista would lie in the dark, a crystal radio he'd built by hand pressed to one ear "to drown out the noise." On other nights, the parents would don their finery to make the rounds of high society and attend opening nights at the theater and the Hungarian Royal Opera House. The Golden Age had been good to Jenő and Rozi Friedman.

"Finally, O Jew, your day is dawning!" József Kiss, son of poor Orthodox parents and acclaimed as turn-of-the-century Hungary's "most popular" poet, exulted in his first collection of verse, published in 1868. "Now you, too, have a fatherland!" By the end of the century, Jews had full religious standing, too. The 1895 Law of Reception elevated Judaism to a "received" religion, recognized by the state.

The Magyar nobility had its reasons for facilitating the rise of a Jewish bourgeoisie. To accomplish such liberal reforms as civil marriage and nationalized education, the aristocrats enlisted Jews to counter the influence of the Catholic clerics. Also, Hungary desperately needed to modernize and industrialize. In the enterprise vacuum that yawned between its complacent nobles and gentry and its wretched peasants, the Jews formed an essential bourgeois class. The Christian noblemen also had political reasons for aiding Jewish assimilation: the nineteenth-century Magyar electorate was 5 percent short of a majority in a multicultural region teeming with restive Germans, Slovaks, Romanians, Ruthenians, Serbians,

Slovenians, Croatians, and other ethnic minorities, all contesting for their rights. The Magyars made up the deficit through artful use of an 1868 "nationalities" law—originally intended as an act of tolerance for minority cultures and languages—to enforce a linguistic Magyarization. Henceforth, anyone who declared Hungarian as their primary language in the national census would be declared a Magyar. Jews, more than other minorities, took the option. By the century's end, more than 75 percent of Hungary's Jews claimed Hungarian as their mother tongue (compared with only 54 percent of its Catholics), and the Magyar population had thus magically risen to 51.4 percent. In a country where voting was limited to educated and propertied taxpayers, affluent Jews in urban districts enjoyed significant electoral clout; in Budapest, Jews were more than 20 percent of the population, and 40 percent of the voters.*

Whatever the self-serving motives of the old aristocracy, the benefits for the bourgeois Jews of Hungary were unparalleled. "No country in Europe was more hospitable to Jewish immigration and assimilation and no country had more enthusiastic support from its Jews than the pre–World War I Hungarian kingdom," prominent historian István Deák observed. And maybe no Jewish population did more to bring its country into the industrial age. By the 1900s, Hungarian Jews had launched and were running most of the country's major banks, heavy industries, mining concerns, and the largest munitions plant. Thirty of the fifty founding members of the National Association of Hungarian Industrialists were Jews. For their contributions, the patriarchs of 346 Hungarian Jewish families were granted the ultimate compliment in the aristocracy-obsessed empire: titled ennoblement.

Wealth was only one aspect of the Golden Age's yield. The era

---

* While Jews made fewer inroads into politics, by the early twentieth century they had been elected to sixteen seats in parliament and served as defense, finance, and justice ministers. In 1913, Ferenc Heltai, a Jew and the nephew of Zionist founder Theodor Herzl, was briefly mayor of Budapest.

also ushered in a remarkable flowering of creative and professional talent. By the 1910s, the 5 percent of the population that was Jewish represented half of Hungary's doctors, 45 percent of its lawyers and journalists, more than a third of its engineers, and a quarter of its artists and writers. Hungarian Jews established, financed, and wrote for many of the nation's important newspapers, literary journals, publishing houses, theaters, cabarets, and cinema, and forged the modern practice of photography.* And they were instrumental in creating a cultural environment in which artists and intellectuals, both Jewish and Christian, could thrive. A notable segment of the gentile literati embraced that collaboration, pinning to it their greatest hopes for a cultural renaissance. "I see before me the prototype of a new people," Christian poet Endre Ady exulted in 1917. "This would be the solution to all our problems and History's outstanding event, if it could be true." And disastrous if it failed: "We either produce a new people," he concluded, "or the deluge will follow."

Hungary's assimilating Jewish population dedicated itself with a formidable intensity to producing that new people. Its most prominent members led a decades-long and wildly successful campaign to "Magyarize" the country, modernizing and promulgating Hungarian as the mother tongue, championing Hungarian handicrafts and viniculture (the worldwide fame of Hungarian Matyó embroidery and Tokáj wine are thanks largely to their Jewish promoters), and organizing the fusion of the three provincial back-

---

* Of all the arts that Hungarian Jews cultivated, photography rose to the forefront, hailed as the country's "first indigenous visual tradition" and its "greatest export." Among the greatest, on a long list of great Hungarian Jewish photographers from the early twentieth century, were Robert Capa, Brassaï, Martin Munkácsi, László Moholy-Nagy, and André Kertész, whose prints my father reproduced for Condé Nast. They were, as well, the pioneers of so many of the craft's innovations: photojournalism, war photography, fashion photography, visual theory, and photomontage. *Modern Photography*'s 1931 list of "The World's Hundred Best Photographs" singled out more works by Hungarians than by any other nationality. "Can we help it," *Coronet* magazine quipped in an issue devoted to Kertész's work, "if the best photographs seem consistently to be produced by Hungarians?"

waters of Buda, Pest, and Óbuda into a city capital that, by the end of the millennium, would be a cultural mecca rivaling Paris and Vienna. "Their contribution to the development of their country was greater than that of any other European Jewish community," historian Jacob Katz wrote. More than anyone else, the Jews invented what it meant to be Hungarian. And with that, invented "a fatherland" into which their day could dawn.

But that dawn, like an Aztec sunrise, demanded a sacrifice, an amputation. Under the terms of the "social contract of assimilation," as historians of the Golden Age call it, Jews were recognized as Hungarians only if they "corrected" themselves. That is, if they betrayed no evidence of being Jewish in appellation, allegiance, attitude, mannerism, speech, or dress. They had to pass. It was a treacherous arrangement. "Perhaps in no other Central European country," István Bibó observed, "was the inner world of the assimilator community as disharmonious, and the cause of Jewish assimilation so burdened by falsehoods and contradictions, as in Hungary."

On New Year's Day of 1896, church bells all over Budapest rang in the start of the "Millennial Jubilee," a nationwide celebration of the thousand-year anniversary of the Magyar Conquest. Several thousand Jews in Budapest gave thanks at the Dohány Street Synagogue, known as the "Israelite Cathedral," a giant temple designed as a basilica, boasting the country's largest organ, a choir, an entrance dominated by a giant rose window, and a facade adorned with *eight*-pointed stars (pointedly not the six-pointed Stars of David). In honor of the Jubilee, Rabbi Sámuel Kohn opened the millennial assembly of the Israelite Magyar Literary Society with the proud declaration that "Israelite" is now but "the adjective of the word Magyar." The Israelite Women's Association hosted a "pre-Lenten" ball in the White Cross Café. And three thousand Jews renounced their family names and adopted Magyar identities as an "offering on the altar of the homeland." By 1918, nearly forty thousand Jews had followed their example, "naturalizing" their names to sound more Magyar. (The poet József Kiss, originally József Klein, was one of them.) Even to call yourself Jewish was too much. They were now, as Jewish community leaders claimed, "Hungarians of the Mosaic persuasion."

Young assimilating Jewish men, in particular, hastened to efface their Jewishness with patriotic displays, dueling scars, and "Christian" sporting feats. They served in disproportionate numbers in World War I (and were nearly 19 percent of army officers), and more than ten thousand gave their lives on the battlefield. Their fathers donated millions of crowns to the war effort. In peacetime, young Jews were the brightest stars of Hungarian sports, and their fathers leading patrons of the nation's athletic teams. Jewish athletes won for Hungary its first Olympic gold medal (in swimming, in 1896), its first world championship (in figure skating), and its only Helms Award for the world's best athlete (a long-distance runner). In the first five Olympic Games, Jewish athletes received five of Hungary's nine individual gold medals (and were nearly 60 percent of the gold-winning team members) and won the country international fame for its fabled fencing team. Attila Petschauer, the Hungarian Jewish prodigy widely regarded as one of the world's top fencers, led his team to two World Championship gold medals and two Olympic gold medals. He was anointed "Hungary's Best Fencer" and "the new D'Artagnan," the Magyars' musketeer.

Zionism would get little traction among bourgeois Jews in Budapest—even though its founding visionaries, Theodor Herzl and Max Nordau, were both sons of Budapest families. Herzl's *The Jewish State*, published in the year of the Millennial Jubilee, generated acclaim and excitement in every nation but his own. "The Prophet Jeremiah calls upon us to serve the welfare of our fatherland," Simon Hevesi, chief rabbi at Budapest's Dohány Street Synagogue, declared at the time. "Zionism is incompatible with the soul of Hungarian Jewry." *Egyenlőség*, then the country's most influential Jewish periodical, advised its readers: "In Hungary,

Zionism can have only one designation: high treason." When Nordau's *Zionism* came out in Hungarian in 1902, its translator, Gyula Gabel, appended a note, observing that most Hungarian Jews have no need for Zionism because they are "happy, emancipated citizens of a chivalrous nation."

The ardor with which turn-of-the-century Jews Magyarized themselves into "our fatherland" often outdid that of their gentile countrymen. As a Hungarian cognoscente at the time remarked, "No one could out-duel, out-ride, out-drink, or out-serenade an assimilated Hungarian Jew!" The Jewish writer Pál Ignotus observed that his "Mosaic" brethren seemed to be "more fervently Magyar than the Magyars themselves." In 1879, Christian novelist Kálmán Mikszáth wrote of the Jewish community in Szeged, Hungary's second-largest city:

> There are no Jews in Szeged any more. . . . Girls in love express their sorrow in Hungarian popular songs, and the portrait of the late rabbi in Jewish homes is covered with a cloth in the red, white, and green colors of the Hungarian flag. The younger generation may even think of Jehovah as an old man wearing a Hungarian short coat with gold lace.

To settle an argument one afternoon—an amiable argument over coffee and seven-layer Viennese cake slices—my father broke into song.

> *I was not born in sunny Hispania*
> *My father came from Rovno Gubernya*
> *But now I'm here, I'm dancing a tango;*
> *Di dee di! Dee di dee di!*
> *I am easily assimilated.*
> *I am so easily assimilated.*

Stripped of its ironies, "The Old Lady's Tango" in Leonard Bernstein's *Candide* could have described much of the Jewish community in Budapest's Golden Age. Until the era crashed. My father, however, meant it to describe her own life in current-day Hungary. "I blend in very well," she said, drying her hands on her apron, a yellow checked print with a frilled hem. "I have had absolutely no difficulties. Don't believe all this nonsense."

"What nonsense?"

"About there still being anti-Semitism here."

"Oh?" Our argument had concerned a small item I'd pointed out in the *Budapest Sun*, the English-language daily. It was an article about a neo-Nazi group putting up posters claiming to be followers of Ferenc Szálasi, the 1940s leader of the Arrow Cross, the Hungarian Nazi Party that ruled the nation in the last months of World War II. The posters were emblazoned with what seemed to be a replica of the Arrow Cross crest, a violation of the government's ban on such symbols. The police regarded the insignia acceptable, the *Sun* reported, because the neo-Nazi group had slightly altered its configuration. My father, a fan of alterations, deemed the news "of no importance."

"What about that glazier you told me about?" I asked. Some years earlier, my father had hired a glass company to install French doors in the living room. Unhappy with the work, my father threatened not to pay—inspiring the glazier to yell, "This is why you people should have all been gassed."

"Waaall," she said now, "but that was an exception. There's really very little anti-Semitism here."

I recalled another "exception" that had occurred on one of my father's earliest scouting trips to post-Communist Budapest in the '80s. After reacquainting himself with the famous pastries at Gerbaud's and paddling in the wave pools at the Hotel Gellért, my father had decided to film a local edifice, or rather, the bombed-out remains of one. The Dohány Street Synagogue, the "Israelite

Cathedral" ornamented with the eight-pointed stars, was still boarded up (as were so many Jewish temples—no wonder we hadn't visited any synagogues on our family vacation to Hungary). A group of locals stopped to watch the American photographer assembling his tripod. They began talking among themselves, assuming he didn't understand Hungarian. He understood all right. "They couldn't see why anyone would want to take pictures of that building," my father recounted. "They were saying 'Look at that rich Jew. Those people ruined Hungary. They took its wealth. The dirty Jews deserved to die.'"

It seemed to me that the Hungary my father had returned to had taken its identity not from the Golden Age of Jewish-Magyar collaboration but from the era immediately following. In the wake of World War I, Hungarian Jews went from being the most assimilated in Europe to being among the most reviled, subject to the earliest anti-Semitic legislation of the new century, deprived by the late '30s of their property, professions, and freedoms, and ultimately targeted by one of the most systematic extermination campaigns of the Holocaust. "Finally, O Jew, your day is dawning," Kiss had crowed in 1868. Three-quarters of a century later, nearly half a million Hungarian Jews would be sent to Auschwitz in the finale of what Winston Churchill described as "probably the greatest and most horrible crime ever committed in the whole history of the world."

Theodor Herzl, for one, had predicted as much. In a 1903 letter to a Hungarian Jewish member of parliament, the founder of Zionism had warned: "The hand of fate shall also seize Hungarian Jewry. And the later this occurs, and the stronger this Jewry becomes, the more cruel and hard shall be the blow, which shall be delivered with greater savagery. There is no escape."

One morning my father summoned me to her office in the attic, where she was seated at her computer, in a blue housedress with orange flowers and terry cloth slippers. A photograph waited on the screen. She'd scanned it in some years earlier, she told me, and saved it to an electronic folder titled "Family." It was dated 1943.

In the picture, three rows of people are arranged for a group portrait. The occasion was a "Golden Jubilee," my father's paternal grandparents' fiftieth wedding anniversary in their well-appointed estate in Kassa. My great-grandfather and great-grandmother, Sámuel and Frida Friedman, are seated in the front row, surrounded by thirteen brothers and sisters, children, and grandchildren. The men are in suits and ties, the women in formal dresses, primped and coiffed. Sámuel is holding a large metal wreath, each of its golden leaves bearing the name of another member in the extensive family tree. At the far left end of the last row, I see a rail-thin boy, who would have then been sixteen years old but who looks much younger. He strikes a hand-in-waistcoat Napoleon pose: my father.

I studied the assembled in their tailored jackets and ivory brooches, this photographic paean to Golden Age prosperity, this un-Photoshoppable testament to a world that had once been, and thought to myself: There are no Jews in Kassa anymore.

9

Ráday 9

"Let's go see the apartment where you grew up," I suggested. We were back in front of the computer. Today it was Hungarian folk-dancing videos and transsexual speech-alteration tutorials. ("How to Develop a Female Voice," by Melanie Anne Phillips: "Nothing gets you read faster than a voice that doesn't match your appearance. . . . Clothes may make the man, but it is voice that makes the woman.")

My father didn't answer.

I repeated the proposal. "You know, on Ráday Street," I said. The one whose Louis XVI furnishings and vitrines stocked with Rosenthal porcelain I'd heard so much about, the "royal apartment."

My father clicked over to her NASA moonshot collection.

"Let's look at some of *your* pictures," I proposed. "The ones you actually took."

"Your mother has those," she said.

Actually, my mother didn't, not anymore. The spring before my first trip to Budapest, a sagging cardboard box held together by

packing tape had arrived at my door in Portland. My mother, in a
spasm of spring cleaning, had mailed me the Faludi picture collection. For years, she'd stored the photos in an old hope chest in her
apartment that also held woolen sweaters and blankets, and when
I unsealed the box, it stank of mothballs. Inside, under trays of
slides of old hiking trips and layers of loose shots that humidity
had turned into clotted sediment, was our one photo album—*Family
Memories* embossed in gilt on its red cover, fading to brown.

Pasted on one page was a photograph of my mother posing in
a billowing bridal gown in the fall of 1957, her face pale and strained.
There were pictures of my mother from the wedding itself, with her
roommate and an uncle as her only witnesses. Her parents, even
her Jewish father (who had changed his family name from Levi to
Lanning), had refused to come, because she was marrying a Jew, and,
worse, marrying him in a synagogue. There were other pictures of
my mother in her early years of housewifery in Queens, and of me
and my brother as infants, then toddlers, then pimply adolescents in
scalloped-cardboard yearbook frames. Where were the pictures of
my father's marital years? The album's fading pages revealed the
traces of a willful erasure. I could see the dark squares where photos had once been glued. My mother had engaged in a little "masking" of her own. Several snapshots were simply ripped down the
middle. Her handiwork was thorough if not deft: she left no record
of my father's two decades of American domesticity.

"Does your mother have that picture of me from when I was a
little child?" my father asked now. "The one where I have long
golden curls?"

I said I didn't think so. Thinking, wasn't your hair always black?

"I'm taking a bath in the kitchen sink. My hair was *blond*. I
look like a little Goldilocks."

I knew one picture that filled the bill, a toddler with light-colored
curls bathing in a kitchen sink. I'd seen it in the *Family Memories*
album. Except the sink was in Queens. The child was me.

As I struggled for an answer, my father moved on to another memory.

"Remember that folk dress I got you?" she said. "When we went to Hungary—as a *family*?" She stressed the last word.

I nodded.

"You hated it!" my father said.

"I did!" I said, absurdly thrilled that she'd remembered.

She laughed and so did I.

"I don't know why you hated that dress so much," she said. "Take a look at this."

She abandoned NASA and scrolled through a sea of folders until she came to one marked "Traditional Folk Costumes," then clicked through many shots of whirling *Csárdás* dancers in beribboned bell skirts and embroidered dirndls, each annotated: "Traditional peasant costumes, 1936," "Hungarian folk dance, 1938 . . ." *Csárdás* dances enjoyed a revival in the same years as Hungarian fascism. The image my father came to rest on was modern day.

"There I am." It was a photo of my father in The Dress, or a dress very much like the one over which we'd had so many pitched battles: the same lace-up bodice, ballooning skirt, and tulip-and-rosebud-dotted apron he insisted I wear to middle school. My father looked to be in mid-dance-step.

I said, "You own one of those?"

"I wish!" she said. "I found a picture of it, on the Internet." And Photoshopped it onto her physique.

I'd wondered whether my latent-female father had tried on my mother's or my clothes when we lived in Yorktown Heights. I asked her directly one afternoon, during one of our coffee-and-cake tête-à-têtes, and received one of her trademark non-reply replies: "Waaall. No. Maybe." Now I wondered if the dress she'd forced me to wear was an outfit she'd wished for herself.

"Why do you like these so much?" I asked now, pointing to the costume on the screen.

"I'm a Hungarian patriot," she said. "It reminds me of the way the country used to be, when I was a little boy."

I saw my opening. "So let's go see the house where you used to live, when you were a little boy."

"There's no point," she said.

"But, I want—"

"I don't want to go all the way over there," she said, as if Pest were a day's journey and not a fifteen-minute drive.

"Anyway, it's unnecessary. You can see it on the Internet." My father hit a few keys on the computer and up popped a photograph of the block that she'd lived on as a boy.

"See," she said, pointing at a partial and blurred shot of a building halfway down a street. "That's my room there," she said, indicating a smudge that might have been a window, three stories up. What caught my attention, though, was the way she'd called up the image. She hadn't typed in the address on Google. She had retrieved the link from a folder on her hard disk marked "Deleted Items." Deleted, but not deleted. My father had an odd way of erasing the past.

When my father first returned to Hungary, he had launched a full-bore campaign to reclaim Ráday 9, as well as Váci 28, the two Pest apartment buildings that had belonged to my grandfather. My father unearthed the original deeds and typed up a letter detailing how the Friedmans' property had been "stolen" by the Communist regime. He delivered his screed to various authorities and each of the building's current occupants. Nothing came of it. Post-Communist Hungary had a restitution system for state-nationalized property, but it was parsimonious in the extreme, a system of vouchers with long delays and paltry payments. In my father's case, two prime-location apartment buildings certainly worth millions were judged worthy of a total reimbursement of $6,500. (My grandfather had been forced to sell the summer villa during the war, making it ineligible for restitution.)

My father wrote in protest to the prime minister's office, the Hungarian justice and agriculture ministers, and several Hungarian MPs, as well as the U.S. embassy, the U.S. ambassador to Hungary, and two U.S. congressmen with Hungarian roots. Those appeals went nowhere, too. Then he joined the conservative-right Independent Smallholders Party—after its leaders started demanding the return of property nationalized under Communism. My father also had a more personal, and older, relationship to the party, which also involved real estate. In 1946, Smallholders leader Ferenc Nagy was elected prime minister in Hungary's first democratic election, a post he held for a little more than a year before the Communists claimed power. Nagy had resided at Ráday 9 since the '30s. He and my grandparents were friendly (too friendly, my father suspected, in the case of my grandmother Rozi, who before the war met Nagy for afternoon confabs in the patisserie on Ráday 9's ground floor). Over the years, Nagy had done several favors for the Friedman family. "Nagy was a great man," my father told me. "They say—and it's true!—he could have straightened up the entire country if it weren't for the Communists. And we had a very good connection with him."

Nothing came of my father's 1990s membership in the Smallholders. When all else failed, he tried to establish a beachhead on Ráday utca another way, investing in a mountaineering-equipment store—in a country with no real mountains. He loaned seed capital to the store's two young entrepreneurs, who were strapped for cash. The shop was located, at my father's urging, just down the block from Ráday 9.

"I'd like to go to the actual place you lived in," I said, predictably.

"There's nothing to see," my father replied, predictably.

She was right in a way. What of her early years could possibly remain after all this time? And yet our proximity to the landmarks of her youth exerted an irresistible pull. Throughout my childhood there had always been the specter of the royal apartment in the 1911 Secession building designed by Gyula Fodor, a prominent Hungarian Jewish architect whose career came to an abrupt end in the 1930s.

"Tell me about your parents," I said.

"There's nothing to tell," my father replied, then returned to the part she'd already told me, many times. "A stupid business, their divorcing. Totally unnecessary. But in the end I brought them together." Her eyes fixed on mine. "*I* brought my parents together," she repeated. *Unlike you*, she meant. It was my turn not to answer.

By 1940, my grandparents' domestic battles had led to separation. Jenő and Rozi, whose marriage had been such a sparkling match, began protracted and acrimonious divorce proceedings. Lawyers were hired, accusations and counteraccusations of infidelities were exchanged. Before Friedman v. Friedman could make it to the docket, a bigger war intervened.

"Did your mother actually have a lover?" I asked.

"Waaall," my father said.

"Well, what?"

"Back then one didn't speak of such things in front of the children. 'Nicht für Kinder!' "

"But you suspected."

"There was a lawyer she ran around with," my father said. And a manufacturer. "Chasing after the rich ones," she said with a grimace. "My mother was a real gold digger."

Jenő also was rumored to have had several affairs, including with their cook and at least one of their maids. "He was always one for the women of the *volk*," my father said approvingly. "This sort of thing was accepted in European society." For men, anyway. The maids were Christian peasant girls. One of them, my father recalled, was named Maryska. She wore "traditional" Magyar attire around the house.

"She put me in one of hers once," my father offered suddenly. A folk dress. "I was probably seven or eight." She looked down at her own skirt and smoothed the pleats.

"It was a little native costume," she continued. "Polka-dotted. Maryska told me I'd make a cute girl."

"And did you?"

"Probably. My mother was always complaining that I looked like a weakling. She'd tell the cook to fatten me up."

"Maybe she was worried about your health."

My father's face darkened. "All my mother worried about was one thing: her appearance."

When my grandparents separated, Jenő moved into the Hotel Astoria, a luxury hotel modeled on the Waldorf-Astoria, and dispatched his estranged wife to a furnished studio. He sent his only child to board with a teacher from the Jewish high school, "because they couldn't decide who I should live with," my father said. The teacher was a "straitlaced" Orthodox Jew, an austere disciplinarian who forced religion on his unhappy young tenant. "Terrible time," my father said, refusing to elaborate. The most I could get out of her was that it was "not good for a child."

The exile lasted for a couple of years. "It was while I was living with that teacher that I almost got hit by the tram," my father said. "Either I was careless, or—"

"Or?" I asked.

"Or I just didn't want to live anymore."

Young István had stepped off the curb to cross the Nagy Körút, the broad Ring Road that runs in a semicircle around inner Pest. "I was standing right across from the National Theater." He was alone and didn't see, or chose not to see, the #6 tram careening around the curve. "And just then, out of nowhere, a hand grabs me and pulls me back to safety." The hand belonged to his father, who happened to be on the same corner at the same time. "It was a *miracle*," she said. "He was my guardian angel." A guardian living the high life at a luxe hotel, I thought, having stowed his son with a religious martinet, his wife in a bed-sit.

While living with the teacher, István turned thirteen. And received from his father the extravagant gift that would spark a lifelong infatuation with film: the Pathé 9.5mm movie camera. The present, it turned out, was in lieu of a parental presence. My father's bar mitzvah ceremony was held that fall in the synagogue at the Jewish high school, the Zsidó Gimnázium. Neither Jenő nor Rozi attended.

"That's awful," I said.

"Waaall, they were too busy with their own problems. Which *they* created."

I suggested we go see the high school, another futile proposal.

"Why?"

"Why?" My voice began to shake. "Because I'd like to see *one thing* that has to do with *your* life in Budapest."

My father turned back to the computer screen and pondered the out-of-focus Google shot of the apartment building on Ráday Street. "This is not a very good picture," she said after a while.

"No," I said. "It isn't."

She pursed her lips. "I told you, it's not my life anymore. It's ancient history."

"I don't care," I said. "I just want to see something. I want to get out of the house."

"You need to calm down," she said. "You are being irrational."

"You are making me irrational," I said, irrationally.

"You don't understand," she said.

"*What* don't I understand?" No answer.

What was I doing here? She seemed to be the same old impenetrable, walled-off person he had always been. As far as I could tell, becoming a woman had only added a barricade, another false front to hide behind. Every road to the interior was blocked by a cardboard cutout of florid femininity, a happy housewife who couldn't wait to get "back to the kitchen," a peasant girl doing the two-step in a Photoshopped dirndl. No wonder my father loved *The Wizard of Oz.* She was that wizard: "Pay no attention to the man behind the curtain."

When I came down to breakfast the next day, she was rummaging through her video library for a copy of *Joy and Revival,* the film she'd made of a Zsidó Gimnázium reunion, a 2001 gathering of the surviving members of my father's high school class in Toronto. "The reunion you didn't come to," she reminded me. We watched it on the jumbo television monitor in the living room.

After a slow pan of the Toronto Four Seasons (as the sound track blasted Brahms's "Academic Festival Overture"), the camera moved on to scenes of aged men hobnobbing over wine and hors d'oeuvres in a hospitality suite. My father makes a brief appearance in a khaki cameraman's vest, clutching a large microphone. The action culminated in a long dinner in a hotel banquet room, where each former classmate of the Zsidó Gymnázium rose in turn to speak, almost exclusively in Hungarian. I understood only a few words: "Bergen-Belsen . . . Buchenwald . . . ghetto . . . SS."

"What are they saying?"

"Waaall, a lot of ancient history," she said. "Anyway, you've seen it." She got up to check the coffee.

I was quiet over breakfast.

"You should try this sausage," my father said, pushing a plate of sweaty sliced links across the table. "*Gyulai kolbász*! Genuine Hungarian."

I said I wasn't hungry. She helped herself to several slices and cast a sidelong glance at her aggrieved daughter.

After a while, she said, "You know, it's not Jewish anymore." She meant the building that once housed the Zsidó Gymnázium. It hadn't been for a while, ever since it was shut down during the war—and reopened afterward as the Royal Catholic Teachers College and Training School. "So, you see, there's nothing to see."

My father pulled into a weedy lot by a tram stop and parked Der
California Exclusive. A few blocks down the street, facing the tracks,
was a Communist-era concrete apartment building, a low-slung
unpainted bunker built above a set of identical garages. A snarl of
satellite dishes hung crookedly from the flat roof. It was hot for an
autumn day, and my father was wearing her "light summer dress,"
blue with white dots, and red-sequined heels, which she complained
pinched her toes, but she wore them anyway. They were her favorite. She called them "my ruby slippers." It was two days before my
return to the United States. I was feeling somewhat cheered, and not
just because I was getting on a plane soon. We were out of the house.

From a tiny balcony on an upper floor, a woman leaned over a
flower box of geraniums and waved. It was Ilonka. I was dispatched
to collect her. Since the operation, my father said, Ilonka's husband
had banished Stefánie from the premises.

The apartment was small and dark, with heavy oversized furniture that made it feel even smaller. Crosses and icon paintings
adorned the walls; a sideboard displayed Madonna figurines. Ilonka's husband, a compact, muscular man with the sort of roughly
misshapen build that comes from a life of manual labor, rose to
greet me. "*Kezét csókolom,*" he said. It was a Hungarian phrase I
knew, an old-fashioned greeting from a man to a woman, which
meant, literally, "I kiss your hand." Ilonka was short and zaftig and
radiated maternal warmth. I noticed she was wearing pearl earrings, a gift from my father from years earlier, when my father was
still a man. She cooed endearments and presented me with a prayer
card from her church, a picture of the Madonna. After a while, she
took my hand and we headed toward the camper.

To my dismay, my father again drove to Castle Hill, to a spot a
stone's throw from the viewing turrets of the Fisherman's Bastion.
Ilonka wanted to show me the celebrated Matthias Church, the

Church of Our Lady. "Waaall," my father said, "Ilonka always has to go to church." On their travels across Europe, the two of them had stopped at every shrine dedicated to Mary, along with many cemeteries, catacombs, and crypts. "Ilonka is a bit of a necrophiliac," my father joked. "But open-minded!" The Matthias Church was the site of the "Mary-wonder" of 1686. During the Battle of Buda between the occupying Ottoman Turks and the "liberating" Holy League, my father related, cannon fire had blasted one of the walls, revealing a hidden votive statue of the Madonna. At the sight of the Virgin Mary, the morale of Muslim Turk soldiers buckled and the city fell to the Holy League that day. "That's the story, anyway," she said. We wandered through the sanctuary's shadowy recesses, my father's ruby slippers clacking on the stone floors. Ilonka lit some candles at Our Lady's shrine.

Afterward, we stopped at an outdoor stand where some elderly women dressed as Gypsies were selling "traditional" Hungarian embroidered pillowcases and handbags that looked suspiciously mass-produced. My father considered some clutch purses. "Perfect for the opera," she said. As we picked through the merchandise, Ilonka recalled how she first learned of my father's interest in feminine attire. "He always wanted to buy me clothes," she told me, my father translating. "And I was always thinking, 'What a gentleman!' But then I realized he really wanted them for himself." One day, she said, they were standing in a department store and she saw my father lingering in the women's sleepwear section. Ilonka picked up a nightgown and cocked her head toward the fitting room. My father stepped into one of the stalls. Ilonka slipped the gown under the door and stood guard while he tried it on. "From then on, we collaborated," Ilonka said. They would pick out outfits together and bring them home—he would model, she would photograph.

"Ilonka helped me design my best costume!" my father interjected. The project had started one night when they were watching *Dinner at Eight*, the 1933 comedy of manners directed by George

Cukor (son of Hungarian Jewish immigrants), with Jean Harlow as the gold-digging chorus girl ("I'm going to be a lady if it kills me!"). My father loved the film, owned copies in Betamax, VHS, and DVD, and watched it at least once a year. When the gold digger's chambermaid appeared on the screen, my father hit the Pause button. The servant girl was dolled up in a French maid's garb, a particularly outlandish version with a velvet-and-lace headdress and a flounce-ridden apron tied in a giant bow. My father asked Ilonka to make a precise drawing of the dress—"Ilonka is a very good draftsman"—and took the results to the Katti Zoób Szalon, a couture design house in Pest run by a former theatrical costume designer, where, for a considerable fee, the outfit was replicated down to the last ruffle. This was the costume my father was modeling in her Screen Saver image.

Ilonka's collaboration continued for the next several years. When my father first ventured into a meeting of the Trans-X club, an Austrian transgender organization that convened periodically at a café in Vienna, Ilonka accompanied him. "He was scared to go alone," she recalled. They sat together on a bench outside the restaurant for a long time, my father said, Ilonka holding his hand while "I screwed up my nerve to go in there." Of the subsequent meeting, my father remembers little, except for a story that one of the club members related over lunch. "When this guy was a boy, he was caught wearing a dress," my father told me. "His father sent him to an officer who was a Nazi—an *actual* Nazi. And this officer beat him. Regularly. To 'cure' him." The story still disturbed her.

For the next two years, my father attended Trans-X events, including a Christmas party ("I brought a very good Hungarian cake") and weekend field trips sponsored by Transgender In Austria, one to a hotel in the south of Sweden, where fashion and beauty consultants dispensed (as the handouts described it) "personal color and style analysis" and designed an "evening dress handmade just for your body," followed by a modeling session before "one of Denmark's hottest photographers." Ilonka came along. "I enjoyed looking at the clothes, the shoes," she told me. "It was like watching a movie." On another jaunt, which Ilonka also joined, club members camped in Croatia and sunbathed topless on the beach. A day into the Croatia trip, my father flew into a rage at one of the campers—"he interrupted a story I was telling about Ilonka"— and packed the VW and drove away. "Ilonka and I went on an excursion without them," my father said. "Aaaand we had a very nice time!"

As we meandered through the cobblestoned streets of the Castle District, Ilonka took my father's arm and spoke for a long time in Hungarian.

"What is she saying?"

"Ilonka's talking about when I went to Thailand." For the operation. "She says she was so upset, she had a heart attack. Waaall, she *thought* she had a heart attack. She had chest pains and went to the hospital. They never figured out what was wrong."

"I always thought he'd come back without doing it," Ilonka told me later. "I thought it was a joke. Had I known, I would have done anything to persuade him not to. When he called me from Thailand, I was shocked. I took it really badly."

A day after my father returned, a despondent Ilonka came over with groceries, and for the next few weeks of my father's recuperation, cooked meals and cleaned house. A maid without a costume. She was one of the few in my father's former circle who stood by her after the operation. "Everyone kept a distance," Ilonka recalled. A former business associate refused to speak to my father, and when Stefi kept calling, he changed his number. The Smallholders Party officials who'd welcomed his membership now shunned her.

"If you hadn't become a woman," I asked my father, "what would have happened with you and Ilonka?"

"Waaall, it was no good—she was taken."

"And if she had divorced? Would you have married her?"

We walked another block before my father answered.

"Ilonka was the woman for me. . . . But she's Catholic. They don't divorce."

Ilonka talked some more. My father laughed, a rueful but sincere laugh. "Ilonka says she always wanted to be a nun. . . . Waaall, and now maybe her wish has come true."

We were done with the Castle District, and the day was half over. As we climbed back in the camper, I floated a proposal. "I'd love to see that mountaineering shop you helped start in Pest." My maneuvering seemed transparent, at least to me. I wasn't interested in the store, only its location—down the street from the royal apartment. To my surprise, my father agreed.

We found a parking space a few blocks away—a feat, given the amount of pavement Der Exclusive required—and strolled down Ráday, which had recently been converted to a pedestrian promenade. The sidewalks were lined with café tables. My father seemed pleased. "When I first came here in '89, it was a dump, filthy, nothing painted since the war," she said. "Only Gypsies lived here." We wandered past boutiques, galleries, a photo shop, then a long strip of trendy bars and restaurants: the Pink Cadillac; Paris, Texas; Top Joy; Drive 911; the Soul Cafe; and the Lizard Café Island of Calmness. Not exactly authentic Hungarian, I thought. The afternoon was warm, the sidewalk tables full. Diners chatted under red and blue café umbrellas branded with American product names: Marlboro, Red Bull. My father led the way to the store.

The shop was bright and smelled of freshly milled wood and new paint. It was also empty of customers. "Business is bad," my father said. The next time I returned to Budapest, the store was gone, replaced by an espresso bar. "And here is the line of shoes I found," my father said, gesturing to a wall of hiking boots by a German manufacturer. "I used to smuggle these in from Germany in my old camper. I hid them in the cabinets under the seat," to avoid paying the tariffs. "I'd just show my American passport and they'd say, 'Go right ahead, Mr. Faludi.'"

I hefted a boot and read the label, Hanwag. "Short for Hans Wagner," my father said, the company's founder. He'd designed the boots for the Third Reich's ski team in the 1936 Olympics. My father had visited Wagner a few times and took him out for beer once when he came to Budapest. "I'd pick up the shoes right from his factory. And you know where it was?"

"Where?"

"Dachau."

Shoes from Dachau. I returned the Hanwag to its stand and suggested we take a walk. Out on the street, I turned left. My father and Ilonka followed. After a block and a half, I gestured to a shabby but once elegant Vienna Secession apartment house across the street. The five-story stone-and-stucco facade was ornamented with sinuous Art Nouveau figures. Just below the roof, three moderne caryatids balanced on fluted columns. On the first floor, a bas relief depicted a mother with her arms wrapped protectively around two children, a girl and a boy. The boy cradled a miniature house in his arms.

"Which window was yours?" I asked.

I waited. My father didn't say anything, but she didn't storm off either. Pedestrians jostled by on the sidewalk. A bus boy clearing café tables paused to inspect us. Ilonka patted my arm. After a while, my father pointed to a small balcony on the third floor.

"I used to raise radishes on the windowsill," she said. She pointed to the double balcony to its right. "That was my parents' terrace." She turned around and looked up at the building behind us. "This was my view," she said. "But it's painted such bright colors now. It used to be very gray. Full of pigeons." I fished my tape recorder out of my bag. My father watched as I fidgeted with the buttons, then turned and lifted her camera up to her eye, aiming it toward the third floor of Ráday 9. She didn't take a picture but kept studying the building through the lens.

"When the war ended," she said, "people came up from the cellars." Including the Friedmans, who had been hiding in a basement of an abandoned apartment building across town. "My father and I went to see if our property was still standing."

It was, but an artillery round had ripped a massive hole through the double balcony and right into the apartment. "You could see the snow and wind blowing through," my father said. "It was very cold."

"What did you do?"

"We went in." The viewfinder was still plastered to her eye. "It was all rubble inside." The shops on the ground floor had been plundered, she recalled, their display cases looted. "Eventually my father found a vacant unit in the building, more or less livable, on the first floor."

"That was fortunate."

"A high-ranking Hungarian officer used to live there. A real Nazi type. He'd fled to Germany, we heard." Later, she said, Small-holders Party leader Ferenc Nagy moved from his flat in the building into the larger Friedman apartment. "He was in the government, so he could get money to do the repairs."

"Shall we cross the street?" I said.

My father lowered the camera. "Why?" I heard a clatter of dishes and the sound of people laughing. The café umbrellas fluttered in a gust of wind.

"To see it better."

"You can see fine from here."

I crossed the street anyway and tried the knob on the heavy front door. The door glass was framed in dark wood and reinforced with a metal lattice in a geometric design. It was locked. I studied the list of names on the gilt-plated building registry.

I sensed a presence and turned to find my father behind me, her lips pressed together in a thin, tight line.

"What are you doing?" she said.

"I'm going to buzz someone." There were a few businesses listed among the tenants—a tax consultant, an ice cream shop, a beauty parlor. I opted for the button next to Várady Szalon. My father pushed my hand away.

"You are bothering people."

"I just want to see—"

"I told you, there's nothing to see."

I hit the buzzer.

"You are making a pest of yourself."

No one answered. I tried the tax consultant.

"Stop it!"

Just then, a man came out of the building. I stuck my foot in the door before it closed.

"Two minutes. Just show me the lobby."

Ilonka, who had followed us across the street, touched my father's elbow and said something in a low voice. They filed in after me into the foyer.

The front hall was refurbished. The red-tiled wainscoting gleamed, and the freshly painted walls glowed a warm creamy yellow, white moldings buffed to a high shine. The interior Art Nouveau friezes had been restored; they ran in a long white panorama down either side of the hallway and across the ceiling. I gazed upon the lithe nudes in playful motion: a girl in ecstatic mid-twirl with arms flung wide; two nubile dancers prancing together with wild abandon, their fingers interlaced; a muscular and naked Adonis reclining with a book. Had these been the daily muses of my father's boyhood?

The beautification project came to an abrupt halt at the end of the corridor. To the right, a dim, sour-smelling stairwell led to the upper floors. Half the lights were burned out. In an alcove under the steps, garbage overflowed from trash bins. Graffiti spattered the walls, which bore a few chipped remnants of a once colorful geometric mosaic. A rusted cage elevator sat at its center, its walls patched with plywood. Directly ahead, the corridor led to a large interior courtyard, open to the sky. Four levels of yellow-brick galleries with floral-ornamented iron railings ran around its sides, like an inverted layer cake. The apartment doors opened onto the galleries. The geometric floor tiles were torn up. Exposed wiring dangled from the walls. A withered plant potted in a plastic canister sat in the center of the courtyard, its spindly stem drooping, half its leaves scattered on the ground.

I picked my way across the shards of tiles, then turned to look back. My father was standing by the potted plant. "The *sukkot* booth was here," she said. "My father would build it right in the courtyard." She was talking about the small temporary hut made of branches to mark the Jewish harvest festival, a tribute to the ephemeral abodes of the Israelites during their forty-year exile in the desert.

"See how dark it gets toward the back of the building?" she said.

I nodded.

"My father was very ingenious. He hung giant mirrors in the courtyard. So all the lower apartments at the back would get the light."

We began to make a slow circuit of the courtyard. The ground-floor shops that had thrived in my father's youth—the patisserie, the furrier, the beauty parlor—were all gone. The storefront that housed the patisserie—where my father used to eat Bavarian pastries (its specialty; the owner was German) and where Rozi Friedman used to take coffee with Ferenc Nagy—was now home to the Várady Szalon. A sandwich sign announced its services in a mongrel Hunglish: KOZMETICA, MASSZAGE, MANICURE, TAROT. Not everything was new. In the opposite corner of the courtyard, behind a padlocked iron grate, a set of cinder-block steps descended into darkness. Bolted to the wall, a small sign with an arrow pointing down the stairs announced, ÓVÓHELY. Bomb shelter. The sign had been hanging there since World War II.

"For a little bit during the war," my father said, pointing to the *szalon* but referring to the vanished confectionary, "I worked here with my friend Tamás—after we couldn't go to school." Tamás Somló was a boy a few years younger than my father, whose family rented one of the apartments in Ráday 9. The Somlós were Jews who converted to Catholicism in the 1930s. When the war came, Tamás's father, the neighborhood pharmacist, was sent to forced labor and then, after returning to Budapest in the fall of 1944, arrested and deported to Mauthausen. "There wasn't much business," my father recalled of István and Tamás's brief wartime stint behind the counter of the German patisserie. "We got to eat the leftover pastries before they got thrown out."

I proposed we go upstairs. My father shook her head and backed toward the front hall. When she reached the alcove with the elevator, she froze.

"Look at what they've done," she said. She pointed an accusatory finger at the oxidizing shell of a once glamorous lift. "It was glass and hand-carved wood, mirrored walls. A beauty." She turned and gestured toward the bare cement of the alcove. "There used to be a beautiful mosaic here. . . . LOOK AT THIS! THEY'VE STOLEN EVERY TILE."

My father whipped around and started toward the foyer. "I need to get the camper," she said over her shoulder. "It's not safe to leave it on the street."

"But couldn't we—"

"I BROUGHT YOU HERE. I SHOWED IT TO YOU. ENOUGH." Her raised voice ricocheted off the bare walls.

"Don't yell at me."

"I wrote them a letter," she said. She had lowered her voice but not her rage.

"Who?"

"The people who live in our apartment. I wrote them that I'm the family owner of this house and they shouldn't buy this property, because the ones who are selling it, it's not theirs to sell. . . . I TOLD YOU THIS. YOU SHOWED NO INTEREST WHATSOEVER."

She turned away and headed down the corridor at a furious pace, her heels clip-clopping on the tiled floor. The street door opened and shut with a heavy thud. Ilonka murmured an apology and scurried after my father. I stood alone in the gloom of the alcove, trying to picture the mirrored walls of the elevator, the giant mirrors my grandfather had hung in the courtyard that once brought light into the dark recesses of my father's youth.

My father was waiting by the camper, her shoulders bunched in a posture I'd known since childhood, and knew to fear. She disabled the alarm and unlocked the doors. Ilonka took the backseat. I envied her refuge. We rode for a long time before my father broke the silence. Our silence. She wasn't the only one in a rage. "I had to get the car," my father said, her jaw tight. "They *steal* things."

My recorder, which I'd forgotten to shut off, caught my subsequent meltdown. I was dismayed when, months later, I transcribed that segment, and not just because for the first ten minutes the traffic had drowned out half the words. I had remembered the drive home as a culmination, the moment when we finally, coherently, grappled with the demon in the room. But when I played the tape, what I heard was a jumble of disconnected words, unfinished sentences, repetitions that went nowhere, dialogue from a Mamet play, or the non-dialogue of my childhood.

SUSAN: . . . only asking . . . few minutes . . .

STEFI: . . . stole the car . . . my house.

SUSAN: . . . don't care . . .

STEFI: . . . nothing to see . . .

SUSAN: . . . not talking . . .

STEFI: ... ringing people's doorbells ...

SUSAN: ... that's not what ...

STEFI: ... We went inside ...

SUSAN: ... not about the house ...

When we had crossed over the Chain Bridge and started the climb through the Buda Hills, the traffic diminished, and the recording was less broken.

STEFI: ... bought the apartment from people in no position to sell it. It's stolen property. Thieves. ... They took what's rightfully mine. And yours. ...

SUSAN: You keep saying that, but I want to—

STEFI: They took it. ... Why should I ... some sentimental voyage? ...

SUSAN: What I'm—

STEFI: ... I'm not interested. ... It was always a dark house.

SUSAN: It's not about the house. ... If you can't talk to me, I—

STEFI: I've talked to you for days. I came here, I found a parking place, I showed you the house.

SUSAN: ... Why can't ... a daughter and her father ... I came here to see if there's anything—

STEFI: I don't want to be in that house.

SUSAN: Stop talking about the fucking house.

STEFI: I was thrown out of my own house. Kicked out by—

SUSAN: That's not—

STEFI: Kicked out by *your mother*.

If this were about a house, it wasn't just the one at Ráday 9. There was the other house, a tract home in an American bedroom community a world and a time away, when she was a parent and

I was a child. We were cruising the quiet back streets when we finally got to that night in Yorktown Heights. The voices on the tape were clear.

STEFI: . . . And you went along with it. When I hadn't done a damn thing.

SUSAN: You—

STEFI: Accused by the whole family, you know? Normal families stick together. They don't fight each other for no reason.

SUSAN: *There was a reason—*

STEFI: A family should stay together. I brought my parents together. *I* saved my family. *You* took your mother's side against me—

SUSAN: Because you—

STEFI: How would you like it if I threw your mother out of the house? How would you like it if a *woman* gets thrown out of her house?

SUSAN: You did—

STEFI: You took your mother's point of view that I should be thrown away, for some reason that she thought up that is not so. Some fantasy. I don't know why.

SUSAN: You attacked—

STEFI: I haven't got any muscles. How could I beat anyone up?

SUSAN: I was there. You—

My father was shouting. I was, too, and also crying. Ilonka reached over the seat and began patting my arm, making soothing, clucking noises. I jerked my arm away.

STEFI: There was no violence. I'm weak.

SUSAN: Then how come—

STEFI: She had the police take me away—when I was
          ABSOLUTELY INNOCENT.

SUSAN: YOU broke down the door. YOU came into—

STEFI: Your mother destroyed my life. She destroyed my family.

SUSAN: . . . YOU, with a knife, attacked—

STEFI: This was a million years ago. There's no need to go back
          to these ancient family things. These are dead things in
          the past. We're different people now.

SUSAN: I'm not—

STEFI: I've forgotten the whole thing. It's like it wasn't even me.

There was a long indecipherable section as a truck went by. Then
the tape cut off.

PART II

10

Something More and Something Other

"Excuse me, are you . . . ?" I debated how to end the sentence: Melanie? Mel?

The woman at the next table was wide-shouldered and sported a Chanel knockoff pantsuit, chunky earrings, and a frosted bob. She had been looking around as if she might be expecting someone.

". . . Melanie?" I settled on.

She shook her head. I sat back down and continued my clandestine inspection of the customers and their putative genders.

I'd been home from Budapest for a week, the last twenty minutes of which I'd spent at the Coffee People on Twenty-Third Avenue in Portland, Oregon, waiting for the arrival of someone I'd never met.

"I'm not sure whether I'll be dressed as a woman or a man," Melanie Myers told me when I set up our meeting. Melanie had been Mel until three years earlier, when he had gone to Thailand to get the same operation as my father, with the same surgeon. Melanie now lived part of the year in Portland, her hometown. "Call

Melanie," my father had advised. "She's practically down the street from you. She would make a good interview for your book." The rest of the year Melanie lived in Phuket, Thailand, where she ran Melanie's Cocoon, a guesthouse for postoperative transsexuals recovering from surgery. My father had stayed there for several weeks after her sex reassignment surgery. Melanie had been on the scene for my father's transit from one sex to another. I'd only known my father as before and after—suburban über-patriarch or ultra-femme hausfrau—separated by an empty moat of many years. Melanie knew the in-between. If I were searching for the fluidity in my father's story, as opposed to the either/or, Melanie might bear witness to my father's most liminal moment.

I scanned the café. Did this "woman" in a dress look like someone who was once a man? Did that "man" in a suit look like a former man who had become a woman and was now a "man" trying to pass as a man? After a while, everyone seemed to be in drag.

Another quarter hour went by. The door of Coffee People swung open to admit a middle-aged man—or "man"—in a shaggy crew cut, wire-rimmed oval glasses, a striped-blue men's dress shirt, and khaki pants. He had a round face and a charming gap between his front teeth that reminded me of Lauren Hutton's. He hesitated a few steps inside the door and looked around.

I stood up, deliberated. "Are you . . . ?" To my relief, he nodded and came over.

"I'm going by Mel now," he said as we shook hands.

"I was a really good-looking guy when I was a man," Mel told me as he settled in with an iced latte. "A real man, I mean . . . I mean, I'm going back to being a man now but"—he rolled his eyes at his own verbal tangle—"picture a football quarterback type. Big strong chin, square jaw, Charlton Heston, Marlboro Man." He pulled out a Palm Pilot and began clicking through pictures, looking for an old photograph.

"Women found me really attractive. But I always dreamed of being a girl. I dreamed of it when I was six years old. I just loved everything about being a woman, the way they got to be treated, pampered, the attention. If I could have gotten that attention as a guy, maybe I wouldn't have done it."

As he spoke, he punched at the buttons on the Palm Pilot. "It's in here somewhere," he said. "I've got a lot of pictures. Hundreds."

"You don't have that square jaw anymore," I said.

"No, I had the jaw flanges cut off and the chin narrowed. I had my whole face redone." He pushed back his hairline to show me. "I had several millimeters of bone taken off my forehead. Titanium pins put in my forehead. Seven millimeters off my nose, seven off my chin. They had to peel off the skin, peel off my face basically."

I winced. "Sounds excruciating."

"I wouldn't have done the surgery if I couldn't have the face," Mel said. "I could never be a clown. If I'm going to be seen in women's clothes, I'm going to be genuine. I had one of the best facial surgeons in the country, Dr. Douglas Ousterhout in San Francisco—he practically invented FFS." Facial feminization surgery. "They say he based it all on his one ideal woman."

Later, I'd look up Ousterhout on the Internet and find before-and-after photographs of his patients, YouTube promotional videos, and patient testimonials to his magic touch. A website developed and run by "Diane," one of his former patients, praised Ousterhout's work and trumpeted FFS as the path to "achieving your dream" and enabling "you to pass as the woman that you are. . . . Dr. Ousterhout will try to improve your appearance so that you feel that you fit back into society as the person you want to see in the mirror."

"It cost thirty-two thousand dollars," Mel said. "For the face surgery, I mean." He spent tens of thousands more for the breast and genital surgery, hair implants, speech therapy, and an extensive new wardrobe. "I was like the poster child for Best Trans Person in Portland."

He held up his Palm Pilot. "See, there I am. Don't recognize me, do you?"

As advertised, the original Mel looked like a high school quarterback.

He clicked some more. "See that?" Three women stood arm and arm in the picture, two petite Thai girls and a Caucasian who towered over them. "I showed this picture to my brother and he said, 'Who's the woman in the middle?' And I said, 'That's *me*.' "

"How did your family handle it?"

Mel was quiet for a moment. "My daughter doesn't speak to me anymore." He looked back down at the Palm Pilot. "I have a picture of her in here somewhere." He searched for a while and then gave up. "This thing has six hundred pictures." He smiled, a sheepish gap-toothed grin. "Most of them are of me. When I first came out, I went overboard. I dressed like eye candy, the best makeup, the most expensive wigs, beautiful clothes from Nordstrom. I got attention all the time."

"And now?"

"Well, I had my dream. It was a great three-year dream. But now it's back to reality."

After the operation, Melanie lost her job as a commercial printing salesman—a firing that she suspected was prompted by her change in sex: "My boss caused me to lose clients by not delivering my orders on time and used that to slide in the knife." Before sales, he'd worked ten years in a lithography darkroom, "manipulating photographs for the big catalogues—Macy's, Nordstrom, Neiman Marcus. I was brightening, darkening, kind of like what you say your father did." The two never connected over their previous work lives: that was in the past. Now Mel was "flat-out broke," in danger of losing his condo, and trying to make ends meet with a part-time

telemarketing gig, selling enrollments to "remote learning opportunities" for an online university. He was desperately looking for more
remunerative employment, and to improve his chances, dressed as
Mel for job interviews. In the sales profession, he noted, a woman
had to contend with sex discrimination.

He was also lonely. He yearned to be reunited with his longtime
Thai girlfriend, who worked as a cocktail waitress in Phuket. She
had planned to move to the United States so they could live together.
But she couldn't stay in the country without a green card—or a
marriage certificate to an American man. Mel wanted to marry her,
but his operation had foreclosed that possibility, or at least it did
in 2004. Besides, he said, "The whole dressing-up-as-a-woman
thrill, I just don't have the same interest in it anymore. It wasn't
real. I was just buying approval." In the last several months, Mel
had begun looking into "getting the papers to change back to
a man."

"But it's what you felt you were?" I asked. "A woman?"

"I don't want to get into that." Mel gave me a sidelong look.
He'd checked into me online, he said. He knew I was a feminist.
Which evidently suggested to him that I didn't believe in gender
distinctions. "But there *are* differences between males and females,"
he said. "There *is* a feminine nature."

"And do you have a feminine nature?"

Mel slowly clicked through another set of pictures on his Palm
Pilot. Melanie in a tube top. Melanie in a miniskirt and stiletto
heels. Melanie in a strapless evening gown. "I don't know," he said
finally. "I used to think so. Now I think there's a spectrum. And
I'm right at the midpoint, a five. I feel that I'm androgynous. . . ."
He paused on a shot of Melanie in shorts, arm in arm with her
girlfriend under some palm trees in Phuket.

"I feel I'm androgynous, but I don't *want* to be," he continued.
His gaze was stricken. "People can't survive without categories.

Even people on the fringes need categories, so they can be on the fringes. You have to have an identity."

————

Portland had been something of a transsexual destination since the early 1990s, when Dr. Toby Meltzer, a local plastic surgeon, was one of only twenty physicians in the country performing sex reassignment surgery. He operated on thousands of patients until, in 2003, conservative owners took over the hospital where he had admitting privileges and Meltzer decamped to Scottsdale, Arizona. When I moved to Portland in the early aughts, I often saw transitioning patients nursing coffee after hormone treatments outside my neighborhood supermarket. Several bars nearby were transsexual redoubts, and the Portland public library's shelves contained an unusual number of volumes dedicated to the transsexual phenomenon. When I returned from my first trip to Budapest, I logged many hours in the library's wood-paneled reading room, under the oil paintings of the city's stern founding fathers, working my way through the collection—305.3. 306.76. 617.520592—the Dewey Decimal classifications where books on gender identity "disorders" and sex reassignment surgery were filed. After a few days prowling the stacks, I had the numbers memorized.

The Portland library's selection of books on male-to-female transsexuals (and there were few then on their female-to-male counterparts) were overwhelmingly autobiographical. That was no anomaly: memoir is the preferred genre of transsexual literature, a particular version of memoir, in which the memories that predate the operation are often cast as belonging to someone else, a person who no longer exists.

That erasure was established in the very first modern transsexual memoir, *Man into Woman*, the 1933 account of Danish artist Einar Wegener's transformation into Lili Elbe: "There could be no past for her. Everything in the past belonged to a person who had vanished, who was dead." Two decades later, Roberta Cowell, a formerly "aggressive male" Spitfire pilot and race-car driver, was erecting the same firewall: "My personality was now entirely a new one," she wrote in *Roberta Cowell's Story*, a recollection that closed with these words: "The past is forgotten, the future doesn't matter, and the glowingly happy present is even better than I had hoped." In *Conundrum*, Jan Morris's classic 1974 chronicle of her transformation from rugged mountaineer and cavalry officer to modest matron, the author pays her last respects before surgery to the soon-to-be-former James: "[I] went to say good-bye to myself in the mirror. We would never meet again." In *Second Serve*, celebrated tennis player Renée Richards (formerly Richard Raskind) said of her 1975 operation, "Dick was turned off." The pain that she felt upon coming to on the surgical table "was Richard Henry Raskind's death throe." The postoperative state was, as so many of these memoirists put it, a "second life," a reboot that reset and replaced the original birth.

The before and after states in the books I read often seemed cast in hell and heaven terms: the before an inferno of self-loathing, self-mutilation, shame, and suicide attempts. "I was trapped, buried alive," decorated soldier and *Chicago Tribune* correspondent Nancy Hunt wrote of her former male physique in her 1978 memoir, *Mirror Image*. "I was condemned to perpetual imprisonment in that loathsome frame." In Roberta Cowell's account, the decades before surgery—a time of "black depression" and "abject misery" when she "envied the insane"—gave way, post-op, to romantic evenings spent in "a perfect dream" with "attentive" gentlemen (who held doors for her and retrieved her gloves) and genteel afternoons chatting with the gentler sex at "an all-woman tea-party." In so many cases, the "after" in these stories appeared to be a blissful round of dinner dates and just-us-girls pajama parties. "I was like a school girl all excited about my first date," Rhonda Hoyman wrote of being "born again" as female in her 1999 memoir, *Rhonda:*

The Woman in Me. "Just like the bride getting ready for her wedding (hopefully I will experience this soon)."

These presto-chango transformations put me in mind of the conversion stories that used to circulate among my evangelical classmates in high school, the *Cross and the Switchblade* formula applied to gender redemption—a rebirth from sinner to saved—or, in gender terms, from deviant lascivious male to demure Angel of the House. "It was obscene, ludicrous, disgusting," Hunt said of herself as a cross-dressing male, an obscenity from which her surgery would spell "deliverance." "I grieved for the others and felt guilty that I should be saved while they were damned," she wrote of her preoperative fellows. "But I rejoiced in my salvation."

Rebirth, especially in the early generation of memoirs, frequently meant coming back to life not just as a woman but as a woman who fit every hoary trope of the Cult of True Womanhood—submissive, chaste, flighty, passive, helpless. In *Man into Woman*, Lili Elbe described herself after the operation as "a completely defenseless creature" who only feels "safe" under the ministrations of her surgeon, "where the strong will of another stands between me and the outside world, as my protector and defender." Genital surgeries and hormone treatments evidently produced not only a new physiology but a new and girlish personality—or rather, an old, old stereotype. Roberta Cowell reported that she was suddenly prone to blushing, wept over schmaltzy films and novels, and developed a "strong maternal instinct," "a new and strong interest in domestic work," handwriting that was "rounder and neater," and a craving for "chocolate creams." Not only that, her "mental processes" slowed and she "found it difficult to summon up will-power when required." A newly acquired incapacity also afflicted Jan Morris, who found herself entranced by male chivalry—and flummoxed by the challenge of screwing in a light-bulb. The former Jim Morris, who had assayed Mount Everest with Sir Edmund Hillary and spent five years in the 9th Queen's Royal

Lancers, acted as if she had trouble putting a car in reverse and opening bottles, and claimed to be "distinctly less forceful," "more retiring, more ready to be led, more passive," and eager to shop for clothes.

> I was even more emotional now. I cried very easily, and was ludicrously susceptible to sadness or flattery. Finding myself rather less interested in great affairs (which are placed in a new perspective, I do assure you, by a change of sex), I acquired a new concern for small ones. My scale of vision seemed to contract. . . .
>
> It is, I think, a simpler vision that I now possess. Perhaps it is nearer a child's.

The women they had always known they were seemed to be the exact sort of girl I'd always thought of as false. I cringed when I discovered, in the appendix to Rhonda Hoyman's 1999 memoir, a section titled "Rhonda's Top 10 Tips!" ("Tip #3: Quit using soap on your face. Start using a skin care cleansing system and moisturizer every day." "Tip #4: Try to match your nail color with the lipstick shade you most often wear, and when possible, coordinate in threes, like your shoes, belt and purse. The key word is: accessorize, accessorize, accessorize.")

I knew some, and would hear more, about the supposed enmity between transsexuals and feminists—or "trans-exclusionary radical feminists" (TERFs), a derogation adopted in the aughts by trans advocates. As far as I could tell, the label fit a few veteran separatists who still wanted to bar transsexuals from the (now defunct) Michigan Womyn's Music Festival or the fans of Janice Raymond's 1978 manifesto, *The Transsexual Empire: The Making of the She-Male*, a book that, in the course of advancing some more subtle thoughts, cast male-to-female transsexuals as surgically engineered monsters threatening to invade female spaces, "supplant the role of women in mothering," and metaphorically "rape" women by appropriating their bodies. I didn't want to fit the mold of cliché feminist decrying cliché transsexuality. But the repeated swipes at feminism in the memoirs I was reading didn't make my nonaligned status any easier. "Liberation from what?" Nancy Hunt wrote of the women's liberation movement in *Mirror Image*. "From the grace and freedom and beauty and emotional spontaneity of womanhood?" It was a verdict that would only crescendo with the years. "This scapegoating of femininity has become the Achilles' heel of the feminist movement," Julia Serano wrote in her popular 2007 manifesto, *Whipping Girl: A Transsexual Woman on Sexism and the Scapegoating of Femininity* (issued by Seal Press, a feminist publishing house). Serano found "the feminist assumption that 'femininity is artificial' " to be "narcissistic," "arrogant," "blatantly misogynistic," and "patronizing toward those for whom femininity simply *feels right*." Serano cast her femininity defense in liberationist terms, but the bullets oddly ricocheted. She attributed feminist antagonism toward traditional femininity to "the fact that many of the women who have most strongly gravitated toward feminism are those who have found traditional feminine gender roles constraining or unnatural. In many cases, this is due to their own inclinations toward exceptional forms of gender expression." Or, put less politely, the old male-chauvinist canard that feminist are feminist because they're unfeminine.

The more I prowled the library stacks that year, and other stacks in the years to come, the more I bridled at these volumes with their Girls-Confidential tone, their cover images of junior-prom ingénues in sweater sets, their chapter titles set in the dainty looping script of old feminine-hygiene ads. The gender identity so many of these chronicles championed was aggressively wholesome, childlike, often prissy, and oddly desexualized. The former man, the authors reported, stalked the exotic lingerie aisles in spasms of shame and agony at his prurience, while the new girl was an innocent maiden of fastidious propriety, grateful to take a man's arm, flustered when a "dirty joke" was told, mortified if her shoes didn't match her purse. I thought of my father and all those "flamboyant" bordello get-ups she'd stowed away in the hallway locker in favor of "sedate" ladies' wear, all those FictionMania sex fantasies she'd printed out and then stashed on closet shelves. Was it really that easy to divorce ego and id, identity and desire? In memoir after memoir, the psychosexual and psychological complexities of an adult had been vanquished; the vamp had become a virgin, with the pre-sexual innocence of a child. (That second childhood, I noticed, was also a staple of so many trans fantasy websites I'd perused. One of FictionMania's largest categories of stories was "Age Regression.") In the 2006 memoir, *Wrapped in Blue: A Journey of Discovery* (cover shot: a profile of a pale blonde, her shoulders draped in blue velvet, clutching a single rose), Donna Rose recalled how thrilled she was with the gifts her mother brought to the hospital to celebrate her transformation: "a pink teddy bear" and "a box of pink bubble gum cigars that said, 'It's a Girl!'" Rose was forty-one at the time.

And my father seventy-six. If I had imagined my library research might bring me closer to an appreciation of her decision, these books were having the opposite effect.

Deirdre McCloskey's 1999 memoir, *Crossing*, began more promisingly: "In contrasting how men and women 'are' I do not mean to recruit sterotypes or essentialisms that have been used to the disadvantage of other women. Women are not always more loving, or less interested in career." And a trans woman with a career, she noted, "tries to keep it and does not in practice dissolve into a 1950s heaven of full-time cookie baking and teatime gossip." Yet even McCloskey, an economics and history professor, went on to truck in stereotypical tropes about male boorishness and ladies "sipping Chablis," "playing house intently," and enjoying cozy "girl-to-girl" talk. She itemized her new womanly ways: hates war stories, bored by sports, reads "women novelists," likes to cook, is eager to make her bed every morning, "dotes on every child she meets," and "loves, just loves, the little favors of womankind, getting a card for someone, making meatloaf for Charles up the street." And loves to shop: "She was just able to resist a beautiful pair of Italian flats full priced at $100." (She told her tale in third person.) One chapter was devoted to makeup: "*Eyeliner*: L'Oréal liquid, the most evocative of her cosmetics. She lines her eyes in 1950s style. . . ."

Was I wrong to flinch? "You have to think about when in their life course they were writing their autobiography," Susan Stryker, an LGBT history professor and male-to-female transsexual, told me when I expressed my discomfort with these sugar-and-spice accounts. "When you are transitioning, it's kind of an adolescence. And things other people dealt with when they were twelve—like, 'Does that eye shadow make me look pretty?' or 'What's my look?'—they are dealing with now. It's almost like being a convert to a new religion." Fair enough: proselyte prose. I remembered my own misadventures with Maybelline. And I also remembered how my ardent adolescent experiments in makeup and affectation were employed as concealer as much as glitter.

Surely there was a more complex drama beneath the crinoline and cinched waists, a narrative involving a particular set of needs, desires, aspirations, fears. If so, it was impossible to divine from these accounts. The one plotline of I-have-always-been-a-woman seemed to be trumping all the other motivations that might reflect the crosscurrents of the human psyche, motivations that weren't exclusively about gender. Where were the memoirs that engaged in some degree of self-inspection? I looked in vain for an account where the author asked, "Could I also be seeking womanhood to reclaim my innocence, be exonerated from the sins of my male past?" Or: "Could I be craving the moral stature that comes with being oppressed?" Or: "Do I want to be a woman to feel special? Celebrated? Loved?" Could that whole nest of an individual's history, all the idiosyncratic struggles, disappointments, and yearnings of a life, really be stuffed so tidily into the bottle labeled

Identity? Since Freud, the art of psychotherapy has been dedicated to teasing apart the many aspects of character that seem, on the surface, unitary. Since the Erikson era, much of the quest for identity appears to have been dedicated to the opposite, to the discounting of psychological complications, to the search for that single broad stroke that explains everything, that will collapse one's entire life story into an identity brand. But what happens when "identity" is used to disown "psychology"? What keeps that brand from becoming the "totalism" that Erikson warned against?

"Each of these adventurers passes directly from one pole of sexual experience to the other," Sandy Stone wrote in her 1991 cri de coeur, "The 'Empire' Strikes Back: A Posttranssexual Manifesto." "If there is any intervening space in the continuum of sexuality, it is invisible. . . . No wonder feminist theorists have been suspicious. Hell, *I'm* suspicious." Stone, a media theorist and male-to-female transsexual, had worked her way through some of the same early trans autobiographies that I had and was similarly dismayed. "All these authors replicate the stereotypical male account of the constitution of woman: Dress, makeup, and delicate fainting at the sight of blood," she wrote. All were "similar in their description of 'woman' as male fetish, as replicating a socially enforced role," and eager to cast themselves as the heroines of a "frogs into princesses" storybook tale. None seemed willing to envision a state of being between hyper-feminine and hyper-masculine. Stone's inquiry would open the door for a new set of transgender writers who challenged the limitations of the literature and who proclaimed themselves "gender outlaws."

"The 'Empire' Strikes Back" was originally intended as a rebuttal to *The Transsexual Empire* (in which Raymond drubbed Stone for having worked at an all-female recording collective in the '70s without revealing that she was once male) and, more broadly, to the handful of '70s feminist separatists who regarded transsexual-

ity (in the words of feminist theologian Mary Daly) as a "Frankenstein phenomenon." In the course of preparing her riposte, Stone
countenanced a lot of the questions ignored in the memoirs I'd
been reading, questions that had bedeviled me in Budapest and
that my father had been intent on evading. What should transsexuals' relationships be to their "former" selves, and what did it
mean to erase your past? By altering your body to "look" like the
sex you believed yourself to be, were you conforming to hide-
bound and sexist conceptions of femininity and masculinity, or
could you use those alterations to suggest that biology was not
destiny, that "trans" could mean not just crossing the gender line
but transcending gender altogether? As long as the currency of
transsexuality was "passing," Stone concluded, transsexuals would
be denying themselves "the ability to authentically represent the
complexities and ambiguities of lived experience." The phrase
recalled to me Erikson's formulation, "the diverse and conflicting stages and aspects of life" that, when renounced or repressed,
led to totalism.

Stone called on her sister trans women to reclaim their actual life
stories and deploy them as battering rams against the concrete walls
of the gender binary. "Transsexuals must take responsibility for all
of their history, to begin to rearticulate their lives not as a series of
erasures, . . . but as a political action begun by reappropriating difference and reclaiming the power of the refigured and reinscribed
body." They should define themselves, Stone proposed, as neither
"women" nor "men," but something mongrel, as representatives of
indeterminate or multiple genders whose existence poses a threat to
the fundamental assumptions of a world restricted to two sexes. In
other words, they should embrace "the promises of monsters" (a
phrase Stone borrowed from her mentor Donna Haraway, the feminist author of "A Cyborg Manifesto"). The very Frankenstein label
that had been hurled at transsexuals might be the source of their

liberation. Seeing beyond the gender binary, Stone declared in the 1999 documentary *Gendernauts*, was "the supreme act . . . because it is the beginning of the path to discovery of self, of our self, of my self, your self, of deeply and importantly who we are."

The "promises of monsters" would inspire another founding member of the new discipline of transgender studies, the LGBT historian Susan Stryker. "I will say this as bluntly as I know how," she wrote in a formative 1994 essay, adopting the epithet that had been hurled at her: "I am a transsexual, and therefore I am a monster." She titled her manifesto "My Words to Victor Frankenstein Above the Village of Chamounix," an allusion to the climactic scene in Mary Shelley's *Frankenstein*, in which the monster finally confronts his creator on the Mer de Glace glacier above the Chamonix Valley. "Words like 'creature,' 'monster,' and 'unnatural' need to be reclaimed by the transgendered," Stryker wrote. "As we rise up from the operating tables of our rebirth, we transsexuals are something more, and something other, than the creatures our makers intended us to be." Like Stone, Stryker believed transsexuals could use their "monstrous" state to expose the artifice of gender dimorphism. By "performing transgender rage" (the subtitle of her 1994 essay), they could lay bare "the constructedness of the natural order," she wrote. "The stigma itself becomes the source of transformative power." Or as she once put it to me with more brio: "We've been made disposable people and fuck that! I model unrepentance."

"If the modern 'problem of identity' is primarily how to construct an identity and keep it solid and stable," Polish sociologist Zygmunt Bauman wrote in 1997, "the postmodern 'problem of identity' is primarily how to avoid fixation and keep the options open." A good number of the new transgender theorists would agree with that. They were academics steeped in post-structuralism, in tune with the post-modern gestalt. But had the gender mavericks kept their options open? For all their assertions of the multiplicities of the gendered state (Stone maintained there were "thousands" of genders), the rebels repeatedly confessed a desire to be one sex only, the one that they had an operation to become, which was always the binary opposite of the one they'd been. Reading these testimonials, I kept hearing Mel's anguished assertion, *"People can't survive without categories."* In *Gender Outlaw*, Kate Bornstein, a performance artist and another pioneering transsexual writer of the new generation, called on her readers to topple the binary with a "revolution" of gender fluidity, a revolt that "recognizes no borders or rules of gender." Yet, even as she declared "I identify as neither male nor female," Bornstein described the devastation she felt when someone she barely knew accidentally referred to her as "him." "The world slowed down, like it does in the movies when someone is getting shot and the filmmaker wants you to feel every bullet enter your body," she wrote. "The words echoed in my ears over and over and over. . . . All the joy sucked out of my life in that instant." Or as Laverne Cox, the transgender star of the television series *Orange Is the New Black*, so adamantly put it, "When a trans woman gets called a man, that is an act of violence."

In the new millennium, all the way into the age of the hit Amazon series *Transparent* and the superstar status of former Olympian Caitlyn Jenner, the insistence on a gender continuum would grow ever louder, even as the adherence to the binary became all the more entrenched. So often in the era of PGP (or "preferred gender pronoun," a stipulation popularized on college campuses) and the fluidity supposedly expressed by choosing your "genderqueer" or "demigirl" or "guydyke" designation, an old-style fundamentalism lurked. In a time when the very idea of "woman" was being denounced as essentialist fantasy, the womanhood of male-to-female transsexuals was asserted as an inviolable absolute.

The postmodern transgender theorists who were seeking to "take responsibility for *all* of their history" weren't insisting on total womanhood in their writings. They weren't claiming to be Athenas sprung from the head of a surgical Dr. Zeus. They were intent on embracing even the "monstrous" aspects of their self-avowedly mongrel gender. Yet so many had carefully scrubbed their former identities from the biographical record, changing (à la Erik Erikson) not only their first but their last names. Why, I wondered, were renegades who "recognize no borders or rules of gender" placing barricades before their past selves and submitting to operations that seemed to enforce a sexual dualism? Or was that dualism only a way station?

In the overheated precincts of the Portland public library one winter's day, I sat fanning myself with my notebook and working my way through the rest of Kate Bornstein's *Gender Outlaw*. Bornstein lamented the "cultural pressure" she felt to jettison her penis to be what society deemed a "real woman." Yet, she went on to say, "Knowing what I know now, I'm real glad I had my surgery, and I'd do it again, just for the comfort I now feel with a constructed vagina." Her book ended with a long prose poem, penned on the occasion of the seventh anniversary of her surgery. In the final stanzas she wrote of her "thrill" when she encountered a girl instead of a boy in the mirror.

She then divulged:

> Girl?
> It's an identity I am working my way out of.

And she argued that, seven years hence, "My girl skin will be lying behind me in the desert," next to all her other cast-off gender allegiances. She would shed her identities, Bornstein contended and thumb her nose at those who "try to label me now."

11

A Lady Is a Lady
Whatever the Case May Be

If the undeclared war of modern transsexuality is between fluidity and binaries, the battle echoed down the decades of twentieth-century sexology. It especially reverberated through the work of two of sexology's commanding generals, Harry Benjamin and Magnus Hirschfeld.

In postwar America, Harry Benjamin would be anointed "the father of transsexualism." He defined the condition's terms and authored its treatment regimen, which for years was known as the Harry Benjamin Standards of Care, and which still reigns. His take on transsexuality was leveraged on a very public creation story that had titillated the world, a story that provided Benjamin, a German emigré and avuncular endocrinologist with a flagging gerontology practice in Manhattan at the time, with a cause and a template. The story belonged to Christine Jorgensen, the first sex-change celebrity.

On December 1, 1952, Benjamin was sixty-seven years old and about to take down his medical shingle when he saw the 72-point all-caps headline on the front page of the New York *Daily News*:

EX-GI BECOMES BLONDE BEAUTY. The story was accompanied by large before and after photographs: George W. Jorgensen Jr., in his army khakis and garrison cap; and Christine, sporting a pin-curled coif, nutria fur coat, and pearl clip earrings. "A Bronx youth, who served two years in the Army during the war and was honorably discharged," the story began, "has been transformed by the wizardry of medical science into a beautiful woman."

The former World War II private had flown to Denmark and, after a series of operations and a legal name change, returned as Christine Jorgensen, alighting at New York's Idlewild Airport to a media frenzy. The *American Weekly*, which paid Jorgensen more than $20,000 for her exclusive account, declared, "The story all America has been waiting for." Evidently it was. According to *Editor & Publisher*, Jorgensen's transformation "received the largest worldwide coverage in the history of newspaper publishing." As historian Joanne Meyerowitz noted in *How Sex Changed*, her authoritative and richly detailed history of transsexuality in the United States, the *Daily News*'s article on Jorgensen was the newspaper's "number-one story of 1953, outpacing in circulation the number-two story on the execution of atomic spy Julius Rosenberg and his wife, Ethel."

One of its avid readers was my father, and the story of Jorgensen's surgery jolted him into a new frame of mind. "It was the first time," she told me, "when I thought, okay, maybe I could just change my sex." The news was also pivotal for Harry Benjamin. The doctor dashed off a letter to Jorgensen to offer his professional assistance. "In my many years of practice of sexology and endocrinology," he wrote, "problems similar to yours have been brought to me frequently." Benjamin had a longstanding interest in sexology and sexual minorities. Nevertheless, before he wrote his letter to Jorgensen, he'd treated fewer than ten patients complaining of gender confusion. (He was better known for dispensing "rejuvenation" hormone therapy to older patients hoping to reclaim their youth.) An introduction between Benjamin and Jorgensen was quickly arranged, brokered by the pulp-romance and sci-fi writer Tiffany Thayer.

Less than a year later, Benjamin published his first tract on transsexuals in the *International Journal of Sexology*. In short order, he claimed credit for inventing the term "transsexualism" (already coined by another doctor) and established himself as the condition's leading authority. With help from a generous donation from a rich patient (who was also seeking a sex-change operation, from female to male), he established the Harry Benjamin Foundation and moved his practice to a larger Park Avenue office. In 1966, Benjamin wrote *The Transsexual Phenomenon*, the first major text on the subject, which would soon be known as the "transsexual bible." By the late '70s, he had treated more than fifteen hundred transsexual clients.

In his first article, Benjamin had described sex as a diverse quality, a "complex variety" that yielded no absolute men and women. But by the time he published the "bible," his thought had shifted toward a medical model for transsexuality more in tune with postwar America's twinned preoccupations: gender conformity and the search for a "true identity."

To determine which transsexuals were eligible for surgery, Benjamin created a classification system, which he called the Sex Orientation Scale, or SOS. He plugged patients into a grid of three "groups" and six "types" of his own devising—from "pseudo transvestite" and "fetishistic transvestite" on one end of the scale to the "true transsexual/moderate intensity" and "true transsexual/high intensity" on the other. According to Benjamin, a preoperative "true" male-to-female transsexual could be identified by several traits: The patient feels he is "trapped in a male body." He "despises his male sex organs." He has "a low libido" (that being feminine) and is "often asexual." He is attracted to men only *as* a woman (the reverse being homosexual).

Benjamin initially regarded these categories as "approximations, schematized and idealized," placeholders until "future studies and observations" came along. But his loose taxonomy was transformed by his successors into a gold standard. By the late '60s, a new generation of university-based clinicians—most notably psychologist John Money and psychiatrists Robert Stoller and Richard Green—were enforcing a more rigid binary and a "preventative" model intended to stamp out early signs of "incongruous gender" in children. Their preoccupation with training patients to express what Money and Green called a "culturally acceptable gender role" befitted the Cold War geopolitics of the time. "The border crossings had become securitized," Susan Stryker told me. "And it became, what do we do with the 'problem' of the nonaligned genders? How do we get them in line?"

By the mid-'70s, more than forty gender identity clinics from Johns Hopkins to the University of Minnesota to Stanford had sprung up to teach "acceptable" gender roles to young children and to diagnose transsexuals and determine whether they should be recommended for surgery. "Some of the doctors," Meyerowitz observed, "actually required their [transsexual] patients to undergo training in conventional gender stereotypes." At the Stanford clinic, "the screening process included a 'rehabilitation' period with workshops on appropriate grooming."

The era's new regimen also gave impetus to the view, which prevails today, that transsexuality has little to do with erotic impulse. The distinction between gender and sex—"Gender is located above, and sex below the belt," Benjamin postulated— became dictum under the new generation of sexologists, who coined the term "gender identity." UCLA psychiatrist Stoller drew a firm line between "gender identity"—what gender one believed oneself to be—and "sexual identity," which was limited to what one did or fantasized doing in bed. By the early '70s, transsexualism was being described in the clinical literature as "a disorder of gender identity," separate from and even antithetical to sexuality. "A single episode of cross-dressing in association with sexual arousal is regarded as sufficient to exclude the diagnosis of transsexualism," Howard J. Baker, a psychiatrist at the UCLA Gender Identity Research Clinic, asserted in 1969 in the *American Journal of Psychiatry*. "Transsexuals," he stated flatly, "never become sexually excited as a result of cross-dressing." Many transsexual advocates guard that border even today. When a 2003 book by a research psychologist suggested that some male-to-female transsexuals were aroused by the idea of themselves as women—a concept known as autogynephilia—the author and his supporters were met with fury.*

As the years passed, Benjamin became increasingly insistent about the need for transsexuals to pass as "normal," meaning that his male-to-female patients (and he mainly treated male-to-female) who qualified for surgery were expected to embody all the clichés of postwar femininity. He, along with the newer cohort of sexologists, was disinclined to accept clients whose exterior appearance and presentation failed to fit an image of the ideal woman or who balked at traditional sex roles. "This includes not only passing as members of the desired sex," Benjamin instructed, "but also accepting the social, economic, and familial consequences of the change." His favored patients were the ones who fulfilled his vision of true womanhood; "my girls," he called them. Benjamin

---

* After Northwestern University psychologist J. Michael Bailey published *The Man Who Would Be Queen*, a group of transgender activists launched a protracted campaign against him, charging him with violating scientific ethics (he was cleared) and practicing psychology without a license (he was again cleared). Rumors were spread about his sexual behavior, and images of his children were posted online with sexually explicit captions (justified as fair turnabout because his work exploited "vulnerable" people). After Anne Lawrence, a physician who calls herself an "autogynephilic transsexual," and Alice Dreger, a bioethicist and longtime advocate for the rights of the intersexed, defended the book, they were likewise hounded and their professional reputations attacked.

and a Los Angeles sex-change surgeon he worked with liked to go to lunch surrounded by their particularly beautiful patients. In Benjamin's case, particularly beautiful meant "Aryan good looks, blond-haired and blue-eyed," recalled Stryker, who conducted oral histories of Benjamin's patients when she was director of the GLBT Historical Society. "He liked to show off his trans arm candy. He took a proprietary, look-what-we-made pride in it all. It was very much a Pygmalion kind of thing."

In Benjamin's own case histories, he cast his clientele in sugar-plum terms: "Ruth" is a "tall, slender woman," he wrote, who "crosses her legs and automatically adjusts her fashionable short skirt as any woman would." "Harriet" is "an attractive young lady" who has "met her Prince Charming" ("a responsible and under-standing older man") and, having relinquished her job for "house-hold duties" and made plans to adopt a child, has achieved "a happy ending." Benjamin's descriptions sometimes sounded like they belonged in a '50s B-movie.

There was, in fact, such a movie: Ed Wood Jr.'s 1953 cult film, *Glen or Glenda*, in which a Benjamin-like psychiatrist supervising the sex change of a Jorgensen-like former GI (played by Wood, himself a lifelong cross-dresser) instructs his patient on "the duty of a woman," "the correct styling for her facial contours," and "the proper walk." Due to the good doctor's tutelage—"A lady is a lady whatever the case may be"—and thanks "to the corrections of medical science," Glenda's case "has a happy ending."

Benjamin's most famous client was only too glad to play the fairy-tale princess. "It is possible that my attachment to the world of make believe was influenced even before I was born," Jorgensen wrote on the first page of her memoir, *Christine Jorgensen: A Personal Autobiography*, "for my paternal grandfather, Charles Gustav Jorgensen, came to this country from Odense, Denmark, the birthplace of Hans Christian Andersen." Jorgensen's allegiance to Andersen startled me, all the more because it wasn't the only parallel with my father. As a young man, Jorgensen relates, he adored marionettes ("I never seemed to tire of manipulating the tiny figures in their fanciful world"), aspired to photography and set up a darkroom at home, and soon set his sights on a career in film. Those ambitions dead-ended in the 1940s in the "cutting library" of RKO-Pathé News in New York, where George Jr. worked in the newsreel's back office, splicing bits of film together to create stock footage. I couldn't help but think of my father's lifelong propensity to cut and splice, in darkrooms on continent after continent.

Two months after her triumphant touchdown at Idlewild Airport, Jorgensen would find herself under attack, thanks to the absence of one "correction of medical science." In April 1953, the *New York Post* published its first installment of a six-part exposé, "The Truth About 'Christine' Jorgensen." She was "a woman in name only," the newspaper held, because she had no female organs. The rest of the media, from *Newsweek* to *True Romance*, piled on. "Jorgensen was no girl at all," *Time* decreed, "only an altered male." If she wouldn't submit to the knife, she couldn't wear the glass slipper. Jorgensen was despondent. Whether in response to the attacks or not, she turned to Harry Benjamin and another physician for a surgical intervention: in a seven-hour operation in the spring of 1954, a plastic surgeon harvested skin grafts from Jorgensen's thighs and fashioned a kind of vagina. The surgery was reportedly a failure by one measure—she told friends that the vaginal canal was too short for intercourse. Worse, the operation dragged on for so long that the anesthesia threatened to wear off, and when an ether mask was hastily applied to keep the patient knocked out, Jorgensen's face was badly burned. "I remember clearly the feelings of dread and terror," she wrote later, "and was far more concerned about facial burns than the complex surgery I'd been through." Jorgensen understood that, whether the equipment worked or not, the most critical test for success as a girl was *looking* like one. "I had to become super-female," she wrote later. "I couldn't have one single masculine trait."

In 1930, Harry Benjamin hosted a prominent German sexologist on his visit to the United States, physician Magnus Hirschfeld. The two men were friends: they had toured the demimonde of Berlin together in the '20s, and when Hirschfeld came to New York he stayed in Benjamin's apartment and gave private lectures in his office. "Benjamin understood himself as a German sexologist in the Hirschfeld tradition," Meyerowitz told me. "They both rejected psychoanalysis; they both advocated for the rights of sexual and gender minorities. They both responded sympathetically to desperate patients." Yet Hirschfeld espoused an ethic directly at odds with the dualism that would come to prevail in the United States later in the century. "The number of actual and imaginable sexual varieties is almost unending," Hirschfeld wrote in 1910. "In each person there is a different mixture of manly and womanly substances, and as we cannot find two leaves alike on a tree, then it is highly unlikely that we will find two humans whose manly and womanly characteristics equally match in kind and number."

In 1919 in Berlin, Hirschfeld established the world's first institute to study sexuality, which issued one of the earliest scientific reports on transsexual surgery. Hirschfeld himself conducted his field studies in the subterranean sexual haunts of Weimar Berlin. He spent years collecting eyewitness observations and distributing detailed questionnaires (ultimately filled out by more than ten thousand people). From this research, and flouting the iron-clad separate-spheres dictates of Wilhelmine Germany, he derived his prime finding: sexual identities were wildly varied and fluid, and defied classification. Categories of sex were "only abstractions, invented extremes." While Hirschfeld constructed categories to aid his work and introduced some of the terminology that would, decades hence, find its way into the *Diagnostic and Statistical Manual of Mental Disorders*, he maintained throughout his life that no one was a "true" sex type; human beings were all to some degree bisexual and bi-gendered, all "sexual intermediaries"— and, because of these endless variations, defined less by their difference than by their shared humanity. At one point, Hirschfeld tried to calculate all the varieties—he arrived at a grand total of 43,046,721—before deciding that number was a gross undercount.

He took the same approach to transvestism, a term that he coined but saw as an "inclination," not a genus. To label someone a transvestite, Hirschfeld argued, was to constrain their experience to too narrow and visual a category, one that could not do justice to the variegations of their internal emotional life. "One disadvantage of the term," he wrote, "is that it describes only the external side, while the internal is limitless." It was this limitlessness that he believed must be taken into account in any political struggle for sexual liberation: "Sexual human rights would have to begin with the acknowledgment that sexualities—in accordance with the doctrine of sexual intermediaries—are as diverse as the number of sexed individuals."

The rights of sexual minorities became Hirschfeld's lifelong cause. For decades he fought to strike down Germany's notorious Paragraph 175, which criminalized male homosexuality, and he convinced the Berlin police to recognize his "transvestite passes," medical certificates he issued to protect cross-dressers from arrest. But he didn't believe one's essence sprang from membership in a sexual or gender category—or any category, racial, religious, or national. Hirschfeld's own selfhood derived from multiple affiliations: he was a homosexual (a fact he neither announced nor denied), a feminist (he was an outspoken and dedicated supporter of women's suffrage and birth control), a scientist, a physician, a socialist, a pacifist, a devotee of German culture, and a secular Jew. The one identity Hirschfeld would admit to was "panhumanist."

> The question: where do you belong? What are you, really, gives me no peace. Were I to pose the question, Are you a German? A Jew? Or a world citizen? My answer would in any case be, "a world citizen." Or all three.

In a journal article in 1923, Hirschfeld remarked that some of his transvestite patients were expressing feelings that might be described as "*seelischer Transsexualismus,*" or spiritual transsexualism, but he wasn't referring to the condition the word denotes today. He never separated out transsexuality as a category or regarded it as an identity. While doctors affiliated with Hirschfeld's institute performed several (rudimentary) sex-change operations, they did so with some reluctance, at the behest of desperate clients threatening severe self-harm. (One male-to-female client later changed her mind and begged to return to manhood, lending support to Hirschfeld's thesis that sexuality was a fluctuating entity.) Hirschfeld was more interested in freeing people to express their own idiosyncratic sexuality than in nailing down which patients belonged to which of two sexes. He was not looking to turn psychological ambiguity into certainty in the flesh.

On May 6, 1933, a little more than three months after Hitler became chancellor, a hundred students from a National Socialist youth league called the Nazi Committee Against the Un-German Spirit pulled up in lorries in front of Hirschfeld's institute. As a brass band blasted martial music, the young thugs stormed and then ransacked the building, smashing furniture and breaking windows, pouring red ink over thousands of manuscripts and confiscating the institute's vast archive of books, photographs, and files. A few days later, a torchlight procession marched to Berlin's Opera Square, bearing the defaced bust of Hirschfeld impaled on a stick, and tossed into a bonfire thousands of the institute's "un-German" volumes. The party's press praised the "Energetic Action against a Poison Shop"; they had "fumigated" the institute run by "the Jew Magnus Hirschfeld."

Hirschfeld, the "world citizen" who embraced all and no identities, was in France at the time, forced into exile. In the years leading up to his flight, fascist gangs had opened fire at his public speaking appearances and physically attacked him in Munich, once fracturing his skull so badly that he was declared dead (allowing him, he noted wryly, "an opportunity" to read his own obituary). Hirschfeld learned of the attack on the institute from a newsreel he watched in a Paris movie theater. He was subsequently stripped of his German citizenship. A year later, devastated by the destruction of his life's work, he died of a heart attack on his sixty-seventh birthday.

Five doctors who had been involved with sexology research at the institute fled the country; another likely died in a concentration camp. They, like a good number of the institute's practitioners, were Jewish. At least one gentile on staff wasn't spared either: the recipient of the first fully completed transsexual operation, Rudolf née Dorchen Richter, who became the institute's longtime live-in maid, disappeared on the day of the attack, likely murdered. Other institute patients were placed on "pink lists," arrested, deported, murdered.

Was the Nazi raid on the institute motivated by hatred of a religious or a sexual identity? Or did the raiders also fear exposure of their own erotic proclivities? The institute's assistant director, Dr. Ludwig Levy-Lenz, later speculated that "we knew too much"; their clientele included Third Reich officials. "Our knowledge of such intimate secrets regarding members of the Nazi Party and our other documentary material . . . was the cause of the complete and utter destruction of the Institute of Sexology."

Hirschfeld's belief that identity divisions were not strictly binary and that desires were intermediary and limitless would find little resonance in Third Reich Germany—or, for that matter, in postwar America. In 1965, the U.S. Congress passed an amendment refining the 1952 Immigration and Nationality Act. The original act had banned immigrants with "psychopathic personalities." The amendment explicitly applied that prohibition to "sexual deviation." The law was upheld by the U.S. Supreme Court in 1967 and remained on the books until 1990.

Twenty-first-century transsexuals still live in a universe bound by Harry Benjamin's protocols. His "Standards of Care" survive in the WPATH (World Professional Association for Transgender Health) Standards of Care, the widely followed guidelines for sex reassignment surgery. Obtaining the surgery under WPATH requires a year's worth of hormone therapy (approved by a therapist), a year of living full-time as the opposite sex, and, most crucially, two separate letters from two mental-health professionals who have independently determined that the patient is "eligible" for surgery. Without these all-important two referrals, WPATH's standards advise surgeons not to operate. Unlike any other "transgressive" group, transsexuals can't transgress without the consent of the authorities.

Altering sex organs means getting an operation, and getting an operation means convincing clinicians to sign off on a diagnosis. That diagnosis is derived from the presumptions and prejudices of twentieth-century "experts" whose claims were often thinly researched and whose suppositions have been vastly amplified in the echo chamber of a clientele eager to say whatever is required to obtain the magic wand of surgery. Since transsexuality first entered the *Diagnostic and Statistical Manual of Mental Disorders* in 1980 (seven years after gay-rights advocates finally managed to get homosexuality out of it), "Transsexualism" has become "Gender Identity Disorder" has become "Gender Dysphoria." In 2013, under pressure to "destigmatize" the transgender population, the authors of the *DSM-V* removed the diagnosis from the "Sexual Dysfunctions" and "Paraphilic Disorders" chapters, albeit not from the manual itself. The practitioners have made endless but largely superficial refinements to the taxonomy, adding and subtracting symptoms and demarcating predisposing and associated factors, primary and secondary types and subtypes. The diagnosis remains a baggy, ill-defined condition, based on theories with tenuous connection to empirical data or actual patient histories.*

With no firm physiological markers to go on, the therapists who issue the all-important two letters must determine eligibility based not on what patients show but on what they tell, and how well they tell it. "Although transsexuality concerns the deliberate transformation of the material body more than any other category catalogued by the American Psychiatric Association's *Diagnostic and Statistical Manual of Mental Disorders*," Jay Prosser, a literature professor and female-to-male transsexual, observed in *Second Skins*, "transsexuality does not symptomize itself in the subject's body, at least not visibly or reliably so. The diagnosis required for this transformation must instead derive from the patient's narrative: narrativization as a transsexual necessarily precedes one's diagnosis as a transsexual; autobiography is transsexuality's

---

* In the smattering of follow-up surveys conducted over the years, most postoperative transsexuals say they don't regret the surgery and are satisfied with the outcome. These surveys, however, lack sufficient numbers and often basic standards of statistical rigor. In 2010, a meta-analysis of all the studies to date warned, "The evidence is of very low quality due to the serious methodological limitations." The one long-term study that did have a significant number of cases (a 2011 Swedish study that followed 324 postoperative transsexuals from 1973 to 2003) reached this conclusion: "Persons with transsexualism, after sex reassignment, have considerably higher risks for mortality, suicidal behaviour, and psychiatric morbidity than the general population. Our findings suggest that sex reassignment, although alleviating gender dysphoria, may not suffice as treatment for transsexualism." How much of this distress is internally generated, and how much imposed by a hostile society, the studies don't say.

proffered symptom." To proceed to the operating room, the patient must tell the therapists the story they want to hear, a story that has barely changed since Harry Benjamin issued his guidelines in 1966.

The tropes, code words, and set pieces this telling requires have long been traded in underground transsexual exchanges, and more recently on electronic forums and chat rooms. "To qualify for surgery," a website for prospective male-to-female transsexuals that I read in 2010 instructed, be sure to emphasize that you suffer from a "persistent feeling of hatred for the male anatomical structures" and that you "absolutely dislike homosexual behavior." In a 2014 online discussion about how to get approval from therapists for hormone treatment and surgery, a successful petitioner explains:

> I lied my ass off to my shrink, either direct lies or lies of omission. I sure as HELL didn't tell him about my drinking problem, nor a word of my recovery issues. I never once told him of any doubts I had, never mentioned my boyfriend (now husband) nor that he is also trans, never mentioned breaking up with my ex. I made sure he saw a happy, well adjusted young girl no matter how stressed I was feeling. . . . I couldn't be open with him, if I was I may still be waiting on that damn letter.

In *How to Change Your Sex*, Lannie Rose, a male-to-female transsexual, counseled others to resist "the urge to game your therapist," while noting how it was done: "The game is simple: just read the stories on a handful of transsexual people's Web sites, and then concoct a story for your therapist that makes you seem similar to them." This is a mode of literary composition that Prosser called replicating "the master narrative" of "transsexuality's classic plot." Sandy Stone described the method more plainly as "learning to lie effectively about one's past."

Concocting such lies, Rose admonished, is "doing your self a big disservice and missing a great opportunity for personal growth." She believed that the strict requirements enforced by unsympathetic therapists were artifacts of the recent past and that, "today, being honest with your therapist should not prevent you from obtaining the treatment you need for your gender dysphoria, regardless of the particulars of your story." Rose's book was first published in 2004, the same year my father had her operation. I wondered how my father had addressed her own particulars.

"Sometimes I wish Harry Benjamin had never existed," Mel Myers told me. "It might have been better if they just let us trans girls suffer in the darkness." Some months after Mel and I met at Coffee People to talk about my father's stay at Melanie's Cocoon, we met for dinner at a Thai restaurant called Miso Happy. "I manipulated my therapist," Mel said over our soup, and elaborated. "I knew all the answers. I'd come out of there like, 'Ha! I nailed that!'" Maybe that wasn't such a victory, he thought now. "The doctors could have guided me better. I wish there were therapists available to help some of us *not* go all the way. Maybe I could've just learned . . ."

"Learned what?" I asked.

"To live with myself."

"Do you think"—I hesitated—"do you think my father shouldn't have had the operation?"

"I can't say why Stefánie was driven to do it," Mel said, "and she was too closed down for me to know." He picked at the remains of a spring roll on his plate. "Of the hundreds of transsexuals I've met, I'd say ten of them probably should have done it. Not that they *shouldn't* transition, but it's just too hard for them. They are always going to have to live as a 'trans person.' They are never going to pass."

In the three weeks that my father stayed at Melanie's Cocoon, she did not impress Mel as someone for whom the transition would be easy. "Actually, I kind of hoped Stefánie wouldn't stay with me," Mel confessed. "I felt kind of threatened around him," he said. "Her," he amended. "Something about her was"—he considered—"overbearing. But I had just opened my guesthouse, and I had to recruit customers. So I went into her hospital room and gave her my pitch. At first she was pretty defensive and looking at me like, 'What sort of a scam is this?' But after a while, she started saying to the nurses, 'Well, maybe I'll stay at Melanie's house.' "

Mel called up some pictures of the Cocoon on his Palm Pilot. It was an airy wood-frame house with a wrap-around porch, ringed with palm trees and banana plants, high on a hill above the beach (high enough to make it through the December 2004 tsunami unscathed). Guests had their own rooms with a private bath. Melanie had decorated the common area with wicker furniture, eight clocks set to different time zones around the world, and inspirational art. The room's signature piece was an oil painting of a naked woman with long blond hair, gazing out a brightly lit window. "She is looking out into a new day," Mel said. "Everybody who's stayed with me identifies with it." Melanie prodded her guests into that new day with field trips to the beach, women's clothing boutiques, nightclubs, and the Phuket FantaSea Show, "The Ultimate Nighttime Cultural Theme Park." (My father would show me the video she bought in the FantaSea gift shop, featuring the park's most popular attractions: a nightly "Cultural Illusion Show" where herds of elephants appear and disappear "at will," a simulated thunder-and-lightning storm, and a photo studio that invited customers to get their pictures taken in "traditional" Thai costumes.)

Melanie's recruitment efforts at the plastic surgery wings of Phuket's hospitals that May paid off. She signed up a half dozen guests, all male-to-female transsexuals. My father was, by far, the oldest. She was also the "most alone," Melanie said. "Stefánie seemed isolated, even more than the others. Maybe it was because of her culture or history, but the others couldn't relate to her. None of the other five wanted to visit with her. I had to push them. I talked her up as 'The Great Hungarian!' "

The other guests, who were in their twenties and thirties and came from the United States, England, and Australia, did not share the Great Hungarian's interests. "Your father arrived with all this equipment, a huge videocam, movies, computer, opera videos. Stefánie wanted to force opera on everybody. She was blasting German opera on these bad speakers. She had all these movies she wanted us to watch, and they were also in German. Stefánie said she'd translate, and I had to tell her not to, that people didn't want that sort of entertainment. And she had a lot of pictures on her computer that she wanted everyone to see, and people got tired of looking at them. At one point I even took her to this luxury hotel for brunch where German people stay, thinking maybe she'd like to check in there. But she stayed for three weeks. And she wanted all this attention."

Mel shot me a self-deprecating grin. "Of course, that's what people accuse *me* of! Always wanting attention!" He laughed. "Transsexuals are . . . we can be wrapped up in ourselves." My father's manner, though, put Mel's guests off for another reason. "Stefánie had this very *dominating* style, like a hammer coming down. I don't think she was being sensitive enough about the niceties of being a woman."

I wasn't sure what this portfolio of "niceties" entailed. And I had surely hated my father's domination growing up. But I was somehow pleased that, whoever my father had become on the operating table, whatever category she'd hoped to join, she was already, incorrigibly, defying the template.

"When Stefánie was staying with me," Mel said, "she talked to me once about being in the war."

"Yes?" I asked, a little jealous that my father was reminiscing with Melanie, and also surprised. Had the butterfly poised to leave her chrysalis for a new life been revisiting his caterpillar past?

Two details had struck Mel. "She said she gave out fake birth certificates. And she said she had an armband with a swastika or something that she would wear, so they wouldn't know she was a Jew."

Mel was dubious but intrigued. "I laughed and I made this remark," Mel said, "and Stefánie gave me kind of an odd look. I couldn't tell if she thought it was funny or not. . . . I said, 'So, you were a trans-Nazi?' "

12

The Mind Is a Black Box

Mel's account of my father's stay in the house where the painted lady "looked out on a new day" had brought my thoughts back around to my father's wartime past. On a subsequent evening in Portland, I paid a visit to a witness who'd known my father in that earlier time, someone my father had also recommended I contact. "Call Otto," she said. "He knows everybody from our school." Otto Szekely had been my father's classmate at the Zsidó Gimnázium, the Jewish high school in Budapest.

Even his pets are Hungarian, I thought, as I followed Szekely, a retired trauma surgeon and anesthesiologist, down the hall and into the dining room of his gracious home in Lake Oswego, with views of Mount Hood and Mount Adams. His two big kuvasz dogs, members of an ancient breed said to have accompanied the Magyars on their conquest of the Carpathian Basin, lumbered after us. "We were just in Budapest," Otto told me as his wife, Margaret, an OR nurse, laid out a sumptuous dinner, a traditional Magyar repast that began with cherry soup and concluded, six courses later, with palacsinta (thin pancakes rolled in fruit jam and dusted with confectioners' sugar). "We visited your father."

"When?" I asked. In early May, he said.

Geranium-planting season. "Wasn't he . . . out of the country?"

"He said he was leaving, I think it was the very next day. He was going to"—Otto struggled to recall the name—"Malaysia?" He found it an odd destination for a vacation. I didn't say anything. If my father hadn't told her classmate about the operation, it didn't seem my place to inform him.

While Margaret served the chicken paprikas, Otto went to a sideboard and retrieved some pictures from their trip to Budapest. In the first one, my father is standing in front of the house in the Buda Hills. As Otto handed it to me, he exchanged a glance with Margaret. "We have a name for that house," he said. "Kafka's Castle." In the next picture, the Szekelys are posed next to an elaborate luncheon spread my father has prepared: herring rolls, goose pâté, sausage and shrimp on openfaced sandwiches. My father's fondness for Danish smorgasbord dated to his years in Copenhagen six decades earlier. The last shot captured my father in his new basement workshop, beside his old Black & Decker saw, wearing khaki trousers and a man's dress shirt and tie. His face is unusually soft and round, with a glossy sheen. He had been taking female hormones for months.

Otto could summon few specifics about my father's years at the Zsidó Gimnázium, other than that István was "small, like me," not athletic, and not very communicative. My teenage father had managed, Otto recalled, to communicate one thing: that the Friedman family "came from wealth" and "owned real estate." Otto gave me the names of a few other classmates who might remember more, but when I called them, their memories were as sparse. Jaacov Steiner, an audiology professor in Tel Aviv, knew the most: he and my father had attended the same schools since they were six years old. "My best friend in the class," my father had described Jaacov to me, though when I asked why, she couldn't come up with anything more than "he was nice to me." Jaacov's memories were less nice. "Your father was something of a troublemaker in the classroom, repeatedly interrupting the teacher," he told me. "A restless and difficult child. But the school put up with it, because of Jenő Friedman's money." He also remembered my father boarding with a teacher, but recalled a different reason than the pending divorce. "The Friedmans had a live-in maid—and your father punched her, twice, very hard in the stomach and legs. The family doctor suggested he be sent to live where he'd be disciplined."

After dinner, Otto ushered me into his study. He settled heavily on the couch, the dogs at his feet. His broad-planed face and bushy eyebrows that arched in two sharp Vs were, I thought, classically Hungarian. He laid out on a table a very few yellowing photographs, the remains of a life interrupted. He shuffled through them slowly and picked up one to show me. It was a yearbook photo, five rows of boys, formal and posed in ties and blazers, on bleachers in front of a brick wall. I recognized a slight boy toward the back with an anxious half-grin, assuming a Napoleon hand-in-vest pose. "Pista," Otto said. My teenage father, in a swank tweed blazer with wide lapels, was the best-dressed of the group. "This is our Class of '45," Otto said, handing me the photo. The "class that never graduated."

"It was a very elite school," he continued, "and the teachers were world class." The Zsidó Gimnázium was famed for its academic erudition, its faculty chockablock with celebrated scholars of mathematics, archaeology, history, linguistics, the classics, and the Hungarian language. Rising anti-Semitism had forced many preeminent Jewish scholars to teach high school. Fears of Jewish "domination" of higher education produced the Numerus Clausus Act of 1920, which placed a restrictive quota on Jewish university students. (The bill was the first anti-Semitic law in interwar Europe.) The list of eminent Hungarians Jews driven abroad by rising discrimination is long and Nobel laureate–studded: among them, mathematician John von Neumann; physicists Eugene Wigner, Leo Szilard, Theodore von Kármán, and Edward Teller; chemist George de Hevesy; and sociologist Karl Mannheim. By the late 1930s, further anti-Jewish legislation would impose a harsh quota on Jewish professors. Among the esteemed Jewish educators who sought employment at the Zsidó Gymnázium were David Rafael Fuchs, Finno-Ugric philologist and member of the Hungarian Academy of Sciences; Salamon Widder, eminent Hebraist; and Mihály Fekete, leading mathematician and later rector of Jerusalem's Hebrew University. The Gimnázium's head of physical education, Zoltán Dückstein, was the Hungarian Olympics coach who had led the nation's team to victories in boxing, fencing, wrestling, and water polo in the 1932 summer games in Los Angeles.

Otto slid a worn finger across the class photo, stopping at each face to identify the boy by his future profession: physicist, chemist, biologist, aeronautics engineer, computer scientist, cardiologist, electrical engineer, psychiatrist, radiologist, museum director, professional athlete memorialized in the Canadian Hall of Fame, billionaire businessman and founder of the world's largest gold-mining company. . . . Those were the ones who survived, of course. Before the war, there were sixty-one boys on the class roster. After, there were fewer than twenty. When Otto organized the class reunion in Toronto in 2001, there were sixteen. "Now there are twelve," Otto said. He looked up, his darkly lined eyes resting on mine. "Your father is the only one who lives in Hungary."

On the day the Germans occupied Budapest, March 19, 1944, the Zsidó Gimnázium sent its students home. Not wanting to cause alarm, the administration said they were being excused to celebrate the birthday of the Father of Hungarian Democracy, Lajos Kossuth. Final report cards were handed out early, starting on April 4, the day before a decree by the Hungarian Ministry of the Interior went into effect requiring Jews to wear the yellow Star of David. Soon after the last graduating class (the Class of '44) took final exams, the Hungarian military commandeered the building as a transit camp for Jewish forced labor.

The teenage Otto aimed to be a poet. In that, he was a true Hungarian, poetry being the most exalted of Magyar arts. Before Otto's father was forced out of his job as financial director of a chemical company—and ultimately taken to his death in Auschwitz—his son borrowed his office typewriter and composed "The Collected Works of Otto Szekely." Otto tried to summon a few of the verses from memory now, in English. In one, a poem about winter, he remembered writing, "The snow is laughing on the smile of the sun." ("The wordplay is better in Hungarian," he said.) In another, an artistic take on rain, he described a downpour as "the death of clouds."

In the summer of '44, Otto wrote his last poem. It was for his sister, who had been forcibly relocated with their mother to one of the city's "Yellow Star" houses, requisitioned apartment buildings that served as wartime holding pens for Budapest Jews in the last year of the war. The houses were intended to be the final stop before deportation. Otto could no longer recall the exact words, but he remembered the parable he used, the story of a wolf who lurks outside a barn while the sheep are sleeping. "I reversed it to say, one day we sheep will be on the outside, and the wolf will be trapped in the barn. I wanted to give her hope." His sister carried the poem up and down the stairs of her Yellow Star house, reading it to the other residents. The poem did lift her spirits, though not her odds. Late in 1944, she was loaded on the last transport from Budapest to Bergen-Belsen, where she died of typhoid fever.

A month and a half before his sister's deportation, seventeen-year-old Otto was rounded up by the Hungarian Arrow Cross and sent into forced labor, digging trenches to halt the progress of the Soviet army. He had no outdoor gear, but "my mother was a magician. She cut my jacket short to make a backpack." And she somehow scrounged enough flour and sugar to make him a batch of cookies. For the next many weeks, he dug in the pouring rain. "You couldn't get dry. At night I just lay right on the ground." The cookies in his backpack turned to mulch. Otto spooned out a speck of dough each day. "It kept me alive."

In the winter of '44, the cookie dough ran out, and his unit was turned west. "There was a bad feeling, because we knew the rumor": heading west, he said, meant heading to a concentration camp. One night as they passed through a village, "we stopped for some reason. I was on the edge of the road and I saw, just by accident, a little gate to a fenced-in yard. I touched it to see if it was open." He extended a finger above the coffee table, pushing on an invisible gate. "And it wasn't locked. I watched. I waited. Waiting, waiting, waiting." When the nearest guards were looking the other way, he slipped through the gate "and I just walked, I didn't know where."

He quickly concocted a new identity, which he proffered whenever he was stopped. "I said I was a Hungarian who had escaped from Romania from the Russians, because there were a lot of Hungarians from Transylvania who were fleeing then." A Christian Hungarian, of course. He had no documents to support this fiction. "But my fear wasn't that I had no papers," he said.

I asked, though I knew.

"That they would tell me to open my fly. That was my main fear."

Many years later, Otto would refuse to have his son circumcised. "I never wanted to put my son in that circumstance."

By the winter of 1944, Budapest was, like so many war-torn European countries, a "city of women." Hungary's capital was also, and notably, a city of Jewish women. In Budapest, 60.1 percent of Jewish women would survive the war, compared with 42.7 percent of men.

Invariably in war, the male enemy is deemed the greater threat (never mind that Hungarian Jews were never the enemy). But also in play was a complex history of fantasies and phobias about Jewish masculinity, centuries in the making and by no means limited to Hungary. The reigning (and contradictory) spectral images of the male Jew—the effeminate castrate who threatened to demoralize Christian manhood, the concupiscent satyr who threatened to despoil Christian virgins, and, of course, the avaricious parasite who threatened to deplete the Christian coffers—resonated throughout Europe. In Trianon-shamed interwar Hungary, the Jewish man was a figure onto whom so many social and economic humiliations and fears were projected. In Dezső Szabó's wildly popular 1919 novel, *The Swept-Away Village*, a young and strapping gentile soldier returns to his Hungarian village after World War I to find his country corrupted by Jews, the town beauty ruined by Jewish lovers (she eventually becomes a prostitute in the "modern Sodom" of Jew-infested Budapest), and his best friend, a Christian poet, rendered insane and impotent by the siren call of (Jewish) cosmopolitan decadence. The hero stands firm against Semitic contamination, marrying a Christian peasant girl and vowing to uphold the ideals of the Magyar countryside, "the cradle of the Hungarian race." To so many gentile Hungarians debilitated by the conditions of the time, the story explained everything: the source of their emasculation resided in the simultaneously lecherous and limp-wristed Jewish urbanite who sashayed through the boulevards of Pest, degrading Christian morals with his sexual infirmities and draining the nation of its wealth and well-being.

One day I was discussing the perception of Jews in Hungarian society with the distinguished Budapest psychoanalyst Judit Mészáros. When we got to the interwar years, she reached for her book, *Ferenczi and Beyond*—about the Budapest School of psychoanalysis—and turned to a reproduction of a 1920s anti-Semitic poster. It depicted a grotesquely fat man with flaking skin, naked except for boots, crouching on bandy legs. He gazes blindly out of spectacles perched over a hooked nose and slobbering lips. A quill pen is tucked behind one ear, another impaled like an arrow in his sagging breasts. Under his left arm hangs a bulging money bag, stamped with a Star of David, spilling gold coins. His right hand reaches for a copy of *Pesti Napló*, a Hungarian newspaper of the time. The lettering above his head reads, "Le az élődi sajtóval!" Down with the Parasite Press!

"What do you notice?" Mészáros asked.

I pointed to the "parasite's" crotch. This pestilential figure had no gonads.

"Yes," she said. "Castrated." She snapped the book shut. "Sometimes," she said, "a single picture condenses everything."

The three "Jewish Laws" passed by the Hungarian Parliament in the late '30s and early '40s devastated Jewish manhood. The first and second laws imposed severe restrictions on professional, managerial, commercial, and industrial employment, eliminating more than 80 percent of jobs for Jewish breadwinners. The third law's "race-protecting" prohibition of intermarriage and extramarital intercourse specifically banned sexual relations between Jewish *men* and gentile women. "After the 'Jewish Laws' caused men to lose their employment and undermined them economically," historian Zoltán Vági and his coauthors observed in *The Holocaust in Hungary: Evolution of a Genocide*, "a unique form of 'emancipation' emerged. The relations between the sexes, gender roles, and the division of labor began to change." Soon, with the inception of forced labor, the male breadwinner would literally vanish from the home.

In March 1939, more than two years before Hungary even entered the war, the Hungarian government declared Jewish men unfit for military action. (The judgment still enraged my father seventy years later. "Israel knocked that idea out flat in the Six-Day War," she exclaimed, slamming her fist on the table. To my father, Israel was among other things an experiment in the restoration of manhood.) Instead, the Hungarian Labor Service System, unique to Hungary, conscripted all male Jews between the ages of twenty and forty-eight (and later, eighteen and forty-eight) into forced work units that served alongside the Hungarian army divisions. (My father was lucky enough not to turn eighteen until November 1945.) Conscripts were deprived of army boots and uniforms (other than yellow armbands identifying them as Jews; white for Jews who were Christian converts). And weapons: designated "unreliables," Jewish men were sent to the front unarmed. When Hungary entered the war, these men provided the slave labor, assigned the most humiliating, punishing, and life-threatening duties. They were barely fed, pitifully clothed, and brutally treated—used in place of dray horses, marched ahead of the regular troops through mine fields, shoved off cliffs and tortured for the delectation of sadistic officers and their troops. Some would argue that forced labor at least kept some of the men out of the ovens. Still, the laborers died in epidemic numbers, forty-two thousand *before* the German occupation.

By the time the Arrow Cross Party took over in the fall of 1944, just about every man who wasn't old or infirm was in military service. Any male on the streets of Budapest without a uniform was suspect. Jewish men, no matter how convincing their false identity papers, risked what was euphemistically known as "trouser inspections" every time they ventured out. Tivadar Soros, the father of philanthropist George Soros, described the daily danger in his wartime memoir, *Masquerade*.

Each district had one or two Arrow Cross buildings whose sole purpose was torture and the "cutting off" of Jewish lives. People suspected of being Jews were taken to these locations to assess their Jewishness. For men the assessment was extremely easy. Documents were of no importance. They had to take off their clothes, and those who were circumcised were unlikely to come out alive. Women had a better chance, because such simple criteria were unavailable.

Soros acquired forged medical certificates for himself and his two sons, which claimed they had been circumcised for "phimosis," a rare condition requiring the removal of constricted foreskin. He knew the documents were unlikely to provide protection. "The foreskin problem," Soros wrote, was "a constant threat haunting our pseudo-Christian lives."

My father's cousin, Dahlia Baral, married a man who would be plagued by the memory of that threat for the rest of his life. When Martin Baral was a boy, his mother attempted to save her two sons from the betraying mark of their religion by arranging for a "fore-skin restoration" surgery. The procedure, conducted in the middle of the war in an abandoned basement by a psychiatrist with limited surgical experience, was a disaster. Martin described it to me one day when he and Dahlia were visiting New York from Sydney, Australia, where they eventually settled after the war. The "so-called operation," he called it. There was no anesthestic. Their mother gave him and his younger brother a slug of vodka and a cigarette. The doctor told everyone to grab an arm and a leg and hold the patients down. "I fainted," Martin told me, "which was a good thing." The operation didn't work, but it did leave the two brothers with raging infections for a year. As it did a third older man they knew, who also had the operation the same day. "Later, some Nazis caught this man on the street, and they pulled his pants down to see if he was a Jew," Martin recalled. They eyed his mauled member. He said it was from syphilis. "And it looked so bad, they believed him. So you could say the operation worked after all."

And my own father? "I was never afraid of that," she said breez-ily when I asked her about the "foreskin problem" of wartime Budapest. "I wasn't an idiot. I knew how to behave. I *never* wore the yellow star."

"But even without the star—" I tried again.

"Waaall, I never got caught," my father said. "It's not relevant." End of discussion.

———

A month after our dinner, Otto Szekely called me. He had received an e-mail from another member of the Class of '45. Attached to the message was an e-mail the man had received from my father, announcing her sex change. Otto wasn't the only recipient; the man had forwarded my father's e-mail to all of the surviving classmates.

Otto didn't know what to think. "The boys have been discussing it," he said of his septuagenarian fellow alumni, "and they think Pista wanted to shock us." Otto scrambled for precedents. "One of the surgeons at the institute I used to work with once did an operation like this," he told me, "but that was for a woman who was born without a vagina but had a uterus." A biological woman, he meant. "It must be some kind of a . . . a pathology of self-conflict," Otto stumbled on, grabbing for medical handholds inside of his expertise to explain my father. "There must be a predetermined psychosomatic syndrome, which could be triggered by an experience early in life. That could make sense." Except it didn't, not to him anyway. "The important thing is that he—, that the conflict—, . . . that it doesn't get more and more in the way of . . ." He left the sentence unfinished. "I can't say I understand."

"Would you care to talk about this over lunch?" I asked.

"It would be a mitzvah."

A few days later Otto eased himself into a banquette at a restaurant in downtown Portland and pushed across the table a sheath of computer printouts. The e-mail from my father that had been forwarded to all the "boys" was less exposition than exhibition—or rather, I thought irritably, exhibitionism. My father had chosen two images to send. In one she was posed in Empress Sisi's imperial garden in Vienna. In the other, she was wearing a platinum blond wig and a red skirt with white lilies. They were the same photographs she had e-mailed me to announce the birth of Stefánie. I felt the stirrings of an obscure resentment. Was I just one of many recipients of this visual form letter?

Some of the classmates had responded with a few choice remarks. To wit: what a ridiculous and embarrassing thing for an old man to do. My rancor instantly attached to a new target. Who were these men, who had barely exchanged two words with my father since 1944, to pass judgment? *They* should be embarrassed, passing around photos like teenagers sniggering over dirty pictures.

Stapled to the photos was another set of e-mails, an exchange between my father and a classmate in Israel. They were several pages in number and entirely text. And all in Hungarian. The only word I could read in my father's e-mail was the last one: "Shalom."

I recognized the correspondent's name, Jaacov Steiner, my father's "best friend" from school. Otto ran his eyes dolefully down the first page of the e-mails. "Steiner writes to your father that he hopes he is satisfied with the operation, and that he has only one question: 'Why wait till now?'"

My father wrote back the next day.

Otto translated the response. "I apologize that I inform you one by one," it began, "but as Stefi I'm a little bit shy now." Otto looked up at me, his vaulted eyebrows arching a notch higher, then returned to the reading. "Honestly I never thought that I would be alive in the twenty-first century, and now I'm here as a relatively pretty lady."

My father's account burbled on in that everything's-coming-up-roses style familiar to me from the early trans memoirs in the Portland library: "The Thai people are all very nice." "In two weeks I had a complete recovery." "I was very satisfied with all the operations in Thailand." "I have had no problems since I got back home." "All my acquaintances are very nice to me now."

The e-mail's last paragraph: "My daughter made many notes here about me and maybe her next book will be about me and the problems of transsexual people. Wishing you a happy New Year. Shalom, Stefi."

Otto thumbed through the pages, looking for something. He found it in a subsequent e-mail, written to him privately from Steiner. Otto had underlined a couple of sentences in red ink.

"Steiner writes here that when Pista was young, his behavior became 'unbearable.' He was acting very aggressive, and because of this, he was sent to live with the teacher. Many times he kicked the live-in maid."

I wondered why Otto had underlined those words. Was he considering whether this childhood incident with the maid could be a factor in my father's latest reinvention? I was dubious. No doubt many privileged children of the era mistreated their servants. It made them obnoxious, but it didn't make them transsexuals.

"I think it was a terrible time in my father's life," I said.

"Yes," Otto said, "Steiner writes that his parents were in a big war over their divorce."

"And the other war," I said. "It must have been terrifying. My father claims to never think about being a Jew in the war," I said, "but I don't buy it."

Otto took off his glasses and ran a hand over his face. "Those of us who survived, we didn't have any 'PTSD syndrome' after the war. I mean, I'm sure we carry psychot—, neurotic—, stress. I have the guilt of a survivor, but I don't—" He stopped and started over. "Maybe on an individual level, if someone gets exposed at a particular period of time, it can enhance, trigger, whatever, that syndrome. The connection exists somewhere at the individual level, but it is very difficult to prove."

"Prove what?" I wasn't following.

"Your father probably had this desire in him as a child, and, by accident, the war came at the same time," Otto said. "I have the feeling you want to find a connection between your father and the Holocaust. But I don't think the Holocaust can *make* someone—"

"I don't think so either," I said.

"It's like with a mass murderer, where they say on TV, 'Oh, this thing happened in his childhood! That explains it!'"

"Otto, I'm not saying the Holocaust explains my father's sex change."

He nodded, somewhat placated. "It's like when, all of a sudden, I have a headache," he said, "and I'll try to figure out why. I'll go back in an associative way, trying to think of what triggered it—and sometimes, if I'm lucky, I figure it out."

"But most of the time you can't," I said. "Most of the time there is no single 'trigger.'"

He was quiet for a few moments. Then he said, "Still, what you are doing, trying to investigate the connections, it's a legitimate idea. It makes good sense." The empirical-minded Dr. Szekely seemed to be in a struggle with the existential Otto. "But if you try to prove it, you may find that you will wind up going on a long, long circle around."

"And wind up where I started."

"Not where you started," he said. "Many facts may come up. But in the end, the mind is a black box."

13

Learn to Forget

My father was seated at the dining-room table, pen in hand, the alumni roster of the Zsidó Gimnázium's Class of '45 before her. She was shuffling the several mimeographed pages and putting an X next to name after name.

"What are you doing?" I asked. Four years had passed since I'd resumed seeing my father. On my subsequent visits, we'd made a few excursions around the city and I'd pried some family history from her. We'd even gone to another of her high school reunions, this one in Budapest. We were there only briefly; she had stormed out, irritated by "all the whining about 'Oh, how we suffered.'" Most of the time, though, we wound up where we were right now, sitting in my father's house.

"What are you doing?" I asked again.

"Marking the people who are dead."

She drew her Xs in an odd sideways fashion. They looked more like crosses. The class roster soon resembled a cemetery—a Christian one.

"These people," she said to me, after a while. "They are just frozen in time. Ghosts." She meant the names that weren't marked with an X, her classmates at the Budapest reunion. "There was one man there who looked so old, he might as well have been dead."

My father ran her finger slowly down the roster one more time, checking to see if she'd missed anybody. She stopped at her own name. She studied it for a moment, then drew a sideways X in the margin.

"What's that for?" I asked.

She shook the pen a few times and reapplied the ink, darkening the X.

"Steven Faludi aaalso," she said. "Steven Faludi is dead."

By 2008, Budapest was no longer terra incognita to me. I knew my way to my father's house, knew the tram and bus schedules, had made some friends in Pest, and had labored through a year's worth of (largely ineffective) Hungarian lessons. Inside the fortress on the hill, some things had changed. My father wasn't conducting compulsory tours of her real and virtual wardrobe. The robe didn't fall open with the same regularity. The visual evidence of her new identity was no longer on 24/7 exhibition. My father's abiding self, though, remained very much resistant and elusive, especially and reliably when it came to matters of history, personal or public. Her inspection of the Zsidó Gymnázium class roster was a rare confrontation with the specters of the past.

My husband and I had rented an apartment that summer in downtown Pest. "It's a stupid thing, not staying in the house," my father complained. And when that didn't work, "You are embarrassing me—in front of everybody." I wasn't sure who "everybody" was—she didn't seem to have a lot of acquaintances—but we stayed in the city, anyway. We'd found a favorite library and a favorite watering hole, and anyway, I was glad to be out of range of my father's still relentless surveillance.

Our rental was in a once showy and still respectable Art Nouveau building, across the street from the opera house. As the season warmed, musicians flung open the windows of the practice studios. We woke many mornings to a celestial mash-up, tenors and trumpeters tuning up for the evening's performance. We'd feel our way down the stairs in the dark—the hall lights were perpetually burned out—and linger over coffee and croissants at the neighborhood café (where the manager, seeing the Americans coming, rushed to play Johnny Cash on her ancient jukebox, drowning out the Verdi). Since the fall of Communism, parts of the city center had undergone frenetic gentrification: the magnificent old Nyugati (Western) Railway Terminal, designed by the architects of the Eiffel Tower, was now in the shadow of the two-million-square-foot WestEnd City Center, the largest mall in Central Europe with two hundred shops, seventy shoe outlets, fifty jewelry stores, a casino and poker club, and a fourteen-screen cinema that played "the latest Hollywood blockbusters." Along the ceremonial thoroughfare of Andrássy Boulevard, the city's Champs-Élysées inaugurated in 1876, upscale chain stores had proliferated: Louis Vuitton, Hugo Boss, Nespresso, wine bars, mobile phone dispensaries, and Internet cafés. But the district where we lived, like so many pockets of Pest, nevertheless showed its age, the stucco facades crumbling, the stair treads bowed by foot traffic, the wizened grandmothers in their faded finery inspecting us from behind lace curtains and window-box geraniums. I'd miss that worn elegance when I returned to the United States and all its prefab uniformity, miss the way every grand-dame edifice on the út or utca wore its history on its face, its beauty munitions-pocked from multiple twentieth-century battles. My delight at the past's insistent presence wasn't universally shared. Alongside a doorway on the street that ran behind the opera house, someone had painted—perhaps in defiance of Nietzsche's observation?—a graffiti message in large Day-Glo letters: "LEARN TO FORGET."

In a funny way, the metropolis's transformation offered a

window on my father's. Like her, the city was attempting a rebirth at an advanced age. Like her, it had undergone an identity makeover from one end of the spectrum to the other. Hungarians had a name for the about-face from Communism to capitalism: they called it "The Change." Wandering the streets of Pest and sitting at my father's table in Buda had a strangely unitary feel. In both places I was watching people engaged in an intense negotiation with the meaning of identity—and the possibility of leaving the past behind, of learning to forget.

On the occasion of one visit, my father had presented me with a gift, a coffee-table book of Hungarian history. Sandwiched between sun-splashed and unsubtly retouched photographs (the Danube an electric blue, the browned-out Great Hungarian Plain as Astroturfed as a putting green), the text proceeded in chronological lockstep from Magyar Conquest through centuries of national martyrdom to the 1989 "Rebirth of Parliamentary Democracy." One historical moment was forgotten. The entirety of World War II had been tucked discreetly, weirdly, in the chapter titled "Hungary in the Inter-War Years," and its casualties enumerated thusly: "40,000 soldiers of the Second Hungarian Army were killed and 70,000 captured by the Soviet troops" and "heavy damage was inflicted on Hungarian towns by the air raids of the Allies." The mass murder of two-thirds of the nation's 825,000 Jews received a parenthetical mention in a dependent clause to a sentence about additional Hungarian troop deployments. Their fate was attributed to "the Gestapo." (Of the persecution and murder of thousands of Roma, there was not a word.) And what of the Hungarian government, gendarmerie, military, and civil service, and the central role they played in the internal evisceration of the last intact Jewish community in Axis Europe? The text was silent.

This was a dodging and masking my father seemed to approve of. The Budapest she wished me to see had the same strange erasure, purposefully scrubbed of the chapter that had left its shrapnel scars on seemingly every building and on my father's character. I thought often of Nobel laureate Imre Kertész's assessment of his former home: "Nothing has been worked through, everything is painted over with pretty colors. Budapest is a city without a memory." When I lured my father into Pest, she gravitated to the generic shopping centers and retail outlets. We walked together only once through the Jewish quarter, site of the infamous and murderous wartime ghetto, and only on the way to her favorite wienerschnitzel restaurant.

On the way back, and at my insistence, we stepped into the Hungarian Jewish Museum, which adjoins the Dohány Street Synagogue in the old Jewish quarter. My father's mood, already sour at this detour, curdled when we reached the Holocaust Room. Alongside deportation rosters and a nation-by-nation breakdown of the toll (Hungary: 565,000 Jews perished) was a large photograph of the Hungarian Regent Miklós Horthy, the same Horthy before whose portrait in the Budapest History Museum my father had stood in adoration. He was shaking hands with Hitler. My request that my father translate the text on some displayed street posters of World War II vintage—grotesque caricatures of rich Jewish men with jug ears and giant hooked noses, their wives in diamond earrings and fur—elicited her customary wave. "This is of no interest," she said. She was ready to go. She glared at a tour guide from Tel Aviv who was orating at the top of his lungs. "Who can think with that braying?" She turned and elbowed her way through the crush of Israeli tourists.

Just before the exit, she jolted to a halt. In front of her on the wall was a photograph, a grainy black-and-white image of a muddy yard in which a group of men in fedoras and raincoats stood behind a small wooden table, observed by a cluster of passersby clutching umbrellas. It was the grounds of the Jewish Maros Street Hospital where, on January 11, 1945, all but one of its ninety-three patients, nurses, and doctors were murdered by the Arrow Cross. In front of the table were three rows of bodies, exhumed from the mass grave by the Soviets a few weeks after the liberation of Budapest. "I was there," my father said quietly. The Soviet soldiers had invited a newly organized youth film club to witness the exhumation. My father was one of the club's charter members.

So many of the pictures of my father's life were missing, lost in the rubble of the Friedman family's fate or torn by his ex-wife from our family album. Or willfully purged from my father's recollection. Here on the museum wall was a moment she couldn't expunge. "The smell," she said, raising her hand to her face. "You could not get it out of your nose."

On occasion as we ambled through her buffed and burnished Budapest, she found herself accosted by the past. One day we were standing outside the brand-new and government-funded House of Terror, a multimedia-experiential museum dedicated to Hungary's twentieth-century torments that, despite its name, did a masterful job of eliding the horror of the Hungarian Holocaust (in favor of showcasing Hungary's victimization by the Soviets). My father was hit by another wartime memory. The forbidding edifice that housed the museum was once the most feared address in Budapest. Andrássy út 60 was the headquarters of the fascist Arrow Cross, and later, under Communism, of the secret police. The building's new House-of-Terror interior (the handiwork of a Hollywood set designer) was heavy on theme-park spectacle, its pounding music, flashing video screens, and pulsating lights calculated to induce maximum fear of the Red menace.

My father and I had sped through the twenty-nine galleries—only two of which (one a hallway) paid any notice to the anti-Jewish blood fest that the Arrow Cross directed from this building—and hurried to the exit. Outside, my father surveyed the boulevard. The history that was absent within the museum had assailed her on the sidewalk. "I was *here*," she said. "Right here. In front of this building. When they brought Szálasi in." In the spring of 1945, the former Arrow Cross leader and Hungarian prime minister, captured by Allied troops, was returned here in shackles. My father's youth film club was invited to watch. Noted movie director Béla Pásztor was there, too, filming Szálasi's capture for a newsreel. "They brought in Szálasi in this cage with iron bars," my father recalled. "And Béla Pásztor—the greaaat Hungarian filmmaker!—went up to him and said, 'Mr. Szálasi, would you be *so good* as to put those hands, which did *so much good*, on those bars, *please*,' and he filmed him." Immediately thereafter, the ex–prime minister was taken to a cell in the basement of Andrássy út 60. He was executed the following March.

My father stood there in the hot sun, ruminating. "Mr. Szálasi," she repeated, relishing the lacerating irony beneath Pásztor's words, "would you be *so good* as to put those hands, which did *so much good*, on those bars, *please*." My father gave a knowing smile. "Waaall," she said, "you know what Pásztor was."

"No, what?"

"A Jew, of course."

After a Saturday evening dinner at Menza, a glossy new restaurant in downtown Pest, my husband and I were strolling down Andrássy Boulevard when we heard a rhythmic martial thumping. The sound of tramping boots drew closer, and a color guard high-stepped toward us on the sidewalk. The flag bearers swept past, pressing us against the Hugo Boss display window. There followed a procession of young men (and a few women) in loose formation, uniformed in black boots, black trousers and vests, and black caps adomed with golden lions and red stripes.

That was my introduction to the Magyar Gárda, the Hungarian Guard, the newly established militia devoted to the "protection of traditions and culture." Its appearance on the most glamorous thoroughfare of Pest was just one manifestation of a mounting national discontent. The much-touted bounty of free enterprise hadn't yielded its promised dividends. After high hopes in the early '90s, Hungary's new market economy cratered and by the mid-aughts lagged behind most of the former Communist-bloc nations. Poverty and unemployment were escalating, and government policies only amplified the blows. As the fiscal crisis deepened, Hungary, unlike every other Eastern European country, cut unemployment assistance, lowered the public minimum wage, and eliminated family supports. At the same time, the country was reeling from massive debt and a currency in free fall. In 2008, Hungary was forced to accept a $25 billion bailout from the International Monetary Fund, the European Union, and the World Bank. Budapest was looking better than when I'd seen it last, but feeling worse. The shiny retail face of "The Change" might imply that old beleaguered Hungary was, as my father would put it, "dead aaalso," a thing of the past. The bitterness on the street said otherwise.

The Gárda was the paramilitary offspring of Jobbik ("The Movement for a Better Hungary"), a young and fast-growing right-wing party established by university students. In 2007, the Gárda inducted its first recruits at the Royal Palace on Castle Hill, before a replica of the Holy Crown of St. Stephen. These and future rites were presided over by leading politicians and blessed by prominent bishops and priests. Six hundred guardsmen had recently taken their vows in Heroes' Square, beside the statues of the Seven Chieftains of the Magyars and the Archangel Gabriel (holding another copy of the Holy Crown), pledging to "defend a physically, spiritually, and intellectually defenseless Hungary." Toward the end of the ceremony, Gábor Vona, a former history teacher and the founder of both the Gárda and Jobbik, rose to remind his troops of their sacred duty: to "save" the "true Hungarians" from humiliations that dated to the end of World War I. "Trianon dismembered the body, the Communists beheaded the nation," Vona told them. "Step by step, we have to rebuild our identity as a nation." What identity was under reconstruction? The Gárda's coat of arms—with its red-and-white "Árpád stripes"—closely resembled the 1940s banner of the fascist Arrow Cross.

"You are making too much of this," my father said when I described the Saturday night goose-stepping through the heart of Pest. "It's not a problem." I wasn't soothed. I remembered a story my father had let slip a few days earlier: She had been coming home on the bus the previous fall when a group of young men with shaved heads got on. "They were coming from some demonstration on Castle Hill," my father said. They started singing an anti-Semitic ditty. My father recognized it; she had heard it as a teenager: "If the head rabbi gets exterminated . . ."

"What did the other passengers do?" I asked.

"Nothing," my father said, momentarily pensive. Then: "Waaall, they were just kids, wanting to upset the grown-ups." Who evidently weren't upset.

One day in her book-lined study on the edge of Buda, sociologist and LGBT-rights expert Judit Takács talked to me about the linked phenomena of Hungary's self-pity and brutality. I had come to her confused on the issue of how "Trianon dismembered the body" could lead so directly to "the head rabbi gets exterminated." "Hungary is a very *normalizing* society, more than others, and it's definitely not inclusive," she told me. "Hungary has this very tragic self view—'We are special because we are the losers of history.' And that self-pitying mentality doesn't lend itself to being welcoming to people who are different."

There was a moment a few years earlier when it looked like Hungary might become more welcoming. In May 2004, the same time that my father had undergone surgery and joined the female gender, the Hungarian government had announced its own transformation and joined the European Union. In both cases, membership in the new "community" involved a display of assimilation: my father had to pass as a woman; Hungary had to pass as a "socially inclusive" state.

Admission to the EU requires that a nation show evidence that its social policies promote "respect for and protection of minorities." Those policies include prohibiting discrimination on the basis of race, religion, ethnicity, age, sex, and (starting in 1998) sexual orientation—and actively monitoring and promoting the equal treatment of marginalized groups. In 2003, Hungarian legislators, intent on making their country one of the first post-Communist bloc nations to join the EU, hurried into law the Equal Treatment Act; in their eagerness to give the EU what it wanted, the parliamentary members kept adding to the list of "protected groups." Ultimately, the bill included twenty protected categories—a list that went beyond the usual concerns of race, religion, and sex to include "family status," "motherhood," "fatherhood," "circumstances of wealth and birth," "social origin," "state of health," "language," "part-time work status," and "trade union representatives." And, remarkably, "gender identity," which two human-rights NGOs managed to slip into the legislation. Hungary became the first nation in the world to guarantee equal protection to transgender people.

On paper. On the street, any urge to celebrate Hungary's declared tolerance was undercut by fear.

Soon after I arrived that summer of 2008, my father threw a party to introduce me to "my new trans friends." I was pleased. For one thing, she was celebrating my presence. She even bought a cake for the occasion, a Sacher torte she had decorated with the message, "Susan—Welcome to Hungary!" For another, it seemed she had found a way to break out of a lifelong isolation. "Before, I was like other men," she said. "I didn't talk to other people. Now I can talk to anybody." Now, not only was she hosting a party; she was trying to assemble what she called, rather hopefully, "the Hungarian trans community."

A few years earlier, my father had stumbled upon TS-Online, at the time the only Hungarian transsexual website. She e-mailed a few of the people who had posted comments and nearly two dozen agreed to get together. My father volunteered her front deck as their gathering place.

At the first meeting, the group settled on a name: the Hungarian Tranny Club. (The term "tranny," regarded as a slur in the United States, had no such resonance in Hungary then.) My father proposed they make it an official organization, registered with the state. Her efforts met with resistance. Some were afraid to have their names on a government list in a hostile society; others felt ambivalent about the very idea of making common cause with other transgender people. "I don't want a 'trans community,' " Jazmin, one of the Tranny Club's reluctant members, told me when we met, clipping the air with a karate chop. "I am not a trans. I am a woman, and that's *it*."

The second meeting of the Hungarian Tranny Club convened at the home of Lorelei, a retired police officer who only used that name when he wore women's clothes; he had not changed his sex and wasn't sure that he wanted to. For now, he considered himself a transvestite and cross-dressed in secret; in his public life, he lived as a man. My father showed up early and received a warm welcome. "Lorelei was glad to have someone his age to talk to!" my father told me. The other club members were decades younger. My father settled into a chair and surveyed Lorelei's living room. "He had a lot of books," she said. "The walls were *lined* with books." My father took a closer look. "And there were all these books about how bad the Jews were. Nazi books. *Mein Kampf*."

Others arrived. "And they looked at the books, too," my father said. "And one of them says, 'Oh, you have *Mein Kampf* aaalso!' And another says, 'There's some good things in that book.'" My father, who had been sitting quietly, spoke up. "Hitler was an idiot," she said. There was an awkward pause. Then, my father recalled, another guest said: "Oh no, Hitler wasn't an idiot. He had some good things to say."

With that, the subject was dropped, and my father presented her research: to set up a state-recognized organization, members had to pay an annual fee of 10,000 forints (about $40 at the time), and at least ten members had to sign a petition requesting official status. At the end of the meeting, the petition was passed around the room. Only five signed it. My father was furious. "They are a bunch of 'fraidy cats." When she got home, she solved the signature problem: "I faked them."

Thus constituted, the Tranny Club soon disbanded. One member, a financial adviser who feared losing clients, announced that she didn't feel "safe" belonging to a club. Lorelei said he didn't want to appear anywhere publicly in a dress. Another member said she didn't want to participate because she was "a married woman." Still another said she was too busy adopting a baby. Then several transsexuals said they didn't want any transvestites in the club.

"You mean you want to *discriminate*?" my father retorted.

In the end, they agreed not to have an organization at all—just a website. One afternoon as we were sitting, per usual, at her computer, my father showed me the club's home page, which she had illustrated with a picture of horses grazing on the Great Hungarian Plain and a photo of herself, posed in her backyard swing. The caption under the picture read, "Stefánie Faludi, Presiding Woman."

My father invited all the former members of the Hungarian Tranny Club to the "Susan—Welcome to Hungary!" brunch. Two accepted: Jazmin and Lorelei. A third guest, also a male-to-female transsexual, was added at the last moment: Tatianna, a Hungarian expat who happened to be visiting the country from Florida. My father filled out the roster with some non-trans guests: two feminist professors she'd met at a literary salon, a young woman who wrote for a weekly city magazine, and the sociologist and LGBT scholar Judit Takács. And Ilonka. "She can help me with the cooking," my father said.

Early that morning, Ilonka arrived with ten bags of groceries and housekeeping supplies. My father had asked her to clean the house, too. While we were setting the table, Tatianna showed up, wrung out from the climb on a blazing hot day. She'd taken the bus from Pest. She was wearing red suede boots, a black knee-length skirt, and, over her henna-red wig, a jaunty wide-brimmed straw hat, which, by the time she arrived at the top of my father's steep street, was perched at a perilous angle. She staggered in the door, batting hat and hair back in place with a devil-may-care swat. At the age of sixty-three, Tatianna wasn't trying to play the ingénue. I liked her at once.

"I nearly *killed* myself coming up your hill," she announced to my father, collapsing into the nearest chair and kicking off her boots. She patted her midriff. "But it's okay, I need to lose some weight." From her purse, she extricated a jumbo bag of mini-Hershey's chocolate bars and passed it around. "Not *too* much weight!" she added.

My father uncorked a bottle of Hungarian pálinka and poured a shot for each of us while Tatianna told her story. This was her fifth trip to Hungary since she'd emigrated to Venezuela with her parents in 1947, when she—then a he—was a toddler. As an adult, still a male, he'd moved to Florida, married and raised two sons, worked as an engineer, and pursued photography and collected cameras in her free time. (Her latest purchase—a big digital camera—dangled from one shoulder.)

"I started wearing women's clothes when I was seven or eight," Tatianna said. "As soon as my parents went to the movies, I'd be in my mother's underwear drawer, I'd be putting on her makeup." In 2006, Tatianna had checked into a hospital in Trinidad, Colorado. "Sex-Change Capital of the World!" she noted. (The late Dr. Stanley Biber, a pioneering sex-reassignment surgeon, performed thousands of sex-change operations there between 1969 and his retirement in 2003, at the age of eighty, after which he was replaced by a surgeon who was herself a transsexual.) Afterward, Tatianna's family refused to recognize her new status. So, Tatianna was still presenting herself as male much of the time, even as her anatomy and every piece of identification in her wallet declared her a woman. Later, when we exchanged e-mails, I noticed she went by a man's name even on the Internet—a name that wasn't her original male name, a new male identity that concealed a new female identity.

"It must be a relief," I ventured, "being away from home and getting to dress how you want."

Tatianna gave a pained laugh. When she'd arrived in Budapest a week earlier, she'd reported to the state agency that issues Hungarian ID papers. (She'd retained her old citizenship, and Hungarian citizens living in Hungary are expected to carry state-issued identification cards.) The state bureaucrats would only recognize her as male, because that's what it said on her original Hungarian birth certificate. The clerk behind the desk "wanted me to take off my wig and all my makeup, right on the spot, so she could take my picture as a 'man.'" Tatianna stood her ground. It took several days of fights with various supervisors up the food chain, but eventually she got her ID.

She pulled out her cell phone and handed it to me. "See?" She had taken a photo of her ID photo with her phone. "Just in case."

"Nice," I said.

My father looked over my shoulder. "Awful," she said. "I had mine taken by a professional."

A racket of stiletto heels on flagstones announced the arrival of

Jazmin. The shoes were silver and matched the polish on her paste-on nails. Jazmin seemed to have adopted the perky persona of an aerobics instructor. She had buff arms. Her bubble-gum pink, off-one-shoulder, faux-torn T-shirt announced, in silver-glitter letters, "Gym Girl!" She was escorted by an equally toned young man in a muscle shirt and gym shorts. "This is my husband," she announced to the other guests. They weren't technically married, but she preferred to describe him that way. Jazmin drew me aside to hear the story of her transformation, enlisting Tatianna as translator.

"I'm very special in this respect," she said, "because for two months, I went into hiding from the whole world. And in this period, I changed myself, all my wardrobes changed, I had my breasts done, I had my FFS"—facial feminization surgery—"I had silicone injections on my cheeks and my forehead, and I had my eyebrows tattooed." The finale occurred in a sex reassignment surgical clinic in Serbia. The operation cost 16,000 euros. "When I woke up, my husband was on his knees by my bed. Because he *knew*. Now I was all woman. This is the meaning of being."

"Of what?"

"Being. Of *my* being. . . . It makes me very happy, this feeling that I only have to snap my fingers and men are at my feet."

I asked if she and her husband had been together long.

"Ten years," she said. "But we never used my penis. We made love another way. My penis was the worst part of my body. I never used it."

Tatianna rolled her eyes. "That's the difference between her and me," Tatianna said to me in English. "I used *my* tool. And I'm not ashamed to say it."

Jazmin said her younger brother had stopped speaking to her since the operation and had forbidden her to come near his children. "He's very Catholic. I told him, 'If God wasn't willing, then it wouldn't have happened.'" He was unconvinced. "I changed," Jazmin said, "but I can't make people change."

"*My* daughter likes me now," my father put in. "She comes to see me."

Jazmin said her husband's family didn't know. "We never told them," she said. He simply presented her one day as the "new" woman in his life. "His parents knew me since I was a boy. But as a woman, they didn't recognize me." Just to be on the safe side, she was introduced to his parents "as the sister of a boy they once knew." Which seemed to work. "They said, 'Oh yes, we see the resemblance.'" Still, there was a tense moment when her husband's parents asked to see Jazmin's baby pictures.

"What did you do?"

Jazmin pulled out her cell phone and called up the picture she had showed them—of herself when she was two years old, naked, and—thanks to Photoshop—sans penis.

Presenting her new self to the staff at the small business she owned required less finesse. Right before the operation, Jazmin had learned that somebody was stealing money from the till. The thievery presented a well-timed opportunity for a fresh start. Everyone was fired. Post-op, she hired a new crew.

"I'm very proud at how these girls take me as a role model," Jazmin said of her female employees. "They try to imitate me—the hair, nails, everything. As a female, I'm representing womanhood."

Soon, she added, she would be representing the ultimate in femininity. "I am going to have a baby," she announced to the guests. "The baby will be God's son."

"Oh, not *God's*, I hope," Tatianna muttered.

"I'm looking for a surrogate," Jazmin continued. "It will be a surrogate mother with my husband's sperm. It's going to cost three to five million forints, but I have another apartment that I'm going to sell."

And then?

"And then, it will be a complete woman's life," she said. "Before I was a transsexual. Now I'm a woman."

My father brought in the cake, decked with candles. As she cut slices of the "Welcome to Hungary" Sacher torte for everyone, she recalled how she had gotten a deliveryman the previous winter to haul her giant Christmas tree all the way into the house. "It's great being a woman," my father said. "I look helpless, and everyone helps me. It's a racket. Women get away with murder!"

Lorelei, who'd arrived at the party two hours late in a wrap-around dress and a choker made of large wooden beads (to hide his Adam's apple), confided that he almost hadn't come. "As soon as I left my apartment, my heartbeat went up," Lorelei said. He feared being seen in a dress. "When it seemed very quiet, I started down." As he entered the lobby, the building's front door swung open and the man who walked in was one of Lorelei's former superior officers. He glanced in Lorelei's direction as he passed, and nodded.

"And he said, '*Kezét csókolom.*'" I kiss your hand.

"He didn't recognize you?" I asked.

Lorelei shook his head. "It made me very happy when he *csókolom*-ed me." Lorelei had only recently dared to appear in women's clothing. "March 6, 2005," he said, his first attempt. He had ventured out of his apartment and descended just one flight before "I was trembling so hard I felt I would have to stop." It took him another nine months to make it to the street. Since he had retired from the police, Lorelei had been working as a security guard. At his job, he wore a man's uniform and a badge with his male name. No one knew his other identity. He preferred to keep it that way.

Hardly surprising, given the political climate. As one of the feminist professors at the table noted, the times were "very very bad for LGBT people." The conservative Fidesz Party and its far-right sidekick, Jobbik, were shooting up in the polls. "Look what happened at the gay pride parade last year," said Judit Takács. Neo-Nazis and skinheads had set upon the marchers. There'd been injuries. "It could be even worse this year," she said. "I'm very worried."

"They need to clean up the parade," my father interjected. "It looks bad with so many raunchy-looking people on the march. It should be *normal* people, not irritants and clowns. We have no right to irritate other people. It doesn't show a good side of minorities. . . ."

"*Stefi!*—" I tried to interrupt.

"You have to do it in a nice way, with a smile," she kept on. "I tell it in a way that they view me as just like them. Otherwise, they are going to go behind your backs and say, 'Who the hell are these people!' It's like what they say about the Orthodox Jews in their awful getup. People look at them and say, 'Who the hell knows *what* they do? Maybe they *are* killing virgin Christians!' "

I glanced over at Lorelei, he of the *Mein Kampf* collection. I wondered what he was thinking. And also, Tatianna. As we were setting the table earlier, Tatianna had told me how she'd found my father through the Trans X club in Vienna. "So I got a phone call from this Stefánie Faludi, and we start talking about this and that, and your father tells me, 'You know, my last name is not really Faludi. It's Friedman.' And I said, 'That's a good thing. Because I'm *that*, too.' " Meaning, Jewish.

"Oh, yes!" my father had replied, Tatianna's remark jogging a memory. "It's like what we'd say during the war, when one Jew met another: '*Én vagyok egy zenész is.*' " I am a musician, too.

Tatianna said she hadn't even known she was a "musician" until she turned twelve. Her parents had converted to Protestantism in the 1930s. It didn't protect them. Tatianna's father was sent to forced labor and then, in December 1944, five months after Tatianna's birth, to Sachsenhausen concentration camp. In the cattle car on the long, terrible ride there, Tatianna's father slipped a postcard between the slats. Miraculously, someone found it lying by the tracks and, even more miraculously, mailed it.

The letter was addressed to his only child, who would later commit it to memory. Tatianna recited it for me now:

To my dear son,
I had to go on a trip. I don't know how long it will take, but I will remember you always.

Your papa

In the last winter of the war, Tatianna's mother had her infant son baptized in a Roman Catholic church, and the two of them moved in with a cousin, a young woman. The building manager's son had a crush on the girl and after she spurned him, he denounced her to an Arrow Cross officer, who pulled out a gun and "killed her right on the spot."

I asked Tatianna how she felt about being back in Hungary. I was remembering the EU-inspired Equal Treatment Act with its landmark protection of "gender identity"—and also the reactions against it. On the floor of the Hungarian Parliament, representatives called the inclusion of that category "a scandalous surprise" and argued that it didn't belong in an antidiscrimination bill because transsexuality was "a birth defect" and "an illness." Conservative MP Sándor Lezsák claimed that guaranteeing equality for the transgendered would require extending the same legal protection to "necrophiliac pathologists or pedophile teachers," people whose "sexual interest turns in the direction of animals," and "all aberrations seen in horror movies." The public view was much the same: opinion polls the year the Equal Treatment Act was being debated reported that 60 percent of the respondents regarded any deviation from the heterosexual norm as either a "sin," a "crime," an "illness," or "deviant." Until 2002, the criminal code defined homosexuality as a "perversion against nature."

"How do I feel about being in Hungary?" Tatianna repeated

my question. Her response had nothing to do with gender. Her fingers floated reflexively to her throat, reaching for something that
wasn't there. "I usually wear a Star of David," she explained. "Here,
I don't."

———

One evening some weeks after the party, my father and I took the
bus up the hairpin switchbacks overlooking the Danube past the
ancient fortifications of Castle Hill. The route circumnavigated
the bulwarks of the Royal Palace and the ceremonial parade
ground presided over by the giant bronze Turul. After the bus
crested the hill, we disembarked. We made our way in the gathering dusk past a stretch of marble and graystone manses, once palaces for nobles, now office space for various state and private
institutions.

The marble foyer we entered was doused in shadow. A few paces
up the ramp, a square of fluorescent light spilled from a Plexiglas
window. My father knocked on the partition, and a man in uniform
and a plastic ID badge hurried out to greet us. The security guard,
Lorelei.

"*Szervusz, Stefi! Szervusz, Susaaan!*" Hello, Stefi! Hello, Susan!
Talking a rapid-fire Hungarian, Lorelei ushered us into his miniature kingdom, a tiny cubicle lined to the ceiling with surveillance
monitors. A slide show of darkened office rooms and corridors and
entryways played on the screens. On a desk were several computer
consoles and two TV sets. The televisions were both playing, one
tuned to the Food Channel, where two chefs with heavily moussed
hair were whipping up a soufflé, the other to *Blue Light*, a police
reality show. Its officers were mid-battle with rioting soccer fans.

"Lorelei says we're just in time," my father told me. "The chimes
are about to play." We filed out to a courtyard behind the building
to hear the evening bells of the Matthias Church.

"In the fifteenth century," my father said, translating Lorelei's recitation, "the pope ordered the ringing of the bells every day all over Europe to pray for victory in the Battle of Belgrade," the battle against the Turks to defend what was then a Hungarian border fort. We stood under a row of ornamental trees on the darkening plaza, listening to the tolling. A sudden wind rattled the leaves.

Lorelei held forth for another minute.

"During the Horthy regime," my father relayed, pointing to the indistinct outlines of a building in the distance, "that was the Ministry of the Interior." The ministry that had planned and directed the destruction of the nation's Jews.

"And that building," my father continued, gesturing farther, "was Gestapo headquarters." She paused. "Waaall," she appended, "one of them."

In the gloaming, I couldn't read her expression.

Overhead, the clouds were turning ominous. Lorelei pointed to a black thunderhead barreling our way. We barely made it inside before the skies let loose.

On the surveillance screens in the dry cocoon of Lorelei's security booth, we watched the rain lash the building's entryways. On the Food Channel, the chefs squirted icing on a seven-layer cake, and the *Blue Light* police turned hoses on the soccer hooligans, who were tearing out rows of stadium seats. The building's security cameras captured the spidery shape of an occasional late-night bureaucrat, scuttling across the monitors.

Lorelei told my father that he'd gone to a dinner-and-dance party at Stone Soup with a few other trans people, but he hadn't liked the location and wouldn't go again.

"On Kazinczy Street," my father told me. Stone Soup was a restaurant in the old Jewish quarter.

Lorelei plunged into a lengthy tale.

"Lorelei says the food was no good there," my father summarized. "Lorelei says they ordered Hungarian pálinka, and the waiter

said, 'There are two kinds here—there is the traditional Hungarian
pálinka and there is the one authorized by the Jewish Community—
and which one do you want to drink?' And they all said, '*Not* the
Jewish pálinka!' "

Another long anecdote followed, of which my father translated
only its conclusion: "So anyway, they had a round of beers and
then they all saluted Germany."

Lorelei reached for his cell phone and held it up to show me a
picture of himself, in a platinum blond wig.

My father said: "Lorelei says, 'You must be shocked to see this
aged man, instead of the elegant girl you met at the brunch.' "

I asked how he'd settled on the name Lorelei.

"He says he wanted a name that keeps distance," my father
translated.

"From what?"

"From bad connotations. In his opinion, Lorelei is a name that
gives some dignity, a delicate, clean-living person. Not some floozy
type. And he says, when he dresses up, he dresses up properly. To
project the image of a true lady. So the name should also be that.
Waaall, sure. Stefánie is also a name of such a lady."

Lorelei turned to one of the several computers and called up a
website that listed names for baby girls. *Sophia, Emma, Isabella,
Emily, Abigail* . . .

"He says he sat here at night for many weeks, searching this
site," my father said. "There are thousands of names, and he selected
many different ones before he decided on Lorelei."

Elizabeth, Charlotte, Audrey, Natalie, Zoe, Victoria, Lily . . .

I pictured Lorelei hunched over the screen here, night after
night, scrolling through the endless list with its cartoon images of
newborns in pink ribbons and mommies in BABY ON BOARD T-shirts.
Here we were in the chamber from which everything was moni-
tored and recorded, where no one could arrive or leave, exit an ele-

vator or take a cigarette break without it registering on Lorelei's security apparatus. No one escaped. And at the heart of all this surveillance was this man in the booth, whose "true" identity no one knew.

Lorelei rolled his swivel chair to a cluttered desk and dug out from under some papers an instruction manual, which he handed to my father.

"Ahhh!" my father said.

They chattered away for a few minutes in Hungarian.

"You see?" my father said, handing it to me. "These are the directions to the video game that I loaned Lorelei."

The manual was titled *Jane's Israeli Air Force.*

"It's one of my flight simulator games," my father said, and I caught a glint in her eye: it was a gift calculated to mess with Lorelei's Luftwaffe allegiances. "You play an Israeli Air Force pilot who shoots at the enemies of the Jewish State," my father said. And you have to choose "a Jewish name."

"How did it go?" I asked.

"Waaall, *I* do it very well," my father said. "I've had a lot of practice. But Lorelei says it was too hard. He kept crashing the plane. He got shot down, and he didn't even know what hit him."

Way to go, Stefi, I thought.

Close to ten, the rain let up. I suggested this might be a good time to leave. We said our farewells and groped our way down the long shadowy corridor to the exit. I imagined Lorelei, back in the booth, watching us on one of his many monitors.

14

Some Kind of Psychic Disturbance

A year before the end of World War II in Europe, the theory of an essential identity that fueled the final solution turned its lethal attention to the Jews of Hungary. That is, anyone "to be regarded as Jewish, if he or she, or at least one of the parents, or at least two of the grandparents were members of the Israelite denomination before the coming into force of the present Law." The "present Law" was the second of the three Jewish Laws passed between 1938 and 1941, a measure that overnight reclassified nearly one hundred thousand Christian converts as members of the Jewish "race."

Beginning on May 15, 1944, an average of 12,000 Jews a day were rounded up in the countryside by Hungarian gendarmes and herded into cattle cars. Within eight weeks, 147 trains delivered 437,402 Hungarian Jews to Auschwitz. In anticipation, the concentration camp's crematoria had been refurbished, furnaces relined, chimneys reinforced with iron rings, and the slave laborers assigned to the special unit servicing the gas chambers quadrupled. Even so, the ovens couldn't handle the immense numbers; bodies were piled in vast open pits and burned, a method that allowed for what the camp commandant called the "disposal" of as many as 9,000 corpses a day. One of every three people murdered in Auschwitz was a Hungarian Jew. The Hungarian Holocaust, its leading historian, Randolph L. Braham, concluded, was "the most concentrated and brutal ghettoization and deportation process of the Nazi's Final Solution program." Hungary's largest cemetery, the saying goes, is a field of grass in Poland.

In many ways, the seeds for this catastrophe had been sown two decades earlier, with the end of the First World War and the signing of the Treaty of Trianon, when the success of assimilated Jews ran up against a ferocious resurgence of anti-Semitism. József Kiss, the poet who had so effusively heralded his coreligionists' emancipation in 1868 ("Finally, O Jew, your day is dawning . . ."), would revise his conclusions. Before his death in 1921, he penned a self-eulogy:

> He was free prey in his homeland
> Disowned, destitute, and homeless
> Maybe the grave will bring him peace
> But maybe even that will reject him.

With Trianon, Hungary shed not only landmass but ethnic diversity. A vast portion of the country's minorities—those restive Romanians, Slovaks, Croatians, Ruthenians, Slovenians—now belonged to other nations carved from its borders. (The persecuted Roma, whose numbers the treaty also shrank, remained politically and economically invisible.) With the exception of ethnic Germans, strongly assimilated yet in their own way outliers, the populace had gone from a roiling rainbow quilt to black and white: Magyar and Jew. One way to read the collapse of the Golden Age—it's what happens when a fluid system becomes binary. Magyars now represented 90 percent of the population. They were no longer the only slightly-less-than-half demographic who needed the Jews to be Magyars in order to construct their majority. The Jews of Hungary now served another purpose, as scapegoats for the "amputation" of the nation, the "mutilated motherland."

Trianon and the subsequent Hungarian humiliation were blamed on the country's Jews—based on the tortured reasoning that, in 1919, many of the leaders of a short-lived Communist regime were Jewish. Even before then, though, after Hungary's defeat in World War I, Hungarian rioters robbed and beat more than six thousand Jews. The violence continued. "The international Jewish mob strives for the complete destruction of dismembered Hungary," the Union of Awakening Hungarians declared in the fall of 1919. "Remove those persistent leeches from your fainting body!" In the weeks after Trianon was signed, the Awakening Hungarians and their compatriots retaliated by murdering Jews in Budapest. By the early '20s, the right-wing union (populated by ex-army officers and university students) boasted one hundred thousand recruits and nearly a third of the members of parliament.

With the collapse of the Communist regime, and in response to its "Red Terror," in which several hundred "counter-revolutionaries" were executed, militia gangs who'd amassed around Horthy's National Army unleashed a "White Terror" that killed roughly one thousand people and targeted Jews in particular. Hundreds of Jews were tortured, lynched, and murdered in anti-Semitic pogroms. Thousands of locals—decommissioned soldiers, peasants, women, and children—joined in the violence. An American military dispatch in the fall of 1919 reported many instances of savagery, including this one:

> Here, the criminals moved on to Diszel, armed with hand-grenades and machine guns. They killed all the Jews there; 4-year-old girls were raped and thrown into the well. Two young girls jumped into the well of their own accord, in order to save their virtue. The soldiers threw hand-grenades after them.

In Budapest, Jewish organizations were attacked and bombed. And so many Jewish students were beaten or hurled down flights of stairs (in one week, 174 had to be hospitalized) that university classes in the capital were temporarily suspended. Nine months after Horthy rode a white horse into Budapest at the head of his National Army—and was then elevated to Regent by the National Assembly (with powers like those of a king)—a fact-finding report to the British Foreign Office observed, "Some of these barbarities as reported by credible witnesses reach a degree of bestiality and horror for which it would be difficult to find a parallel." A year later, the new Regent Horthy gave blanket amnesty to the White Terror perpetrators who, "because of their national enthusiasm, in the interest of the nation, committed certain acts."

In interwar Hungary, the shtetl Jews with their exotic-seeming habits and dress were no longer the prime objects of anti-Semitic suspicion. Now it was the secular Jews, the least exotic, the most accommodating, the "so easily assimilated"—and with that was opened a new conversation on the finer nuances of identity. "We were satisfied with the externalities of clothing and speech," Gyula Szekfű wrote in 1920 in *Three Generations*, his influential anti-Semitic assault on Western liberalism, "and thus we fell prey to the gravest mistake: . . . we mistook language for nationality, Hungarian chatter for Hungarianness, the transient, deceptive exterior for the immortal soul." The deceiver was the Magyarized Jew, applauded for decades for "correcting" his alien nature, but now, in the popular parlance of the time, "the hidden Jew," whose disguise fooled no one. "Why must the Jews hide their race?" interwar populist writer and politician Péter Veres asked. "Have they truly shameful racial characteristics? . . . Assimilation is a hundred times more difficult for the Jews than for any other race. The more they desire it, the more difficult it becomes, for their nervous false conformity is one of their main characteristics."

In '20s Hungary, there were to be two species—one pseudo, one true—and the pseudo-Hungarians needed to be expelled for the true Hungarians to thrive. "Hungarians and Jews," the popular writer László Németh wrote in 1927, the year of my father's birth, "are like two laboratory animals that history has sewn together in a skin graft to see which one will poison the other."

The assimilated Jews of Hungary responded to the mounting animus by trying all the harder to assimilate. The authors of the 1929 *Hungarian Jewish Lexicon* attempted to appeal to detractors by itemizing all the Jewish good works in support of the Hungarian state and the Horthy regime, all the acts of devotion to Magyar culture, all the ways that Jews had absorbed and been remade by "European-Christian civilization" (assimilated Jews, the lexicon asserted, even showed a measurable increase in skull size). "For decades prior to the horrible tragedy of their physical annihilation," historian Raphael Patai wrote in *The Jews of Hungary*, "the Hungarian Jews lived the psychological tragedy of unrequited love, of being rejected, at times politely, at others brutally, by the people of whom they so desperately wanted to be part." The more their affections went unreciprocated, the more the Jews of Hungary tried to prove their fealty as loyal Magyars, with tormented results.

That torment had been building for decades in so many of the new nation states of Central and Eastern Europe. "With the deepening crisis of assimilation in the late nineteenth century," Hungarian historian Viktor Karády wrote, "all forms of modern Jewish identity became saddled with some kind of psychic disturbance." Karády enumerated the symptoms of that disturbance: "an aversion" to the past (what my father called "ancient history"); exhibitions of extreme self-hatred "invariably directed against 'archaic' Jews who rejected 'progress'" (what my father called those "Orthodox Jews in their awful getup"); and "grotesque forms" of compensatory behavior, including "maximal conformism in dress and public self-presentation," "imitating Christian traits that turned out to be utterly improbable, pointless or misplaced," and "proclamations of chauvinist bombast" (or what my father would call being "100 percent Hungarian"). The impossible contradictions of self-denial and self-presentation led to a terrible irony. "The need to pay constant heed to fitting in," Karády wrote, "paradoxically drove those engaged in such strategies of concealment to an obsessional preoccupation with identity."

As the '20s and '30s unfolded and Hungarian Jews were terrorized by anti-Semitic militias and subjected to punishing anti-Semitic laws that stripped them of their basic rights, the Jewish leadership repeatedly rebuffed offers of aid from international human-rights and Jewish organizations as "foreign intervention"—and entreated these groups to help reverse the terms of the Treaty of Trianon instead. In 1934, the Israelite Congregation of Pest passed a resolution rejecting any alliance with outside Jewish groups and proclaimed, "We cling indomitably to our Magyardom, and we cannot allow this to be interfered with by foreign, international currents, even praiseworthy ones." Hungarian Jewish leaders would continue to refuse outside help until 1939, when it was far too late.

In the end, Magyardom would avail them nothing, even to the most decorated. In the winter of 1942, Attila Petschauer, the Olympian fencing star of 1928 and 1932, Hungary's "new D'Artagnan," was deported to a forced labor battalion in the Ukraine. On the Eastern Front, his champion status would spell his undoing. Sports chronicler Peter Horvitz gave one account of Petschauer's last hours:

> One day, from among the Hungarian officers guarding his unit, Attila recognized a lieutenant colonel as an old friend from the Amsterdam Olympics, Kalman Cseh, who had participated as an equestrian. Attila called out to Cseh, who recognized him. The Hungarian officer turned to one of his ordinates and said, "Make things hot for the Jew!" The great Olympian who had brought honor to Hungary was ordered to undress in the frigid weather and climb a tree. Then he was ordered to sing like a rooster. He was

then sprayed with water, which froze to his naked flesh. He died shortly thereafter on January 20, 1943. These tragic events were witnessed by Károly Karpati, a Jewish wrestler from Hungary who in 1936, before Hitler's own eyes, defeated the German National Champion to capture the gold medal of the Berlin Olympics.

At the end of a cascade of identity creations and identity breakdowns was the Jew. Under Habsburg rule, the Magyars, in order to maintain their political authority as Magyars, needed the Jews to be Magyars. After Trianon, the Magyars, in order to know who the Magyars were, needed the Jews to be Jews. And the Jews, having assimilated into Hungarianism (a concept they had done so much to create), had no identity to fall back on.

"Who is a Hungarian?" There seemed to be only one answer. The Hungarian was not a Jew.

On the morning that my father showed me the photo of my great-grandparents' "Golden Jubilee," I'd asked her to identify the well-dressed people in the picture. They were my relatives, but I'd never met any of them. My father slowly ran a finger across the faces as she named them, though not by their names. "Shot in a house. Killed in a brick factory. Died in a cattle car. Gassed in Auschwitz. Gassed in Auschwitz. Gassed. Gassed. Gassed . . ."

Only three of the fifteen pictured survived the war.

My paternal grandfather's hometown of Kassa, home to one of the largest Jewish communities in the country, was among the first to ghettoize and deport its population. More than twelve thousand Jews from the northeastern city and its neighboring rural hamlets were herded into brickyards and loaded onto trains. (When a seventeen-year-old girl tried to flee, she was killed and her naked body displayed as a lesson to others.) Kassa was also the railway hub for the transports to Auschwitz and other Polish concentration camps, the transfer point where cattle cars from all over Hungary were turned over to the Germans. That transfer was memorialized by Goebbels's Ministry of Propaganda in a so-called documentary intended to demonstrate the Germans' "humanitarian" approach— by contrasting it with the brutality of the Hungarians. After shots of Magyar gendarmes—whipping children, beating women, and ripping off their victims' wedding bands—the film showed German Red Cross nurses rushing into the freight cars to administer to the victims. The Florence Nightingale performance was staged. The cruelty of the Hungarian gendarmes was all too real.

Fifty-six members of the Friedman-Schwarcz family of Kassa, my grandfather Jenő's side of our family, were killed during the deportations. My great-grandfather Sámuel—the paterfamilias celebrating his wedding anniversary only months earlier—died in the brickyards. One of his grandsons was my father's cousin Viktor Schwarcz, a retired chemist who lives in Prague and was nearing ninety when we met. Viktor showed me Sámuel's "dying paper." He kept it swathed in layers of protective plastic. The official notice, dated May 25, 1944, lists Sámuel's cause of death as "heart attack." A "lie," Viktor told me, of a sort; if there was a heart attack, it was induced by the seventy-seven-year-old's savage beating by Hungarian gendarmes. "They wanted to know where the rich Jew was hiding his gold." By the time the Jews of Kassa were deported, teen-aged Viktor Schwarcz was already in forced labor on the Eastern Front. He eventually escaped and joined the Red Army. At the end of the war, he returned to Kassa to find the house rifled of its worldly goods. There was no gold to recover, except for a gold-plated garland he found in the cellar: the commemorative wreath of Sámuel and Frida Friedman's Golden Jubilee. At the end of our visit together, Viktor said he'd decided to give it to me: "In remembrance of our family." He apologized for its tarnished state. "You can see where the gold is going away," he said, rubbing a finger along the discolored metal leaves. That wasn't what bothered me. The names on the leaves were faded, almost unreadable. *The Friedman family,* I thought, *was going away.*

It was the same with the other side of the family. Two years before Sámuel Friedman's death, the deportations of the region's Jews had reached my grandmother's birthplace, the Grünbergers' ancestral town of Spišské Podhradie, "The Place under the Beautiful Castle." The once Hungarian hamlet was now ruled by Slovakia, where deportations began earlier. Gendarmes and paramilitary guards rounded up the hundreds of Jews living in the town and the surrounding area and sent them to concentration camps in Poland, where most were immediately put to death. The abbot at the Spišské Podhradie monastery shielded a few Jews, as did one Greek Orthodox priest in a nearby village. Others did nothing.

The last surviving sibling of my grandmother Rozi, Alexander Gordon (who changed his name from Grünberger after the war), gave me a series of photographs that recorded the day of the deportation, May 28, 1942. They had been taken by his Christian schoolmate. Several of the pictures were shot from ground level, others from the vantage of an upper-floor window, providing a vista on the town square. They show a long row of horse-drawn hay wagons, laden with older men, women, and children, who are swathed, despite the warmth of the day, in layers of coats, hats, and sweaters. They were only allowed to bring what they could wear. The perimeter is lined with spectators, Christian villagers, children playing at their feet. As the wagons pass the monastery, a townswoman waves to her Jewish friend who she may or may not know is being taken to her death. The woman in the wagon waves back. In the last shot, guards congregate in front of a house in their dark uniforms and high boots, rifles strapped to their shoulders, some of them laughing and chatting. Standing stiffly in their midst, somber and isolated, is an older man in a jacket and tie, a fedora on his head, a walking stick in his hand. I'd seen his face in family portraits of special occasions. Leopold Grünberger, my great-grandfather.

I wondered why he wasn't in the wagons. Alexander Gordon explained: "My father was granted an 'exception,' " along with his wife, Sidonia. "Only a few Jews had exceptions. Like if you were producing something that was important to the Germans." In Leopold's case, he was making the lumber in the town's biggest industry. On this day, he was being made to preside over the destruction of his own community.

The "exception" would be rendered meaningless when the Germans occupied Slovakia in the fall of 1944. Leopold and Sidonia fled into the countryside, where their son Alexander encountered them one last time. He'd been in a forced labor camp during the deportations and had fled to join the Slovak National Uprising. After the revolt failed and he was lying low with false documents in a small village, Alexander heard rumors that his parents were hiding in the forest and, after days of searching, found them huddled with twenty others in a woodsman's shack. "The Germans are coming," Alexander told them. He begged his parents to keep themselves hidden. His mother asked for his shirt. "She wanted to wash it," Alexander said. Sidonia scrubbed the garment as best she could and hung it near the fire. When it was dry enough to wear, she told him, "Go! Go! Save yourself." Alexander fled. The following day, an SS unit descended on the hut and sent all of its inhabitants to concentration camps in Germany: Leopold to Sachsenhausen, Sidonia to Ravensbrück.

Alexander presented me with a document, several pages long. It was a list of names, composed on a manual typewriter by a functionary: a roster of the lost Jews of Spišské Podhradie. The fastidious bureaucratic record listed the dead alphabetically, followed by date of birth, concentration camp, date of death. There were 416 names on the list, all but 20 of the Jews who had been residents of

Spišské Podhradie. Nos. 135 and 136 were Leopold and Sidonia Grünberger.

When Adolf Eichmann came to Budapest on March 19, 1944, the first day of the German occupation, to oversee the "Jewish Question" in Hungary, he arrived with ten to twelve officers and an administrative staff (including secretaries, cooks, and chauffeurs) of a mere two hundred—and with no clear authority to direct the Hungarian government. "What was unique about the German regime in Hungary," Hungarian historian György Ránki observed, "was that a relatively large degree of national sovereignty was left in the hands of the [Hungarian] government, even more than had been done anywhere else in Europe, including Denmark." Denmark had famously used its sovereignty to resist the anti-Jewish dictates of its occupiers. With only a handful of SS officers in the entire country, the Hungarian officialdom would seem to have been in an even stronger position to counter German edicts, but right from the start it chose otherwise. When the SS and the Gestapo arrested hundreds of prominent and professional Jews in Budapest in the first two weeks of the occupation—and interned them in the rabbinical seminary building where my father had attended elementary school—neither the parliament nor Regent Horthy protested. Every branch of Hungarian lawmaking and law enforcement would fall into line. Eichmann was startled, if pleased, by the occupied state's willingness, even enthusiasm. "Hungary was the only European country to encourage us relentlessly," he said later. "They were never satisfied with the rate of the deportations; no matter how much we speeded it up, they always found us too slow." He had no objections, of course: "Everything went like a dream."

The Hungarian government hastened to mobilize all its muscle in service of the Final Solution. The Hungarian Ministry of the Interior drew up the plans. One ministry undersecretary, László Endre, urged Eichmann (successfully) to quadruple the number of Jewish transports. Eichmann liked to joke that Endre "wanted to eat the Jews with paprika." Less than three weeks into the German occupation, local authorities received the ministry's order to ghettoize and deport their Jewish citizens. "The Royal Hungarian Government," the decree began, "will soon have the country purged of Jews."

A very few county and municipal officials refused to participate. They were the exception. "If any local administration deviated from the national directives," historian Elek Karsai noted in his study of the management of the Hungarian deportations, "they were aimed at exceeding the target: either by implementing the government decrees ahead of schedule or by taking more severe and harsher measures than required." The eagerness of government functionaries was matched by the nation's civilians. In the first eight days of the Nazi occupation in Budapest, Hungarian citizens filed 30,000 denunciations against hidden Jews and Jewish property, compared with 350 in the first *years* of German-occupied Holland.

In short order the Hungarian government would issue more than one hundred anti-Jewish decrees: Jews were not allowed to travel, own cars or bicycles, or make use of radios or phones. Jews were not allowed to publish books, nor could any books they'd already published be sold. (The April 1944 decree, "Concerning the Protection of Hungarian Intellectual Life from the Literary Works of Jewish Authors," ordered such works shredded or publicly burned. One such bonfire in Budapest consumed 447,627 volumes, "the equivalent," Braham noted, "of 22 fully loaded freight cars.") Jews were not allowed to employ Christian servants, or wear school or military uniforms, or swim in pools or public baths, or patronize bars, restaurants, catering services, cafés, espresso stands, or pastry shops.

My grandfather's car, the lace-curtained Renault with the dashboard vase for one rose, was confiscated and the Christian maid, governess, and cook let go. At Ráday 9, the ground-floor shops—

the furrier, beauty parlor, and patisserie—were off-limits to the family who owned the building. Not that they owned it any longer. Transactions of property by Jews were invalidated, assets seized, safe-deposit boxes sealed, commercial and industrial establishments shut down or assigned to Christian managers. In any case, the Friedman family was no longer living at Ráday 9. By then, my father was boarding with his disciplinarian teacher, Rozi was residing at her furnished studio, and Jenő was living at the Hotel Astoria. (He would soon have to find other lodgings; after the German occupation, the Astoria became a Gestapo headquarters.) Still another decree forbade Jews to purchase butter, eggs, rice, any meat except beef, or—that essential of Hungarian cuisine—paprika. By fall, Jewish rations had fallen to starvation levels. My father recalls slipping into the pastry shop at Ráday 9—by then abandoned—and running his fingers along the display counter, searching for crumbs.

The Jews of Budapest were the last in the country slated for transport to Auschwitz. In preparation, on June 16, 1944, 250,000 Budapest Jews were told they had three days to abandon their homes and move into one of the two thousand apartment buildings selected as "Yellow Star" houses. They were to leave their furnishings behind, to be enjoyed by the new Christian tenants.

My grandmother Rozi wound up in a Yellow Star house in a bleak section of southern Pest. She shared her room with a dozen others. The occupants were forbidden to have guests or speak with people through their windows and could leave only for a very few designated hours to buy food (riding to stores only on the last car of the tram). My father saw his mother once during her months in the Star house. He regretted the visit. Shortly after he'd slipped inside, the police came and sealed the doors. "They wouldn't let anyone out," my father said. He waited till night, then "climbed to the rooftop, and walked from roof to roof until I found an open door and got away." He never went back. "I wasn't going to get trapped in any stupid Star house."

At some point in the late spring of 1944, my father and my grandfather returned to Ráday 9 and holed up in the apartment of a gentile physician. The doctor had taken his family to their vacation home in Lake Balaton and invited Jenő and István to stay in the empty flat. Father and son hunkered down there for two months, curtains drawn, lights dimmed, listening to the BBC "very quietly" on the radio. Then the tenants returned. My father decamped to the streets and a series of hiding places. My grandfather Jenő relocated, too—briefly to the homes of friends and then to what had been, only a short while earlier, his other Budapest property. The apartment building at Váci 28 had been requisitioned as a Yellow Star house. A regulation foot-high Star of David, displayed on a black background, now hung over its entrance. Jenő bedded down in a former maid's room.

On July 7, just as the deportations were to commence in Budapest, Regent Horthy announced a halt in what he called "the transfer." He made the decision for various reasons—among them, the degenerating military situation, the mounting appeals from Allied and neutral powers, and the pleas of world leaders. The Jewish population of Budapest was, for the time being, spared, an act that forever elevated Horthy in the estimation of not only my father but of many of the capital's Jews, who attributed their survival to the Regent.

Horthy's order to halt the deportation of Budapest's Jews proved a brief reprieve—"the false spring," it would be called in retrospect, though it spanned from late summer into fall. On October 15, after Horthy announced that he had signed an armistice with the Soviet Union, the Germans launched Operation Panzerfaust, kidnapping Horthy's son and forcing the Regent's resignation and imprisonment. Horthy abdicated in favor of the Germans' handpicked new head of state, Ferenc Szálasi, the leader of the fascist Arrow Cross Party. A former army officer, fervid anti-Semite, and Magyar nationalist (though only partly Magyar himself), Szálasi promulgated an incoherent ideology he called "Hungarism." (During a prison stint in 1938, and "with the help of the Bible," he had worked out Jesus's family tree and concluded that Jesus was not a Jew but a "Godvanian," an imaginary race that he believed to be related to the Magyars.) Szálasi was from Kassa.

The new prime minister promptly set to eliminating the Budapest Jews, seeking to resume the deportations in early November (*after* Himmler had ordered them halted). Szálasi's Arrow Cross troops—mostly young men, many with criminal records ("primitive shoemaker types," my father said, "and not too bright")—carried out a full-bore, if increasingly freelance, Judenfrei extermination program that killed many thousands of the city's Jews and sent nearly eighty thousand on death marches to the Austrian border. In late November 1944, the Arrow Cross regime ordered the city's surviving Jews herded out of the Yellow Star houses and into the newly designated ghetto, a hastily walled-off deathtrap erected in the heart of the old Jewish quarter. In an area of only 0.1 square miles, soon teeming with rats, raw sewage, and typhus, seventy thousand Jews were incarcerated. Little food came in, no garbage came out. By December, the thousands of corpses stacked in the courtyards of buildings (including the Dohány Street Synagogue) had fused into blocks of ice.

My father moved from hiding place to hiding place. For a while, he took refuge in an old barracks on the outskirts of Buda that doubled as an airplane graveyard. The Hungarian army used the parade grounds to store the mangled hulks of shot-down Allied bombers. At night, my father would bed down on one of the abandoned military cots. Whenever the coast was clear, she told me, "I would sneak into the cockpits, and pretend I was a bomber pilot." Long before my father developed a passion for Microsoft flight videos, young István was simulating takeoffs and landings. Army officers finally chased him out, and he found a new hiding spot on the edge of Pest in a Christian neighborhood. By then, he had acquired, via the Zionist underground, an armband that belonged to one of the Hungarian Nazi-aligned parties.

While my father was piloting downed planes and roaming the streets with fascist regalia and an incriminating lack of foreskin, my grandparents had reunited, albeit by accident. They both happened to seek shelter in one of the "protected houses" along the river by St. Stephen's Park, an area that came to be known as the International Ghetto. Starting in the late summer of 1944, the neutral legations of Sweden, Switzerland, Portugal, Spain, and the Vatican began issuing tens of thousands of official-looking safe-conduct passes and protective passports that (theoretically) shielded the city's Jews from deportation. The non-aligned diplomatic missions declared several dozen apartment buildings in the city as safe zones. Rozi and Jenő wound up independently taking refuge in the same Swiss protected house on Pozsonyi út, a couple blocks from the Danube. They shared a room with about forty other people, including my father's cousin, Judit (later Yudit) Yarden, and her parents.

That late fall and winter, armed gangs of Arrow Cross adherents took a particular malicious pleasure in invading the protected houses—they regarded the occupants as privileged Jews and thus even more tempting targets. Soon the "protected" were being hauled off, some to be interrogated and beaten in Arrow Cross detention centers, others forced on death marches. Thousands more were taken to the Danube and shot into the river. To save on bullets, Arrow Cross gunmen tied people together—often family members— shot one into the river, and let the sinking corpse drown the rest.

My father heard reports of the shootings. One day, she said (in one of the detail-free childhood anecdotes my father had proferred in my youth, an anecdote I'd never known whether to believe), a teenaged Pista had shown up at the Swiss protected house where his parents were living and, displaying his Hungarian Nazi armband, "saaaved" them.

"Which house?" I asked one afternoon in Buda. We were sitting in her dining room over the remains of coffee and cake. I laid out a city street map on the dining-room table and pointed to the half-dozen-block area where most of the protected houses were grouped.

"Waaall," my father said, "one of those buildings. I don't remember."

"Why don't we go over there and see?" I pressed. A stupid question.

"No point," she said, shoving the map aside.

She diverted the conversation to one of the few topics from the past she didn't mind revisiting—her own father's excellent taste. "My father was always very classy," she said, ticking off a list of examples I'd heard many times: the custom-made suits ("beautiful fabric he ordered from England"), the classics he kept in his study's glass display cases ("very fine, elegant bound editions"), the Renault with the lace-curtained rear window and the dashboard flower vase.

"Pretty stylish," I said, wearily pushing the crumbs around on my plate and wishing she'd move on.

"Waaall," she laughed, "of course, my father didn't know what to do when the car broke down!"

"Not a grease monkey, huh?"

"No, but he did take a course on auto repair once. Aaand"—the finger aloft, her digital exclamation point—"he bought overalls to wear when he would go for his class at the garage. Gray, with a matching gray cap. I was a similar size. So I wore it."

"You fixed the car?"

"No!"

"For what then?"

"Vadász Street."

"What?"

"You're not listening!"

I was. I just wasn't getting it, though I should have. In 2004, when my father was leading the guided tour of her feminine wardrobe on my first visit to the Buda house, she had pointed out the one outfit from her former life that hadn't been exiled to the armoire of male castoffs. Hanging in her bedroom closet was a pair of white overalls, carefully pressed and preserved in a dry-cleaning bag. It was the uniform my father had worn as a volunteer for the Yorktown Heights Ambulance Corps. I remembered the nights he was on call; he'd wear the uniform around the house, starched and ironed. I was startled that he'd held on to it, and perplexed by its significance. What was this conflation of clothing and saving, regalia and rescue?

15

The Grand Hotel Royal

"Vadász Street," my father repeated. She was referring to the "Glass House," a former glass factory turned Swiss protected building at Vadász utca 29, where clandestine Zionist youth organizations had set up shop in the fall of 1944. The youth groups printed and distributed tens of thousands of false identity papers, helped smuggle Jews to the Romanian border, and tried to collect useful information to aid the Allied effort. After the Arrow Cross take-over, the young Zionists also began collecting fascist party uniforms and armbands to wear while gathering intelligence and distributing forged documents. Their numbers were small—maybe a few hundred, one of the smallest such movements in Central Europe—and many were refugees from Slovakia and Poland.

My father joined Betar, a Zionist youth organization, at the behest of his seventeen-year-old cousin, Frigyes "Friczi" Schwarcz, who had come to the city in 1944 intent on instigating an armed resistance. The two young men shared an abandoned apartment briefly, before Friczi decamped to a "bunker" on the outskirts of Pest to organize an uprising. Soon thereafter, neighbors denounced him and his handful of young bunker-mates, and they were all killed. "They were going to 'fight the Nazis!' " my father scoffed. "They didn't even know how to use a gun. Friczi wanted to be a hero. And he didn't survive."

My father continued to work sporadically with Betar. "I had this one contact. He'd get in touch and give me a task—like, go spy on some building where the Nazis were. I'd wear my father's overalls and cap."

"Why?"

My father gave me one of her you-idiot looks. "Because, *as I told you*, they were gray. The Luftwaffe color. I acted like I was a Luftwaffe mechanic, working for the Nazis."

"That worked?" I doubted it.

"It worked quite well." And it led, she said, to "an even more absurd happening." One day, the Betar contact asked my father to spy on an elementary school that had been commandeered by the SS and was now occupied by the Gestapo and the Arrow Cross. "They would take people in there to question them and beat them up," my father said. His job was to try to find out who was being held.

"It turned out it was *my* elementary school." The school housed in the Rabbinical Seminary of Hungary, which my father had attended until he was ten. "I put on my 'uniform' and went over there with my false papers, and I volunteered to be one of the guards on night duty. Waaall, these Arrow Cross guys were not too bright! They were happy someone came to help them."

"What did you find out?"

"Nothing significant. It wasn't that long. Maybe a week. . . . But no one suspected me of being Jewish. I didn't act like that."

"Like what?"

"Like doing stupid things." Her voice was rising. "Like taking 'protection' papers from some diplomats who couldn't really do anything." She meant her parents. "Like moving into a 'protected' house and saying, 'Oh, now we're protected!' " She affected a fey tone as she spoke these last words. "Waaall, okay," she conceded, "maybe they were for a little time. . . . But then I had to get them out of there."

I reached for my notebook. "How?"

"I've told you all that."

"Not the details."

She studied her empty plate for a while. "What do you want to know?"

"That day . . . were you wearing the overalls?" It was a dumb question, but a safe one; she liked to talk about clothes.

"No, I just wore the armband. And an Arrow Cross hat." She wanted to pass that day as a Hungarian Nazi, not a German officer. "And I had a gun."

"A gun?"

"Just an old army rifle. I probably got that from someone at Vadász. I do know it didn't have any bullets!" Not that it would have mattered, my father noted. Like Friczi, young István didn't know how to shoot.

"And they let you in?"

"I was armed, so it was all correct." He told the guard at the front door that he had orders to take away the Friedmans. "I acted mean, but not *too* mean. I didn't overdo it."

"They weren't suspicious?" I had trouble imagining this.

"I told you, I know how to fake things." She rose to her feet and began swinging her arms. "I marched upstairs, hup two, hup two, and I pushed open the door and yelled, 'Is there a Jenő Friedman in here? And his wife? Send those goddam Jews out here! And they can't bring anything!' " She waved a fist in the air, brandishing an invisible rifle.

"And they were in there?"

"There were as many people as could fit," she recalled of the room, "all crammed up" against one another, "old people, sick people, little children." He remembered their stares. "They all felt sorry for my parents," she said. "They thought, 'Oh, this Naaazi is going to kill the poor Friedmans!'" My father said he ordered his parents toward the door. As they were heading down the corridor, an elderly Jewish man sidled up. "He wanted to know if I could get him false papers." That is, he recognized the young man in the fascist armband as a fellow Jew. "I yelled at him, 'Get out of here or I'll take you, too!'" The man backed away, and my father marched his parents down the stairs at gunpoint.

"When we went past the guard at the front door, I gave the salute, and I shouted, 'Long live Szálasi!'" My father dusted crumbs off her doily placemat. "And that's how I brought the family together."

Afterward, father, mother, and son set up housekeeping in the winter of 1944 in an abandoned flat on the outskirts of Pest. They were now, according to the false papers my father had obtained from the Zionist youth resistance, the "Fabians," Catholic refugees from the Romanian town of Brașov. When the long Siege of Budapest began, a few days after Christmas, a bomb fell directly across the street, shattering every window in the unit. The Fabians retreated to the cellar, where they spent the rest of the war. "When we came up from the basement," my father recalled, "a man was upstairs and he started shouting, 'I am the rightful owner of this house!' We told him, 'Calm down, calm down! We're not staying.' Then he introduced himself, and you know what his name turned out to be? Friedman."

My father studied my hand flying across the notepad. "When you write about my life story," she said, "this would be a great story to include. Aaand"—she lifted a finger aloft—"it's aaalso true."

Was any of it? Or was this another one of my father's fairy tales? Had the trick photographer tricked the Arrow Cross—or was she tricking me? How could I begin to assess the truth of a story whose very point was to confirm the storyteller as an extremely effective liar?

On several of my earlier trips to Budapest, I'd wasted a good deal of time trying to research the larger family history, to ferret out the written annals to go along with the pitifully few photographs I had found of the Friedman-Grünberger tribe. There weren't many repositories to ferret in. The Hungarian Holocaust Memorial Center in Budapest had opened only in 2004, and when I visited, its tiny research staff had little to offer. They told me to write each of my relatives' names, along with their places and dates of birth, on forms that they would "file in our system."

For what purpose? I asked.

"So then we have their names on file."

They suggested I try the Hungarian Jewish Archives. "But I don't know if you'll find anything," one of the researchers said. "It's a little disorganized."

The archives, an annex of the Hungarian Jewish Museum, was in the old Jewish quarter, attached to the Dohány Street Synagogue. Entering from the museum's exhibit hall required negotiating an elaborate series of twists and turns through spottily lit corridors and staircases. The labyrinth dead-ended in an imposing set of double doors. I gave a timid rap, and a woman in a white lab coat let me in. She was Zsuzsanna Toronyi, the archives' director.

The cramped interior was made more so by the old tomes and stacks of moldering periodicals piled to perilous heights around the room. Sagging shelves looked like they could give way at any moment under a riot of cardboard boxes with handwritten labels. I eyed the out-of-order sign on the copy machine with dismay. Toronyi advised me that there was little the archives could offer in the way of family records, but when I said my father had attended the elementary school at the Rabbinical Seminary, she led me through the maze of boxes and, as if by internal divining rod, plucked a book in an instant from the chaos. *The Rabbinical Seminary of Budapest, 1877–1977: A Centennial Volume* began with a proud recounting of its inauguration "in the presence of the members of the Hungarian parliament and government." Its instructors were "not only to teach Judaism but also to foster Hungarian patriotism among their co-religionists by disseminating the language and culture of Hungary." I skimmed through the account of its "modern" curriculum and the lists of its many internationally known graduates. Eventually, the book got around to the Holocaust.

"In spite of World War II," the text intoned, the seminary's educators "continued their work, hoping that the horror of the European war would not touch them." A vain wish. Less than twenty-four hours after the Germans occupied Hungary, the building "was confiscated by the SS, to serve as a transit prison for thousands of Jews on their tragic way to the extermination camps." As I read further into this chilling chapter—the plundering of the seminary's 300,000-volume library, the destruction of the rector's lifework of research, the Arrow Cross's artillery position on the roof, and, ultimately, the bombardment of the building itself—Toronyi appeared at my side to offer another text. It was decrepit and much thumbed, its pages loose in the bindings. "You might find your family members in here," she said.

The volume's title was *Counted Remnant: Register of the Jewish Survivors in Budapest*, published a year after the end of the war. The register had been assembled by the Hungarian Section of the World Jewish Congress and the Jewish Agency for Palestine, which had deployed 402 people to search 35,082 houses in Budapest in the summer of 1945, looking for living Jews. The resulting book listed survivors in alphabetical order, along with their birthplace, birth date, mother's maiden name, and the address where they had been located. The data had been gathered in a hurry and

rushed into print in hopes of aiding the search for missing relatives, and was not the most accurate or complete of records. Dates
and spellings were often approximate. Still, I knew when I found
it. As my finger landed on the fading tiny print, and despite the
stifling summer heat, I shivered:

"Friedmann István, Bpest, 1932, Grünbaum Rózsi, VIII, Víg
u. 15."

I tried to place my young father at 15 Víg Street, a good twenty-
minute walk from Ráday 9 in the once aristocratic Palace District.
What was he doing and thinking that day? Had the census taker
gotten his birth year wrong, or was he already lying about his age?
I pored over the entry for a long time, as if its contents might yield
a secret code. But they were just words on a page.

I flipped to the front to read the registry's introduction. It began
with an epigraph from Deuteronomy: "*And the Lord shall scatter
you among the nations, and ye shall be left few in number. . . .*"
And went on to offer this counsel:

> Everybody turning over the leaves of this book should realize the
> significance of the fact that also above the will of the power which
> thought itself to be the strongest there is a higher jurisdiction, pre-
> venting the innocent from being entirely exterminated. But he
> should also realize the heavy burden pressing down upon each
> single person who is figuring in this book: the dreadful memories
> of the past, the frightful dreariness of the present, and the unsolved
> problems of the future.
>
> For we all who remained are now standing here in the world,
> plundered, humiliated in our human dignity, with souls harassed
> to death, and alone.

I closed the volume slowly, distressed that my turning the crumbling pages had loosened several more leaves. I thanked the
kindly Toronyi and pushed through the double doors.

Minutes into my departure, I realized I was lost. In my befuddle-
ment, I'd forgotten the complicated directions from the archives to
the museum. I turned down one corridor, then another, up one set
of turreted stairs, then down again. Every route dead-ended in a
locked chicken-wire gate. I knew these were security cages to protect the museum's valuables. I knew it was 2008, yet I could not
quell the panic. I began running in circles through the maze, rattling
doorknobs. Every one was locked. Down a passageway I heard
the sound of a radio. I traced it to its source and banged on the
door. A stooped elderly man opened it a crack and marveled at the
hysterical American woman on the other side. "Out?" I said, pointing. "Out?" He took my arm and led me to the exit.

Some months later I would read how, in the winter of 1944,
several inmates of the city's fenced-in Jewish ghetto who were
slated for deportation escaped by squeezing through a narrow,
hand-dug breach in the perimeter—through a wall of the building
that now housed the Jewish Museum and Archives. As the authors
of *Jewish Budapest* noted, "The Jewish Museum was the single
tiny chink in the wall of the Pest ghetto."

One afternoon I managed to lure my father out of the house with
the promise of sweets. I suggested we check out a pastry shop in
Pest known for its Viennese tortes. Its appeal to me was the address,
not the menu. It was near the Grand Hotel Royal and the spot
where my father said that she, as a teenage boy, had been grabbed
off the street by an Arrow Cross officer and almost killed in a cellar. This was another of the anecdotes my father had told me as a
child. Or at least the Royal was the place where she said it "probably" had happened. The hotel was a storied establishment.
Opened in 1896 in honor of the Millennial Jubilee, its French
Renaissance palatial quarters had boasted a spa, a *cour d'honneur*
with palm garden and a "royal ballroom," where Béla Bartók reg-

ularly conducted concerts. The Royal was requisitioned during the war by both the Arrow Cross and the SS. The patisserie was a couple of blocks away.

Over two Dobos tortes, an eight-layer sugar mountain of sponge cake and chocolate buttercream, to which my father insisted on adding a snowcap of whipped cream, I did my best to steer the conversation to the drama that may or may not have unfolded down the street more than sixty years earlier. My father did her best to steer it away.

"The Urania was maaarvelous," she said, a fork overloaded with whipped cream poised in midair. The Urania National Film Theater, an early cinema with a lavishly gilded and mirrored Moorish interior, was another landmark from my father's childhood, a Taj Mahal that young István used to haunt. "It had mostly first-run German movies. Waaall, it was German owned. And I also used to go to the Savoy Theater, near where we lived on Ráday. I got free tickets there because my father had 'befriended' the ticket lady. Waaall, he had many lady friends."

"And the Hotel Royal . . ."

"Then after the Urania," my father plowed on, "I'd go to the film rental shop next door." She recalled its furnishings: richly embroidered upholstery in gold and red threads, velvet drapes, brocaded walls. "You could get all the old silent films there. Sixteen millimeters. I rented *Metropolis*, all the great classics. It was just a *jewel*. It was"—she stopped to summon the proper word; her eyes had a childlike glimmer; I'd rarely seen her so enchanted—"like being inside a music box."

"Were you already making your own films then?" I asked.

"Now, *this* is an interesting story," my father said. "The nine-and-a-half-millimeter Pathé my father gave me had a perforation in the middle of the film, a stupid thing." The sprocket holes were between the frames, "right in the middle of the picture! Waaall, the French have to make something completely different for no purpose. But don't write that down. We don't want to offend the French!

So anyway, I bought a sixteen-millimeter camera, and a sixteen-millimeter projector, too. I bought the camera from a Hungarian engineer who had manufactured it himself. In his cellar! He copied the American Bell & Howell model. He sold it cheaper to me because I was a kid. And later I aaalso managed to acquire a Swiss Bolex movie camera."

"When was this?"

"In the '40s." In the middle of the war, my teenage father was out shopping for better film equipment.

"I'd also go to this Hungarian filmmakers' society," she continued. "They called themselves the Amateur Narrow-Film Group, because they used the narrower sixteen-millimeter film." The society, she recalled, "was full of fascists." My father was unfazed. "I was so interested in amateur films, I'd go all the time. *This* interested me, not the stupid Nazis."

"Did they know you were Jewish?"

"I didn't tell them."

After the war, my father would be one of the first members of another moviemaking group, the youth film club sponsored by the Hungarian Communist Party. Young István suggested the site of its first clubhouse: the abandoned offices of the German Nazi film archives in Pest. And proposed its first activity: splicing the 16mm newsreels left behind there into counter-narratives. "You know, Eisenstein film theory," my father said. "We turned them from Nazi to *anti*-Nazi films."

I said that sounded like a gratifying exercise.

"The power of editing!" she said. "Waaall, I have to edit everything I do."

She got up and went to retrieve her purse, which she'd hung on the coatrack across the room.

"You shouldn't leave that there," I said.

"Why not?"

"It will be stolen," I said. And thought, here I go again with the purse.

We paid the bill and wandered down the street. As we passed the Royal, I suggested we take a look inside.

The marbled entrance faced a sweeping staircase and, beyond it, a six-story glass atrium. The Grand Hotel Royal was now the Corinthia Hotel Budapest, a five-star resort run by a multinational chain based in Malta. A brochure on the information desk trumpeted the building's transformation into "the very best in 21st century spa luxury" with "levels of comfort and convenience" that are "all reassuringly up to date." In the lobby, a series of captioned photographs recounted the hotel's history, with one elision; the exhibit's chronology leaped from 1928 to the anti-Communist uprising of 1956. From the sports bar down the hall came the shouts of fans and the flicker of large-screen TVs. A soccer match was under way.

I turned to look at my father, and she was shaking her head.

"No," she said. "No, no, no!" She pivoted on a heel and headed back toward the grand revolving door.

"What's—?"

"This isn't it," she said. "This isn't where it happened." I started after her. Had it happened at all?

On the sidewalk, she paced back and forth. After a while, she crossed to the other side of the wide curving Ring Road, called Erzsébet körút in this segment, and headed south. I followed. Two blocks later, she came to a halt on the corner of Wesselényi utca.

"This is where I turned left onto the *körút*," she said. "There were dead bodies lying all over on the sidewalk here, dead horses, frozen, and"—she rotated in a slow circle, eyeing a line of rundown apartment buildings—"my God, there it is." She stared up at a four-story faux stone edifice with Gothic arched windows and soot-blackened gargoyles. Two carved owls perched over the front portal, which was embossed with a coat of arms of crossed hooks that looked eerily like a swastika. A homeless man with a crutch was sleeping on the front ledge. The windows were covered in wrought-iron bars.

"All these years," she said, eyes locked on the owls. "All these years I thought it was the Royal."

The entry door was unlocked. We went inside.

A smell of mildew pervaded. In the foyer, three bare bulbs dangled from a chain, one of them burned out. We passed through the main hall—where a shop selling "Western cowboy boots with spurs" was shuttered—and proceeded to a gloomy interior courtyard, girdled by three floors of arcaded galleries with groin-vaulted ceilings. I felt like we'd wandered into a Romanesque monastery. The place was deathly quiet.

My father took a few tentative steps up the first set of worn concrete stairs. Then she came around and started down the staircase that led to the cellar. She didn't get far. The way was barred by a locked metal cage.

"I was going to get food at Váci 28," she began. The Christian building manager, the Friedmans' former employee, had agreed to sell young Pista a small portion of lard and beans if he could make it over there. "I shouldn't have gone on the big *körút*, that was my mistake."

As he had passed the building, my father recalled, a young man in an Arrow Cross uniform had waved him over. My father recalled the man's words: "'Brother!'—they always called each other that—'Brother! Why are you wearing that armband. Don't you know the two parties are united?'" The Arrow Cross and the Hungarian Renewal-National Socialists, another fascist party, had recently combined forces and were all now wearing the Arrow Cross crest. My father was sporting the wrong insignia. "I acted very confident and said, 'Oh, yaaas, brother, I know! I'll go get a new armband.'"

The guard ordered my father to go inside and report to the cellar. My father went in, then paused before the stairwell. The building was a hive of Arrow Cross activity, armed young men striding through the corridors. He heard gunshots. "They were shooting people in the basement." The Royal was where the Arrow Cross displayed its public face. This was the place, one of several in the city, where executions were carried out.

My father demonstrated what happened next. "I made like I was going down"—she took a few steps toward the locked metal cage—"but I saw no one was looking, so I went up and around." She strode purposefully up the first flight, as if heading for an appointment, and stopped at a shadowy recess at the bend of the stairs. "I stayed there awhile." She pressed herself flat against the wall, the floral pattern of her dress fading into the gloom. We waited. A door slammed upstairs, and I jumped.

"How long?" I asked, mainly to break the tension.

My father didn't move. I thought she was going to reenact the interval, rather than describe it, but then she said, "Long enough so the guard would think I was doing what he said." She eased away from the wall. "I took off my armband, and then I marched back down." She demonstrated, goose-stepping stiffly down the stairs in her heels. "I went past the guard and gave the Nazi greeting"— she shifted her purse to the other shoulder and shot out her arm in illustration—"and I said, 'Thank you very much, *brother*!' and I walked away." Either the guard was a different one from the one who'd ordered him in, or my father's confident posture, even sans armband, had convinced him that István Friedman had passed his credentials check and was, indeed, a "brother."

"And then?"

"And then I went to Váci út and collected the lard and beans."

16

Smitten in the Hinder Parts

"You can always tell it's my name day," my father said to me as we climbed the steps of the block-long cathedral. She meant her former "name day," the feast day of the saint who shared her former name. "Because no one's at work," she explained. St. Stephen's Day is a state holiday. Every August 20, the entire country pays homage— starting with early-morning Holy Mass and ending with late-night fireworks—to the canonized first king of Hungary.

The gilded dome of St. Stephen's Basilica is one of the city's most visible beacons: at exactly ninety-six meters tall—in honor of 896, the supposed year of the Magyar Conquest—it is one of the two tallest buildings in the city. (The other, the Hungarian Parliament, is also exactly ninety-six meters high; government regulations mandate that no city structure exceed in height that prized number.) The basilica's construction involved three architects, five decades, and fifty types of marble. Once inside, we struggled to get our bearings in the vast and echoing darkness. The ornately carved wooden pews can seat eighty-five hundred worshippers. I could just make out the main altar, where a giant marbled figure of Saint

Stephen presided, the archangel Gabriel hovering above, clutching the Holy Crown.

"Where is it?" I asked my father.

She nodded toward the far left of the altar, where a long queue had formed. We joined it. Half an hour later, we arrived at the guards' station. A velvet rope swung aside and we were admitted to the Chapel of the Holy Right. Paintings of various saints adorned the chamber. Against the far wall, the object we came to see was shrouded in shadow. You had to drop 200 forints in a coin box to illuminate it. The lights went up on what looked like a jewel-studded dollhouse, a heavily ornamented golden reliquary encased in a glass sarcophagus. Inside the arches of the miniature shrine was an amputated hand: Hungary's cherished Christian relic, the Holy Right, the mummified right hand of Saint Stephen. It was the miracle-dispensing hand with which the dying king is said to have lifted the Holy Crown of Hungary in 1038 and pledged his throne to the Virgin Mary. After a minute, the light shut off.

On August 20, 1990, and in celebration of the fall of heathen Communism and the restoration of Christianity, the Holy Right was allowed out of its sepulcher for what would become an annual excursion. Actually, it led a parade. Priests bearing aloft the relic in its sealed glass case headed up a procession, tens of thousands of people marching through the streets of Budapest. Hundreds of thousands more watched the live broadcast on television.

The post-Communist preoccupation with Saint Stephen's hand was part of a larger reconstruction of a mythological history, the myth of Hungary as originally and quintessentially Christian.* The Communist regime had suppressed religious practice of all stripes. After 1949, the government ceased collecting religious affiliation in

---

* Never mind that Jews likely predated the Magyars in the Carpathian Basin, and that when the Magyar chieftains did arrive, their legions included several Jewish Kabar and Khazar contingents: the Magyar Conquest was a Magyar-Jewish alliance.

the national census and omitted religion from identity cards. Citizens were supposed to be Communists, first and last. The suppression of religion led to a new erasure for Hungary's embattled Jews. In 1989, the year marking the end of Communist rule, Hungarian historian Peter Kende published a book on Hungarian Jewry that included a chapter titled, "Are There Jews in Hungary Today?" It was a reasonable question. When the post-Communist Hungarian census restored religious affiliation to its count, the results were as follows in 1992: Roman Catholics, 67.8 percent; Calvinists, 20.9 percent; Lutherans, 4.2 percent; Jews, 0 percent.

Many parents had gone to great lengths to conceal Jewish roots from their children. A 1985 study of children of Holocaust survivors living in Hungary found that they generally stumbled upon their religious origins by accident or happenstance when they were teenagers or older, often when an incident shook loose a parent's confession. It was a phenomenon so commonplace the study's authors gave it a name: "How I Came to Know That I Am Jewish."

After my parents' divorce, my father became a devotee of televangelism. The Christian Broadcast Network was his lifeline, and he recorded scores of sermons by Robert Schuller, Pat Robertson, Jerry Falwell, and many more, with the exception of Jim Bakker, whom he deemed "an idiot." The *Hour of Power* telecast from the Crystal Cathedral played on his thirteen-inch Panasonic TV every Sunday. He put the TV on a lazy Susan so he could watch while he was cooking, or eating, or in bed. He would interrupt the marathon viewing sessions to expound to visitors on Christian morality and "family values." A favorite topic: the abomination of divorce.

My father's evangelical fervor amplified an older fascination with Christianity. Before the divorce, Sunday afternoons in our living room were wall-of-sound masses, baroque sacred music, fugues, passions, requiems. Between records, my father would deliver wearying sermons on the finer points of liturgical history. He would sometimes sing along with the chorus, in German. I sat across from him, desperate to flee, pretending to study the English translation in the liner notes. ("O Lamb of God, wholly innocent / Slaughtered on the trunk of the Cross, / Patient through all ages, / No matter how much provoked.")

The only high holidays we celebrated were Christian ones. At Christmas, my father strung lights across the front of our house and installed a large and fastidiously decorated tree in our living room. (One year the decor was a "Danish theme," with live candles; an errant taper nearly burned the house down.) We'd assemble for a family photo session, posed with fruit cake or tins of Christmas cookies, which my father insisted my mother bake. Bach's *Christmas Oratorio* or its equivalent issued from the stereo system. On Easter, he'd enlist us in a pilgrimage to a Roman Catholic—or Greek Ortho-dox or Russian Orthodox—church that he'd heard hosted an especially resplendent resurrection ritual. He just liked "the pag-eantry of the church fathers," he said, the men of the cloth parading their supreme spiritual authority. After services, as the ecclesiastics processed in their vestments swinging incense censers, my father would capture the pomp and circumstance on film. His desire to commit Christian rites to celluloid was long-standing. A few weeks after receiving the Pathé camera as his bar mitzvah present, young István had set out for Esztergom, the Hungarian seat of the Roman Catholic Church, so he could "make a movie" of churchgoers filing into the largest cathedral (and building) in the country, the Primatial Basilica of the Blessed Virgin Mary Assumed into Heaven.

My father never attended a service at the lone synagogue in York-town Heights. He did, though, pay a call on its offices one day in 1976—to see if the young rabbi could stop my mother from seek-ing a divorce. "And you know what he said?" my father asked me as we were sitting in front of her computer. We had been looking at photographs of Hungarian cathedrals. "Waaall, Mr. Faludi"—my father delivered the rabbi's remarks in a high-pitched register—"in modern Judaism, divorce is something that has to be considered." Whenever my father got on the subject of Jewish male authorities she'd encountered—whether American Reform rabbis or Orthodox caftan wearers or wartime Judenrat representatives—her impersonations turned mincing.

One summer afternoon when we had taken our coffee to the deck, my father went into yet another of her mocking imitations of the Budapest Jewish community elders who wouldn't help her reclaim the family property after her return to Hungary: "Oh, we can't *do* anything, Mr. Faludi," she said, channeling Minnie Mouse. "We have to make *nice* with the authorities." My father was wearing a rosebud-print housecoat and bedroom slippers—"my hausfrau outfit," she called it—which only heightened the contradictions. Here was a Jewish man-turned-woman making fun of Jewish men for not being manly enough.

One night, my father and I attended a concert performance of Halévy's *La Juive* (*The Jewess*) in the Dohány Synagogue, the "Israelite Cathedral" with the organ and eight-pointed stars that stood at the spot that once marked the entrance to the ghetto. On the way in, my father hesitated at the foldout table heaped with loaner yarmulkes. "No, not for women!" she announced, exclamatory finger in the air, and we proceeded to the main sanctuary, where the opera would be performed officially for the first time in Hungary since 1937. The story was typical convoluted libretto fare, with all the plot twists dependent on mistaken identity between Jews and Christians. A Jewish goldsmith raises the daughter of a cardinal as if she were his own daughter, and when she's grown, the cardinal (who doesn't know that "Rachel" is really his daughter) condemns her to death for falling in love with a Christian prince (who has led her to believe he is a Jew). The goldsmith could save Rachel by revealing that she actually is, by bloodlines anyway, a Christian, but he stays mum and the girl dies in a boiling pot of oil, into which the goldsmith soon follows.

My father was annoyed that we had to sit so far back. Almost half the pews were cordoned off and marked RESERVED FOR VIPS.

"All the *biiig alte kockers*," she said derisively. As we squeezed into the middle of a back row, I was aware of people inspecting my father, some unkindly. She seemed aware of it, too.

"Do I need rouge?" she asked me, scrounging in her pocket-book for a compact mirror.

She was wearing her red sheath dress, with black heels and a black scarf with big red cabbage roses and she carried a black pocketbook. ("You can't bring a white pocketbook to the opera," she'd advised me earlier in the evening.)

"No, you look fine."

"Look at all those fat Jewish men with their big bellies and their gold rings and watches," my father said, gesturing to the reserved pews. She couldn't seem to get off the subject, and her voice kept getting louder. "They think they're so important sitting there in the VIP section with all their gold."

People were turning around. The concert, sponsored by the Jewish Summer Festival, was a tourist attraction—not particularly well attended by Hungarians—and evidently a fair number of the tourists understood English.

"Stefi, could you lower your voice?"

My father fussed with her scarf and then leaned over to deliver a stage whisper into my ear. "I know what they are thinking," she said, sotto voce. "They are looking at me and saying, 'There's an overdressed shiksa.'"

I was mindful of Otto Szekely's injunction not to conflate religion and gender. There were times when my father seemed intent on making that difficult.

———

In 1922, Hans Blüher, early Nazi ideologue and champion of a German state based on the manly bonds of a theoretical *Männerbund*, spelled out the sexual distinction between the Aryan and Jewish "races." "The association between male character and the essence of being German," he said, "and between the feminine and servile character with the Jewish is a direct intuition of the German people, which becomes more definite from day to day."

These canards were aimed at one sex in particular. The feminization of the "race" seemed to render "the Jewess," particularly of the assimilated and affluent variety, all the more attractive. Even when she was vilified, as she was in the interwar years, it was more often as a seductress, not a failed woman. Generally, she was regarded as beautiful. Visiting Budapest in 1913, the French writer André Duboscq wrote approvingly: "The Jewish women stand out with the voluptuousness of their becoming curves and little gaudy outfits: they flag their hats with feathers and ribbons. One might see them every day at the promenade." That promenade took place each weekend in Budapest along the Corso, the boardwalk on the Pest side of the Danube. My grandparents and their son used to walk up and down there, too, every Saturday after morning services. In 1908, Budapest journalist Jenő Heltai observed that among the upwardly mobile Jewish couples he knew, the men couldn't hide their origins, but "Jewishness did not show on their wives." When it did, it only added to their erotic appeal. Hungarian poet Endre Ady, whose wealthy married mistress and muse was Jewish, exalted "the blood-red lips" of Jewry's "honeyed women." In his 1912 novel in verse, *Margita Wants to Live*, Ady declared "the Jewish girl" to be "a symbol of the new, / fine Hungarian times that hasten to come / . . . Hungaria and Margita are almost one."

In Budapest, thanks to the superior education of the bourgeois

"Jewess" (by the turn of the century, 48 percent of the city's female university students were Jewish) and her cultural appetites (well-off Jewish women quickly became leading consumers of the capital's arts-and-leisure market), every theater, concert hall, and publishing house in the late nineteenth and early twentieth centuries was hungry for her business. She was also more likely than her male counterpart to marry a Christian of higher social status. A striking number of prominent men of the Christian upper crust (including Baron Géza Fejérváry, Hungary's prime minister in the early 1900s) and the Christian intelligentsia (Béla Bartók, Zoltán Kodály, and Gyula Krúdy among them) had Jewish wives. (An anti-Semitic interwar writer unhappily reported that he had counted twenty-six gentile aristocrats with the most ancient lineage who had married the daughters of Jewish industrialists.) The Jewess was more than a tolerated assimilant; she was an exemplar of modern Hungarian femininity. As historian Viktor Karády noted in the Hungarian Jewish Museum's catalogue for its 2002 exhibition "The Jewess," the Jews of fin de siècle Hungary played an "extraordinarily important" role in defining and legitimating "the behavioral model of the Western middle-class woman."

Still, as the hoary expression went, "A Jewess is no Jew." Leading Christian male writers of the time in Hungary and throughout Central Europe, while extolling the Jewess's "proud beauty," simultaneously mocked her Jewish husband's "ridiculous and unhandsome appearance." Jewish men were said to be plagued by the female ailments of hysteria and neurasthenia, prone to fainting spells and tubercular pallor (along with flat feet, varicose veins, and hemorrhoids), lacking in reproductive vigor, afflicted with venereal disease, and beset by sexual "abnormalities" of an effeminate and submissive nature. The new age gave these slanders a scientific sheen. "There is a relatively high incidence of homosexuality among the Jews," Alexander Pilcz, a leading Viennese psychiatrist in the early 1900s and author of the standard textbook on "racial psychiatry," held. Also, he claimed, a high rate of drug addiction and "periodic insanity." The theoreticians of the day based their conclusions on such "facts" as a Jewish man's arm span being less than his height, and thus like a woman's. Such were the flimsy premises buttressing a resilient prejudice: "a widespread sensibility," as historian Daniel Boyarin put it in his thought-provoking book *Unheroic Conduct,* "that being Jewish in our culture renders a boy effeminate."

Oskar Panizza, a German psychiatrist-turned-writer, described the type in his 1893 novella, *The Operated Jew.* The antihero of this "horrifying comedy," as Panizza characterized his handiwork, is Itzig Faitel, "a small, squat man" with a gimpy walk, a "cowardly" voice, contorted spine and legs, and a chest puffed like a "chicken breast." Vowing to remake his physique and "become such a fine gentilman just like a goymenera and to geeve up all fizonimie of Jewishness" (as Panizza's rendition of Yiddish has been translated into English), Faitel hires a team of speech specialists, anatomists, and orthopedists. His crooked bones are broken and reset, his kinky black hair turned into "the golden locks of a child," and a barbed-wire cage strapped to his pelvis to eliminate a swishy walk. Then, in exchange for "a great deal of money," seven women from the Black Forest provide a "Christian blood" infusion. Faitel climbs into a bathtub, cuts open an artery, and injects himself with their donation until he falls into a coma. When he awakes, the transformation is complete and Faitel can now "pretend to be a normal human being." He has his "papers changed," adopts the name Siegfried Freudenstern, and announces his engagement to a "beautiful flaxen-haired" Christian girl. At the wedding feast, though, the groom downs too many glasses of champagne (Jews can't handle their drink) and as he rises to deliver his toast, the oh-so-laboriously constructed facade cracks. Out leaps a "monster," who "began clicking his tongue, gurgling, and tottering back and forth while making disgusting, lascivious, and bestial canine movements with his rear end." The horrified guests watch as Faitel's straight blond strands begin to curl and then turn black; his limbs go spastic and crooked; and "a terrible smell spread in the room, forcing those people who were still hesitating at the exit, to flee while holding their noses." Itzig had not so easily assimilated.

Panizza's tale partook of a very long tradition. In the 1180 chronicle *History of Jerusalem*, Cardinal Jacques de Vitry maintained that Jewish men "have become weak and unwarlike even as women, and it is said that they have a flux of blood every month. God has smitten them in the hinder parts, and put them to perpetual shame." Bernard de Gordon's *Lilium Medicinae*, a medical text of the early fourteenth century, set forth a typical diagnosis: the "immoderate flow of blood" in Jewish men was the result of their unmanly "idleness" and "fear and anxiety"—as well as, of course, a "divine punishment" for killing Christ. As the fourteenth-century treatise by Italian encyclopaedist and physician Cecco d'Ascoli asserted, "After the death of Christ, all Jewish men, like women, suffer menstruation."

Such loss of blood required replenishment. In medieval Europe, Jews had long been accused of slaughtering virgin children (mainly prepubescent boys) and using their blood for ritualistic purposes. But starting around the fifteenth century, particular allegations began to recur: Jewish men, it was said, were seeking Christian blood to treat their menstrual bleeding, their flagging fertility, and their "wound of circumcision." Jewish men of means, it was said, coated themselves with gentile blood on their wedding day. These beliefs seemed to take especial hold in Hungary. In 1494 in the Hungarian city of Nagyszombat, fourteen Jews were charged with drinking the blood of a Christian girl to stanch their "excessive bleeding" from circumcision, "arouse" their lovemaking, and "cure" their "monthly menses." They were tortured, then burned at the stake. (Four decades later, the citizens of the same town pursued the same charge against another local Jew and succeeded in having the city's entire Jewish population expelled "for all times" by royal edict.) In 1529 in the Hungarian town of Bazin, Jewish men were burned to death following claims that they had killed a nine-year-old boy, cutting off his penis and testicles, and sucking out his blood with quills and small reeds. (The boy was later found in Vienna, alive and unmolested.) Even in the modern era in Hungary, as Joshua Trachtenberg noted in *The Devil and the Jew*, a conviction held sway "that Jews annually strangle a child or a virgin with their phylacteries, draw off the blood and smear the genitalia of their children with it to make them fertile." Accusations of ritual murder—or "blood libel"—plagued Jewish communities in Central Europe in general, and Hungary in particular, late into the nineteenth century.

In early April 1882, a month after a fourteen-year-old Christian peasant girl disappeared in the northeastern Hungarian town of Tiszaeszlár, Jewish men in the local synagogue were accused of slitting her throat so they could mix her blood into their Passover matzohs. The girl's body was found two months later floating in the river, bearing no signs of violence; forensic examiners later concluded she had drowned, likely a suicide. The accused were eventually acquitted. Nevertheless, the incident became one of Europe's last and most sensational ritual-murder accusations, evidence that the Golden Age was already under siege. The "Tiszaeszlár affair" launched the continent's first anti-Semitic party, the Országos Antiszemita Párt, and provoked a nationwide wave of anti-Jewish hysteria and violence; mobs in two hundred cities and villages attacked Jews. To this day, as ethnographers discovered when they canvassed the region, many still believe that the Jews of Tiszaeszlár murdered a Christian teenager to get her blood. (In 2012, a right-wing MP rose in Parliament to protest that the Tiszaeszlár Affair had been "whitewashed" by Hungary's "Jewry and its then leaders.") Cases like Tiszaeszlár made the equation explicit. Jews were dangerous precisely because of their weakness, which required them to prey on the vitality of healthier races. Blood libel, by conflating effeminacy and aggression through the body of the Jewish man, served as a linchpin between religious hatred and sexual phobia.

Anti-Semitism has many wellsprings, but the Jewishness that threatened the modern fascist state wasn't only Jewishness as religion. It was also Jewishness as gender. German publisher Theodor Fritsch crystallized the threat early on in his 1893 bestselling tome, *The Anti-Semitic Catechism*: "The Jew simply has a different sexuality from the Teutons; he can't and won't understand them. And when he tries to transfer his own attitudes to the Germans, this can lead to the destruction of the German soul." (In the Viennese slang of the time, "the Jew" was, literally, the clitoris, and female masturbation was "playing with the Jew.") A few decades later, when the future Nazi interior minister Wilhelm Frick introduced a bill in the Reichstag in 1930 to castrate gay men, he dubbed homosexuality "that Jewish pestilence." Heinrich Himmler famously proclaimed Germany "a masculine state" and cinched that connection: "The conspiracy of homosexuals must be viewed side by side with the world Jewish conspiracy. . . . Both are bent on destroying the German state and race." By then, as historian Sander Gilman observed, Europe had "witnessed not just the emergence of the modern Jew but the emergence also of the modern homosexual." The twin births were "more than historical coincidence," Gilman wrote. "Modern Jewishness became as much a category of gender as race." It was something that Freud had suspected as well, years earlier, when he wrote in his 1909 analysis of a boy who feared the loss of his penis, "The castration complex is the deepest unconscious root of anti-Semitism."

The belief in Jewish male effeminacy would be internalized and promulgated by a host of leading Jewish writers, scholars, doctors, and politicians of the modern era. Ethnologist and rabbi Adolf Jellinek: "The Jews belong as one of those tribes that are both more feminine and have come to represent the feminine among other peoples. A juxtaposition of the Jew and the woman will persuade the reader of the truth of the ethnographic thesis." Physician Heinrich Singer: "In general it is clear in examining the body of the Jew that the Jew most approaches the body type of the female." Weimar industrialist and statesman Walther Rathenau, reproaching his fellow Jews in "Hear, O Israel": "Look in the mirror! . . . If you recognize your poorly constructed frame—the high shoulders, the clumsy feet, the soft roundedness of form—as signs of bodily decadence, you will, for a few generations, work for your external rebirth." And famously, Viennese philosopher and wunderkind Otto Weininger, whose 1903 bestselling sensation, *Sex and Character*, spelled out the equation between religion and gender most baldly: "The Jewish race is pervasively feminine. . . . The Jews are much more feminine than Aryans . . . and the manliest Jew may be taken for a female." Weininger tried to escape his own verdict by converting to Protestantism—and more covertly (it seemed) sampling sex-gland extracts to fortify the heterosexual virility he feared was flagging. In any event, the cure didn't relieve a deeper despondency. In a testimonial that he titled "Condemnation," he likened himself to a shuttered house: "What does it look like inside this house? A wild desperate activity, a slow terrifying realization in the dark, an eternal clearing-out of things. Do not ask how it looks inside the house." A year later, in 1903, having moved to a rented room in the house where Beethoven had died, he wrote a letter to his father and brother announcing his imminent death, and then, at the age of twenty-three, shot himself in the chest. A few decades later, Weininger's ideas would enjoy a second coming under the Third Reich: its propaganda office quoted from his book in radio broadcasts, and Hitler, a great fan, declared of Weininger, "There was one decent Jew, and he killed himself."

What had been the cost, I wondered, to one striving-to-assimilate Jewish boy growing up in such a system, under such an ethic?

Young István had come of age in a culture where the men of his "race" were slandered as neurasthenic sissies and the women petted as paragons of feminine grace. As a child, he'd watched as his "diva" mother blended in so effortlessly in her furs and jewels, charming her way through the Budapest social scene and flirting with the future Christian prime minister at Ráday 9's German patisserie. And then as a teenager, he'd witnessed his man-about-town "cultured" father reduced to a fearful fugitive, unable to save his family when that liquid brew of distorted identities calcified into racial genocide. Surely the experience would have taken a toll.

My father admitted to none. Anyway, she maintained, whatever rage she might have felt in the past was dissolved by her new incarnation, her latest identity. "Why would I be angry?" she said. "Everyone is very nice to me. I am accepted better now as a woman than I ever was as a man."

"And as a Jew?"

The dismissive hand swatted the air. "No one sees me as a Jew," she said. "Because *I* don't see me as a Jew."

I was dubious. I remembered from my youth all her earlier pro-testations that seemed to protest too much: the oversized Christmas tree with its giant nativity star, the Little-Drummer-Boy greeting cards, the booming oratorios, the annual pilgrimages to Easter Holy Mass. I didn't buy her claims of equanimity now any more than then.

When I was a teenager, my best friend, a devout Catholic, became enamored of the Charismatic Renewal movement. Its adherents gathered in the social room in the local St. Patrick's Church to call on the Holy Spirit for prophecy and faith healing. I tagged along a few times to watch the spectacle at what were largely female prayer meetings, the suburban housewives and their daughters speaking in tongues and laying on hands to cure the afflicted. As always, I regarded myself as the inquiring reporter, on the lookout for a story. The senior parish priest, a crotchety traditionalist who took a dim view of glossolalia, had retired by the time the Charismatic Renewal craze took hold, and a young and more sympathetic Rock Hudson idol had assumed his place and pulpit. My friend and her mother, perhaps hoping I'd be inspired to convert, arranged for me to have a personal audience with the priest. I mentioned the invitation to my mother. She made the mistake of mentioning it to my father. She found the prospect amusing. He did not.

As I was drifting off to sleep that night, my door flew open. My father stormed in. "I created you," he shouted as he yanked me out of bed. He grabbed me by the neck and began knocking my head against the floor. His torrent of wrath was largely incoherent, but his point was clear—that he wouldn't have a Catholic child. "I created you," he repeated as my head hit the boards. "And I can destroy you."

Thus did one daughter come to know that her father was a Jew.

17

The Subtle Poison of Adjustment

My father broke into a run, pounding across the plaza to the entrance of a ten-story commercial building a few blocks from the Danube on the Buda side of the river, skirt rustling, black pumps clacking on the concrete. She jammed a leg in the glass door just as it was closing behind a mail carrier. We had arrived at her doctor's office.

"They lock the entrance," she called over her shoulder. "*Come on.*" We took the elevator to an upper floor.

The physician's quarters were at the end of a long tatty corridor. The interior wasn't much better. In the waiting area, two sagging vinyl couches were pushed up against opposing walls. The scruffy carpet was balding and matched the mud color of the couches. A line of baby photos was thumbtacked to one wall. There was no reception window and no receptionist.

"Where did you find this doctor?" I asked.

"Phone book," my father said. She settled on a couch and leaned down to adjust her white anklets, which she was wearing over her nylons. "He takes good care of me, because, you know, he brings babies into the world. . . . Waaall, I give him a big bribe." She meant a tip, or the euphemistic term of art, a *paraszolvencia* or "pseudo-solution" payment, standard practice in a country where doctors are poorly paid, even in Budapest's tonier districts.

"How much?" I asked.

"Ten thousand forints." A $40 gratuity.

I flipped through the few periodicals stacked on a chipped end table. They were back issues of sailing magazines.

"Don't you want one of these?" My father was pointing at the baby pictures.

I pretended not to hear, and studied the large plaque to the right of them: DR. MISLEY ENDRE, SZÜLÉSZET-NŐGYÓGYÁSZAT. Dr. Endre Misley, Obstetrics and Gynecology.

The inner door swung open before she could ask me again. A very tan and silver-haired gent in an Izod shirt and doctor's smock greeted us.

"*Kezét csókolom*," he said to me. I kiss your hand. And then, turning to my father, "*Kezét csókolom.*"

My father grinned and gave me a nudge. We followed the gynecologist into his consulting room, a small space with a cluttered desk and a credenza lined with sports trophies. My father settled her pocketbook on her lap and began chatting away in Hungarian. The bronzed Dr. Misley beamed and nodded affably. After a while, he made some notes on a prescription pad, tore out the sheet, and handed it to my father. A refill for her estrogen. That was the thing we'd come for. My father deposited the slip in her purse.

"I was just telling Dr. Misley," my father said, turning to me, "that I am the 'mother' of you." She made air quotes with her fingers. Pause. "Who is *not* a mother."

"Who?"

"*You*. Not yet anyway."

How did he get those trophies? I asked. I was changing the subject.

"Dr. Misley is a *greaaat* yachtsman," my father explained. "He has a twenty-foot boat, and he's won many prizes."

She translated her flattery to Captain Misley, who beamed some more.

"He sails in Bavaria," my father continued. "Waaall, he's German."

My father turned back to Dr. Misley and carried on for a while, pointing a finger at me from time to time.

"I'm telling him about your problem," she said.

"I don't have a problem."

"There may be physical reasons."

"There are no—"

"My mother smoked when she was pregnant," my father interrupted. "Maybe that's why."

"Why what?"

My father gestured toward her body. "Why I'm so weak. She had that miscarriage, you know."

Dr. Misley put away his prescription pad. I pulled out my reporter's notebook.

"Can I ask a few questions?"

Dr. Misley indicated, through my father, that he was amenable.

"Do you see a difference, since the operation?"

The doctor dawdled with his answer.

"He says my face is very nice now," my father translated. "He says I have very few wrinkles for a man my age. This is hormones, but also genes." She reached over and patted my face. "You have the genes, too."

"What I meant," I said, "was, does Dr. Misley see a difference in your *personality*?"

The reply was longer in coming.

"Dr. Misley says that I'm a happy man," my father related. "A happy *person*," she corrected herself. "Dr. Misley says this is very important, because we don't know how many years a life brings, but at least a person must live it in happiness."

Dr. Misley, I thought, dispenses platitudes as well as pharmaceuticals.

"Is my father one of your more"—I turned over adjectives in my mind—"unusual patients?"

The answer came back through the linguistic bucket brigade. "He says he has one even more unusual. He brought into the world a girl who was twelve years old."

This did sound unusual.

"The *patient* was twelve years old," my father amended. "She came to the hospital and she didn't know she was pregnant. He had to cut open that thing."

"What thing?"

"You know, where the vagina is."

"The hymen?"

"Right."

I still wasn't following.

"Sperm got smeared on her somehow," my father related. "There was a little hole in the hymen. The sperm got in."

Somehow? My father conferred again with the doctor.

"The girl got raped."

My pen froze over my notepad.

Another round of Hungarian.

"It was her father," my father said.

"Christ," I said.

Dr. Misley continued beaming.

Doctor and patient chatted for another long stretch. From time to time, my father chuckled. No translation was forthcoming, and after a while I retired my notebook.

"Dr. Misley wants to know how old you are," my father said.

"Forty-nine." And thought, peevishly: *Don't you know?*

The two conferred.

"He says you look much younger," my father said. "Like me," she added.

And then, after a few more minutes: "Dr. Misley says that he once had a patient who had her first baby past forty-eight. . . . So this is your last chance. Dr. Misley wants to know if you've tried fertility treatments."

"I don't—"

"And if you've ever been pregnant before."

"Not"—I hesitated—"no."

"Dr. Misley says you should monitor your ovulation."

The gynecologist reached into a drawer and pulled out a small plastic device shaped like a kazoo.

"You spit into it," my father translated, "and it tells you on the days you are impregnable."

Impregnable?

"Whether you can have a baby." My father elbowed me. "Okay, deaaar, he says now he can do the exam."

"No thanks," I said.

"But he's got free time."

"I don't want an examination."

"You want to come back?"

"No, I—."

"He says he can recommend another doctor, if you don't feel comfortable with him."

The doctor reached into his desk and handed me a flyer, an advertisement for Mini Mikroszóp, the ovulation monitor. On the front, in girlish pink script, and in English, it said, "Maybe Baby."

"It will only take ten minutes," my father said.

"No!"

My father snatched up her purse and headed for the door, her face contracting into a familiar scowl.

We rode the elevator in silence. Downstairs, we stopped at the pharmacy—she had to pick up her hormones—and found our place at the end of a long queue. A cranky clerk behind the counter took her time filling the order, eyeing my father doubtfully.

I could feel my father appraising me.

"This business of no children," she said. "It's not normal."

Normal? At a crucial point in my early twenties, being able to end a pregnancy had restored to me what I regarded as normal life. I remembered that it saved me. I also remembered an older woman I was close to, someone I much admired, whose life was devastated by not being able to do the same. In the mid-1950s, she had sought the help of a back-alley abortionist, and the horrors that ensued—the botched operation, a life-threatening delivery, late-term, to a long-dead fetus—was a trauma that haunted her the rest of her life. The story of her ordeal fed my young feminism.

When the prescription was finally ready, my father snatched it from the counter and flung herself through the door. I had to hurry not to lose her as she clacked furiously down a warren of back streets, her white pocketbook swinging like a mainsail from the gaff of a bunched shoulder. At one point she disappeared around a corner, and I was overcome with a childlike terror of being lost, left to wander forever amid incomprehensible signage and surly drug-store attendants.

I caught sight of the flapping purse again just as she was making the turn onto the broad thoroughfare of Margit körút. She was swallowed up by a sea of shoppers, pouring in and out of that 105,000-square-meter temple to post-Communist freedom, the Mammut Mall. ("Mammut Mall I," that is. Mammut II, equally mammoth, was under construction on the next block.) At least here, I consoled myself, I could read the signs. (EXTREME DIGITAL, CINEMA CITY, D.I.V.A., ROYAL CROISSANT . . .) At least I knew we were only a few minutes from our destination: Moszkva tér, the city's huge and hugely ugly outdoor transport junction still bearing at the time its Communist-era appellation. Six tram lines, eighteen bus lines, and a major subway line intersected here. By the time we arrived, I'd closed the gap. I followed at my father's heels as she crossed several sets of railroad tracks and came to rest on the platform for the #59, the tram that headed toward the district where she lived. Some minutes into our wait, my father broke the silence.

"Everything reproduces," she said. "Birds, bees, even these little weeds in the ground." She gestured toward a tuft of crabgrass, pushing through a crack in the pavement.

I looked down the tracks, willing the tram to come.

"Without children, your existence has no meaning." And, when I didn't answer: "Your books will stop selling. People will forget all about what you wrote."

I kept my eyes on the rails.

"It's the most important thing," she said.

I turned to face her.

"Family," she finished.

If family meant so much, I thought and didn't say, why had she cut herself off from the one she was born into and the one she'd sired? Wasn't she still cutting herself off—"I'm *Stefi* now"—from her whole fraught history as a troubled son and embattled husband and father.

But what if something else was going on? "My daughter likes me now," my father had told her new trans friends at the party she hosted in my honor. "She comes to see me." In the article about my father in *Replika*, the interviewer had asked about her relationship with her family since the operation. "My daughter was very happy about it," my father had replied. "She came here right after the surgery. Before that, you know, due to the separation of sexes, even between father and daughter, we were further away from each other." I thought of an observation Ilonka made to me: "I believe your father was attracted to me because he was attracted to being a member of my *family*." I thought of the headline in the article in *Mások*: "*Stefánia, a családapa*," Stefánia, the Father.

As we stood waiting for the tram on the platform at Moszkva tér, my father's words rattled in my head. Why hadn't I come years earlier? An ear-piercing screech of metal wheels announced the approach of the tram. My father fixed a sharp eye on me. "You are ending the family," she said. "When a family gets discontinued, it's suicide—for all these people who lived, all these people who came before you." She wasn't wrong, I thought. I had denied her family. Not just by failing to have children, but by letting our estrangement drag on for so many years. It was the latter that caused me shame.

The #59 squealed to a halt in front of us. I told my father I'd come by the next morning. I was heading back to Pest for the evening. We studied each other for a moment, then I leaned over and gave her an awkward hug good-bye. She climbed up the steps, steadying herself with the railings. The train was brightly illuminated, and through its series of windows, like frames in a strip of film, I followed my father's progress down the aisle to a seat. She arranged her pocketbook on her lap, folded her hands on top of the clasp, and stared straight ahead. I lingered on the platform, hoping she'd look out and see me waving, but she didn't. Then the doors closed and the train clanked around the curve, carrying my father out of the brightness of Moszkva tér to her fenced-in kingdom in the Buda Hills, where the view was more obscure.

Midway through Mary Shelley's 1818 classic horror story, Dr. Frankenstein is hiking near the base of Mont Blanc, above the village of Chamonix, when he spies a figure approaching across the glacial expanse of the Mer de Glace, bounding across crevasses with a superhuman speed. As the shape draws near, Dr. Frankenstein realizes "that it was the wretch whom I had created. I trembled with rage and horror, resolving to wait his approach and then close with him in mortal combat." But the monster doesn't want to fight. He wants to tell his story. It's a tale of disconsolate travels through a world of humans who despise and flee from him, and culminates in his discovery, peering through a chink in his hiding place at an adjoining rustic cottage, of a tender domestic circle. He spends a full year spying on the happy family, making a careful study of all their customs and relations:

> I heard of the difference of sexes, and the birth and growth of children, how the father doted on the smiles of the infant, and the lively sallies of the older child, how all the life and cares of the mother were wrapped up in the precious charge, how the mind of youth expanded and gained knowledge, of brother, sister, and all the various relationships which bind one human being to another in mutual bonds.

The knowledge that he will never have such bonds fills the monster with despair, and then a murderous rage. "No father had watched my infant days, no mother had blessed me with smiles and caresses," he berates his creator, "or if they had, all my past life was now a blot, a blind vacancy in which I distinguished nothing. . . . I had never yet seen a being resembling me or who claimed any intercourse with me. What was I?"

The author of *Frankenstein* denied her creation relief. Family was a complicated quotient for Mary Shelley. Her mother, famous feminist Mary Wollstonecraft, had tried to commit suicide after the father of her first child deserted her, and had died giving birth to her second, Mary. Mary's lover, Percy Shelley, had chased after other women even as she had grieved the death of their premature newborn and composed her famous tale. In the narrative Mary Shelley concocted, Dr. Frankenstein first agrees to make a monster Eve for his tortured Adam, then recants, destroying his progeny's only hope for happiness.

"A family should stay together," my father had yelled the day we drove home from our abortive visit to her childhood apartment at Ráday 9. "Normal families stick together." I wondered: Had my father ever felt like a member of any family? Or had she only stolen glimpses, peering through the chink of her camera viewfinder?

In the fall of 1976, the year of the U.S. Bicentennial, my mother declared her independence. She filed for divorce.

My father fought it with everything he had. When pity didn't work—he turned a minor hernia operation into a battle wound ("You are doing this to an injured man," he yelled at my mother one night, yanking open his pajama drawstring to display his scar)—he tried intimidation. One Sunday afternoon, I heard shouting and a scuffle. I came out of my room to see my father charging toward my mother with one of our Scandinavian "moderne" dining-room chairs hoisted over his head. He brought the chair down on her back. I ran up and jumped him from behind and, not knowing what else to do, covered his eyes like I was riding a run-amok horse. My mother escaped out the back door.

I no longer recall the precise order of things that fall and winter. The restraining order my mother obtained and that my father ignored. The Thanksgiving weekend she took her children to New York City and we holed up in someone's apartment. The afternoon some days after we returned, when he hurled a hiking boot at her head. My mother got another restraining order. He ignored it. My mother tried to make a citizen's arrest. No charges were filed. Then there was the mysterious car that would park some evenings outside our house, and drive away when we approached. Had my father hired a private eye to spy on us?

The night my father dragged me out of bed and hit my head against the floor was only one of the threatening episodes from that season: My father standing in the driveway, screaming at me "I disown you," for taking my mother's side. My father, in a rage that someone left a box of matches in the cellar, striking them in our faces: "You could have started a fire!" Another weekend toward evening, sometime in late autumn: My father has pulled out the ingredients for Hungarian *lecsó* and is slicing sausage and green peppers with a knife. He calls me into the kitchen. "Where's your mother?" he asks. I say I don't know. My mother left the house early in the morning and has yet to return. "You *do* know." He whips around, knife in hand. "You know what I could do to her?" I go into the hallway and put on my sneakers. My father follows. "Where are you going?" Running, I say, and I do. I run the several blocks to a friend's home and phone my mother. My father is right. I do know where she is. When I leave half an hour later, it's getting dark, but I can make out the figure in the shadows across the street from my friend's house, watching.

Another night, I wake to someone shaking me. It is my father, who is now living in a studio in Manhattan. He has climbed in a window. My mother has changed the locks. "Where is she?" he demands. My mother has gone to a friend's in the city. He stands there, staring, then heads down the hall to the master bedroom. A half hour passes. I go to find him. Every drawer of my mother's dresser has been yanked out and plundered. He is seated on the floor, surrounded by file folders he's found in a box in her closet, going through their contents, examining every page. *What are you doing?* "Getting evidence," he says, and slams the door in my face.

Some weeks later, I come home from school and see a massive bouquet of bloodred roses lying on the dining-room table.

"Who sent the roses?" I ask my mother.

"Your father." He delivered them himself. He told her "the family" needs to come first. The roses lie on the table, unwrapped, their red petals fading to brown. Eventually, I throw them out.

My father's violence had been concentrated in that one exceptional season, during my parents' divorce. Yet what erupted then had been churning beneath the surface for a long time. His rage was a preexisting condition, so ancient it semed foundational. The collapse of the marriage shook the rubble of earlier catastrophes. The first traumatic marital breakdown my father had suffered was his parents', which had left young István abandoned in a time of global terror. For more than twenty years, ever since he'd come to the United States at the end of 1953, my father had struggled to fit himself into the ready-made template of American husband and dad—until his marriage fell apart just as his parents' marriage had, and his estranged wife deposed him not just from a home but from an identity.

My parents first met at a cocktail party in Greenwich Village in 1957. My father had been invited there by some Hungarian Jewish émigrés he'd met on the Upper West Side, where he was renting a basement room with a half window looking out on overflowing trash bins. Since he'd arrived in New York, he'd held a series of darkroom and technical jobs in the photo departments of Manhattan advertising agencies, perfecting shots of satisfied shoppers and happy families. "In the darkroom, I'd always listen to this Hungarian-American radio program," my father recalled. "I was so excited the day I heard on the radio about '56," the Hungarian uprising against Soviet rule. "I was thinking, maybe I could go back." Eighteen days later, the uprising collapsed.

His first job, at $35 a week, was as a darkroom assistant at a photo studio in the city's Diamond District, designing food ads. "We cheated," my father recalled, "greasing up the cold cuts so they looked better." He made extra money at night with an unofficial assignment, photographing attractive young women his boss met in nightclubs. "He'd have me take their pictures in sexy lingerie or naked while he and his friends watched," my father told me. "It was in very bad taste, pornographic." After two years, he left for Illustrators Incorporated, where he designed images for the *Saturday Evening Post* with an epidiascope, an optical projector. He projected photos of ur-domestic Americana—Mom in an apron serving Thanksgiving dinner, Dad in his armchair smoking a pipe—onto the illustrators' drawing boards, "so that everything came out *real*-looking." In his own real life, he wolfed down a sandwich at a cheap Broadway deli that catered to freshly arrived Eastern European immigrants, then went home to the room by the garbage cans.

Late that night at the Greenwich Village party, my father overcame his shyness enough to ask my mother to dance. He invited her to the Tanglewood Music Festival the following weekend to hear a jazz concert. He preferred classical but figured that proposing jazz would make him sound "more American." That Sunday they drove to the Berkshires in my father's 1955 Ford convertible, "red and white, a really flashy thing," my father said. Another prop in his new red-white-and-blue performance. Six weeks later they married in Congregation Rodeph Sholom, a Reform synagogue on Eighty-Third Street, over the objections of her parents.

"Such a hurry to get married!" I said to my father one evening in Budapest.

A shrug. "It seemed like the thing to do," she said. Then, "Your mother wanted to." My father's uncle Ernő, who had emigrated to New York years earlier, was his one family witness at the ceremony. There was no honeymoon: the ad agency where my father projected shots of family joy wouldn't give him the time off. Half a year later, the newlyweds marked the occasion with a long weekend in Niagara Falls. It was another "thing to do."

In short order, my father had attained the big-box model of the postwar American Dream, male division: the house in the suburbs, the commuter job in the city, the stay-at-home wife, the two children and a dog, the quarter-acre lawn with dog house and playset and perimeter white-picket fence, all built in his home workshop in the cellar. The realization of such comfort and security and order must have astounded him. But the security was booby-trapped. Organization-Man America was a store-bought landscape—kitschified, prettified, market-ready—whose images of cowboy-rugged indi-vidualism and Father-Knows-Best authority masked a simpering Hallmark sameness. "The American Male: Why Is He Afraid to Be Different?" *Look* magazine's headline asked in its 1958 series on the debilitated postwar man (later issued as a book, *The Decline of the American Male*). The article's composite character was "Gary Gray," a compliant suburban husband and dad who had swallowed the "subtle poison of adjustment and conformity," and who one win-ter morning "awakened and realized he had forgotten how to say the word 'I.'"

The emblem of the embattled American self, circa 1950s, was a browbeaten, emasculated male, returned from heroic combat only to fall prey to the domesticating forces of consumerism and "mom-ism" and "mass society" homogenization, an ex-GI turned cringing cream puff, the aproned epicene dad in *Rebel Without a Cause* delivering dinner trays to his domineering wife. In "The Crisis of American Masculinity," Arthur Schlesinger Jr.'s influential 1958 *Esquire* essay, the social critic singled out one news event as "impressive evidence" of that crisis—indeed, its embodiment. "It appears no accident," he wrote, "that the changing of sex—the Christine Jorgensen phenomenon—so fascinates our newspaper editors and readers." Coming across Schlesinger's words all these years later, I considered my father's odyssey as a twentieth-century Zelig, present at the identity Götterdämmerung of fascist Europe, present again as the question of the age took on new form in postwar America. In both times and places, and whatever ideolo-gies were in play, the politics on the surface hid a roiling conflation of identity and gender. As both European Jew and American Dad, my father's manhood had been doubted, distorted, and besmirched.

"The key to the recovery of masculinity lies rather in the prob-lem of identity," Schlesinger concluded in that 1958 article. "When a person begins to find out *who* he is, he is likely to find out rather soon what sex he is."

———

By the 1970s, my father's cinematic productions of American domesticity—the home movies of our first family Christmas, our first Easter, our first strained family visit to the Florida Keys to visit my mother's disapproving parents—had declined into sporadic snapshots more Diane Arbus than Norman Rockwell. I found a bunch of them at the bottom of the mothball-ridden box of photos my mother had mailed me—a dank clump of stills, color fading, edges curling, a disorderly chronicle of familial decline.

On my return from one of my visits to Budapest, I spent the better part of an afternoon trying to get those photos to lie flat on my desk; as soon as I lifted my hand they'd recoil, as if ashamed of what they revealed. Here were my parents on a browning front lawn: my mother looking worn and seated in a sagging lawn chair; my father kneeling nervously at her side, sporting scraggly sideburns and a mullet-like mane that made him look more Tutankhamen than Tom Jones. Another photo: the family gathered around the picnic table on the back porch, funereal over half-eaten hot dogs. And: my brother and me on our chipped concrete front stoop, him in a crooked homemade haircut and mismatched hand-me-downs, me in equally crooked cat-eye glasses with the stems held together with adhesive tape.

The box contained several shots of our house, its faux rusticated shingled exterior now genuinely weather-beaten—or rather, putrefied, an ulcerated mess of scaling paint and mold, the shutters at alarming angles. A picture of the backyard captures a tarp over a pit in the ground—what was once the Japanese goldfish pond—and the understructure of the porch, its wood beams eaten through with dry rot. In a shot looking down from the top of the drive, you can see foot-high weeds, flourishing in the macadam in front of the garage door. Which dates it to the late '70s—after my father moved out. My non-driving mother had no need of a car.

"The Fall of the House of Usher," she used to say back then, as mice (or worse) scrabbled back and forth audibly in the attic. Porch railings mulched and came away in our hands, termites swarmed around the rotted windowsills, and, one by one, the kitchen linoleum tiles came unglued and stayed that way. One day, in a stab at imposing order, I collected the tile shards and stacked them in a corner. It's hard to look at these pictures now and not revisit the disintegration of a family on the brink. The camera only documented what had been there all along, a marriage whose foundations, constructed from the cheap materials of convention and fear, had been buckling for years.

The fissures first became evident on the hiking trail. After my adolescent rebellion eliminated me as a trekking partner, my father had enlisted my mother. Unlike his grumpy teenage daughter, his wife discovered that she adored the great outdoors. For a few years, she was my father's regular wilderness companion. In 1973, after months of training, they flew to Mexico and assailed the volcanic slopes of Popocatépetl and Pico de Orizaba, the country's two highest peaks. Henceforth, mountaineering, their one shared pleasure, became the stage set of their crack-up. The Mexico trip was the last they took together.

The way my father explained it to me later was: "Your mother wanted to do different mountains—the more *minor* peaks." In fact, she was an intrepid hiker. When the four of us were caught in a blizzard on a climb to the first hut of the Matterhorn, my mother was the only one who thrilled to the experience—as evidenced by a photograph that she framed and kept on display in her apartment for years after the divorce: she stands in the foreground in a thin windbreaker and kerchief, her face turned up to greet the snow as if it's a glorious blast of sun, while her miserable teenage daughter cowers behind her, glaring at her sodden desert boots. My mother didn't want "different mountains." She wanted different company.

A dozen yellow containers of Ektachrome slides bear testament to the fatal divergence. One box is marked, in my mother's handwriting, with her initials, denoting that these are shots of one of her summer solo treks. Inside is slide after slide of my mother in the Austrian Alps, striding up steep trails, scrambling over boulders, bundled in her orange 60/40 parka in a rainstorm, waving from a peak. She is tan, her calves muscular, her hair in girlish braids, and her face—so drawn and despairing in those wedding and early marriage pictures—illuminated with a kind of stunned joy. She is forty-four but looks younger than in the photos from her early twenties. Rarely alone, she is laughing, sharing food with the other hikers in her group, lounging on a rock soaking up the sun, clinking beer glasses in a candlelit hut. One day, armed with a handheld viewfinder, I worked my way through all the slides of my mother's Austria trip and her other independent vacation through the Dolomites in northeastern Italy. I know Paul Simon meant the lyrics in "Kodachrome" to be ironic, yet an ingenuous version kept burbling through my head as I peered into the plastic window at my suddenly alive, suddenly-in-color mother, released for two weeks from the drab walls of her marriage. "They give us those nice bright colors. . . . Makes you think all the world's a sunny day, oh yeah . . ." Four more years would pass before the divorce, but the whole story was right there in the viewfinder, visible to any but the blind.

I opened the other boxes, the ones that held slides of my father's solitary travels during that same period. Dozens of transparencies from his first summer in the French Alps featured what looked like an identical shot: a vast river of white ice filled the bottom half of the frame, an iron-black mass of rock the top, its leviathan shanks blotting out the sun. In all, I found only two pictures in which my father appears, both taken during his second summer trip, when he hired a guide to lead him on several alpine climbs. In one of them he is posed by a cliff face, holding an ice ax. In the other, he is a dot in an endless field of snow. No one else is in the frame. The slides were also shot with color film, not that you could tell.

"Where was that?" I asked my father, describing an image from the first trip. We were talking over the phone.

"Chamonix," my father said. He didn't stay in the village long. "I was ten days in a mountain hut. I was by myself. I even hiked by myself. When you're alone"—she stopped—"it's a funny feeling."

"Funny?"

"Like humanity had ceased. Like you were the only human being on earth. Like the whole world had been bombed and you were left all alone. . . . Waaall"—I could picture her hand, brushing away my remark before I made it—"I was careful not to do anything too risky."

My father had hiked up from the village "to the base of Mont Blanc. What a mountain, indescribable. . . ."

So that was the menacing mass of iron. And the empty field of white, the famous four-mile glacier that flows along Mont Blanc's northern flank, the Mer de Glace. My father's route was the same as the one that Mary Shelley's creature followed, on the day he confronted his creator. After we got off the phone, I pulled *Frankenstein* off my shelf, the novel that had inspired, among so many others, Susan Stryker, whose manifesto had framed her transgender identity in terms of that lonely figure on the Mer de Glace: "I will say this as bluntly as I know how," Stryker wrote in "My Words to Victor Frankenstein Above the Village of Chamounix." "I am a transsexual, and therefore I am a monster."

I spent the rest of the afternoon leafing through my copy of Shelley's horror story. "Am I not alone, miserably alone?" the monster says that day above Chamonix. "The desert mountains and dreary glaciers are my refuge. I have wandered here many days. . . ."

Several weeks after the divorce was finalized, my father loaded up his camper with as many of his possessions as he could fit and all of his mountaineering gear, and headed west. He had decided to leave everything behind and live a bare-bones existence as a rock-climbing guide in Colorado. Before he reached the Pennsylvania Turnpike, he turned back.

18

You're Out of the Woods

On my father's eighty-third birthday, I found myself at the Jewish Museum in Manhattan, where a tribute to Harry Houdini had just opened. The exhibit chronicled the celebrated escape artist's self-transformation, via the newly minted arts of photography and film, from impoverished Hungarian émigré to "American icon." Along the way, Houdini had shed his name (Erik Weisz), his Budapest nativity (claiming Appleton, Wisconsin, where his family moved when he was four, as his birthplace), and his patrimony (after Rabbi Mayer Sámuel Weisz was fired from Appleton's Reform synagogue for failing to assimilate, his son decided to become a magician). The museum show's centerpiece was the immigrant packing trunk in which Houdini—shackled, bagged, and locked inside—had performed his first famous act, "The Metamorphosis Illusion." His wife Bess would pull the curtain closed and, when it was drawn back seconds later, Houdini stood miraculously free, Bess now bound and imprisoned in the wood-and-metal chest. Houdini went on to ever grander escapes—breaking free of ropes slung from skyscrapers, straitjackets suspended from cranes, stocks lowered into a "Chinese Water Torture Cell," crates dropped to the bottom of the East River.

On the way out of the museum, I stopped in the gift shop and flipped through the picture postcards. Most of them showcased the barrel-chested illusionist picking locks and springing from iron cages—often in the nude (to prove he had nothing to hide), his manacled hands arranged to conceal his private parts. One card featured a glamour shot, the master magician as Valentino—his eyebrows tweezed to perfect arches, his black hair oiled flat and parted in the middle, his eyes come-hither coals. I bought it as a birthday greeting for a Houdini fan in Hungary who I knew would like it.

Before my father came to the United States and before he and then she embarked on subsequent reinventions—American dad, Magyar repatriate, "overdressed shiksa"—there was a time when it seemed István Faludi had escaped the identity grid altogether. In the spring of 1948, my twenty-year-old father boarded the *Carina*, a former U.S. liberty ship turned Norwegian freighter docked in the port of Göteborg on Sweden's western coast, and crossed the ocean to Brazil. It was a miraculous escape from an impossible trap. To be a Hungarian Jew in the 1940s was to be bound head to toe, locked in a trunk, dropped to the bottom of the deepest river on Earth. Through a set of ingenious contortions and illusions, my father had managed to wriggle free of his chains.

The Brazil my father entered in 1948 was a country with a national identity wholly at odds with the one he'd just left. "The experiment of Brazil, with its complete and conscious negation of all colour and racial distinctions, represents by its obvious success perhaps the most important contribution toward the liquidation of a mania that has brought more disruption and unhappiness into our world than any other," my father's beloved author Stefan Zweig wrote in 1941. Zweig, like my father, was a Central European Jew who'd fled a war-ravaged continent for Brazil, a country whose inclusive ethos filled the writer, at least in 1941, with "infinite relief." In *Brazil, Land of the Future*, Zweig set out his reasons for believing that his new homeland "demands not only the attention but the admiration of the whole world":

> The allegedly destructive principle of race mixture, this horror, this "sin against the blood" of our obsessed race theoreticians, is here consciously used as a process of cementing national culture. On this foundation a nation has been building itself up, slowly but surely, for four hundred years; and the adaptation to the same climate, to the same living conditions, has created a thoroughly individual type, lacking in all the "degenerate" characteristics against which race fanatics try to warn us.

Zweig elided certain historical evidence that ran contrary to his Panglossian image of Brazil, like the importation of millions of African slaves, the enslavement of the indigenous population, and the prewar dictatorship's less-than-welcoming stance toward Jewish refugees. Still, the vision of Brazilian nationality that pertained when Zweig arrived was a world away from the racial purity fixations of Nazi Europe, and its hopeful intermingling antipodal to Zionism. If anything, it suggested the "panhumanist" model Magnus Hirschfeld had in mind when he declared himself a "world citizen." To Zweig, Brazil held out the promise that there would be no need to withdraw to a bunkered Jewish state, that it was possible to melt away the hatreds of the past by "continuous assimilation through perpetual interbreeding." No one could lay exclusive claim to being a "true" Brazilian, Zweig exulted, "because there is nothing more typical of a Brazilian than that he is a man without a history."

———

I learned some of the details of my father's escape from Hungary on the afternoon she decided to show me my "inheritance." I followed her down the wooden steps and through the garage to the cellar door, which she unlocked with one of the many keys on her jailer's-sized ring. When we stepped through the portal, the first thing I saw was a familiar display of sanders and power drills and the DeWalt radial arm saw: my father's old Black & Decker home workshop. It was arranged exactly as it had been in our basement in Yorktown Heights.

She ran her hand under the workbench peg-board covered with tools and retrieved another key, hanging by a string from a nail, and carried it over to a large steel cabinet. "This is my 'safe,'" my father said. "I keep my valuables in here because it's fireproof." When the metal doors swung open, though, there wasn't much to see except a cardboard carton. She retrieved the box and set it on her old worktable. Here was the lockbox I'd sought since I'd first come into the house, the repository containing the relics of István's past.

"If anything happens to me, you should know where this is," my father said. She lifted the lid and rooted through yellowing papers and sepia photographs, and extracted two small square documents on crumbling parchment paper, covered with official-looking stamps and a sea of daunting Hungarian; *Telekjegyzőkönyv* was one of the shorter words. They were my grandfather's deeds to the two apartment buildings he'd owned in Pest, at Ráday utca 9 and Váci út 28. The property titles were dated, respectively, April 24, 1925, and May 4, 1925, and the purchase prices listed as 2,500,000,000 and 3,000,000,000 korona, the hyperinflated currency of post–World War I Hungary.

"This is our property that the Communists stole from us—after the war."

"You mean, after the Hungarians stole it," I said, ever the historical spoilsport to my father's mythography, "*during* the war."

"No *deaaar*, the Communists. The *Soviet* Communists." She

returned to her inspection of the documents. "What you are talking about is without significance," she said. "The Communists came in after the war and took away private property that belonged to *Hungarians*."

She lifted another document from the box and laid it on the table. It looked like a handbill, palm-sized and printed on heavy stock. Under a Latin inscription, a line of typed words and hand-written entries ran down the side. "My high school report card," she noted.

"Are those your grades?" I thrilled to this rare aperture into my father's school days.

"A 'good' in Hungarian language and literature. Aaand in 'religious ethics'!"

She returned the card to the box and held up a square of parchment. A birth certificate.

"István Károly Friedman," she read out loud. "Born November 1, 1927, to Jenő Friedman, thirty-three years of age, and Rozália Grünberger Friedman, twenty-four years of age." Under the birth name were two notations: "—*Fiú.*—*Izr.*"—Boy.—Israelite. Until the Communist era, all birth certificates listed religion. On the back was an addendum, noting that the name Friedman had been officially changed to Faludi in 1946. Another document: István's old passport. The original date on the inside cover was July 5, 1946. The photo was of a very young and slender man, with a pencil-thin mustache and dark, unfathomable eyes.

My father pointed to the mustache. "My disguise," she said. "My father grew a mustache, too—in the war. But that was because he didn't want to look Jewish."

"And you?"

No response. Then, "I never looked Jewish."

With this passport my eighteen-year-old father left postwar Hungary in 1946 with his equally youthful business partner, Tibor Jablonszky; they had met a year earlier at the youth film club

backed by the Communist Party. The two young men were heading for Denmark—the first stop on what would eventually be a
journey halfway around the world—armed with freshly printed
business cards and letterhead with their new company logo. My
father still had a few sheets of the stationery he'd designed, embossed
with a tiny plane flying over a large movie reel, next to the name
of their new enterprise, Jablonszky & Faludi, a film "export-import"
company.

Jablonszky & Faludi was more import than export. The new
Hungarian Communist film agency, known as Mafirt, was looking
to replenish the nation's movie stock, destroyed in the bombings.
Less than a year after the war, my father and Tibor approached
Mafirt with a proposition: send Jablonszky & Faludi to Scandina-
via to collect new films. "The guys at Mafirt said they could get us
a permit," my father recalled, "but they warned us, 'Don't bring
anything that will offend the Russians.' We told them, 'Oh no, we
wouldn't dream of it!'"

The two intended to travel by train to Denmark, but rail service
still went no farther than Vienna. For weeks, they wandered
around Budapest looking for someone who could give them a ride
to Copenhagen. They were joined by a third young member of the
youth film club, Tamás Somló, the Jewish boy who lived at Ráday
9, whose pharmacist father had been deported to Mauthausen.

After one memorable night on the town, the three young men
wound up at the Kit Kat Club in Pest. "A wild place," my father
recalled, gazing at the passport picture of her mustachioed young self.
"It was where you'd go to pick up prostitutes." They followed some
women to a flea-bitten hotel, where my father had his first sexual
experience. "One dollar, with everything included!" The night at the
Kit Kat Club was a milestone in my father's life for another reason.
"We met this Dane in the men's room," my father said. A bloodied
Dane, thanks to certain nationality confusions. "He had been shot
by a Russian who thought he was a Nazi because he was wearing

a uniform, but it was the Danish Red Cross uniform," my father explained. "Waaall, everyone was drunk. Anyway, the bullet only grazed him." The Dane introduced the three young men to his Red Cross coworkers, who were traveling around Central Europe in a truck, distributing food to children. My father saw an opportunity. "I told them we were filmmakers and that we could make a film of them doing all their *vaaary* good works."

My father and Tibor set out the next day with the Danish Red Cross (Tamás stayed behind temporarily to take his high school exams) and passed through the northwestern countryside of Hungary and into Austria, cameras rolling. "We made a big show of it," my father recalled. "We said the film labs in Hungary were no good anymore, but if they took us to Denmark, we could develop the movie there."

"What happened to that movie?"

A sly smile played across my father's face. "It was all a deceit. We didn't have any film in our camera."

The Red Cross workers had to spend several weeks in Vienna before they hit the road, and my father and Tibor ran out of money. My father wrote home for funds; Jenő mailed his son a few Napoleon gold coins—Hungarian currency was worthless at that point. My father had to rinse the coins off in the sink. "They were all sticky because my father sent them hidden in a box of prunes." She thought for a second. "'Sun Ripe Prunes!' That's what it said on the box. Funny, what you remember." The coins were soon spent. It was my father's idea to see if the two hungry young men could get a meal from the American Jewish Joint Distribution Committee, which was providing relief rations for Holocaust refugees. "So we went over there and asked for help packages. And they said to me, 'Well, you're okay, but you' "—meaning Tibor—" 'you're not Jewish!' "

Which was correct. Tibor was Catholic.

"But how did they know?"

"Waaall, he was blond. The man from the Joint said, 'You know, we can easily check this—come into the next room.' " He was proposing Tibor drop his trousers—a turnabout on every Jewish man's wartime fear. Tibor feigned outrage. "He said, 'I have *never* been so insulted in my entire life! I am *one hundred percent* Jewish!' And the man said, 'All right, all right, don't get excited.' " Tibor got his care package.

When the Red Cross aid workers finally finished their rounds, they made good on their end of the deal. They told the two young filmmakers to report to the Danish Red Cross villa in Vienna on the morning of December 3, 1946, where "a luxury sedan" would be waiting to take them to Denmark. The sedan belonged to a "rich exporter," my father recalled, and was piloted by a cantankerous chauffeur with no sense of direction—"which wasn't good because the roads through Germany were dangerous."

My father returned to her rummage in the box. After a while, she extracted a thin file folder. It was titled, in my father's hand, "Letters from the Past." There were only two inside, the first a couple of paragraphs long, the other five dense pages of single-spaced Hungarian. She handed me the longer document. "This might be of interest to you." The paper clip holding the pages together had rusted to the disintegrating onion skin. The dateline read, "Copenhagen 1946, Christmas Eve."

My father translated the first paragraph:

Dear Parents, Baba, Tomi, Eva, Misi,
With one toothbrush, and two slightly crinkled trousers in our hands, we have arrived in heaven. Now we are sitting here above the clouds in the heart of Copenhagen and, shaking off the circulating chaos of our experiences, we are trying to describe faithfully to you everything that has happened to us. . . .

"I wrote this with Tibor," my father said. It was their first letter home, a narrative of their exodus across post-Nazi Europe, a chronicle of escape.

> In the morning greyness on the third of December 1946,
> a mysterious taxi stopped in front of the villa of the
> Danish Red Cross in Vienna. From inside of the car emerged
> two sleepy young men, followed by many suitcases, typing
> machine, film projector, and blankets. These young men
> were us.

I could see the scene before me more lucidly than if I were studying a photograph. My father had conjured this picture on her daughter's occupational tool of choice, the "typing machine." A machine that as a young man he had evidently found essential enough to his aspirations to haul across three countries. At my urging, the translation continued:

> We paid the driver with half a kilogram of bacon meat,
> after which we sat comfortably on our pile of luggage and
> smoked a Chesterfield. It was pleasant weather, cold and rainy.
> Next to us in an opened garage there were two cars: a small Opel
> and a Steyer. We studied them, guessing in which one we will
> travel. After we smoked a couple of cigarettes, it was light. In the
> villa, life started, and they discovered us, sitting on our luggage.
> They immediately invited us in for a cup of tea. In the villa,
> which was furnished with American luxury, in a dining room
> partitioned by a heavy curtain, they left us with a ten-course
> breakfast. The beginning was very promising.

At "half past eight," a gleaming apple-green sedan "curved into the drive." A Danish Red Cross nurse, "Froken" (Miss) Lund, who "looked like an English lady," squeezed into the front seat, next to the chauffeur and the wealthy exporter (a "smoking capitalist"), and my father and Tibor climbed in back, clutching two briefcases "containing Danish dictionaries and language books, a map, twenty packs of American cigarettes, a bottle of real Bolognese liqueur, a package of Czech saccharine, two pairs of shoes, half a kilogram butter, two horse riding sticks, Danish salami, cheese, and a toothbrush in a case."

Riding sticks? I asked.

"Sure," my father said. "And jodhpurs. We were gentlemen of the nobility." Pretending to be, anyway. The driver, whom my father and Tibor dubbed "Mr. Na-Na," for his crankiness, instantly got lost, and it was nearly dusk by the time they passed through Hitler's hometown of Linz and, soon thereafter, arrived at the checkpoint between the Russian and American zones. Several hours and many wrong turns later, they passed into Germany.

> Falling asleep while crossing a dull landscape, we woke to realize that we were lost in Nuremberg. The city, dumped to the ground, was dead. The old houses with their small windows made the impression of a huge prison.

They had entered the medieval city center, where, in one hour on January 2, 1945, bombing missions by the British Royal Air Force and the U.S. Army Air Forces had obliterated 90 percent of the buildings and killed eighteen hundred civilians. After additional attacks a month later, more than six thousand residents would be dead. "We let Mr. Na-Na wander around the dead city. After which we took out our map and led ourselves out from the vale of tears."

By nightfall they were in what remained of Hamburg, where, over a few months beginning in late July 1943, Allied bombings code-named Operation Gomorrah unleashed a firestorm that flattened the city (including the blocks of buildings whose sale had

yielded the Friedmans such wealth) and killed more than thirty
thousand civilians.

Among the huge cranes, tanks, and docks, a spooky road led
us to a residential district, where mountains of burned houses,
coming down on top of each other, showed us a picture of evil
destruction. Kilometer after kilometer, we saw only rubble
everywhere. Only a few intact buildings rose above the ruins,
like lighthouses in the sea.

By three a.m., they had passed through "the land-of-no-one"
and arrived at the Danish border:

The red-and-white striped checkpoint pike lifted slowly in front
of us. As we looked around, on the other side of the glass wall
everything seemed implausible and dreamlike. We were standing
in front of a white building, which resembled a small castle with
its many little towers. In between our car and the building there
was a traffic island, on which three border guards were walking,
all dressed in light blue uniforms, with arms linked together,
stepping together, as in an operetta scene.

For the happy ending to be perfect, we opened a good-
smelling pack of Chesterfields and we offered this prohibited
goods to the operetta army. Then we sat back in the car and,
saying good-bye to the men, we started our triumph. After the
first kilometer we opened a liqueur. Our co-travelers were
sharing our happiness and were greeting us in Danish: *Velkome
til Danmark!* Meanwhile we drove along glamorous, clean roads,
surrounded by white beautiful small houses, like in a fairy tale.
After the big happiness and the liqueur we fell asleep.

The driver dropped my father and Tibor Jablonszky at the
western port town of Esbjerg and the two young men boarded

a train, heading east, then, at Nyborg, a "supermodern" ferry to Copenhagen.

> Copenhagen is so wonderful and there is never enough of it—huge, modern houses with glamorous flats and beautiful shop windows. On its wonderful, wide, never-ending, straight boulevards there are many cars. There are rows of automats on the streets everywhere. From buttered bread to caviar, from candy to cake, and from Gillette to pocket lamps, everything is available day and night, from twenty-five ore to two crowns. We keep our eyes open and we are very active. We hope we succeed. Currently we are negotiating with a couple of big Danish filmmaking factories. We watch movies from morning till the evening. . . .
> We send lot of kisses to everybody,
>
>   Pista, Tibi

My father returned the "letter from the past" to its folder.

"This is so well written!" I exclaimed.

"Waaall, we wrote it in the style of P. Howard," my father said. P. Howard, aka Jenő Rejtő, was a Hungarian pulp-fiction writer whose detective-fiction parodies peopled with tricksters were wildly popular in my father's youth. My father remained a fan. She had a large selection of P. Howard novels on her bookshelf. "He wrote so it would sound like he was a British writer who'd been translated into Hungarian," my father explained. A British *Christian* writer, that is. Rejtő had to hide his religion after the wartime laws banned publication of Jewish authors. In the late fall of 1942, an Arrow Cross–affiliated newspaper revealed the true identity of "P. Howard." Rejtő was sent to a forced labor camp in the Ukraine. Within weeks, he was dead.

My father's own tricksterism would lead to a happier outcome. In the weeks after his arrival in Denmark, István and Tibor traveled from Copenhagen to Stockholm and on to London. They hit a dozen film distribution companies and brokered deals for fifteen movies "with nothing bad about Russians." The haul included *Caesar and Cleopatra*, *Odd Man Out*, and, my father's favorite, *Ditte, Child of Man*, a Danish melodrama about a girl abandoned by her depraved mother. Then, having enlisted a Copenhagen film lab to make reproductions, my father and Tibor flew home—temporarily, they hoped—to collect their commission from Mafirt. At the Budapest airport, they were stopped by customs officers, who confiscated their passports. "They told us, 'You are of military age. You have to go into the army.' "

My father thought otherwise. He had no intention of serving in a military that, less than two years ago, had enslaved his "race" in forced labor and sent them unarmed to their deaths. The next day, the door of the Mafirt office flew open and in stormed a very indignant young man. "I told them, 'Oh, this is a vaaary big problem! The people at the film lab in Copenhagen will only turn over the copies to *us*! The situation is hopeless unless we go back.' " He delivered the same message at the Communist Party headquarters, along with a promise to set up a new Communist Hungarian consulate in Copenhagen—he would be "chairman" and Tibor "cultural attaché." "I knew what they wanted to hear." Evidently so, because a few days later the two young men had their passports back and were on a plane to Denmark.

They found a room in a widow's home in Copenhagen. "It was in the back and had a view of a garden," my father recalled. "We each had our own bed. Aaand our own duvet." Untold luxury for two war-deprived Hungarians. And soon, they had two local teenage girls in their beds, a few hours after meeting them on a street corner. "The Danes are very relaxed," my father recalled appreciatively.

My father sought help to extend their stay, appealing to former Ráday 9 tenant Ferenc Nagy, the Smallholders Party leader who had flirted with Rozi and who had become prime minister in 1946. Nagy pulled some strings to make it happen. Some months later, my father again turned to Nagy—this time to assist his young friend from Ráday 9, fellow film-club member Tamás Somló, in procuring a passport to come to Denmark. Again, Nagy came through. I was beginning to understand why a half century later my father would turn to the rightist Smallholders Party for help reclaiming the family property.

By 1948, the three young men were getting threatening letters for overstaying their visas. The Communist Party had forced Nagy out of office a half year earlier, and he'd fled to the United States. The ex–Smallholders leader wrote one more letter, from Virginia, at István's request. My father kept a copy of the certified Danish translation of Nagy's missive in her lockbox, preserved in a ziplock bag:

> I, former Hungarian prime minister Ferenc Nagy, now living in Herndon, Va., USA, certify that I know well the movie operator István Faludi. He has, in the time I was prime minister, received his traveling pass at my request so that he and his companions Tibor Jablonszky and Tamás Somló should realize travel abroad. Because of this fact, the above persons cannot return to Hungary, which is under complete Communist rule, since in that case it would expose them to the Communist regime's persecution. I ask the corresponding competent authorities to show understanding and goodwill for István Faludi and his comrades' case.
>
> —Ferenc Nagy, Herndon, Va., April 14, 1948

By then, Tamás Somló had moved on to Stockholm with a Swedish girlfriend. The Hungarian Communist government no longer wanted Western films. The boys' days in Denmark were numbered.

One evening in Copenhagen, Tibor and my father attended a

lecture sponsored by a Brazilian tourist agency. "They showed this little filmstrip, with these beautiful shots of Copacabana Beach." The very next day my father stopped in at the Brazilian consulate and asked how he could visit the country. The man behind the counter inspected his passport and told him it wasn't valid for South America. "And so I said to myself, Okay, I'll make it so it will be valid." He drew what seemed like an official-looking insignia and submitted it to a printer. "I said, 'We have this little company and we need this for our office stamp. And we need it tomorrow morning.'" The printer wanted to know what the words said in the drawing. "I told him, 'Oh, it's just Hungarian.' Then he wasn't too interested." What it said was, "This visa is valid for North and South America."

My father flipped through the passport until she got to the page with the stamp. "You see here, where I scribbled some French on it?" she said. "And I crossed out North America—to make it look more legitimate. Waaall, by then I had a lot of practice."

"Practice?"

"Faking things."

A few weeks later, my father and Tibor took the train to the west coast of Sweden and, after a customs official studied their passports and found them "legitimate," boarded the *Carina*. They were on their way to the white beaches of Copacabana. The ocean crossing took two and a half weeks.

"I remember when I first saw Rio," my father said. Her eyes had a dreamy cast. "It was late afternoon. It was like the mountains and the sky touched. And then the ship radio started blaring ads." She rattled off a Portuguese jingle.

"What's that?"

"'Jump out of bed with the will to live, because your stomach is cleared!'"

"You still remember it."

"Back then there weren't so many commercials."

The two young men spent their first days wandering the beach and investigating a favela. "Not only that, we took a camera," my father recalled. "People said to us, 'Oh, you'll be in *danger!*' But we didn't care." For the survivors of a world war, danger was a relative concept.

Whatever the virtues of Brazilian race-blindness, my father and Tibor needed a job—and they would turn to Hungarian expatriates to find one. "We went to see this guy named Glausius, who was *vaaary* Hungarian," my father said, "and not Jewish." Glausius introduced them to two brothers, "who were hairdressers for ladies in Copacabana." They were, likewise, *very* Hungarian. "The older brother, he ate bacon in the Hungarian style—bread, bacon, paprika, and onion in one hand, and a knife in the other, and he'd cut a big slab and eat it off the knife. A real Magyar peasant!"

The chain of happenstance continued. The peasant happened to do the hair of the wife of a U.S. Air Force colonel from Texas— he invited the two hungry young men over for dinner ("Big steaks on the grill!")—and the colonel happened to be advising the Brazilian government's Institute of Geography and Statistics, which had been trying, unsuccessfully, to convert U.S. Air Force aerial surveillance photographs of Brazil so they could be used to design maps. My father met with the institute's cartographer and proposed a way to reconfigure the images without losing any detail. His method worked, and my father and Tibor were hired into the institute's photographic unit.

"Actually, we *were* the photographic unit," my father said. "And then, when Tamás came, we were three."

Tamás Somló had taken a circuitous route to Brazil. With the help of his Swedish girlfriend's father (who was eager to put space between his daughter and her refugee beau), Tamás had obtained a temporary visa to Buenos Aires, where he was stuck for nearly a year washing dishes, until my father landed him a visa and a job at the geographic institute. "I told the director," my father recalled,

"Tamás is an *indispensable* member of the 'Hungarian photographic team'!"

My father reached for the "Letters from the Past" folder, and the only other piece of correspondence it contained, dated "Rio, 1950": a letter from Pista Faludi in Rio de Janeiro to Tomi Somló in Buenos Aires. The occasion was Tamás's imminent arrival in Brazil.

Dear Tomi,

We were very happy to receive your letter, in which you inform us that we cannot escape from your wonderful presence. The entire country of Brazil is mourning with us from the crocodiles of the Amazonas to the pampas of Del and on the second of January they will all pull the black flag and declare siege. Next year they will even elect a new president because Dutra will not take responsibility for the country if you are here.

I suppose this was another attempt at P. Howard/Jenő Rejtő flair. Still, the debonair and wisecracking voice that sprang from the yellowing foolscap startled me. Where had this gregarious young man fled to?

We find it very clever that you arrive at one a.m. In this case no one will notice that you arrive and you can travel the couple-of-hundred-meter-long distance between our home and the airport without getting a heat stroke. Don't worry if you don't speak the language yet, because nowadays Rio is inhabited by so many Hungarians, that addressing someone in Portuguese is showing off. Now the most important thing is that you arrive safe, and we can discuss everything else when you are here. . . . No matter if you arrive to Santos Dumont or Galeao airport, we will figure it out here.

With hot (35°C) love,
Pista

A handwritten addendum at the bottom of the page read: "Bring addresses of blond women—Tibor."

At first, the three slept for free in the office. Eventually Tamás rented a room in Copacabana, and my father and Tibor shared a small house on Glória Hill in Rio, beneath the Church of Our Lady of the Glory of the Outerio. Usually, though, the young men were out in the outback, traveling one-on-one with a research scientist or a guide or sometimes entirely alone, photographing the immense ecological and human diversity of the fifth-largest nation in the world. "A lot of these places you could only get to by horseback or plane," my father recalled. He crisscrossed the backcountry of Mato Grosso, the subtropical jungles of Paraná, the plateaus and savannas of Goiás, and the rain forests of the Amazon, which he and a guide navigated in a tiny wooden boat when a promised ship didn't arrive, all the way to Manaus, where the young István was enraptured to find the Teatro Amazonas, the lavish opera house built with rubber baron money in the late nineteenth century. My father recalled photographing trees "the size of skyscrapers," rivers that "seemed like oceans." Other times he would accompany the institute's researchers on their sociological rounds, making a visual record of rubber tappers and cocoa workers, African shamans performing ancient spirit dances, and nomadic gauchos hunting wild cattle in the Cerrado. The last would linger in my father's imagination. "The cowboys would ride on these little horses, and they were covered from head to toe with leather, like a suit of armor!" she marveled. "Their horses wore it, too. They had to or they'd get torn to pieces by the *caatinga*." Bushes with punishing thorns. "They were like medieval knights. I wanted that uniform."

"Where *are* your Brazil photographs?"

She didn't know. They had disappeared, along with a couple of large film reels marked "Brazil" that I vaguely recalled gathering dust for many years on a bookshelf in Yorktown Heights. When my father arrived in Brazil, he was still entertaining dreams of a moviemaking career—"the famous Hungarian director!" He convinced the geographic institute that it "really needed a photographic *and* a filmmaking unit," and he went in search of a movie camera—"a real one, not something for amateurs." In Rio, he found a former cameraman, an ex-Nazi who had fled to Brazil, with an Askania to sell. My father was delighted. The Askania, then the height of modern technology, was a 35mm camera light enough to carry on your shoulder, and a favorite of one of his moviemaking idols. "The same camera Leni Riefenstahl used to film Hitler in the 1936 Olympics!"

My father's directorial debut was a documentary of a landmark construction project on the São Francisco River, Brazil's first large power plant, the Paulo Afonso Hydroelectric Complex, fueled by a natural 260-foot waterfall. "I had this idea that I'd be Cecil B. DeMille," my father said. He arranged for a construction crane to hoist him in an aerial lift to film a fancy tracking shot. "Somewhere, there's a photograph of me in that bucket." He also commissioned a two-seat open-cockpit biplane from the air force base in Bahia. "We flew through a canyon and sometimes we went underground, through these cave tunnels." Aboveground, they dodged vultures. "If you hit one, the plane would crash—and there were plenty circling around." Vultures were such a problem, "they even had a saying: '*Urubu pousou na minha sorte!*'" (A vulture has landed on my luck!)

Off-hours, he and the other two young Hungarians played cards at the home of the institute's secretary-general, Christovam Leite de Castro. "A nobleman," my father said, "and very friendly to us. He was our patron." When not socializing with aristocrats, the trio trolled for women on the beach and in the brothels. "I got gonorrhea once from one of these houses of ill repute." My father sought relief in a pharmacy in Rio. "They took me in the back and gave me

a huge penicillin shot." For a while, the three young men were partial to a particular brothel in Copacabana called The Palace. "The
name was a bit of an exaggeration," my father said. The place was
a pit. "The 'madam' was this transvestite named Jesus, and he also
ran a bar on the ground floor." My father, never a big drinker, liked
to order rounds there, so "I could yell, 'Jesus, get me a beer!' " Tibor
got involved with an Indian woman he'd picked up on the beach;
her name was Irene, but he called her Inca. She worked in their
house as a maid. For a while, my father went out with a part-African,
part-Indian woman he met at Carnaval, also a housekeeper, whom
he favored because she was "smart and easygoing."

During the Carnaval festivities, my father dressed up, generally
as a French sailor. "I had this very colorful striped polo. I was very
convincing, because I was so skinny." He augmented the sailor
image with a pet he'd acquired soon after his arrival: an Amazon
green parrot. The bird had a particular skill, learned from a nanny
in the neighborhood who was always calling a child: "He could
imitate a woman's voice really well!" My father named the bird
Loira, Portuguese for Blondie. "Blondie was green, but he had a
yellow spot on his forehead." The parrot lived on the porch of the
house—in a cage, but my father left the door open. "Loira could
say, 'Loira wants a coffee.' And I would dunk some cake in coffee,
and he would eat it."

"Were you tempted to cross-dress?" I asked, thinking of Carnaval's ample opportunities to assume any costume without judgment.
"Brazil is one of the most sexually relaxed places on Earth."

My father shot me a skeptical look. "I don't like to be *too*
relaxed," she said. "Anyway, I couldn't. Tibor and I shared the house.
And he wasn't that way."

In 1950, Tibor applied for a visa to the United States and
suggested my father apply, too. "I wasn't too keen on it," my father
said. "I was happy where I was." The United States had a tight quota

on Hungarian immigrants at the time, but three years later, the visas came through. "By then, Tibor didn't want to go—but I did."

A new regime had taken charge and my father's "patron" at the institute, the nobleman, had been replaced. "The new boss was a military attaché," my father said. "Military men are all horse's asses." There was another issue. "The new guy didn't like 'foreigners,'" my father said. In Hungary, "foreigners" was code for Jews. "I knew it could be bad for me." He accepted the visa and made preparations to leave.

His Hungarian compatriots remained in Brazil. Tamás would thrive. He went on to direct the news department of TV Rio and launch his own production company, making commercials for Coca-Cola, IBM, and major advertising agencies. Last my father had heard, some decades earlier, Tamás was on his second marriage, to a beautiful concert pianist. "I don't even know if he's alive." Recently, my father said, she had dug up her old address books and tried all the phone numbers she had for Tamás. They were disconnected.

Tibor's fate she did know, and it was not a happy one. After my father left, Tibor moved in with "Inca." He continued to work at the geographic institute, but with a listlessness that eventually turned to permanent despair. He drank heavily, mostly whiskey. In 1967, he died from cirrhosis of the liver. Just before he died, Tibor married Inca. He wanted her to inherit his government pension.

"Tibor should never have left Hungary—he was not like me and Tamás," my father said. That is, not a "so-easily-assimilated" Jew. "Tibor couldn't function outside Hungary. People like him, when the root is cut, they wither and die. I didn't have these problems."

Yet my father's most treasured memory of Brazil involved a search for that root. On an expedition to the state of São Paulo, he'd heard rumors of a hidden community of a particular ethnicity, flourishing deep in the bush. He hired a jeep driver to haul him down barely passable dirt tracks and, after many teeth-rattling days and false leads, he found what he was looking for: Árpád-falva, Árpád Village, a tiny Hungarian colony near the Paraná River. It was named for the tribal chief who led the Magyar Conquest into the Carpathian Basin.

The village's three hundred residents had immigrated in the 1920s, built a church (named, of course, St. Stephen's) and a school where, for many years, all instruction was in Hungarian. My father was especially entranced by one extended family of Hungarian farmers, so many kinfolk that after he assembled them in front of one of their houses—"a very traditional Hungarian cottage with a thatched roof"—he needed an extra-wide lens to get everyone in the frame. Something about my father's description reminded me of the one picture she kept in her computer folder marked "Family," the 1943 photograph of the Friedman clan, gathered for Sámuel and Frida's Golden Jubilee.

"I loved that Hungarian family," my father said, pensive. "I wish I had those photos."

A few weeks after I returned home, I did a Google search for Tamás Somló's stepdaughter. My father had said she might be in the United States. As it turned out, she was on Facebook. Within a few days, I had Tamás's phone number. He was alive and well and retired in Brasília.

"Your father helped me a lot to leave Hungary," Tamás told me when we talked. "And to come to Brazil. And to get a job." My father got him that job, Tamás recalled, by claiming that he was a "seasoned" photographer. (In fact, Tamás had no experience in professional photography and had to do a frantic stealth study after he arrived.) Tamás still had the letter my father wrote to land him a visa. "I owe him a lot." He suggested I contact a senior researcher at the current-day geographic institute in Rio, who had written a scholarly treatise on the Hungarian trio and the formative role they had played in shaping Brazilian photography. "They brought a new kind of vision to photographing people and land-scapes," Vera Lucia Cortes Abrantes, the researcher, told me when we spoke. "They left a precious legacy." As it happened, that legacy was now on electronic display. The institute had begun digitizing the photos from that era and posting them on a website.

A half hour later, I was sitting at my computer, dumbfounded by what was before me: the visual record of a body of work that I'd presumed was lost forever, summoned with a few keystrokes. Late into the evening, I typed "Faludi" over and over again into the box marked "Fotógrafo" and downloaded scores of brooding vis-tas, sun-bleached ports, flea-bitten villages, leathery farmers and cowboys and fishermen, barefoot children with ragged clothes and bloated bellies. They suggested a documentarian's sensibility, WPA, not Condé Nast. The gaze behind the camera was observant, unsparing. The cache included three photos of the extended Hun-garian family in Árpádfalva, lined up several rows deep before a thatch-roofed cottage, dressed in faded European frocks, button-down shirts, and fedoras.

I downloaded the pictures and sent them to my father. A few days later, she sent me back an e-mail, with two of the photos attached. One was of Árpádfalva. She had enlarged it several times, my father explained in her annotation, so I could see the details that proved the house to be a "true Hungarian Village Hut." The other shot, which she captioned "Picture from My Past," was a photo of the São Francisco River threading through a deep can-yon, the river over which my father as a young man had flown all those years ago when filming the construction of the Paulo Afonso dam. In the picture, a canary-yellow two-seater fighter jet zoomed over the canyon. Perched on the far cliff were two vultures, hun-grily eyeing the plane. It took me a moment to realize I was the recipient of a gag. My father couldn't let pass an opportunity to Photoshop.

———

Brazil's freedom was oxygen that not every European expatriate could breathe, even its most celebrated Jewish refugee. Stefan Zweig finished another book a year after his ecstatic *Brazil, Land of the Future*, and *The World of Yesterday* may have expressed more truthfully his state of mind: it was an elegy for an epoch lost forever. In its pages, he set down a succinct diagnosis of his terminal condition: "I belong nowhere, and everywhere am a stranger." On February 22, 1942, less than a week after attending Carnaval, Stefan Zweig and his second wife, Lotte, killed themselves with massive overdoses of sleeping pills.

And what had been the relationship between my young father and the Land of the Future, the land of "hot (35 degree) love," where no matter what went wrong, nothing would go wrong, because "we will figure it out here"? "In Brazil, I had a great life," my father told me. "The climate was wonderful, I had a solid job with a lot of freedom, I was making movies. They even gave me a VIP card that got me in everywhere. State receptions! Executive banquets! And there was no discrimination. No one ever asked me in Brazil if I was a Jew." If there was a fairy-tale chapter to my father's otherwise constricted and disappointed life, it would seem to be here in the lush abundance of one of the most ecologically diverse countries on earth. In the movie version of my father's story, this is where the film goes from black and white to living color.

Back in Yorktown Heights when *The Wizard of Oz* enjoyed its annual television broadcast, my father never missed a showing. He seemed as rapt as his children. The movie belonged to the storybook side of my childhood, of a piece with my father's confectionary constructions—the marionette theater, the train set with its elaborate Odense toy town of cottages and churches, the lavishly illustrated Hans Christian Andersen anthologies that lined the shelves. My own favorite scene in *Oz* was the one where Dorothy and her companions shake off the fatal slumber of the Deadly Poppy Field and, linking arms, skip toward the glittering gates of the Emerald City. I thrilled to the song that accompanied their liberation, no doubt because liberation was what I craved.

> You're out of the woods,
> You're out of the dark,
> You're out of the night.
> Step into the sun,
> Step into the light. . . .
>
> Hold onto your breath
> Hold onto your heart,
> Hold onto your hope.
> March up to the gate
> And bid it o-pen. . . .

Now I think that anthem more rightly belonged to my father, the sound track to her South American years. Whenever I'd mention to an expatriated Hungarian Jew that my father had returned to their homeland, I'd always get the same horrified response: "How could he go back to Hungary?" I had another question: how could he have left Brazil? He'd escaped from the abattoir of identity-turned-death-sentence and skipped into one of the freest places on the face of the earth. He'd gone from a world of enforced and fatal racial classifications to a land of none. If identity is what you choose to be, not the thing you can't escape, then my father's arrival in Rio ushered in a period when every choice was open to him, occupationally, religiously, racially, sexually. He was free, more than free. He could take flight. The fantasy he'd had for himself, the desire he'd engraved on Jablonszky & Faludi letterhead—with a soaring plane and an unspooling reel of film—had come true. Why did he forsake it?

Partly it seemed for love, his infatuation with the one woman he knew in the United States, a childhood sweetheart, a Hungarian Jew who had survived a death march and found her way to New York after the war. "I often feel like crying that I cannot be with you," he wrote from Rio. "Believe me, You are the only being with whom I have a serious emotional bond." In one letter he enclosed a photograph of himself: the dashing film director in a bow tie and jacket, framing a shot with his tripod. "Time, however, somehow passes, because I always have a lot of work, and while one is young all kinds of entertainment are possible, which however do not sustain the spirit. You know I'm entering the age when one starts to be seriously preoccupied with thoughts about marriage and family," a state he philosophized about. "Man, being a social animal, needs family and a sexual partner," he wrote. "I don't really believe in the possibility of a perfectly happy married life with a foreign woman brought up in a different milieu, though there are exceptions and one can, as a last resort, modify oneself as well."

So there was that—his longing for a future with a woman of his "milieu" held within it a longing for a vanished prewar past, as miraculously preserved as an Árpádfalva in a Brazilian forest. "Do you still remember the harvest fair, the Disznófő and the Normafa, summer vacations and winter skiing?" he wrote. "Those were beautiful times, full of variation. I remember you had a Skoda and we had a Renault and once I was on a vacation near the Balaton and I invited you to come play 'Swallows and Amazons' with me on a real sailboat, but the contemporary spirit did not allow for such naughty acts."

On the very last day of 1953, my father boarded a Braniff International flight for the United States. He descended from the DC-6 Cloudmaster at Idlewild Airport many hours later, carrying a formal tie and dinner jacket in his suitcase. It was New Year's Eve and he had anticipated ringing in 1954 with his old flame. She, however, had plans for the evening—with her fiancé, an American GI. "I guess she couldn't resist the American man in uniform," my father told me wanly one night in Buda. In a matter of hours, Braniff's Cloudmaster had transported him from expectancy to disappointment, from the freewheeling polymorphism of mid-century Brazil to the gender demarcations of postwar America.

Blondie, the parrot with the golden topknot, accompanied my father to the United States. "They made me leave him in quarantine for a while," my father said, "but finally I got him back." By then, my father had moved into a dreary studio on the west side of Manhattan. "I was at work every day. The poor thing was so lonesome. He was used to living on a sunny veranda. Now he was locked into a dark room all day with no sound." The bird languished, stopped channeling the woman's voice, then stopped eating. My father came home one day to find Blondie dead in his cage.

19

The Transformation of the Patient Is Without a Doubt

"What's this?" I said.

It was another day in the attic, and we were at our routine, me in the folding chair, my notebook open, my father presiding from behind her desk, going through a manila folder marked "Changes." It contained the paperwork of her operation, including the letter I'd just asked her about, two pages of single-spaced Hungarian text with an official-looking medical logo at the top, above the heading:

Pszichológiai vélemény
Név: Faludi István Károly
Szül.: 1927. 11. 01.

A "psychological opinion," my father's name and birth date.

She made a scoffing sound. "Just life history. Things I told her." She turned to the second page, perused it quickly. "But it's no good." She swept the letter aside. "That psychologist didn't know what she was talking about."

"So, this is . . . what?"

"An idiotic thing. Not relevant."

"One of the letters you submitted to the surgeon?" I meant, one of the all-important two letters stipulated under the Harry Benjamin Standards of Care, the protocols first devised by "the father of transsexualism" in the 1960s for treating transsexuals, which have since become the World Professional Association for Transgender Health Standards of Care. Those standards call for written evaluations from two independent mental-health professionals, verifying the patient's eligibility for surgery.

"I *told* you, it's not relevant."

I pulled the letter toward me and studied the incomprehensible type.

"Originally, I had the idea I'd have the operation on November first," my father said as she continued to rummage through the file. "On my birthday. It would be a rebirth." But a year of hormone treatment is customary before surgery, and my father had barely begun the regimen. "So now my birthday is May seventh."

"Aha!" My father had found what she was looking for. This was a document she was eager for me to inspect—once she got it out of its protective wrappings. The extraction took a while: she kept it in a plastic sheath inside a hardback folder bound in elastic straps. It seemed to be some sort of diploma.

"Beautiful!" my father said, handing it over to me with a flourish, then leaning over my shoulder to admire it. "You see how nice and official it is? With that stamp, too." She pointed to the imprint of a blue medical cross, floating over a blue ocean wave. "Signed by Dr. Sanguan Kunaporn himself. The great magician!" The document was titled, in English, in all caps, "POST-OPERATIVE MEDICAL CERTIFICATE." Its declaration, also in English, was sloppily typed, whether due to language difficulties or assembly-line haste, I couldn't say. It read as follows:

May 22, 2004

To whom it may concern,

This is to certify that MR. ISTVAN FALUDI, born on November 1, 1937, H.N. 05-04 009626, was admitted to this hospital from May 6 to May 22, 2004. She underwent irreversible two-stage male to female sex reassignment surgeries on May 7, 2004 at Bangkok Phuket Hospital, Phuket, Thailand. The surgeries were successfully completed. All male genitalia including gonads have been removed and MR. ISTVAN now has female external genitalia that includes labia major, labia minor, clitoris and vaginal canal. She may now assume female gender.

Yours sincerely,

Sanguan Kunaporn, M.D.

Thai Cert. Board of Plastic & Reconstructive Surgery

"Nineteen thirty-seven?" I said.

"Yaaas"—she had altered the birth date on her medical records, shedding a decade—"they might not have operated on someone of my advanced age."

She returned to the filing cabinet in search of more folders. I returned to studying the cast-aside letter from the psychologist who "didn't know what she was talking about." I looked up at my father. Her back was to me. I looked down at the letter.

Who was I in that moment? Girl reporter, snooping on her own family member? My father's daughter, exhibiting the same craftiness and stealth? A common thief? It wasn't an act I would have condoned in my professional life. And yet, as my hand slid the letter soundlessly across the desk, I was already formulating my rationale: You think you can alter your story? Fine. I intend to document mine.

———

"Susaaan!" My father was standing at the foot of the stairs. "Susaaan!" I had retreated to my room with a book, intent on five minutes alone. Then, reveille. "Susaaan! Come here! I want you to see this."

"See what?"

"Just come down. It's on the screen."

I dreaded the summons to her monitor, never knowing which of her obsessions would be on display: her favorite Leni Riefenstahl films, her favorite mountaineering films, her favorite Leni Riefenstahl *in* mountaineering films, her favorite Wagner opera productions, her favorite hagiographies of Hungarian martyrs, her favorite NASA videos of simulated Mars landings.

"Susaaan! Come look!"

She was waiting for me in the hallway in the Little Red Riding Hood bathrobe. Reluctantly I followed into the living room.

"Sit there," she said, waving the remote control toward one of the Naugahyde movie-screening chairs. She settled in the other one and hit the Play button. Nothing happened, a not unusual occurrence. She went over to the recalcitrant VCR player and began twisting at knobs, pulling at wires, then peering in the slot with a flashlight.

"It was working fine a second ago." Pause. "Did you touch the remote control?"

"I just got here!"

"Waaall, don't touch it," my father said. She peered behind the VCR player. "Oh wait a minute, wait a minute, maybe we need to switch from Channel 3 to Channel 4." I braced myself, for the verbal torrent. "Okay, no, no, wait, it may be the cable is in the wrong jack. Yes, that must be it. No, yes, waaall. . . . Aaah-haaa!, Okay, so now this one goes to 'Line Out,' so if we move it to Line In,' no, yes, wait, now that's the other wire that needs to . . ."

"I think you need to click where it says 'VCR' on the remote control."

"No, *deaaar*, that's not the problem." A filibuster on the intricacies of A/V input-output plugs followed.

I reached over and hit the VCR button. The video began to roll. My father inspected me doubtfully, then sat back down.

On the TV screen, an operating theater appeared. The camera wheeled around, then zoomed in on a bloody midsection. A surgery was under way. Hers.

"I don't want to see this."

"It's well done," my father said. "I sent a copy to my endocrinologist, and he found it very interesting."

I said I didn't care. "I still don't want to see it."

But I sat there watching anyway. All I could think of was a cooking show, Julia Child in surgical scrubs: *Slice the fish lengthwise. Fillet with a well-sharpened paring knife. Set aside the skin for later. . . .* At least Julia would have been armed with a stiff drink.

After a few minutes, I studied the floor.

"You're not watching!"

I raised my head, keeping my eyelids at half-mast. Which didn't block the sound track, a tinkly "inspirational" medley that repeated every ten seconds.

"It's Thai pop," my father said. "They put it on there for me."

"They" being the Thai hospital staff who had agreed, at my father's request, to record the surgical procedure with her video equipment. "They only did the highlights," my father said. The film clicked off. I got up and left the room.

My father chose surgery in Thailand largely for the cost: $8,000, a third of the tab in Europe or the United States. She found Dr. Sanguan Kunaporn, a sex-reassignment surgeon at Bangkok Phuket Hospital, the same place she'd acquired most of her preoperative knowledge about transsexuality: the Internet.

A driver from the hospital collected my father at the airport. Steven had a lot of luggage. Along with an extensive double wardrobe—men's clothes for before, women's clothes for after— he had in tow all the cargo that would later alarm the denizens of Melanie's Cocoon: several cameras, a tripod, a videocam, a computer and DVD player, and a suitcase full of films, music, and opera recordings: *Das Boot, Otello, Don Carlo, The Abduction from the Seraglio, The Land of Smiles* . . .

The Land of Smiles?

"Franz Lehár's operetta," my father told me. "*Das Land des Lächelns.*" She reviewed the plot: a Viennese countess weds a Chinese prince but flees his palace when she realizes he must take other wives; the prince is heartbroken but abides by his local custom: "No matter what, you must always smile! '*Immer nur lächeln*'!" Lehár was Hungarian.

The operetta's credo was hardly a Hungarian sentiment. In my visits to Budapest, I'd come to recognize a certain sulky melancholy in the Hungarian personality. (It takes one to know one.) "*Sírva vigad a magyar,*" as the old maxim went: "Magyars take their pleasures mournfully." If nations were known by their gestures, Hungary's would be Das Land der Sullen Shoulder Shrug.

"They call Thailand 'The Land of Smiles,'" my father said. "And it's true—people are always smiling at you."

"That's nice."

"Waaaall, they don't really mean it. . . . But they know how to fake it." A high compliment, coming from my father.

The afternoon he arrived, my father went looking for a Buddhist monastery. "I wanted a monk to bless me." He found a temple nearby, but was informed that the monks were too busy. My father decided he'd just have to rely on the blessings of another faith: "Before I left, I told Ilonka to pray for me in church."

After an electrocardiogram and a stress test, my father unpacked in one of the "tastefully decorated private rooms" or "VIP suites," as the hospital's promotional packet billed them. He set up his computer on a bedside table. The packet had also advertised excellent Internet service, but he couldn't get the computer to connect, and the hospital staff wasn't much help. "They just smiled a lot," my father said, and told him the server might be down. It never came up. At first my father was upset, but after a while he decided it didn't matter. "There was no one I needed to e-mail."

At eight p.m. the first evening, Dr. Sanguan stopped by the room to discuss the logistics. The operation, he told my father, has two phases. Stage One, an eight-hour procedure, would take place the next morning: it would begin with the breast augmentation, then move on to the "vaginoplasty" (the creation of a vaginal tunnel), the "penectomy" (the removal of the penis), the "orchidectomy" (the castration of the testes), the "labiaplasty" (the construction of a clitoris, clitoris hood, and labia minora), and the "urethroplasty" (the creation of a new pathway for urination). Dr. Sanguan specialized in male-to-female surgery. The doctor reviewed the procedure with my father: He collects the tissue and nerves from the penis and the prepuce, or foreskin, and fashions them into female sexual organs. The top of the penile glans becomes the "Neo-Clitoris"; the underside, the inner section of the labia minora. The scrotum he sets aside for safekeeping. Later, he peels the scrotal skin and puts it on ice—or, as the literature the hospital provides puts it, "safely refrigerated at 4 degrees Celsius (approximately 39 degrees Fahrenheit), where it will remain healthy for up to three weeks."

Seven days after the first set of operations comes Stage Two, the skin graft to line the vaginal tunnel. The scrotal tissue is retrieved from the hospital refrigerator and thoroughly scraped of hair follicles—"thus preventing hair growth inside the vagina." Dr. Sanguan said that by grafting the penile and scrotal skin, he generally can create a "Neo-Vagina" with a depth of four to five inches, but sometimes that's "not enough skin" and then he would have to resort to other options.

"Not enough?" I asked.

"Like if you are circumcised," my father said.

If additional "harvesting" is necessary, the patient must undergo one of three increasingly tricky procedures. They are detailed on Dr. Sanguan's website. The least invasive is a "full thickness skin graft": the surgeon cuts "excess" flesh from the patient's stomach, hip, or groin. But sometimes this method doesn't suffice, and the surgeon has to resort to option two, a "split thickness skin graft," in which he makes a deep gouge in the patient's thighs or buttocks, leaving a scar of "eight to sixteen square inches" that looks like "a deep abrasion or burn injury." Sometimes that doesn't work either, and then he asks the patient to wait six months and return for a "secondary colon vaginoplasty"—a section of the patient's lower intestine is removed and sutured onto the Neo-Vagina. The patient winds up, Dr. Sanguan's literature relates, with "a scar similar to that for women who have given birth by Cesarean [*sic*] Section." The procedure can lead to numerous "complications," among them "leakage of anastomoses" (a leaking intestine, which can cause life-threatening infections), "fistulas" (another dangerous condition in which small tunnels form between organs that shouldn't be connected, like the colon and the bladder), and, in some cases, "temporary colostomy cannot be avoided."

Dr. Sanguan skips over such details in the YouTube informational video I watched, attesting to his skills as a sex-reassignment surgeon. (By the time it was posted, in 2010, he'd operated on more than seven hundred male-to-female patients.) "You will be happy," he assures prospective clients in halting English. "You will go back with a beautiful face, beautiful body, beautiful breasts, with very inexpensive cost, spend just thousands of dollars, not ten thousands of dollars. . . . Please feel free to come to Phuket for any surgery you dream for."

The night before the surgery, my father said, Dr. Sanguan asked a few questions about his general health. Then he took out a plastic container and spread its contents on a tray: gelatinous discs of breast implants, arranged in ascending sizes. My father picked the largest. "I had brought some padded bras with me that I used to stuff to make them look even bigger," my father told me. "I even had a very nice Victoria's Secret bra, bright pink. But after the operation, they were all too small."

My father gave me a sideways glance.

"You could use them."

I said I didn't think so.

"It's a waste of money for them to just sit in a drawer. Take them home with you."

"No!"

The morning of May 7, orderlies wheeled my father into the operating theater in Bangkok Phuket Hospital's plastic surgery wing. About ten hours later, she awoke in a recovery room. She was immobilized, catheterized, in great pain, and alone. "No one came and no one came," my father told me. "The bed felt so hard." My father's back hurt so much, she thought she was lying on stone. When a nurse finally materialized, my father begged her to find a new mattress.

Stage Two, seven days later, was supposed to be the easier operation. It didn't even require general anesthesia, just a local.

My father lay under a floodlight, numbed from the waist down. When she lifted her head, she could just make out Dr. Sanguan at the foot of the bed, pulling hairs out of her former scrotum. "I am lying there under these harsh bright lamps," my father told me, recalling it in the present tense, as if it were still happening, as if it might never stop happening. "They are all doing their work around me. No one is saying a word to me. And all of a sudden, I get this horrible feeling. This horrible realization. No one can see me. I've disappeared. *Maybe I'm dead*." After a while, my father's terror-stricken eyes caught the attention of a nurse. She told my father to take some long, deep breaths, and rearranged the pillows so she wasn't staring straight into the surgical lamps. Gradually, the panic subsided. Later, my father asked one of the other nurses about it. "She said it was probably a reaction to my feeling nothing beneath my waist. She told me, 'It's like half of you isn't there.'"

My father showed me a photograph of herself, a few days after the second operation. She is lying on her side in a hospital gown, her face a waxy sheen. She looks up at the camera with that strained half-smile.

A week into the recovery, Dr. Sanguan arrived with bad news: the penile tissue wasn't sufficient to fashion all the female body parts. He told my father that after several more weeks of recovery, she would have to return for a "full thickness skin graft." In the meantime, she had to find a place to wait in Phuket. Which was how my father came to stay at Melanie's Cocoon.

Melanie's other guests, my father recalled, were half her age: "One of them came with a boyfriend, with an engagement ring! And there was one who was a real whiner, crying all the time." Another guest later had good reason to cry. Her vaginoplasty hadn't worked; her scrotal tissue had thawed during a hospital blackout. She had to fly back to have the procedure redone.

"The youngest one there," my father said, "he was always talking—*she* was always talking—about how she'd told her psychiatrist she just wants to be a woman like her mother, *not* independent. She wants to be a good housewife, and make the sandwiches for her husband. She said she had her bridal gown all picked out."

"And a groom?"

"Waaall"—my father rolled her eyes—"he said—*she* said— she had a couple of guys in mind back home. But then she said she thought one of the nurses in the hospital liked her, so maybe she'd run off with him. The nurse was probably just being nice without meaning it."

Land of Smiles.

My father's skin graft worked and, after ten more days of rest, she was informed she could go home and start "a new life."

"I already *told* you," my father said. "It's *irrelevant*." We were back in her office under the eaves. I was asking about the psychologist whose letter was never submitted, the letter that I'd secreted in my purse.

"Why?"

"I didn't send it in." An airy wave of the hand. "There was no need. The other therapist was a higher rank. He was a university professor."

The other therapist, a professor of psychotherapy at Semmelweis University, was the second mental-health professional my father had sought out for an evaluation. And he, my father said, had approved the operation.

"But don't you need *two* evaluations?"

"That first psychologist, she was some lady shrink," my father continued, ignoring the question. "I had to go see her in an *insane asylum*. Full of old ladies, draaagging themselves around in bathrobes. It was someplace way out of town. She was probably put there because she was no good."

"And what happened?"

"She asked me a lot of questions. But she didn't know what she was talking about." Or rather, my father didn't like what she had to say.

My father went to the file cabinet and pulled out the "Changes" folder again. I hoped she wasn't looking for the letter I'd filched.

She extracted a short, typed piece of correspondence and handed it over to me with an I-told-you-so look.

"This is the one that matters. Dr. Simon is the ranking authority." Dr. Lajos Simon, the Semelweiss professor.

"And what did Dr. Simon think of the psychologist's letter?"

"He told me that it would make trouble for me."

"Because she didn't recommend you for surgery?"

"Waaall," my father said, "Dr. Simon probably knew that lady shrink was some kind of nut."

She unfolded Simon's letter and began to translate it.

The patient has decided about three years ago that he was going to operate himself over as a woman. Two years ago the patient has started feminine hormone treatment in Vienna. . . .

"Waaall, technically, it was only nine months," my father annotated. Not the one year of pre-op hormone therapy that is the minimum recommended by the Standards of Care.

. . . According to what the patient has informed me, he has in the past, since childhood, changed clothing regularly into women's clothes.

"You see? 'Changed clothing regularly.' You have to say that."

"But did you?"

"Maybe. Yeah, a little bit. I said it, but it's aaalso true."

The translation resumed.

The patient has lived in a conventional marriage. He has informed me that he has two children, who are healthy. He was divorced in 1973 and then he lived alone in the U.S. and Hungary. During this time, he has had regular heterosexual relations . . .

"Actually," she interjected, "it's more accurate to say that during that time I had *no* sexual relations." And was divorced, more accurately, in 1977. Later, the report continued,

> . . . he also openly wore feminine clothes, filling the feminine role in certain circumstances.

I wondered what "certain circumstances" meant. The Standards of Care stipulate that sex-reassignment candidates should live "continuously" and for a minimum of a year as the opposite gender before progressing to surgery, a period referred to more colloquially as "RLE," or Real Life Experience.

"Did you?" I asked.

"Waaall, sometimes at home, when I'd take pictures of myself."

"I mean, out in the world, '*Real Life Experience*,'" I said.

She thought about it.

"Once in Vienna, I wore a dress to a restaurant."

"And?"

"And I was very convincing. The waiter said, '*Ja, meine gnädige Frau*! I will bring your Wienerschnitzel right away!'"

"But aren't you supposed to—?"

My father cut me off. "Now, here's the important part." My father pointed to the words toward the bottom of the page under *Velemény* (Opinion), *Transzexualizmus, F64.0*. "What he's saying here is that the personal examination of the patient by the psychologists have concluded that the patient suffers a transsexual identity crisis."

"But the first psychologist didn't reach that conclusion."

"It's *irrelevant*," my father said. "Dr. Simon was my psychologist."

"You saw him regularly?"

"Just to get the letter. I don't need psychiatry. Maybe I visited him three or four times, but the rest were just friendly visits. He was a good guy, *funny*, too."

"Oh?"

"When he walked me out to the waiting room, there was a woman sitting there, and I said to her, '*Kezét csókolom.*'" I kiss your hand. "Dr. Simon started laughing, and he said, 'You've got a lot to learn!'"

I looked at Simon's letter again. I couldn't decipher the Hungarian. But I could read the date: 2004, Július 8.

"This was written . . . two months *after* your operation."

My father took her time responding.

"He wrote this after I got back from Thailand. For the Motherbook," the Hungarian birth registry. "So I could get my name changed on my birth certificate."

Like the Red Queen, I thought: Sentence first, verdict afterward.

"See, it says right here"—my father translated the last paragraph of the letter:

> The patient does not currently have male sex organs. However the female organs have been successfully formed. The petition for name change is justified and I recommend the acceptance of the request.

"But . . ."

"I gave Dr. Simon some money. Ten thousand forints. On top of his fee." Which was 8,000 forints. A 125 percent tip. A generous "pseudo-solution."

"So you didn't have a letter from Dr. Simon before the operation?"

"Correct."

"And you didn't send in the letter from the psychologist?"

"Correct."

"So how is it that you were able to have the surgery?"

"Aaah!" My father swiveled around to his computer and began clicking through electronic files.

"See?"

On the screen was an e-mail exchange, in English.

Feb. 26, 2003

From: Steven C. Faludi

To: Dr. Sanguan Kunaporn:

Your web page informations are quite clear. In addition I would like to know what are the minimum required preparations for SRS [Sex Reassignment Surgery], as in Hungary the psychological and medical examinations are not as readily available as for example in the United States. I am an older person and in excellent health.

And the reply:

March 14, 2003

Dear Steven

Thank you for your mail.

I understand your limitation. Do you have anyone like your wife, your friends that can send me a letter to tell me about your transition. Also, I need you to send me your photos. Do you live full time as a woman and have female hormone or not?

Regards

Sanguan Kunaporn

Years later Dr. Sanguan and I would have an exchange of phone calls and e-mails, and he would elaborate on his procedures and protocols. Before 2009, he said, when the Thailand Medical Council tightened regulations, he offered sex-reassignment surgery to Thai patients based on his own judgment, but for "foreigner TS"— transsexuals—"I like to follow Harry Benjamin criteria. . . . So I ask them to send me a letter of support from their psychiatrist or therapist before [I] accept them as a good candidate for SRS." With an exception: Some people, he wrote me, even those who have lived and been accepted as the other gender for a long time, "struggle to get the letter from the psychiatrist." He continued: "These people would have never had peace in their lives until death because they had no chance to get SRS in their home country. So for humanitarian view, I open a small window for these people, if they can send me a letter from their friends or close relatives, I will consider to do SRS for them, even I might face the lawsuit if there is something unexpected later."

My father took full advantage of Dr. Sanguan's humanitarian proclivities.

"So," she told me, "I said to myself, *Ilonka* could be 'my friend.'"
She hit a few more keys on her computer. "See?"

I peered over her shoulder. On the screen was a typed letter, set in a feathery italic font. My father had e-mailed it—from his own e-mail address—to the surgeon on March 23, 2003:

Dear Mr. Kunaporn,
I am writing this letter as a recommendation for Ms. Stephanie Faludi whom I know well since 1989, when she came to live in Hungary. At that time he came as a man and a mountain climber. I have helped him after he moved into his new house. We have developed a close relationship, that has lasted all these years. As I am married I could only see Steven once a week, but we went away on many occasions, also on summer vacations. He always took the female role and dress. I did not mind this. The last two years we have joined a Transsexual Club in Vienna Austria and went together to their evenings, dances, picnics and hikes, which I have also enjoyed. Recently we have discussed the possibility of a gender reassignment for him, that he is now considering. When Stephanie is in a foreign country she always dresses as a woman

and passes as such without any problems. Her health is good and
I hope it will remain well, also in the future. With friendly
greetings Ilonka—.

I had no trouble reading this note. Like the e-mail exchange between my father and the surgeon, the letter was in English. My father gave me a slow, satisfied smile. The cat who swallowed the canary. Ilonka doesn't speak English.

"I wrote the letter. And put her signature on it."

"That's—"

"See how I typed it in this italic script? It looks more feminine that way." She considered her handiwork. "It's very well written. This is *my* literature." Then: "I'm a fake. But a good one!"

"Dr. Sanguan bought it?"

"He just wrote back: Does she know that after your operation, you won't be able to have sex as a man and woman?" "Ilonka" wrote back at once, assuring the doctor that she didn't mind. Two days later, Dr. Sanguan e-mailed the good news: "I will accept you as a candidate for SRS."

One bit of my father's falsifications nearly came back to bite her. To change her Hungarian birth certificate and passport, my father had to submit the Post-Operative Medical Certificate—the surgeon's fancy document with the blue-cross stamp—as proof of her new sex. But thanks to my father's lying about her actual age, that document now listed a date of birth that didn't match the original birth certificate by ten years. So my father performed another alteration. "I made a very nice full-color copy," she said. She rummaged through the "Changes" folder again and presented me with the doctored version of Dr. Sanguan's certificate. "The blue stamp came out perfectly. No one could tell the difference."

The difference being that the birth date now read, with the original typing replicated down to the skipped spaces, "born on November 1, 1927."

My father studied the final sentence of the document and read it out loud with slow relish. "'She—may—now—ass-ume—fe-male—gen—der.'"

"It's like in *The Wizard of Oz*," my father said.

"How's that?"

"When the house lands on the Wicked Witch of the East, and the coroner reads the proclamation." The coroner of Munchkin Land—whose verdict my father now singsonged from memory, affecting a high-pitched nasality:

> And she's not only merely dead,
> She's really most sincerely dead!

"*She*'s your old self?" I asked.

No answer.

If my father had cast Steven as the witch in the fairy tale of her life, who was Stefánie? I had an inkling. On the first anniversary of her surgery, she sent me an e-mail with a link to a book she recommended I buy, a new biography of Hans Christian Andersen. My father signed the note, "Love from Stefánie," and beside her name pasted in a photograph—of a swan.

She may now assume female gender. I handed the certificate back to my father, who read it once more before returning it to the protective plastic sheath and inserting the sheath into the hardback folder with elastic straps to hold it steady. She stored it that way, she said, to avoid "damage."

"When I got back from Thailand, I carried it with me in my purse." She'd carried it, she said, for months. "Just in case."

"In case of ... ?"

"It's important to have the *correct* papers. Otherwise, you could get into problems."

What sort of problems? I asked. For the second time in my father's life, she was roaming around Budapest with an altered ID.

She gave me one of those Hungarian shrugs and changed the subject.

Back home, I sent the psychological report I'd pinched from my father's office to a friend who knows software. He'd offered to run the document through a computer translation program. Such things were still primitive then, but he had found one on the Web that claimed to convert Magyar into English.

"Ugh," he wrote in an e-mail accompanying the translation, "it's a bust."

A tantalizing bust, though: a gusher of gibberish with an occasional spurt of nonsensically arranged English words.

> Rasps spondee, rasps kerdesekre valaszolva tell, that novel loves operaltatni selves. . . .
>
> Hazassagukat Jonathan they were keeping, for it against him sauce ban runaway tole . . .
>
> Kisgyerekkent very slack it had been, unloved tussle . . .

Maybe it had been a mistake to pick translation software with the name of the world's most unbreakable encryption. The program was titled Enigma, presumably after the German device that enciphered and deciphered the Nazi's secret code. I read on:

> Gannet jo module, Jewish people there had been. Bud there is not. . . . THE deceive trance szexualisokkal alakitott who connections this time acquainting the simile Hungarian kozossegekkel. About your child elhatarozasarol not could ugy think about . . .

A few weeks later, I called my father's old high school classmate, the retired trauma surgeon and anesthesiologist Otto Szekely.

We met at a café in downtown Portland. Over lunch we talked about Otto's various postretirement endeavors—he was taking classes at the local university on Renaissance drama and studying the latest breakthroughs in genetics. He had recently participated in the opening ceremonies of Portland's Holocaust memorial, placing the names of his father and sister among those inscribed on the memorial wall. "It was something I could do to honor them."

As we were lingering over coffee, I fished the purloined document out of my purse and pushed it across the table.

"Would you translate this?"

Otto studied the subject heading at the top of the page:

Pszichológiai vélemény
Név: Faludi István Károly
Szül.: 1927. 11. 01.

Otto read through both pages without speaking. He looked up and over his glasses with a frown of disapproval. I thought he was dismayed I'd absconded with the letter, but that wasn't it. "This psychologist is writing in a very German type of way," he said. "It's not good Hungarian."

Then he started translating.

"Part I of the evaluation," Otto said. "He has titled it 'Exploration.'"

"She," I said.

"What?"

"The psychologist is a woman." Perhaps it was the usual Magyar confusion with gendered pronouns.

Under "Exploration," Otto told me, the psychologist wrote of my father: "His appearance is conventionally dressed, a little bit of a feminine man. He is partially spontaneous in answering the questions. He would like to have a sex-change operation from a man to a woman. . . . He was dreaming about this for a long time but because of his financial responsibility for his children, he couldn't do it."

"Hardly," I sniped, under my breath. I had paid my own way through college, with the help of an Elks National Foundation scholarship and a federal loan, and support from my mother. My father hadn't contributed anything. "Responsibility?"

The furrows in Otto's forehead deepened. "His parents were well-to-do Jewish people," he read. "During the war he joined the underground and that way he was able to obtain false papers and rescue his parents and himself. Later, his parents emigrated to Israel and they died there."

Otto reached under his glasses and rubbed his eyes. "I don't think he's a Jew."

"Who?"

"The *psychologist*." I blinked, surprised. I'd asked about the gender identity of my father, and Otto was speculating on the religious identity of the shrink.

"This is very much simplified," he said, "this idea of 'joining' the 'underground.' This psychologist doesn't understand the Hungarian Jewish situation."

He slid his glasses back on his nose and continued reading: "His relationship with his parents was good. As a small child he was very girlish. He didn't like to fight. He avoided the boys' activities. In secret, he wore his mother's dresses. Their maid also often dressed him as a girl."

Otto raised his head and we exchanged a wordless glance.

The "Exploration" whipped through my father's biography: the two years in Denmark, the five in Brazil, his emigration to the United States at the end of 1953. "In 1957, he says he got married to a German-origin American girl."

German origin? One of my mother's grandparents was German. Is this how my father saw her? I wondered why the psychologist found this significant enough to include in a document that was only a page and a half long.

Otto continued: "They had two children. He felt that the marriage was good, but despite this fact, his wife divorced him. According to his story, he still doesn't know the reason for the divorce. . . . He feels his relationship with his children is good, and in spite of geographical distance, they keep in contact."

Otto translated the "Exploration's" last paragraph:

> From the sexual point of view, he was always attracted to females. He has sexual relationships with women only. Until the beginning of the hormone treatment, he led an active heterosexual life. However, during his marriage, it happened sometimes he secretly took his wife's dresses. . . . He doesn't know whether after the sex change he will be attracted to men or women.

Part II was titled "Examination." It recounted the outcome of various psychological and personality tests that the psychologist had conducted on my father, including—how quaint!—a Rorschach.

> The tests don't show any sign of psychosis or bizarre appearance and aggressive signs. However, some signs of circular thinking can be found. The whole result of these test materials are impregnated with an uncertainty of or about identity and searching for identity. . . . But this is not circumscribed to the psychosexual areas only. It characterizes the behavior and the disharmony of the desires. . . .

"Oh, this awful *Germanic* language," Otto groaned.

> His psychological condition can be characterized as different in activity—open or branching—which shows up in sexual fantasies and behavior. Primarily, the preference of impersonal eroticism is present, which is associated with the experience of feelings of guilt.

We arrived at Part III, "Vélemény," or Opinion, the all-important determination of whether the patient is eligible for surgery:

> Based on my examination and various tests, it can be stated the psychosexual development is disordered. However, a straightforward indication of transsexuality cannot be verified without doubt. A fetishistic or transvestite type of identity disorder can be supposed. No conception and aim can be explored in relation to the future for the sex change. From a psychological point of view and taking into consideration the age of the patient, the experience of rebuilding a new identity and adaptation to it after surgery seems problematic.

"The language here is very ambiguous," Otto said. "But I think what this psychologist is trying to say is that he doesn't think—*she* doesn't think—that your father knows what he wants to do. Or who he wants to be."

PART III

20

Pity, O God, the Hungarian

Several years after my father had flown to Thailand to establish his gender identity "without a doubt," Hungary's identity crisis, building since 1989, reached its own Rubicon. The crisis was, in its own way, as "disordered" and "problematic" as my father's, with all the insistence of a generation raised to believe it was one thing, Soviet-subject Communist, only to discover that it had been something else all along. "Step by step," as Gábor Vona, the founder of the far-right Jobbik Party and Magyar Gárda militia, had declared to his followers in 2008, "we have to rebuild our identity as a nation." That summons proved to be one of Jobbik's greatest draws, especially among the younger electorate. (Nearly half of Jobbik's voters in the 2010 national election were under thirty-five.) In a survey of Jobbik's Facebook fans, the party's supporters chose this phrase as one of their top three reasons for backing Jobbik: "the protection of identity."

That quest for nationhood played out not as an intermediary adjustment or evolutionary progression, but as a thoroughgoing renunciation of one self-definition to assert its opposite. The identity that the post-1989 generation was seeking to assume was 180 degrees from the one it had been born into, an abrupt flip from atheist Bolshevik to Christian authoritarian. By the late 2000s, Kuruc.info, a far-right electronic portal, had become a popular news site for young Hungarians; reactionary heavy-metal bands were rocketing to the top of the charts; and the extremist Szent Korona Rádió (Holy Crown Radio) ranked as one of the nation's top ten online stations. These were the forums where young Internet-savvy Hungarians were flocking to defend a "true" Magyar self. When Hungarian sociologist Pál Tamás reviewed the 2008 results of a general population poll, he was alarmed by what he found: a surge in extreme rightist sentiments and a profound longing for a reigning strongman. Three-quarters of the respondents agreed with this statement: "We need a resolute leader who rules this country with an iron fist." Such views were now so widespread, Tamás wrote, that "in some sense, we can hardly call these extreme anymore."

Totalism, Erik Erikson had cautioned, could set in when the search for identity becomes an insistence on a "category-to-be-made-absolute," displacing psychological complexity and self-awareness. Instead of teasing out the component desires and conflicts and injuries that shape a personality, instead of inspecting (and con-fronting) the social and economic conditions and history that form and deform individual lives, identity could dangle the dangerous panacea of a single global fix. Could a nation succumb to the same temptation? What happens when a government champions a unitary image as a substitute for reckoning with its country's real historical baggage and grappling with its citizens' real problems? The politi-cal equivalent of totalism was totalitarianism.

It was no mystery why my father had deep-sixed her psycho-logical report: it blocked her path to the operating room. But I suspected there were other reasons. Its analysis had concentrated on the particulars, on details from a past my father preferred to keep buried. And it highlighted contradictions in a psychology— what transgender writer Sandy Stone would describe as "the complexities and ambiguities of lived experience"—that my father did not want examined. The larger questions the report raised were the very ones my father hoped to quash with a category-to-be-made-absolute surgery. The psychologist saw a patient troubled by "disharmony of the desires," whose "impersonal eroticism" was entangled with "feelings of guilt" and whose mental landscape was "impregnated with an uncertainty" that ranged far beyond sexuality and gender. What my father wanted the psychologist to see and validate was a patient whose conflicts were either contained within or irrelevant to a single problem of identity, which could be resolved with a physical solution.

"There's no 'problem,'" my father told me. It was the summer of 2010, a few months after the national election, and we were sitting in her living room, watching the news on her giant television set. She was talking about her nation's politics. "It's democracy in action," she said.

In the wake of the country's humiliating fiscal collapse and rampaging rates of poverty and unemployment, the Hungarian right had swept the ballot. The Fidesz Party, which had undergone a wholesale transformation from liberal to conservative, landed commanding victories even in historically more left-leaning Budapest and in virtually all the local and county governments. The far-right Jobbik Party won nearly a fifth of the electorate and a quarter of voters between the ages of eighteen and twenty-nine, making it the nation's third-largest party. It was hard to look at the results and not see the elections as a shadow play haunted by ghosts from Hungary's darkest years.

My father voted for Fidesz.

Now we watched as more than a thousand black-shirted supporters of the Magyar Gárda who had rallied in the capital's Erzsébet Square paraded before the news cameras, hurling bottles at police and brandishing air guns. Or rather, these were black-shirted supporters of the Új Magyar Gárda, the *New* Hungarian Guard. A year earlier, the courts had ruled that the Gárda had "overstepped" its constitutional rights as an association and ordered it dissolved. Unfazed, the guard reorganized under a new name, declaring itself a "civil service association" dedicated to "cultural and nation-building" activities, and carried on as before.

"It *is* a problem," I retorted. "The Gárda are terrorizing innocent people." She waved away the remark and scootched her chair closer to the TV screen, where several Jobbik MPs and a priest were extolling the demonstrators, who marched with raised fists beneath the "Árpád stripes" banner that so closely resembled the Arrow Cross flag.

"Terrorizing *your* people," I added.

Since its inauguration, the Gárda, along with a proliferating constellation of other far-right groups, had been pursuing an ever more aggressive campaign against the two identities it regarded as "foreign" threats to Magyar selfhood. They were the same two identities the Hungarian fascist authorities had sought to purge from the nation in 1944, Jew and Roma. Throughout the aughts, the assault would intensify: Jewish cemeteries were desecrated, monuments mutilated, synagogues vandalized, worshippers beaten, religious leaders accosted. In the countryside, vigilante "patrols" beset Roma villages. Black-booted thugs—some armed with whips, axes, and snarling dogs—harangued residents and hurled slurs and threats like this one, caught on a cell-phone video: "Dirty Gypsies! We should exterminate all the Roma and their children." In 2012, after the patrols stormed the streets of a town north of Budapest for two months (while the police largely turned a blind eye), the Red Cross evacuated six busloads of traumatized Romani women and children. Between 2008 and 2012, a human-rights organization recorded more than sixty hate crimes against Roma citizens: beatings, shootings, arson, and the deaths of seven adults and two children. More than a third of the attacks involved firearms, Molotov cocktails, or hand grenades. In Budapest, hate crimes were also accruing against Jews: a ticket office in a Jewish district torched, the home of a prominent rabbi stoned on Passover, bloodied pigs' feet hung around the neck of the statue of Swedish Holocaust hero Raoul Wallenberg in St. Stephen's Park. These insults were less alarming to some Hungarian cultural observers than the proliferating reformulations of history: Holocaust denial, rehabilitation of the Horthy regime, a poisonously coded politics.

Rightist politicians lent their support, both tacit and open. During the campaign for the 2010 national election, Jobbik announced its alliance with a far-right Hungarian police union that declared anti-Semitism to be "the duty of every Hungarian homeland lover" and instructed its forces to "prepare for armed battle against the Jews." The cover of the election eve issue of *Barikád*, Jobbik's party magazine, displayed a photomontage of the statue of Saint Gellért, the patron saint of Budapest, holding a menorah instead of a cross over the capital. The caption read, "Wake up, Budapest! Is this what you want?" Csanád Szegedi, Jobbik's twenty-eight-year-old vice chairman, was particularly voluble, accusing Jews of desecrating Hungarian national symbols, conducting "massive real estate purchases" throughout Hungary "to bring in Israeli residents," and entering into an alliance with the Roma to turn "pure" Hungarians into a minority in their own nation. Szegedi demanded that Roma families be forced out of their homes and "sealed off" in "public order protection camps." By 2012, Jobbik's deputy parliamentary leader Márton Gyöngyösi was pressing for another sort of roundup. On the floor of the parliament, he called on the government to draw up a list of Jewish residents "who, indeed, pose a national security risk" to Hungary.

The party made no apologies for its explosive rhetoric. Jobbik deputy chair Levente Murányi told the media he was proud to be a "Nazi, a fascist, an anti-Semite if that is what is necessary to represent the true Hungarian interests and the sanctity of the thousand-year-old Hungarian state." His words resonated: public opinion polls found that the proportion of Hungarians who felt extreme antipathy for Jews had doubled between 2003 and 2010. Hungary now ranked as one of the most anti-Semitic nations in the European Union. Among young adults, that hostility was at its highest levels since the fall of Communism: by 2013, one-third of Hungarian citizens between the ages of eighteen and thirty-nine were telling pollsters they harbored animosity toward Jews. Sociologist András Kovács, the leading researcher on contemporary anti-Semitic attitudes in Hungary, observed that anti-Semitism was operating as an "identity peg," symbolically useful to bond people who were drawn to the right wing for many conflicting reasons. The "primary function" of anti-Semitism for parties like Jobbik, Kovács concluded, is to make "members of the group recognizable to each other"—that is, "to establish a common identity." Earlier generations had used anti-Semitism as a way to express their opposition to modernity; "nowadays," Kovács wrote, "Hungarian antisemitism on the extreme right seems to serve as code for the political identity of those who oppose the system of parliamentary democracy." To be a Hungarian rightist in the 2000s, as in the years leading up to World War II, was *not* to be a Jew.

"How can you watch this?" I said to my father as the "new" Magyar Gárda marched through Erzsébet Square.

"Should they have shot the Nazis when they marched in Skokie?" my father said. "Should the American police exterminate the Klan?"

"Dad, I wasn't saying they should be *killed*."

"It's a democratic country now. They were freely elected."

"No one elected the Magyar Gárda."

"Waaall," my father said, "we elected the Fidesz Party. And Fidesz will put Hungary back on a good path. Viktor Orbán"—Fidesz's founder and now Hungary's prime minister—"will stand up to all these EU people who are bankrupting the country with their stupid policies."

"And Jobbik?" I parried.

On the first day of the new parliamentary session, Jobbik leader Gábor Vona had stepped up to take the oath of office—and flipped into Superman mode, whipping off his suit jacket and puffing out his chest to the cameras. He was wearing the black vest and symbols of the old and banned Magyar Gárda. A few Socialist ministers objected to the stunt. The governing Fidesz leadership ignored them.

"Fidesz will keep Jobbik in line," my father said. "It's like with the Regent Horthy. He kept the extremists in check."

Until, of course, he didn't.

Anyway, my father said, Fidesz had promised to stop the corrupt handouts of real estate. "Maybe we will finally get our property back."

I doubted it.

Under the Fidesz administration, the economy continued its free fall, poverty soared, social support services were slashed, and professionals fled the country in droves. By the end of Fidesz's first term in 2014, a third of the population was living at or below the subsistence level, child poverty was growing faster than in any other country in the European Union, and more than a fourth of citizens were "seriously deprived" (that is, unable to pay for such basics as rent, home heat, or groceries). Nearly a half million citizens

had left the country, a sixfold increase in emigration since Fidesz
had taken power. A third of the expatriates were college-educated.
The brain drain hit all professional sectors: medicine, science,
finance, academe, culture. By 2015, there was an alarming short-
age of physicians, health care workers, engineers, and computer
scientists. "We have become a country of emigrants," a headline
lamented. Emblematic was psychiatric care. A mental-health crisis,
aggravated in no small measure by socio-economic distress, afflicted
the nation at the very time when thousands of psychiatrists, psychologists, and psychiatric nurses—grossly underpaid, despite
"pseudo-solution" gratuities—were decamping. Severe austerity
measures had driven the national hospital system to the brink of
bankruptcy. Earlier and without explanation, the state had shut
down the nation's premier institute for psychiatric training, treatment, and research (established by Franz Josef in 1868) and eliminated 25 percent of the nation's acute psychiatric hospital beds.
The cutbacks were hardly due to lack of demand: Hungary has
one of the highest rates in the EU of depression, alcoholism, bipo-
lar disorder, and suicide. As these rates rose even higher in the new
millennium, the psychiatrists available to treat them would shrink
by 40 percent.

Faced with such real problems, the Fidesz regime peddled the
pseudo-solution elixir of identity. Within weeks of Fidesz's victory at
the polls, the new government had moved to grant "ethnic Hungarians" outside its borders (that is, Hungarians supposedly "stranded"
in the Trianon successor states) the right to Hungarian citizenship,
and declared June 4 (the day the Treaty of Trianon was signed) the
Day of National Cohesion, mounting countrywide demonstrations
of Magyar folk dances, handicrafts, and cuisine to "strengthen
national identity." Fidesz legislators championed municipal initia-
tives on "what it means to be Hungarian," and took pains to define
who was not Hungarian. The Hungarian Parliament renamed streets
and erected monuments to "Hungarian patriots," more than a few

with a fascist past. Reviving the authoritarian state seemed to be an integral part of reviving Hungarian selfhood.

In 2015, the Fidesz government sponsored a billboard campaign accusing foreign invaders of "taking" Hungarian jobs and conducted a survey on "immigration and terrorism" that fanned the flames with such leading questions as "Do you agree with the Hungarian government that instead of migrants, we should support families and their future babies?" Prime Minister Orbán ordered the construction of a thirteen-foot razor-wire fence along the 110-mile border with Serbia to keep out refugees (and soon after, another one on the border with Croatia). That summer the feared wave arrived, and the fence famously didn't hold. Orbán greeted the scandal of thousands of migrants stranded at the Serbian border and in the Keleti train station in Budapest with a military response and declarations like "We want to preserve the Hungarian Hungary" and "Those arriving have been raised in another religion and represent a radically different culture. Most of them are not Christians." Hungarian police herded the migrants into holding pens and locked them in train cars without drinking water. "They tell them that the train is going to Austria and then take them to a camp instead," Robert Frölich, chief rabbi of the Dohány Street Synagogue, told the *New York Times* that September. "I don't think the police got instructions from the government to do it this way, but it is very similar to what happened to Jews in the 1940s."

There were other echoes: The Orbán administration, which my father had counted on to curb Jobbik's worst instincts, moved quickly after the 2010 election to pass a battery of laws that undermined the independence of the courts, the central bank, the national elections commission, the media, and a host of government oversight bodies. The Hungarian Constitution was rewritten, expanding the powers of the state, curtailing civil liberties, defining life as beginning at conception, and forbidding same-sex marriage. Its preamble ("the National Credo") enshrined the

"Holy Crown" of Saint Stephen as the embodiment of national "unity" and recognized "the role of Christianity in preserving our nationhood."

The government began aggressively firing the heads of cultural and academic institutions (a notable number of them Jews or liberal intellectuals suspected of a "foreign" mind-set) and installing in their stead true believers in the Magyar way. The new Fidesz mayor of Budapest replaced the director of the New Theater with an unapologetic anti-Semite and Jobbik adherent, who vowed to liberate the stage from a "degenerate, sickly, liberal hegemony" and "instill patriotic values" with programming that would feature only "pure" Hungarian plays. (His first, though abandoned, choice: a notorious anti-Semite's play, "The Sixth Coffin," which blamed the Jews for Trianon.) When a Fidesz minister handed out government awards in 2013 to "those who represent the best of the nation" in the arts and sciences, the prizes went to several anti-Semitic reactionaries, including the guitarist for the neo-Nazi band Kárpátia, who had composed the official anthem of the Magyar Gárda militia. Most Fidesz officials were careful to speak in euphemisms, but not always: Zsolt Bayer, a founding member of the party and a personal friend of the prime minister, published a scabrous attack on three prominent Jews who had been critical of Fidesz policies (including Hungarian-born concert pianist András Schiff). Bayer equated one of the critics with "stinking excrement" and expressed his regret that they "were not all buried up to their necks in the forest of Orgovány," the site of a 1919 pogrom.

Jobbik officeholders rarely bothered to conceal their anti-Semitism. "Hitler was right in everything," one Jobbik MP pronounced, "except he made a mistake with this holocaust thing which is a weapon in the hands of the Jewry." The Jews, he added, "are people of Satan." Krisztina Morvai, Jobbik's declared future nominee for president and one of its best-known figures (though she claimed to be independent of the party), announced that "we will not allow Hungary to become a second Palestine." She advised Hungarian Jews, "Your kind's time is over." While serving as an elected representative to the European Parliament, Morvai wrote an open letter to the Israeli ambassador to Hungary in which she said she "rejoiced" over Israeli deaths in the country's war in Gaza: "I wish all of you lice-infested, dirty murderers will receive Hamas's 'kisses.'" After a conservative Jewish expatriate (who styled himself a "proud Hungarian Jew") expressed dismay over Morvai's remarks, he received the following response from her: "Your kind expect that if you fart our kind stands at attention and caters to all your wishes. It's time to learn: we no longer oblige! We hold our heads high and no longer tolerate the terror your kind imposes on us." In conclusion, Morvai advised all of "the so-called proud Hungarian Jews" to "go back to playing with their tiny little circumcised tails rather than vilifying me."

By the time of that exchange, Morvai had pulled off her own identity reinvention. She had begun her public life as a progressive lawyer. She was the author of Hungary's first and groundbreaking book on domestic violence (*Terror in the Family*), organized the nation's first association to fight violence against women, and, in the early '90s, represented four women who had killed their battering husbands with a self-defense argument. From 2003 to 2006, she served as the Hungarian representative to the UN Convention on the Elimination of All Forms of Discrimination Against Women. Before she was the poster girl for Jobbik intolerance, Krisztina Morvai was a ranking feminist.

And claimed she still was one. Jobbik and the Magyar Gárda, she maintained when I interviewed her at her home several months after the 2010 elections, were packed with "strong and revolutionary" women. "In the Gárda, which is pictured as the most extremist fascist Nazi organization in the history of the world," she told me, "there are lots of women, and most of them I would say are very conscious of women's equality." In fact, they were joining the

Gárda for liberationist reasons, "to say, 'I'm going to defend myself and other vulnerable people.'" She rattled off the names of Jobbik leaders whose marriages she regarded as "model" equal partnerships. ("You call Gábor"—Jobbik founder Gábor Vona—"and often, he's like, 'I just picked up my child from the pediatrician.'") As I left, Morvai handed me a gift: a huge coffee-table book titled *The Beauties of Historic Hungary*, containing glossy photographs of the "former Counties of the Hungarian Holy Crown" lost to the Treaty of Trianon. On the ride home, I opened to the title page and read her inscription: "To Susan Faludi, in sisterhood and with love, Morvai Krisztina."

"I'm getting all these e-mail attacks about how I'm not a 'true Hungarian,'" Katalin Lévai told me. It was two years before the fateful 2010 elections. I was having coffee in the Pest theater district with the Socialist Party representative to the European Parliament. The day was warm and we had grabbed one of the remaining outdoor tables at Mai Manó café, named for the royal court photographer of the Austro-Hungarian Empire, a seminal figure in Hungarian photography (and a Jew), who had worked and lived in the building. In 2003, the then governing Socialist Party had appointed Lévai its equality minister. She was the first to hold that post.

"I'm very worried about what is happening in this country," she said. "The nation is being divided into two kinds of people, the 'good Hungarians' and the 'bad Hungarians.' And the 'bad Hungarians' are all of those who are not crying over Trianon every day, or who are Jewish or Roma or feminist." Under that ideology, the "good Hungarians" are the ones who have actually been discriminated against and deserve "special care." That belief had deep roots. "The Habsburg Monarchy cultivated this idea of Hungarians being taken care of by the nobility," Lévai said. "And then the Com-

munist regime continued that under the state. Being 'taken care of' "
by those in power—"this is the key to the Hungarian mentality."

A few weeks earlier, Lévai had agreed to give the keynote speech
for the upcoming Gay Pride Festival in Budapest. When the news hit
the press, she was deluged with threats and hate messages. For championing LGBT rights, she told me, "they are calling me a 'dirty Jew.' "

As we were finishing our espressos, Lévai asked, "Do you know
the words to the 'Himnusz'?" She was speaking of the Hungarian
national anthem. When I said I didn't, she broke into song, and the
verse she sang was a reminder that the need to be "taken care of"
could have its flip side, a desire for victimization:

> Isten, áldd meg a magyart
> Jó kedvvel, bőséggel,
> Nyújts feléje védő kart,
> Ha küzd ellenséggel;
> Bal sors akit régen tép, . . .

"It is asking God to protect the Hungarian, to protect us
from"—she struggled to find the right words—"it's very hard to
translate. It means, when we Hungarians fight against the enemy,
we have this terrible fate which has tortured us for a long time. We've
suffered enough for our future and our past, so please God, protect
us." She continued to the concluding verse:

> Szánd meg Isten a magyart
> Kit vészek hányának,
> Nyújts feléje védő kart
> Tengerén kínjának.
> Bal sors akit régen tép,
> Hozz rá víg esztendőt,
> Megbűnhődte már e nép
> A múltat s jövendőt.

Pity, O God, the Hungarian
Who is tossed by waves of danger
Extend over him your guarding arm
On his misery's seas.
Long torn by ill fate
Bring upon him a joyous year
This people has suffered for
Past and future.

"When I've gone to football matches in Europe," Lévai said, "I'm always struck by the difference. Other countries have anthems that express the determination of their people, the power of their people—they're optimistic and proud. And ours is quite the contrary. It's very sad and defensive. Self-pitying." She recommended I study it. "If you understand the Hungarian anthem, you understand the Hungarian soul."

"Are you going to be in the parade?" I asked. We were washing dishes in my father's kitchen. It was a week after my conversation with Lévai.

"Waaall"—my father took her time drying her hands on her frilled yellow apron—"no."

"Why not?" I asked. We were talking about the one annual public showing of Hungary's LGBT population, the Budapest Gay Pride Parade—or rather, as of this year, the Budapest Gay Dignity Procession. The organizers had changed the name to counter charges that they were taking pride in *not* being Hungarian. The march was scheduled for July 5, a few weeks hence.

"I did it once," my father said.

"So?"

"So, I don't need to do it again. It's boring."

I didn't buy that. "The grande dame of the gay parade!" she'd exulted two years earlier, after the 2006 march. "Waaall, old dame, anyway!" She'd sent me pictures she'd taken with young revelers, and she couldn't stop talking about it. Boring?

"It's the signature event of the LGBT community, *your* community. Don't you want to be there?"

She gave her signature wave.

"It's an irritant. Some of the transes don't dress tastefully, you know?"

I didn't know. But I knew enough about the parade's reception to be secretly relieved she was planning on missing it.

My father stacked the plates in the cupboard. She wiped down the counters, slowly, and took her time folding the matching yellow floral dish towels. Then she met my eye. "There could be trouble," she said.

The previous year, right-wing thugs had attacked the paraders as they marched down Andrássy Boulevard and beat up revelers at the after party at Buddha Beach, two so severely that they had to be hospitalized. The police were conspicuously absent. According to a subsequent investigation by Amnesty International, a parade member who called the police was told that, having chosen to participate in the march, she "should take its consequences." On the streets of Pest that day, two assertions of identity had collided, with bloody consequences for one of them.

In the weeks leading up to this year's procession, the signs were even more ominous. The Hungarian right-wing media and blogosphere were roiling with fury. The "communiqué" issued by the rightist Hunnia organization and the Sixty-Four Counties Youth Movement was typical:

> We will not permit aberrant foreigners of this or that color to force their alien and sick world on Hungary. We hereby publicly declare that we, ourselves, will defend the Hungarian capital. . . . During these days, we Hungarian patriots will recall the Battle of Pressburg

in which the forces of our founding father, Prince Árpád, inflicted
a crushing defeat upon the western armies.

The Battle of Pressburg took place in 907.

Jobbik parliamentary members attempted to ban the parade
(and, later, introduced legislation to make the "promotion of
sexual deviations," including "homosexuality, transsexuality, trans-
vestitism, bisexuality, and pedophile behaviors," punishable by up to
eight years in prison). In June, the Budapest police chief tried to can-
cel the parade, claiming that the march might "impede the circula-
tion of mass transit and vehicle traffic." The ban was rescinded after
an international protest by LGBT and human-rights organizations.

That same month, the far-right website Kuruc.info posted the
names and addresses of LGBT gathering spots in Budapest. A
few days later, a gay bar and bathhouse, both on the website's
list, were firebombed. Kuruc hailed the attacks in a post titled,
"Cleansing Fire Licks Another Mini Sodom." By then, more than
a dozen Hungarian far-right groups were mobilizing against the
march. The Hungarian Self-Defense Movement (known by its
Hungarian acronym, MÖM) announced its intent to attack the
parade "out of self-defense" and appealed to "all Hungarians" to
"expel the pederast horde once and for all." A soccer-fan club
promised to meet the marchers "with weapons if we must, with
bare hands if we must, but we will not let things stand as they
are!" On Jobbik's website a warning appeared that invoked Levit-
icus 20:13: "If a man lies with a man as one lies with a woman,
both of them have done what is detestable. They must be put to
death; their blood will be on their own heads."

The night before the 2008 Gay Dignity Procession, and after
another protest by human-rights groups over the lack of security
measures, the Budapest police installed high metal fences at the

starting point of the parade and deployed two thousand officers along the route. The barricade, along with the water cannons and tear gas the officers wielded, failed to deter the assault.

Bands of self-styled "Hungarian patriots" broke through the fences and hurled smoke bombs, firecrackers, cobblestones, bottles, acid-filled eggs, rotting food, and feces. They accosted parade-goers and policemen alike, beat up a well-known liberal radio reporter, and attacked a Roma entertainer slated to perform at the parade's concert. They slapped and spat at a Socialist politician who was on record as supporting the march, and set on one vehicle with particular furor, smashing its windows: the car carrying former equality minister Katalin Lévai and Gábor Szetey, the Socialist human-resources secretary and the first openly gay government official. On the street, marchers tried to shield themselves from the fusillade with their placards and rainbow-colored umbrellas. Many fled through an underground tunnel to the nearest subway station.

The opening ceremonies of the Gay Pride Festival had been held a few days earlier in a downtown theater. Lévai delivered the key-note speech. She talked about the rights and the desires of LGBT people to build a community by making their "identity" public. "A community," she said, "may only find dignity if it becomes visible." But the threats convinced many, like my father, to stay home. More police officers policed the event than there were marchers marching. In the years to come, the parade would literally be placed out of sight: the police banned spectators and cordoned off the route a full block to either side.

In the course of the Dignity Procession, the predictable epithets were hurled—"dirty queers," "filthy fags," "perverts rot in hell," and so on. One particular chant seemed to capture the crowd's fancy. It was heard all along the parade route: "Buzikat a Dunába, zsidókat meg utána." Faggots into the Danube, followed by the Jews.

———

Pronouncing such categorical death sentences required being very certain of one's own category. To document the "purity" of his own Hungarian blood, one Jobbik parliamentary minister even submitted to a DNA test with a medical diagnostic company and posted the reassuring results on a far-right website: "No genetic trace of Jewish or Roma ancestors." Not all were so fortunate. Jobbik vice chairman Csanád Szegedi, the reliable fount of anti-Semitic assertions, bragged that he could trace his "thousand-year-old" Hungarian family ancestry back to the original Magyar tribes. Then, in 2010, some political adversaries went looking for dirt, and found it in a local registry of vital statistics: his grandmother's birth certificate. In 1944, Szegedi's maternal grandmother had been deported to Auschwitz. She was the sole survivor of her extended Jewish family. After the war, she had concealed her religion. Thus did Csanád Szegedi come to know that he was a Jew.

The grandmother's damning birth certificate was uploaded to a far-right website, and Szegedi resigned from Jobbik. The party demanded he also abandon his post in the European Parliament, and one Jobbik official told Szegedi that really only one solution would suffice: "The best thing that could happen now is for someone to shoot you in the head, and for you to be reborn as an eighteen-year-old without any Jewish origins."

Szegedi tried to finesse his new status. "The important thing is the way one behaves as a Hungarian." He was not really a Jew, he said, just someone with "ancestry of Jewish origin—because I declare myself 100 percent Hungarian." Some months later, Szegedi issued another statement, informing the media that he had been learning Hebrew, attending Shabbat services every Friday at an Orthodox synagogue, and eating kosher. He was now, he announced, Dovid Szegedi. "This is my true identity."

When I asked my father what she thought about the Szegedi flap, she considered for a few moments, then burst into song.

Erger, Berger, Sósberger!
Minden Zsidó gazember.
Nincs semmi baj.
Mert az Imrédy sem gaj.
Haj!

"This is the song we used to sing about Imrédy's little 'problem,'" my father said. She was talking about an earlier and equally rabid anti-Semitic political leader, Prime Minister Béla Imrédy, who, in 1939, had fainted dead away over the news, likewise uncovered by a rival, of his Jewish origins. Imrédy had championed the anti-Jewish laws of the late '30s that defined Jewishness along genetic bloodlines. The tune my father was remembering reworked the words of an anti-Semitic ditty popular in interwar Hungary. "The first line is just nonsense words, like 'Hickory Dickory Dock,'" my father explained. In truth, it was all fairly nonsensical. She sang it again in English:

Erger, Berger, Sósberger!
All Jews are buggers!
No troubles, however.
Because Imrédy is no goy.
Wow!

"What Szegedi did is absolutely right," my father said. She was talking about his belated embrace of Judaism. "Because it is his ancestry, his *family's* ancestry."

A family ancestry that my father shared but had seemingly disavowed.

"Is it his 'true identity'?" I asked.

"Waaall—"

"What does that mean to you?" I pressed.

"Identity is"—she deliberated—"it's what society accepts for you. You have to behave in a way that people *accept*, otherwise you have enemies. That's what I do—and I have no problems."

21

All the Female Steps

I was startled to hear my father espouse the importance of family ancestry, she who had for so many years rejected and renounced her closest kin. My father's alienation from her parents was an open family wound that still disturbed the peace of the extended Grünberger clan. Just how open was made clear to me one afternoon in 2010 in Basel. I'd come to talk to my ninety-five-year-old uncle, retired pediatric pulmonologist and my grandmother's only living sibling, Alexander Gordon (formerly Sándor Grünberger). "All the family was angry at Pista!" Alexander burst out suddenly. We were drinking shots of homemade slivovitz in the Gordons' cozy flat on Clarastrasse, a few blocks from the Three Kings Hotel where Zionist founder and Hungarian expatriate Theodor Herzl was famously photographed on the balcony during the first World Zionist Congress in 1897. Alexander's wife, Vera, sat beside me on the sofa, plying us with cake and cookies. "Your grandmother Rozi," Alexander said, "she was always crying, 'Why do I have a son who doesn't want to know anything about his mother?' Pista didn't write to her, he didn't speak to her, nothing! It was a big conflict within the whole family." Alexander recalled the day when, on a trip to New York City in the late 1970s, he'd finally confronted my father. "I said to Pista, 'Why, why? Why are you not caring about your mamma?'" No answer. "He just said, 'We don't speak about it.'" Alexander threw his arms in the air. "And after Rozi died, all he wanted was the documents for those apartment buildings. You don't speak to your mother, and then after you come and you want houses?" Alexander seemed to be addressing my father directly, as if his nephew Pista were sitting on the couch instead of me. "My mamma is dead, and you, you have the possibility to have contact with your mother and you don't do it? What are you? What is your character?"

Vera tried to calm her husband. "You have to understand," she said to me. "Pista had a terrible childhood. And his parents used him in the divorce in a very terrible way. They put him in a place no child should be." She related a story that had made the rounds among the women in the family. "Jenő had your father hide behind the stove—to watch Rozi when Jenő wasn't at home, and report if she was with one of her boyfriends. He wanted Pista to get information he could use in the divorce—he was using Pista as a witness." Alexander listened, then waved his hand in dismissal. I recognized the gesture.

That visit, I'd stayed with Alexander and Vera's son, Peter Gordon, and his wife, Helga. They were kind and forbearing. Peter was a pediatrician who devoted long hours to refugee patients from Turkey and the former Yugoslavia; Helga, a new mother, had a sympathetic nature that invited confidences. "Your father came to see us in Basel after the operation," Helga said one morning, "and she told all kinds of things to me. She said when she was a boy, she saw her mother in bed with another man." And another thing: "Your father said that when he was ten or eleven, Rozi caught him in her corset and panties and slip. And she beat him." It was for this transgression, Helga suspected, that my father was sent to live with the religious teacher, "to be straightened out," since the usual straightening-out methods employed at home weren't working. Rozi's preferred form of punishment, my father told Helga, was to lock her young son "in a dark room."

When I repeated some of these stories to my father, she dismissed them as "gossip" and "stupid things," and refused to say more. I didn't know how much credence to give them, or what they explained, if anything. Why had my father, who claimed she had rescued her parents from imminent death during the war, disowned them afterward and during their long senescence in Israel? Was Pista the wartime savior of manipulative and neglectful parents, or the ungrateful son who'd abandoned them? And if my father's fight was with her parents, why had she cut herself off from the rest of the family?

Though not from everyone. My father maintained contact with one relative: Peter Gordon.

On one of my early visits to Budapest, Peter had arrived on a predawn flight from Basel, bearing a cache of my father's favorite Swiss chocolate.

"Peeeeeter!" my father had greeted him at the door, "I was just telling Susan. I have found family pictures."

If Peter was the only Grünberger my father spoke to, that was largely thanks to Peter's efforts, which stretched back decades. When Peter was completing his medical residency at Long Island Jewish Hospital and Mount Sinai Beth Israel Medical Center in the '70s, he made a point of visiting my father. After my parents' divorce, Peter looked in on his distressed cousin and often took him to dinner. And right after my father had returned from Thailand, Peter had come to Budapest to make sure she was in good health. For all of my father's harangues about the failure of our family to "stay together," here was one kinsman who was a paragon of fidelity.

The family pictures my father had "found" hadn't exactly been lost. They'd been remanded to the cardboard carton in the fireproof steel cabinet in the basement, the same lockbox where she kept the deeds to her father's old Budapest real estate.

"Pictures aaand a letter," my father said to Peter, "about Susan's birth! I'll get them."

My father's heels click-clacked down and up the basement stairs. She emerged with the carton in her arms and extracted from it a small sandwich baggie, containing a very few yellowing snapshots. She handed me one of them—of a nattily dressed middle-aged man in a tuxedo, a silk hankie folded crisply in his lapel, doing the two-step with an attractive young woman in a black chiffon gown. "That's my father," she said, "dancing with"—she paused, for dramatic effect—"an unknown lady! He got around!" She pulled out a second picture. "That's me with my father." A boy of about eight or nine holds the hand of his unsmiling parent; the two are dressed in matching dress shirts and trench coats.

I picked up the plastic bag and pulled out a stack of faded snapshots: A stylish woman wearing a checked skirt, low heels with white anklets and a fashionable brimmed cap sits on a camel. The same woman poses beside the Great Sphinx of Giza. The woman again, mingling with a Bedouin encampment, bumping along on a donkey, strolling in the desert beside a Libyan constable, a leather pocketbook dangling from one arm. The photos are dated 1936, when Rozi and Jenő had taken an extended cruise and tour of southern Europe, North Africa, and the Middle East. "And they visited Palestine," my father said.

"And—?" My father had never mentioned this trip to me, and I waited in vain for her elaboration.

Later I'd hear accounts from relatives of the journey, Rozi and Jenő's passage around the rim of the Mediterranean on the luxury liner *Palestina*, with ports of call and side trips, including Naples, Genoa, Trieste, Venice, Luxor, Pompeii, Istanbul, Rhodes, Beirut,

Cairo, Alexandria, Haifa, Jaffa, and Tel Aviv. "A love boat cruise," my father's cousin Hanna Spiegel characterized it, "without the love part." They were "leading the La Dolce Vita life," my father's cousin Dahlia Baral said. But the couple was already battling, and catastrophe waited in the wings. In the shots of Rozi disembarking at various Mediterranean ports, warships guard the harbors. Aboard the *Palestina* en route from Greece to Haifa, the Friedmans took a snapshot for the family album of an on-deck service by fellow passenger Rabbi Meir Bar-Ilan, a year before the founding father of the Religious Zionist movement squared off against the British partition plan and seven years before his desperate 1943 mission to Washington, D.C., to plead for the rescue of Europe's Jewry. The second honeymoon recorded in the photographs was perched on the brink of political and personal collapse, a family soon to be decimated by war, a marriage about to implode, a son about to become an urchin on the streets of Budapest. Already, that child was alone: on their weeks-long excursion, Rozi and Jenő left young István behind.

Poking through the box of artifacts and photos now, an older Stefánie rendered a succinct verdict on her parents' first visit to Palestine. "They didn't like it," she said crisply. "But that's not what I want to show you." She handed me two pictures of buildings, my grandfather's Budapest properties.

"Here's Váci 28, as it looked after the war," she said. "It wasn't bombed or anything, a miracle. And this is Ráday 9, as it looks now."

"Can you apply for—what is it called—restitution?" Peter asked. "Or does that not exist in Hungary?"

"Waaall, it exists," my father said. She turned back to the box and began rifling through papers. "But it isn't worth anything." My father had rejected the government's offer of a $6,500 voucher in "compensation" for the buildings.

"So, you didn't—?"

"The oldest law of Hungary says no one has the right to take away somebody's property," my father exclaimed, the color rising in her face. "And that goes back to the days of Saint Stephen in the year 1000." (My father had actually pasted the relevant passage from St. Stephen's Law into her real estate dossier: "We decide in our kingly power that every man has the right to divide his own property or give that property to his wife, sons, daughters, or the church, and after his death no one shall attempt to question it.") My father was now shouting. "Why should I hand it over to robbers— for a few pennies?"

Peter nodded, carefully noncommital.

"Susan"—my father rattled my shoulder—"I have proof of our possession. That they wanted to rob us. I have a whole dossier on it—that I wrote that I want the houses back, not some stupid small change." She turned to Peter. "And it was the *correct* thing to do."

"Sure," Peter said.

My father sat back in her chair, arms crossed, lips pursed, eyes on the floor. A tense silence descended over the dining room. I went into the kitchen and came back with the coffeepot. I broke off a chunk of Lindt chocolate and put it on her plate. My father studied it for a few moments, then took a bite. "The Swiss know their chocolate," she said. "Not like that horrible Hershey's." She gave me a mildly accusing look, as if I, as a U.S. citizen, was responsible for the poor quality of American candy bars. She ate another square. Revived, she returned to the box and came up with a thin bundle of letters, in pale blue airmail envelopes with American and Israeli postmarks. I scooted my chair closer as she slowly unfolded each missive and reviewed its contents, reading under her breath in Hungarian and muttering a running report on her progress, or lack thereof, in English. "Ahhh, here we go! . . . Oh, wait, nooo, that's the wrong one."

She came to a note with familiar handwriting on it. "Aha!" Then, after a long pause, "Noooo. This one is after your birth. It says here, 'Susan is growing well and is in good health.'" My mother's words, written to my grandmother Rozi in Israel.

My father put my mother's letter on the table and I reached for it. She snatched it away.

"Don't! You'll get them all out of order."

Out of the box came a small Hebrew prayer book.

"This belonged to my mother," she said, holding up the worn palm-sized volume with gilt-edged pages and a cloth cover.

I leaned in. How had it wound up in my father's possession?

"Did *you* ever consider moving to Israel?" I asked. "To be closer . . . to family?"

"God no," my father said. "I went to Israel once. In 1990, right before I moved back to Hungary. Three days."

Another trip I didn't know about. "Three days?"

"Haaated it."

"Your mother was still alive?" I asked.

"Oh, yes," my father said. A shadow of dismay played on her face. "She conducted me to the cemetery to see my father's grave. There she was, all fat and rosy, when poor Father's last days, he was so thin and pasty, like a ghost." Jenő, who suffered from chronic lung ailments, had died twenty-three years earlier, one day after the end of the Six-Day War.

"So that's when she gave you all these things?" I gestured to the stash on the table.

"No!" my father said. "I got them years after she died. These are the things *they* wouldn't give me."

"Who?"

"The family members who live in Israel. They wouldn't give me the deeds to the Budapest houses. *Our* houses. For *four years* they wouldn't give them. They told a pack of lies."

"What sort of lies?"

"I told you, *lies*." I waited. "That my father was on bad terms with me. That he didn't want me to have the deeds. Which was a *lie.* My father would never have said that. My father wanted me to have the property. My father loved me."

She dove back into the cardboard box, still looking for my "birth letter." Finally, she found it. "We are reporting a great family pleasure," she read. I looked over her shoulder and, with a start, saw that the letter was in Hungarian and recognized the handwriting. This was a letter to Rozi from my father, not my mother. All these years I'd been under the impression that my father had never written to her, that he was not, as Alexander put it, "caring about his mamma."

"We have had—a small daughter," my father said, pausing between phrases to parse the translation. "Her name is Susan Faludi. She is—6 pounds, 6 ounces—in weight—a very good looking little girl. She has—nice light hair—and large blue eyes.—Mother and the child—are in good health.—Everything is prepared—at home.—Here the spring has come—and pretty soon—we will take the little Zsuzsi—into the fresh air—I work a lot—I hope you are well—and you won't be mad—if for a while I don't write—but here it is—sometimes—so much excitement—I don't feel like—writing letters."

She stopped and began folding the paper along its ancient creases.

"Is that the end?" I said.

My father hesitated, her face darkening. "Yeah, yeah," she said finally. "Then it just goes, 'I greet you with much love, etc.' As they say."

"Did she write back?" I asked. "Where are her letters?"

There was no answer. My father dropped the letter back in the box.

That night, Der California Exclusive careened down a dark and potholed boulevard along the river. It was pouring rain and we were lost, though my father wouldn't admit it. We were south of the city, in a bleak stretch on the Pest side. From what I could see— and the lack of streetlights made seeing a challenge—most of the buildings we passed were boarded up. Peter sat on the front passenger side, politely offering driving suggestions. "Stefi, I think you might want to turn around—this is very far south of the address." And a little later, "Stefi, I don't think you want to turn there."

From the backseat, less delicately: "Dad, Jesus, you're going the wrong way down a one-way street!"

My father yanked at the wheel and the van lurched over the curb.

We were looking for a former factory on Soroksári út, in the old manufacturing sector. Old and godforsaken. Was this what remained of the grand Communist dream to convert Hungary into an industrial behemoth? The *Blade Runner* mise-en-scène reminded me of the gutted urbanscape of the city's old Jewish quarter, where young squatters had recently set up improvisational social clubs in the rubble. "Ruin bars," they called them. Which more or less described our destination. My father had asked us to come with her to a transsexual *buli*, or party, a disco dance in an abandoned factory. Considering the violence that had greeted the Budapest Gay Dignity Procession, the out-of-the-way venue seemed like a smart move.

Disco was hardly my father's dance of choice. A year earlier, she had signed up for ballroom dancing at Eklektika Restolounge, a "lesbian friendly" bistro in Budapest that was offering same-sex group lessons in its back room. The offer was short-lived; the café's young clientele wasn't so interested and the lessons were soon discontinued. My father hired the instructor to coach her privately. "I told him, I want to know all the female steps," she said. "*Only* the women's parts."

After a half hour of wrong turns down unlit thoroughfares, we arrived at our destination, a hulking brick and cement structure on the far side of a giant and mostly empty parking lot. There were fewer than a dozen cars. My father seemed nervous. She stalled for time in the Exclusive, checking and rechecking her hair and makeup in the rearview mirror. A heavy rain drummed on the camper's roof. "My dress is going to be soaked," she lamented. She had worn her red sleeveless sheath for the occasion and her "ruby slippers." I handed her my umbrella. I was dressed in jeans and a T-shirt. Peter had on what I would come to think of as his uniform, as I never saw him in anything else: a sweater vest and khakis. We made a run for it.

We were drenched by the time we found the one unlocked door. A set of steep worn cement steps led up to what was once a locker room and dressing area for employees. The walls and floors were tile. A row of rusting shower heads ran along one side. I eyed them with a certain atavistic paranoia. At one end of the room, bedsheets had been pinned to clotheslines to create a few private spaces. Each of the curtained cubicles announced its purpose with a hand-drawn sign, attached to the drapery with a safety pin. "Makeup room," my father translated. I peeked inside and saw a vanity mirror and a pink-cushioned stool. "Changing room," said another. And in the farthest corner: "Conversation nook"—containing a couple of gone-to-seed armchairs and a listing end table. Posted all over were warning signs, in a universal language: a camera with a line drawn through it, a prohibition my father ordinarily would have deplored.

At the door, we were each handed a ticket for a complimentary drink. The "bar" offered only soft and fruit drinks. I turned in my chit and received a Dixie cup of pear juice. At the other end of the room, a stage had been jury-rigged with boards and a bolt of red velour hung from a ceiling pipe. Repurposed Christmas decorations—hanks of tinsel and blinking colored lights—dangled overhead. American techno music blasted from the speakers. The dance floor was empty.

The partygoers hovered in the periphery in a kind of centrifugal isolation. A few had retired to the folding chairs that ringed the dance floor, clutching cell phones. Nobody was talking, not that you could be heard above the decibels. Across the room, a statuesque platinum blonde in a sequined cocktail dress teetered on stilettos. Under the strobe light, I caught glimpses of off-the-shoulder gowns, coiffed updos, sculpted décolletage. I thought of what Jazmin, one of the reluctant members of the Hungarian Tranny Club, had told me at my father's house party: "I don't want a 'trans community.' I am not a trans. I am a woman."

In the center of the factory's converted locker room, a mirrored disco ball started spinning, an enticement to the dance floor. Nobody made a move. My father cast about for a familiar face. Seeing none, she led the way to a corner sofa. We perched in a row, me in the middle. "THEY ARE SUPPOSED TO HAVE A STAGE SHOW," my father yelled over the booming speakers. "IT STARTS AT MIDNIGHT." I checked my wristwatch. It was ten o'clock.

I turned to Peter and began to apologize. Surely there were more pleasant ways to spend his one evening in Budapest than being pummeled by '80s dance music. Peter said he didn't mind. He looked exhausted. "Maybe this is the youth your father never had," he volunteered. I said I didn't think so, and then wondered why I was being such a wet blanket. Much to my amazement, my father had fallen into conversation, or at least a monologue, with a partygoer seated on her other side. "Chloe," as she identified herself, sported a teased red wig, tube top, and vinyl micro-mini.

"WHAT ARE YOU TWO TALKING ABOUT?" I shouted. Michael Jackson's "Thriller" was drowning out every other word.

"ME, OF COURSE!" my father said. "I'M TELLING CHLOE ABOUT MY SURGERY."

My father's interlocutor pointed to her cell phone and said something in Hungarian.

"WHAT?" my father said.

Chloe repeated her words at full bellow.

"WHAT DID SHE SAY?" I yelled in my father's ear.

"CHLOE SAYS, 'THIS IS A PICTURE OF ME!' "

Chloe held up her phone. On the screen was a photo of herself posed in a field of flowers. She talked some more in Hungarian.

"CHLOE SAYS SHE IS A COMPUTER PROGRAMMER," my father relayed, before shouting something back.

"WHAT DID YOU SAY?"

"I SAID, 'GOOD, MAYBE YOU CAN FIX MY COMPUTER!' "

Chloe nodded, then fell silent. The conversation had reached its terminus, or maybe terminal.

I went to get another pear juice, but the bar had run out. My head was beginning to pound. I retreated to the "Conversation Nook," where no one was conversing, and collapsed for a few minutes on one of the foam-spewing armchairs, hands over ears. Midnight came and went without a stage show. By then, Peter had drifted off. His chin sagged on his chest. I envied his oblivion.

From the speakers, Army of Lovers was belting out its gay-liberation anthem and Eurochart hit, "Sexual Revolution":

> Love is love let's come together
> Love is free it lasts forever

"WHY ISN'T ANYONE DANCING?" I asked my father, as the hands on my watch inched toward one a.m.

She shrugged and her mouth moved.

"WHAT?"

"I SAID, 'THEY ARE TOO SHY.' "

For all the flamboyant outfits, the room was a sea of reticence. It was half past one when, one by one, a few guests steeled their nerve and ventured onto the dance floor. For a quarter hour, my father studied their movements. Then she handed me her purse and joined them.

I watched as she and eventually a half-dozen others gyrated in place, each in their own bubble, dancing by themselves. My mind traveled to the weekends in my adolescence when my father had tried to teach me how to dance the waltz, and then excoriated me for leading.

Peter woke up. "Where's your father?" he said.

I gestured toward the dance floor. Stefi was hopping tentatively on one heel, then the other. She looked so alone out there. Everyone looked so alone. I handed Peter my father's purse—and my own—and got up off the couch.

My father and I circled around each other for a few minutes. Then I put out my hand and she took it. I couldn't teach her the "female steps" to a Viennese waltz, but I'd done my time in New York's Limelight. I knew what to do with Michael Jackson. I led her through a few moves and soon we were swinging each other around. It occurred to me that I hadn't danced like this in ages. It occurred to me that I was having a good time.

I glanced over at the couch, where Peter was doing his best, through drooping eyelids, to stay awake. He gave me a drowsy smile. I looked back at my father. She was grinning, and not that anxious half-grin she so often had on her face. I held up my arm and she twirled underneath it like a pro.

22

Paid Up

"What we have here is a lot of broken things," Hanna Spiegel said, teetering on a stepladder in her bedroom, wrestling with a bulky package lodged on the upper shelf of her closet. She was talking about family.

"None of the Grünbergers are in good relations. We were left so few of us—and to end like this? It is something impossible to understand. The whole family is in bad connection." She climbed another step on the ladder and stuck her head inside the shelf. "But your father, he has broken *every* connection. He has broken with everyone. All these years, he did not want to know his parents. And why? It is the great family mystery." She gave the recalcitrant object in the closet several more yanks, then pivoted to meet my gaze. "And now, this thing"—she was referring to the news I had brought her, of my father's operation—"now he breaks even the connection with himself." The package came free. I followed my father's cousin into her living room in Kfar Saba, a small city outside Tel Aviv. The name means "Grandfather's Village."

Hanna placed the taped and trussed mystery lump on the table and began unwinding its dust-laden layers of cardboard, plastic, and tissue paper, as if unraveling a mummy. When she had folded back the final sheath, she reached inside and handed me the contents. I staggered with the weight.

"That's your grandmother's fur coat," she said. "Well, one of them. The *least* nice one." Rozi and Jenő Grünberger had arrived in Israel in the spring of 1955 with little money and no prospects. They moved into a bleak apartment in a poor neighborhood for off-the-boat immigrants in Ramat Gan, a satellite of Tel Aviv. Jenő found work as a part-time bookkeeper; his paycheck didn't cover the bills. "Rozi had to get this job in a factory that made these plastic aprons with tails around them, ugly like I don't know what," Hanna said. "It was so dreadful for her. Because she was a *lady*." Rozi wheedled money from her wealthier male relatives and did her best to keep up appearances. "A new dress must be worn to every occasion, and your shoes had to be according to your pocketbook, everything to match," Hanna recalled. At home, Rozi maintained a set of color-coordinated wash and dust cloths, each designated for a different chore. "Your grandmother would have a big fight with every maid. It was always, 'She doesn't know how to *clean*!' Your grandmother kept her apartment like a museum, like something in a Martha Stewart magazine." Eventually Rozi convinced various male relatives to buy her nearly a dozen custom-made fur coats, stoles, and wraps, talismen of her previous pampered existence as a haute-bourgeois princess. Several were minks, from the celebrated Israeli furrier house of Stefan Braun (Rozi's sister's husband was Braun's accountant). The fur that wound up in Hanna's closet was unborn lamb. Its sleeves were wide and flared, like angel's wings, and its custom-made fasteners designed to close on the inside for maximum aesthetic appeal.

I laid the heavy garment on the dining-room table and ran my fingers along the perfectly cut fur panels, the fine, almost invisible stitching. The coat seemed so alien in this tropical room with its AC and modern furnishings, as though it had wandered in from another realm, a lost but regal lamb far from its Mitteleuropean flock. For all that, it breathed a greater ghost of my grandmother than anything I'd ever encountered. Rozi and I never met.

I had been in Kfar Saba close to a week, staying with Hanna and her husband, Yair, in their apartment. It was an indication of that "bad connection," my father's but also mine, that I had trouble answering the standard questions El Al's security screeners ask at boarding: "Who are your relatives in Israel? Where do they live? When's the last time you talked to them? . . ." I'd found Hanna not through family introductions but on JewishGen.org, a genealogical Internet site for researching and locating Jewish ancestors. A few days after I'd posted a query, an exclamatory e-mail appeared in my in-box:

> hi! it is a big surprise—a letter from my second cousin.a grand-
> daughter of my aunt-Rosalia faludi grunberger!!! i took care of her
> for several years till her death. I am the daughter of Julius
> grunberger—your grandmothers brother. . . . i am happy that
> you found me!, hanna spiegel.

She was my father's first cousin, though she felt more like mine, both in temperament (feminist) and age (only eight years older than me). Hanna was an art therapist for traumatized combat veterans; Yair, who had lost vision in one eye and hearing in both ears in the 1970 War of Attrition, worked for the Israel Defense Forces.

After Hanna had returned this family relic to its cardboard sarcaphogus, she opened a few rumpled baggies and cascaded old photographs onto the coffee table. It was a ritual I'd grow accustomed to in the time I spent with the Grünberger and Friedman diaspora in Kfar Saba, Tel Aviv, and Netanya, and in Basel, Prague, and New York. Everyone had their cache of photos, their visual evidence of Old World elegance and decorum, stored in plastic bags in shoe boxes and manila envelopes in bureau drawers. The black-and-white snapshots, some mounted on postcard pasteboard, showcased women in furs and heels, men with walking canes and watch fobs, posing at the mountain spas, beach resorts, ski lodges, and five-star hotels of interwar Central Europe. And a few showed a small boy in a double-breasted jacket and matching shorts or a cashmere coat and tie or a pair of custom-made lederhosen, peeking in from the edge of the frame, cavorting on the running board of a Renault, gazing from behind a rock at a beribboned girl, clutching his father's pipe and resting a tentative hand on a cousin's shoulder: Pista, as he would have been known to everyone else in these photos.

Here was the whole extended, entwined family tree, branching on the Grünberger side from the great trunk of Leopold and Sidonia and the brood they raised in the grand house in Spišské Podhradie, except that the tree's leaves now lay fallen haphazardly onto one coffee table or another. And so I was introduced to my relatives, one by arbitrary one, in order of appearance as their images were pulled from the pile.

A fashionable woman leans on a man's arm in a square in Venice or poses before a pyramid in Egypt—the glamorous Grünberger girls, Rozi and her three sisters on their honeymoons and vacations and shopping sprees. "They were always in a quarrel over who was the most beautiful," Hanna said. The girls were raised to be "accomplished," in a nonthreatening, finishing-school sort of way, tutored in dance and tennis, French and piano. Their real calling was to be lovely ornaments, capable of drawing wealthy husbands who would keep them ornamented—and protected. Which is why, Hanna noted, every one of them married a man a decade older.

All four sisters survived the war, though none without scars. Gabriella, the third sister, lost her husband—he was deported to Sachsenhausen, worked nearly to death, and then shot into a mass grave. On a train heading to Miskolcs, one of her husband's former employees recognized Gabriella and her daughter, Marika, and denounced them to the authorities. Mother and child were dragged out at the next stop and sent to Ravensbrück, later to Bergen-Belsen.

Hanna extracted several more snapshots from the pile. "Here's Árpád," she said. A dapper man with a cleft chin, looking sharp in a tailored suit and fedora, strolls along a boardwalk in the Czech spa town of Carlsbad in 1937, slaloms down a ski slope with friends in the High Tatras, poses in his backyard with his family, one protective hand on his wife's shoulder, the other on his daughter's, a little girl in braids and bows. Árpád, the oldest of Leopold and Sidonia's four sons, who "ran the wood business with your great-grandfather," Hanna said, and who would die with his wife, Margit, and daughter, Verushka, in 1944, when the house in which they'd taken refuge with other Jewish partisans was shot up by the SS, then doused with gasoline and burned to the ground. It was only seven years since his Carlsbad promenade. Árpád's cleft chin, I registered, was just like my father's, and mine.

"And here's your grandmother again," Hanna said, handing me another photograph of Rozi, in a veiled cloche and bejeweled, posing with her husband, Jenő, an austere presence in a formal dark suit and bowler hat, and her son, wearing a double-breasted coat with brass buttons.

I'd seen many photos of Rozi. When I went to Tel Aviv to visit my father's cousin Marika Barbash (who, with her mother, Gabriella, survived Bergen-Belsen), she pulled from her grocery bag of pictures some shots of Rozi and Jenő taken in a studio, Rozi in a black dress, pearl necklace, and matching pearl earrings. "Always with the pearls," Marika observed.

Hanna pulled out several more photos from this period: Rozi on a shopping trip in Italy, laden with purchases; Rozi dressed for a night on the town in one of her minks and sporting an elaborate coiffure. "Rozi was very beautiful, with many lovers, and every night she was going to the theater or the opera," Hanna said. "Pista would be brought in before she left to get his good-night kiss, and that was it. Night after night, he was alone in the house with the nanny. It was like a royal family. Pista had everything—private teachers, governesses, expensive toys—but there were no parents there." One picture recorded a rare domestic scene: Rozi is seated on the emerald-velvet love seat in the salon at Ráday 9, the room my father described as being furnished in a "Louis the XVI style." Seated awkwardly on her lap, as if someone has just plunked him there for the picture, is a toddler in a Little Lord Fauntleroy outfit, white kneesocks and tiny polished lace-up boots. The photograph captures an equivocal look on Rozi's face; she peers down at the child on her lap as if she isn't entirely sure what his relation to her might be. My father, clutching a teddy bear, pivots away from his mother and stares into the camera. "My father visited Rozi when Pista was five or six years old," Hanna said, "and he told me he thought to himself, 'This is a very sad child.' He could see he had no love."

"Pista was a very intelligent, clever boy," Yudit Yarden told me. Yudit was my father's cousin from the paternal side of the family, the Friedman side. During the early years of the war, Yudit and her parents had lived in the apartment building my grandfather owned at Váci 28 and vacationed at the Friedman summer villa in the Buda Hills, where the two children swam in the pool and played together in the big yard. When I visited her small assisted-living flat in Netanya, a coastal town in northern Israel, Yudit was eighty. She greeted me like a long-lost friend: "Dear Susaaan, you come! My heart it's made so warm!" Her English was as eloquent in its brokenness as her face was beautiful in its age.

"Pista knew everything," Yudit recalled over cherry brandy and a groaning platter of pastries. "He read a lot, and of technical things he was also very talented, very sophisticated." He showed her how to take photographs and make films. "He was always rationalist, always working with the brain, not the emotions. He was very"—

she struggled for the English word and closed her hand in a fist—
"shut. Like the face in poker. You couldn't guess what was it he
thought." She remembered something else from those summers.
"Rozi didn't spend time with her child. Once I heard from Pista
that his mother will come, and I was . . . astonished. They were not
warm parents."

And Jenő? I asked.

"Jenő was cold," Yudit said. "A *gvir*"—Yiddish for rich man—"a
big prestige person in the Jewish community in Budapest. But he
was . . . pedant. Very critical of Pista. Very very critical." And when
he wasn't critical, he was absent. "Pista was forced to care for himself. He was awfully alone. He had two homes but not really any
home." She fixed me with her mournful wide eyes. "It's a wound he
never will be able to cure it."

And yet, it wasn't the abandonment of Pista by Rozi and Jenő
that posed what Hanna called "the great family mystery." It was
Pista's abandonment of his mother.

"He was Rozi's only child and he wouldn't even speak to
her," Marika told me one afternoon, as we sat drinking tea in her
spanking-new condominium in Tel Aviv. The AC blasted frigid air.
Overhead on a shelf were a few surviving heirlooms: a set of silver candlestick holders and a porcelain dancer in regal frills, ready
for a Habsburg minuet.

"She lost two children, you know," Marika said.

I said my father had told me that Rozi had miscarried once.

"Not *miscarriage*, and not *one*," Marika said. "They were two
live births." According to family recollection, one of the babies
lived a short while, the other close to a year.

"And then she finally has a child who lives—and he won't talk
to her," Marika said. "She suffered. Because of your father. It was
her tragedy." Marika recalled my father's three-day visit to Tel
Aviv in 1990. He put a stone on his father Jenő's grave, met briefly
with relatives to discuss the possibility of reclaiming the apartments

in Budapest, and left. "He wanted houses, not people," Marika said.

A couple of years after his brief touchdown in Israel, my father invited Rozi, by then eighty-nine years old, to visit him in Budapest. The news rippled to the far reaches of the Grünberger family. "It was the *big event*," my father's cousin Dahlia Baral, who was living in Australia then, told me. "Steven has called at last! We all thought that the Messianic days are approaching and here to stay."

And then, Rozi returned from Hungary—her leg in a massive cast. She had fallen on the front stoop of my father's house in the Buda Hills and shattered her leg. My father had taken her to St. János Hospital, the closest medical facility. Rozi was put in a room with someone who screamed in agony night and day. My father enlisted Ilonka to tend to Rozi for the several weeks that she was recovering in the house. Ilonka described the experience to me as "the most awful month of my life." She recalled Rozi screaming at my father all day long and treating Ilonka like the maid. "She would yell, 'Bring in "the girl"!'" And she remembered my father screaming back at his mother: "You neglected me. You never loved me."

Rozi's surgery was a mess. "An operation like from the days of Franz Josef," Marika said. The surgeon patched her leg together with a giant nail that soon began breaking through the skin. A hospital in Tel Aviv had to redo the entire operation. "Your father wanted her back to Israel as quick as possible," Marika said. As soon as she could travel, he booked her a return ticket. "Rozi said, 'He got rid of me.' She was devastated. Everything she had lost, it all came up again."

"It was sad," Marika went on, "but Rozi dealt with it. She cut herself off from things." She made a chop-chop motion with her hands. "You know about her will," she added.

No, I said, I didn't.

"It said, 'And for my son, only one shekel.'"

Marika's anecdote was correct concerning the generational

rejection but wrong in the details, as I discovered when I talked to Hanna, who had nursed Rozi through her final decline and sorted her papers after her death. Hanna said my father had indeed been cut off but that Rozi wasn't the offender: "Your grandfather wrote the will." Hanna recalled the words Jenő had set down in the 1960s, when the lira, not the shekel, was the basic coin of Israeli currency. They appeared on the last page of the will, at the bottom of a list of inheritors and the percentages each would receive: "To my son, István Faludi, one lira." The man my father had mythologized as "my guardian angel" had left his only child spare change.

Early in my visit to Tel Aviv, after Marika and her cousin Dahlia had led me on a tour of the Arab market in Jaffa, we stopped to take in the view of the harbor. We'd been talking about family history and about my father's sex change. I'd just finished telling them about the night my father and I went to see *La Juive* at the Dohány synagogue, and my father's assessment of the wealthy Jewish *alte kockers* in the audience: "They are looking at me and saying, 'There's an overdressed shiksa.' "

Marika considered. "Maybe he was thinking, if you change one thing, you change the other." She meant gender and religion. "The two go together."

"But you know what?" Dahlia said, shaking her head furiously. "It doesn't work. Once a Jew, always a Jew. You can't escape it. You can't, you can't, you can't, you can't."

I leaned against the railing, gazing out to the Mediterranean. Marika touched my arm. "Your father did something heroic," she said. "He saved his parents from the Arrow Cross."

I was electrified. I'd lived with his boast since childhood. This was my first confirmation.

"Rozi told me," Marika said. "She was very proud of it."

More confirmation would come to me on that trip. Yudit Yarden spent much of 1944 in Váci 28, my grandfather's building, which was by then a Yellow Star house. In early November of that year, after the Arrow Cross took over, the Yardens fled to a Swiss protected house. There they shared a room with forty others, including Rozi and Jenő, the estranged couple tossed back together by the vicissitudes of war. Yudit vividly recalled the bitter cold her family endured in the unheated room. She remembered, too, the absence of food, the sound of shooting by the river, and the rumors that the Arrow Cross were invading protected houses. In her memories of the Swiss safe house, one day in particular stood out—the day my father, impersonating an Arrow Cross guard, came and "took your grandparents away."

As Yudit told me this story, just as when Marika related the story she'd heard from Rozi, I wondered once again how this spectacular display of filial devotion could coexist with a lifetime of estrangement.

My father's cousin Peter Gordon recalled the showdown, back in the late '70s, when he and his father Alexander had visited my father in New York. Alexander had begun questioning his nephew Pista: Why did he neglect Rozi? How could he be so cold to his own mother? "What are you? What is your character?" When Alexander kept pressing, my father exploded. Peter remembered the words my father had yelled: "When I saved my parents during the war, I was paid up, and that was *it*. I owed them nothing anymore."

As it turned out, my teenage father's rescue of his parents wasn't his only act of valor. Some days later, Yudit's father, Gyula Yarden, was also taken from the Swiss protected house—by an actual Arrow Cross officer—and held in a detention center. Yudit remembered the destination as Andrássy út 60, the main headquarters of the Arrow Cross, but she wasn't positive. Days went by with no news. "We were . . . desperated," Yudit told me. She and her mother sought out Jenő and Rozi Friedman for support, but the couple made it plain there was nothing they could, or would, do. Then, a few days later, Yudit's father returned to the Swiss protected house. "I think he was tortured by the fascists very hard," Yudit told me, "because after that he always had big troubles with his legs and stomach." But she could only speculate. "I know nothing for sure, because he never would speak of it." He would speak of only one thing: how he was able to escape.

Yudit leaned forward and rested her gnarled hands on my knees. "I must tell you that your father was very brave at 1944," she said. "He saved my father from death." She told me what her father had told her: Pista had marched into the building where the Arrow Cross was holding Gyula Yarden and announced, "I am taking this man to execution." Pista was wearing an armband and carrying a rifle. Yudit's father "went a step before him, and Pista walked after him with the gun. . . . And he brought him back to the Swiss house."

The Yardens were astonished at his nerve, and by something else. "My father couldn't understand it," Yudit said. "Why they didn't think he was Jewish? Because Pista had a very Jewish face."

If I found the possibility of my father invading the fortress at Andrássy 60 mind-boggling, my father, for her part, found it inaccurate. "She's not remembering it right," she said when I relayed Yudit's story. My father recalled rescuing Gyula Yarden not from Arrow Cross headquarters but from the walled-in ghetto in Budapest's old Jewish quarter. "It wasn't that hard to get into the ghetto," she told me. "They weren't very organized." My father, whose accounts of wartime valor I'd always suspected of inflation, was downplaying her courage.

23

Getting Away with It

"Can I ask you a question?' My father and I were sitting on her deck. It was a perfect late summer afternoon in June 2010. Bees were making lazy circles around the sugar bowl and coffee cups. A woodpecker was tapping away overhead, fruitlessly—he was drilling for grubs on my father's satellite dish. My father was in one of her rare expansive moods, holding forth into my recorder on past adventures in '60s Manhattan, '50s Rio de Janeiro, '40s Copenhagen. I was glad for it. There were times when she was not as sanguine about our mutual project.

"I see what you are doing," she had said to me one morning as we sat in front of her computer. The subject was Richard Avedon's photography, but not the high-fashion Avedon shots that my father had spent so many years printing and color converting for Condé Nast. "I was at Avedon's studio one day, and he had those pictures of his father," she said. "They were frightening."

What my father had seen were the famous portraits that Avedon took of his ailing parent between 1969 and 1973, chronicling in excruciating clarity and detail, under unforgiving light drained of sentiment, his father's long and terrible surrender to cancer. Avedon had hoped the portraits would, among other things, repair their relationship; they had been estranged for many years. As Avedon tried to explain in a letter to his father, he was hoping to show him as he really was. "When you pose for a photograph, it's behind a smile that isn't yours," he wrote. "You are angry and hungry and alive. What I value in you is that intensity. . . . Do you understand?" Whether he understood or not is hard to say. After Jacob Israel Avedon died, his son's letter was found in the inside pocket of his best suit—the suit he never wore.

"I see what you are doing," my father had said to me that morning in front of the computer. She gestured to my pen, racing across my notebook. "Just what Avedon did."

Yet in 2010 we seemed to be collaborating better than ever. She resorted only occasionally to her wall-of-words defensive maneuver. One morning of the visit, she presented me with a color print of the two of us. It was a photograph my husband had taken two years earlier. In the shot, my father and I are seated close to each other at the deck table, my father holding forth, me leaning forward, pen poised to catch every word in my reporter's notepad. We are both laughing. "This is a very nice picture," my father said as she handed it to me. "You are a very thorough interviewer, aaand"—the finger held aloft in exclamatory mode—"a good writer." She had captioned the photo with a Latin phrase she remembered from her classical training at her old Jewish high school: "*Verba volant scripta manent*," "spoken words fly away, written words remain."

As my father finished off her slice of Black Forest cake and nursed an espresso on the deck, it seemed as good a time as any to push into thornier territory.

"Can I ask you a question?"

"Sure," she said, puzzled that I was seeking permission. "You are aaalways asking questions."

"Well, this is a hard one." My voice squeaked, betraying my

anxiety. I wasn't sure what I would be unleashing. I checked the red light on my recorder.

My father picked at crumbs from her plate. The woodpecker made another assay of the satellite dish.

"What happened that night?"

"Which night?"

"In Yorktown, in '76. The night you broke into the house." I delivered these words to the placemat. I left unsaid: the night you nearly killed the man my mother was dating. My heart was pounding.

When I looked up, my father was still picking lackadaisically at the crumbs.

"That's an *easy* question," she said. "I wanted to throw him out of the house, of course."

"How'd you even know he was there?"

My father considered. "Maybe the private eye told me."

"So," I pounced, a bad imitation of Perry Mason, "you *did* hire a detective."

"Sure," my father said, unperturbed. "But he wasn't much use. And a terrible photographer. His pictures were useless. Now, if I had been taking the pictures, I would—"

I returned us to the scene of the crime. "So, you got to the house and—"

"And I punctured his tires. So he wouldn't escape."

I walked her through what came next: the door crashing open, the stomping footfall on the stairs. The bloodcurdling scream on the landing. "Were you furious? Frightened?"

"I wouldn't say *furious*."

"You gave this terrifying yell."

"To *frighten*," my father said, "but he wasn't afraid. He came at me."

"Okay," I said, "but you had a baseball bat."

"The baseball bat, that was a stupid thing," she said. "I wanted to protect myself. But then he hit me. Let that be a lesson to me! Like Jesus said, 'A man is going to be killed by a sword if he raises the sword.' Or something like that." Despite the shelves of *Hour of Power* videos, the New Testament was not my father's strong suit.

The lighthearted tone unnerved me. My questions seemed to bounce off her bonhomie. I felt like the woodpecker, hammering at steel.

"And you stabbed him," I prompted.

"He came at me, and I knew I wouldn't be effective. I can't handle a baseball bat. If I was strong and muscular, I would have beat him out of the house with it, but I had no such fantasies. I let the bat drop. And he hit me. And to defend myself, I got out my Swiss Army knife. Which isn't really a lethal weapon. But I made him bleed a little."

"*A little?*"

"I stabbed him a couple of times. But I didn't direct it into his chest, not where the heart is." She was quiet for a moment. "It was dangerous," she said. "They say that you could bleed to death that way. But eventually he got to the hospital. The police came. And the ambulance. You remember the ambulance I used to go with, to save people?"

I hadn't forgotten my father's years as an EMT volunteer.

"The driver who came was the same one I used to ride with."

My father recalled how he climbed in the back; he had been "injured," too, a cut on the head. "Waaall, it was just a superficial wound." Once it was bandaged, "the police came and took me to jail."

Where, I noted, he was granted bail before morning.

"Yes, and then I went right back to the city and had a picture taken, with me bleeding and everything."

"What for?"

"For proof," she said. "What else?"

"When I phoned 911 that night," I said, "the dispatcher told me that someone had already called to report an incident." Now some pieces were falling into place. "That was you, wasn't it?"

"Sure."

"But why?" Why call the cops before you commit the crime?

"I wanted the *proof*," she said. "The police took me away. It was all right. "I wanted to set up a precedent. With witnesses."

I didn't get it.

"I was creating an incident."

"What, like a staged event?"

"Yaaas. And it looked good, the enraged husband trying to chase the—what do you call it—in dramatic terms, the 'seducer.'" My father made air quotes with her fingers. "I set up this whole thing. To establish that she brought a man into the house, and I was the 'wronged husband.'" Another air quote.

"It looked like there was a fight over jealousy, you know," my father continued, "and that I'm the house's owner and married to this woman, and I was beating the guy out of the house and he resisted it. I created an incident. But nobody could *prove* I created an incident."

To what end?

"Proof of so-called 'in-fi-del-i-ty.'" More air quotes. "Waaall, she didn't get any alimony."

"You mean you put on this whole show so you wouldn't have to pay alimony?"

"No! The point was"—she batted at one of the circling bees, exasperated by my slow comprehension—"okay, sure, I didn't have to pay. But that wasn't . . ." Her face looked suddenly leaden.

"There was one time I got very sick," she said. "At the end of the divorce. I had these pains all over. Pretty soon I couldn't walk. I never had anything like that in my life." By then, my father had been exiled from the house and was living in Manhattan. "Finally, I called a taxi and told the driver to take me to this doctor I knew—Dr. Kraus, he worked on rock climbers." Hans Kraus, "the father of sports medicine," was also the unofficial founder of rock climbing in the United States, having pioneered the sport on the cliff faces of the Shawangunk Mountains, where my father and I used to spend our weekends. An Austrian Jew who had fled Nazi Europe in the '30s, Kraus was past seventy, "semiretired," by the time my father came calling.

"What did he do?"

"Some sort of electrical treatment, with a machine. I went several times. Eventually I began to be better."

I thought of the language my father had insisted on inserting in the divorce decree: that my mother's withdrawal of affections had "caused the defendant to receive medical treatment and become ill."

"What was wrong with you?"

My father shrugged. "Dr. Kraus didn't say."

"What do *you* think was wrong?"

My father looked at me and her face crumpled. "Despite everything I tried, it all collapsed. I was—broken. I was"—she groped for a more precise term to describe her condition—"abandoned." She gazed into her coffee cup. "I didn't want the divorce. I was trying to show that it was forced on me."

Show who?

"I was trying to make your mother forget the whole thing," she said. "To throw out this whole stupid thing of breaking up the family. I was trying to keep the family together."

Had the home invasion all been kabuki? In my effort to establish who my father really was, had I mistaken artifice for essence? But I'd heard his howls, and the rage I'd heard was genuine. The blood I'd cleaned off the floor wasn't from surface wounds but from stabbings deep in the stomach. And his violence wasn't confined to one incident. "*I created you, and I can destroy you.*" I'd felt his wrath the night he'd hit my head against the floor for my religious infidelity. Could *that* be bracketed by air quotes, too? Or was there another side that was "aaalso true"?

One evening, my father, my husband, and I headed to Horgász-tanya Vendéglő, the Fish-Farm Inn, a restaurant in Buda close to the Danube where my father liked to order the *halászlé*, a traditional spicy fish soup larded with enough paprika to burn out your brain on the first sip. The last time we'd gone, I had committed the gau-cherie of ordering a glass of water to counteract the pound and a half of high-octane paprika floating in my soup. Worse, I had ordered my water with ice. My father had lambasted me. "*Ice cubes?*" she had pronounced with revulsion. "No European with any *class* would be caught dead putting those tacky things in a drink." Every time I reached for the glass, she would start up again, declar-ing herself "embarrassed" to be seen with such a boorish dinner partner.

"Maybe we could try a new place tonight."

No dice. My father was a stick-in-the-mud when it came to restaurants. I followed her crankily into the dining hall, its walls festooned with drift nets, floats, and anchors. An entire dinghy with oars still attached hung from the ceiling. "Tacky," I thought to myself.

"I love this place," my father said, and I practically lip-synched the next words along with her: "It's *aaauthentic* Hungarian." She wasn't just referring to the cuisine. She loved the old-school waiters, elderly gents with formal manners, greeting my father with courtly deference and pulling out her chair, kissing her hand with a "*Kezét csókolom.*"

It seemed unlikely to me that she looked particularly womanly to the waiters. As usual, my father wasn't wearing a wig. She had her white purse slung like a sailor's duffel over her blue double-breasted

captain's jacket, an ocean-faring motif for a seafood dinner perhaps, though more Admiral Horthy than Empress Sisi.

My father tilted her pate coquettishly and chatted away to the
grizzled server, who was all smiles and obsequious nods.

When the waiter left the table, I remarked on his deference.

"Waaall, they have to '*csókolom*' me now."

"Why 'have to'?"

"Because," she said, "I'm tough."

We opened the heavy tasseled menus. I decided to exercise some
toughness of my own. I announced I was forgoing the fish soup.

"Susan is such a picky eater," my father grumbled to my husband.
"When Tibor and I were in Vienna, we hardly ate either, but that's
because we didn't have any money." One of her time-out-of-joint
remarks. A conversation with her was like a ride in a run-amok
submersible. One minute you were bobbing on the surface; the
next you were trawling the ocean floor, or, in this case, traveling
through her adventures in Austria in 1946.

The waiter returned and set a large glass of water on my placemat.

My father had ordered it for me, a liquid olive branch. "But I
told him," my father said, "'*No ice!*'"

I said maybe I'd try the fish soup, after all.

"It's made the *correct* way here," my father said. "*Halászlé* should
only be made with *river* fish, because Hungary is a landlocked nation.
Or lake fish. But *never* saltwater. It can be carp, perch, catfish. . . .
Now the Tisza River has excellent fishing. . . . Lake Balaton can
also be . . ."

"Have you been back to Balaton?" my husband interjected, to
foreshorten the ichthyology disquisition.

". . . Balaton's the largest freshwater lake in Europe," my father
continued. "Waaall, the largest in *Central* Europe, but it's known
for . . ."

The waiter arrived with the soup, in a cast-iron kettle hanging from a flimsy tripod. He removed the lid with an ostentatious flour-ish and began ladling out its contents, starting with my father's bowl.

"Ladies first!" my father quipped. She looked pleased with her own sophistry—a trickster mocking and simultaneously enforcing convention. I stirred the fire-engine broth in my bowl. A carp head floated to the top. Across the table, my father took several happy slurps, savoring the burn.

"Balaton," she said after a while. "That's how we ended up hearing it on the radio."

"Excuse me?"

"The doctor and his family at Ráday 9. They lived on the sec-ond floor. But they went to Lake Balaton that summer."

Another dive into history—now it was the late spring and early summer of '44, the time when Jenő Friedman and his sixteen-year-old son took cover in the doctor's apartment, hiding behind drawn curtains, listening "very quietly" to the BBC on the radio. "That's how we heard the Germans had taken away the Jews of Kassa," she said now. My grandfather's hometown. "My father, he started to cry. He told me, 'They have killed my parents.'"

She ladled out another serving of soup. The BBC's report, she added, wasn't entirely a bolt from the blue. Weeks earlier, "my father had heard something bad was going to happen out there."

"So did Jenő try to get his parents out of Kassa?" I asked.

"Waaall, he sent Gaal." Gaal was the groundskeeper for Ráday 9. "He paid Gaal to go to Kassa and sort of check things out." A wasted investment. Gaal was back in a hurry. "He said there was nothing he could do."

"Did Jenő consider going himself?"

My father studied the tablecloth and said nothing.

"Aaanywaaay," she said finally, "he couldn't have known." That they would be murdered, she meant. "It was something that had never happened before."

"*You* did something," I said. "You saved your parents."

"My cousin Friczi and those Betar guys he was with, they were going to 'save' people, too." He was referring to the Zionist uprising hatched in a Budapest "bunker" that ended in disaster. "They didn't even know how to use a gun. Foolishness."

"But didn't you," I persisted, "have a gun you didn't know how to use when you marched up the stairs of the Swiss protected house? Wasn't that 'foolishness,' too?"

"Yaaas, but my gun wasn't loaded."

"So?"

"So, it's very simple. I *believed* it. So they believed it. I took part in their game. If you believe you are whoever you pretend to be, you're halfway saved. But if you act funny, if you act afraid, you're halfway to the gas chamber."

My father folded her napkin carefully and put it on the table. "Waaall, I have these wisdoms," she said. "But I believe them!"

For dessert, my father ordered *gesztenyepüré*—a traditional Hungarian delicacy, chestnuts pureed through a potato ricer into "noodles" and then laced with rum and vanilla. Seeing the name shook loose a surprisingly nostalgic association: my father sometimes made the dish on Sunday afternoons in Yorktown. The restaurant purée arrived in a gigantic goblet, crowned with a minaret of whipped cream.

"This role-playing during the war," my father said as she tackled the towering confection, "that was a similar process."

"To what?"

"I can sit down with anyone now, and he kisses my hand. It strengthened me for life that I did these things back then. That I could live as not myself but as a non-Jewish person. And that I could get away with it. So now I can do this other thing." Meaning her change in sex. "Because if you are convinced you are this other person, everybody else will be convinced. . . . I impersonate myself."

"So, what you're doing now," I asked, "is that playing another 'role,' too?"

"I was role-playing as a *man*," she said, "but I wasn't totally accepted by women as a capital-letter-'M' man. I didn't have the wherewithal. Now as a woman, I'm not role-playing anymore. I don't have to."

"Because this is who you were all along? This is your true self?"

"Waaall, it's who I am *now*," she said. "Since the operation. I have developed another personality."

With a difference from the wartime attempt, I thought. As a Jewish young man in Nazi Europe, no matter how brilliant the performance, no matter how convincingly he wore the Arrow Cross armband or gave the "Heil Szálasi!" salute, my father still had to live with the terrifying knowledge that his enemies always held the trump card: the minute they ordered him to the back room and pulled down his pants, it was over. This time she had declared herself a woman, and if the gender police took her in the back room, she could prove it.

"Which has been easier for you," I asked, "to be accepted as a woman after being born a man, or to be accepted as a Magyar after being born a Jew?"

My father thought about it for a few moments, holding her spoon before her like a hand mirror. "As a woman," she said. "Because I *am* a woman—with a birth certificate that says I'm a woman. So I must be a woman."

My father polished off the remains of the *gesztenyepüré*.

"So, is the inquisition over now?" She grinned and waved her spoon at me. "The Lives and Crimes of Stefánie Faludi! Oh my God!"

We filed out past the dust-laden fishing nets and into the night air. The Danube lay before us, obsidian in darkness. My father tugged at my sleeve.

"*Getting away with it*," she said. "Susaaan, don't forget that line. That's the key to it all. Because a lot of people got discovered that they were Jewish, and they were shot."

"It's a beautiful day," I said to my father. We'd been looking for hours at the latest videos she'd received from NASA, and I was desperate to get outside. "Why don't we take a walk in Pest?" I said, and then added, with as casual an air as I could muster, "You can show me the Kazinczy Street Synagogue"—the synagogue where my father and his parents had gone to services every Saturday morning.

"I've *told* you, I already went once to the Jewish quarter. I took Ilonka and we ate at that kosher restaurant. Such bland food! There's nothing more to see."

"But you didn't go to see your synagogue."

"Why would I want to do that? It was ruined."

"But they've rebuilt it." Albeit only recently—the synagogue had sat in its wartime rubble for decades and reopened only a few years ago.

"Waaall, it can't be the same as it was."

"How do you know if you've never been?"

Silence.

"Don't you want to see the place you went every weekend— *with your family?*"

"Waaall, my father wouldn't go to Dohány Synagogue because it had an organ. Too Christian."

I know, I said. "You told me."

"After services, we would walk down Kazinczy utca to Rákóczi út, to the Corso, and then we'd walk up and down, promenaaading." My father's slippered feet scuffed the floor, back and forth, in time with the memory. "The Christians promenaded there on Sunday, the Jews on Saturday," my father said. "Then we'd go home, and the maid would get the warmed *cholent* out of the oven from the bakery downstairs."

I nodded. I'd heard the story many times. It seemed like a good moment to close the deal. "So, let's go to the synagogue—we can walk on the Corso after."

My father considered.

"Yaaas, but," she said, "we can't. It's the Pentecost."

What?

"The *Pentecost*, deaaar. The end of the Easter season."

A synagogue closed for a Christian holiday? Unlikely. "Anyway," I pointed out, "today is Monday." The Pentecost was the day before.

"It's 'Pentecost Monday,' " my father said.

I pulled the keyboard onto my lap and speed-typed "Kazinczy Street Synagogue" into Google. I was looking for a phone number to prove her wrong. The website of the "Hidden Treasures Tours of Jewish Budapest" listed the synagogue's visiting hours—Monday–Thurs., 10–3:30—and noted that it closed only for Jewish High Holidays and "Hungarian national holidays," a phrase that was highlighted. When I clicked on the text, the list of federal Magyar holidays popped up. My father looked over my shoulder and pointed to a notation halfway down the page: *Pünkösdhétfő*, the Monday after Pentecost.

"I *told* you," she said smugly.

Two days later, I came down to breakfast and found on the kitchen counter, next to the coffee cups awaiting their morning brew, a slip of scrap paper. My father had jotted some notes on it in her looping Old European script, some Hungarian words I couldn't read, followed by "10–15:30."

She came into the room, dressed in a pale blue sheath and carrying her white pocketbook. "I was thinking," she said. "This might be a good day to go to Kazinczy."

You don't approach the Kazinczy Street Synagogue so much as stumble on it. The Orthodox house of worship is wedged into a corner of a maze of narrow streets and cobblestoned courtyards. If the Dohány Synagogue was the Versailles version of worship— its diva splendor primping before a wide plaza for maximum visibility—Kazinczy was its vestpocket secret sister.

The enclosed, almost medieval warren enveloping the synagogue was once a self-sufficient Orthodox community, containing the shul, *mikveh*, winter prayer room, kosher restaurant, kosher poultry butchery, kosher dairy, matzoh factory, apartments owned by the Orthodox community, outdoor wedding chuppah, an open water pipe for Jews to cast their sins into the sea on Rosh Hashanah, and a Jewish burial society. The morning we approached, the streets were deserted; the sound of our heels on the cobbled pavement echoed off the high stone walls. I followed my father up the four marble steps to the exposed red-brick facade with its high-arched windows and carved stone battlements. Above the wrought-iron doors was a prominently displayed symbol. Unlike Dohány's, this star had six, not eight, points. Inscribed in the frieze was Jacob's cry upon waking from his dream, the words displayed in Hebrew lettering: "This is none other than the abode of God, and that is the gateway to Heaven."

The interior was, in point of fact, heavenly, an exquisite chamber of serenity, eggshell-blue frescoes with menorahs and Stars of David on the walls, shafts of soothing blue light piercing the reticulated floral windows set into the ceiling. The floor plan was traditional, with the rostrum, or bimah, in the center of the room, and two staircases leading to the upper two galleries, the seating for women. There was no organ.

We had made it only a few steps past the threshhold when a short balding man in a knee-length gray coat and a *chai* symbol dangling from a chain around his neck hurried over to see who was disturbing the peace. He was the shammes, the synagogue's caretaker, and we were his first and, at least for the time that we were there, his only visitors that day. He glanced at my father, then reached into a basket and fished out a plain blue cloth. My father studied it with momentary perplexity. Then the shammes leaned over and draped it around my father's bare shoulders. The color, I noted, matched her dress.

I asked how big the current congregation was. My father translated and the shammes said that the building could seat 500 men downstairs, 500 women in the galleries, but that most services were attended by no more than 150 people in the summer—many of them foreign visitors—and as few as 30 in the winter. "The community is very small because a lot of people living here during Communism lost their Jewishness," he said. "They were afraid they would lose their jobs and endanger their families if they would go to synagogue. . . . And, of course, many were killed or deported in the Shoah." He pointed to a framed image hanging by the entrance: a photograph of the ruins of the synagogue in 1944, a heap of splintered wood, shattered glass.

My father revealed that she came here as a child. The shammes brightened. They began to reminisce. They discussed the synagogue's former illustrious rabbi, Koppel Reich, who presided over the 1905 convention that codified the rules of the Hungarian Orthodox community and, at 89, was elected representative to the Upper House of the Hungarian Parliament in 1927, the year of my father's birth. My father recalled how the synagogue used to be "air conditioned" in the summer—with buckets of ice poured inside the floor vents. "Very modern!" And she remembered the crabby shammes who was always shushing the children.

"He was this giant, with a long beard," my father said. "He would scare the kids to death, yelling, '*Shah! Shah!*' "

The shammes laughed. "We still do!" he said.

After a while, the caretaker returned to his duties and invited us to make ourselves at home. My father and I wandered up the aisle.

"Where did you used to sit?" I asked.

"Ssshh!" my father said. "It's a good thing he doesn't understand English."

I realized my stupidity: my father used to sit downstairs.

We toured the perimeter, admiring the wall frescoes ("The colors are even brighter than when I was a child!" my father marveled), and paying our respects to Rabbi Reich's chair, which stood to the left of the ark, retired in homage to his eminence. After a while, my father walked down the right aisle. She stopped at the fourth center row, deliberating. Then she made her way to the fifth chair and sat down. I followed and perched beside her.

"These were the Friedman seats," she said in a low voice, patting the arms of my chair and hers: Jenő's and István's. Rozi sat upstairs. Congregants paid for specific seats, my father explained, and the better the location, the more they cost. These were considered to be among the best. She reached in front and lifted the lid of a small wooden compartment. "This is where we'd keep our prayer books and tallis."

My father touched her head, a nervous gesture. "I've never been in a synagogue without a kippah," she said. "It's okay, I get used to things in ten minutes."

She pulled the blue cloth tighter around her shoulders. "At first, I didn't know why he was giving me this shawl," she said. "I thought I was supposed to cover my head, like a burka. I thought, Oh my God, I'm in the wrong place!"

We both laughed and then we sat for a few moments in companionable silence, gazing at the gleaming marble-columned enclosure of the ark, and the bas-relief emblem above it, of two hands held out to deliver the ancient Sabbath benediction. My father held out her own hands in imitation, then lifted them above my head.

"*Ye'varech'echa Adonoy ve'yish'merecha,*" she said. "*Ya'ir*

Adonoy panav eilecha viy' chuneka. Yisa Adonoy panav eilecha, ve'yasim lecha shalom."

My father's religiously illiterate daughter had to ask for a translation.

"May God bless you and protect you. May God's face shine toward you and show you favor. May God look favorably upon you and grant you peace."

It was the blessing parents said over their children on Sabbath. There were other blessings that were specific for sons or daughters, my father said, but this was the one for both sexes.

She fell silent again.

"I was very upset that time," she said after a while. "In Yorktown. . . . When you wanted to see the priest to become a Christian."

I waited. We had never discussed that night. I had never brought it up. I'd figured she'd long ago filed it in that mental safe-deposit case of memories she refused to revisit.

I created you. And I can destroy you.

"Do you remember what you said to me?" I asked.

"I remember exactly what I said," she answered. "That they exterminated the Jews. And how could you do this?"

I didn't correct her. Whatever the actual words, I understood, this is what they meant to her.

She looked down at her hands, resting now in her lap. "I shouldn't have been so angry," she said.

I reached over and squeezed her wrist. "It's okay," I said.

A few minutes later, we stood up and made our way to the entrance. My father had remembered a café she was partial to, just a short walk from here, outside the old Jewish quarter. "They make excellent Viennese cakes."

24

The Pregnancy of the World

In 2014, *Time* magazine hailed the "Transgender Tipping Point" in a cover story that, with a thousand concurring stories from all corners of the media, enshrined gender identity as the cutting edge of civil rights. That same year, the United Nations passed a resolution condemning discrimination and violence based on gender identity, and governmental bodies from the Danish and Dutch parliaments to the New York state legislature and New York City mayoral office proclaimed the right of citizens to change their birth certificates to match their chosen gender, even without surgery.

The drumroll continued into 2015, when President Obama tweeted Caitlyn Jenner to commend her "courage" (hours after she appeared in a satin corset on the cover of *Vanity Fair*), and transgender rights became a slogan on the presidential campaign trail. In the media, trans identity was fast solidifying into an emblematic narrative, with all the requisite tropes of victimization, heroism, and celebrity. Rarely did the fanfare convey the daily texture of complicated ordinary lives.

In the summer of that year, I received a letter from Mel Myers, who, back when he was Melanie, ran Melanie's Cocoon, the guest house in Phuket, Thailand, where my father had recovered from her operation in 2004. Mel had finally succeeded in moving his longtime Thai girlfriend to the United States, but at a cost. "When it came time to bring her to America and get married, I had to transition back to male," Mel wrote. "My facial feminization surgery is covered with a beard, my reassignment surgery makes bathroom trips awkward, and I cover my beautiful breasts with loose fitting clothes." He said that sometimes he wished he'd continued as Melanie and sometimes he wished he'd hadn't had the operation in the first place, "now that I find myself living in limbo. . . . I had my previous life as a male, I had my life as Melanie, and now I have my life as neither male nor female or both female and male." He remembered the time when she, as Melanie, had served as "a poster child of sorts, someone who trans girls would look to for guidance and encouragement," but those days were in the past.

He and his now wife had opened a Thai restaurant in the suburbs, and Mel was making ends meet working for the TriMet transit authority. "I see all walks of life driving a city bus. They're little snapshots of humanity, like a quick line sketch of life, it catches life's essence. I see myself reflected sometimes. It is enlightening sometimes and sometimes it is kind of scary," he wrote. "I gave up a lot to be who I am."

Back in my father's motherland, as in the U.S. media, questions of identity were in full flower. The ruling Fidesz Party celebrated 2014 as the rebirth of Hungarian identity. That spring, the rightist party won the national elections again, and handily—with an assist from the newly minted media law, which stifled the independence of state-financed media, and with the manipulation of electoral rules that allowed Fidesz to secure a two-thirds parliamentary majority with only 44.5 percent of the vote. Jobbik, the openly anti-Semitic and anti-Roma party, expanded its base even further, nearly edging out the long-standing Socialist Party in the Hungarian Parliament and becoming the most popular far-right party in the European Union.

Fidesz also swept the European Parliament election that year (and Jobbik came in second). And in the municipal elections that fall, Fidesz won control of every county assembly and all but one of the largest cities, including Budapest. When the polls closed in October, Fidesz leaders celebrated their party's electoral trifecta. "Three is the Hungarian truth," Prime Minister Viktor Orbán exulted in a speech that day, invoking the (Latin) maxim that "everything that comes in threes is perfect." The party's triple victory, Orbán declared, solidified a national "unity" and would "make Hungary great in the next four years."

Four months earlier, the Hungarian Supreme Court had issued a ruling in support of the identity prerogatives of the political right. The court found that a TV news channel had violated the media law's ban on opinionated press commentary by describing the far-right Jobbik as . . . far right. Jobbik's lawyers had argued that "far right" didn't fit the party's chosen identity, which was "Christian nationalist." The judges concurred: "Jobbik doesn't consider itself an extreme-right party, thus referring to it with the adjective 'far right' constitutes an act of expressing an opinion, making it possible for the viewer to associate it with a radical movement and induce a negative impression." The court's ruling continued, in words that could have been lifted from the identity-sensitive speech codes of a college campus or the "Preferred Gender Pronoun" directives of the blogosphere: "Even a single word, a single epithet, may exert influence on the viewer."

On the world stage, criticism of the Hungarian government was reaching a fever pitch: the European Commission had threatened to take legal action against Hungary for undermining the independence of its judiciary and central bank; fifty U.S. congressmen had signed a letter to Orbán demanding that he condemn Jobbik's "anti-Semitic and homophobic positions"; and media outlets around the globe were calling the nation an "autocracy," the "EU's only dictatorship," and, in the words of one German newpaper, the new "Führerstaat." Orbán was eager to turn the page. His administration hired the high-powered New York public relations firm of Burson-Marsteller to reengineer its image. The Hungarian government vowed to prove its critics wrong: it would make 2014 "Holocaust Remembrance Year," officially commemorating the seventieth anniversary of the destruction of Hungarian Jewry. "2014 must be the year for facing up to the fact and for apologizing," János Lázár, Orbán's state secretary and chief administrator of the initiative, asserted at a press conference to unveil the nation's makeover. "We must make the apology a part of our national identity." To that end, Fidesz announced that it would open a new museum about Jewish persecution in Hungary and erect memorials and exhibitions to pay respect to the ordeal of Hungarian Jews.

But plans for a Jewish-friendly "national identity" year were soon unraveling. To direct the new museum of Jewish persecution— the House of Fates (installed in a defunct train station and devoted exclusively to "child victims")—the government appointed Mária Schmidt, Orbán's historical adviser who also directed the House of Terror, the museum that had shrunk the Holocaust to a footnote. After Jewish organizations protested her selection, Schmidt unleashed a full-throated attack on these "left-liberal opinion leaders" who use "intellectual terror" and "prescribe whom we can mourn and whom we can't, for whom we can shed a tear and for whom we can't." By such behavior, "they exclude themselves from our national community." Meanwhile, the Orbán government inaugurated another establishment, the Veritas Research Institute for History, to produce a history of Hungary's last century that would "strengthen national identity." Placed at its helm was right-wing military historian Sándor Szakály, who promptly declared that the 1941 Hungarian government's deportation of eighteen thousand

Jews to the Ukraine (where they were massacred by SS and Ukrainian militia) was just "a police action against aliens."

Then the prime minister's office unveiled plans for a monument to be erected during Holocaust Remembrance Year in Freedom Square, dedicated to "all the victims of the 19 March 1944 German invasion of Hungary." What "all" meant became clear when the government issued a drawing of the monument's design: An imperial eagle representing the Third Reich savagely descends on an innocent and helpless Hungary in the form of the archangel Gabriel. Prime Minister Orbán described the monument as "morally precise and immaculate."

Some months after the monument's erection, I would stop on my way through Freedom Square to inspect the results. The swooping German eagle was even more supersized than the drawing had suggested, and more garish, a cartoon bird of prey with armor-plate feathers. The archangel Gabriel was a supplicant, hands held up in surrender, his delicate and bare-breasted frame a study in feminine vulnerability and innocence. Pity, O God, the Hungarian. A few feet away, a homemade counter-memorial by Holocaust survivors and the families of victims protested that assertion of innocence with a display of cracked eyeglasses, empty suitcases, and photographs of murdered relatives.

The ruling party responded to such criticism with outrage. János Lázár, the state secretary who had promised that 2014 would be a year of "apologizing" for the Holocaust, accused Jewish leaders of ruining the government's commemoration and "fomenting discord between Hungarians and Jews who have lived in unity and symbiosis for centuries." The House of Fates director Mária Schmidt chimed in again with her own tirade: "To let international Jewish organizations have a say without having contributed a single penny to the costs of setting up the institution is contrary to the responsibility of the sovereign Hungarian state for its own past, present, and future." Those who disagree "fail to understand that this time we are dealing with our very identity."

In August 2014, a month before I was due to fly to Budapest, I got an e-mail from my father. It contained a link, which read: www.szimsalom.hu. I called up the Web page, but it was a sea of Hungarian—and a bit of Hebrew.

"What's this?" I wrote back. I received no answer. My father, for all her enthusiasm for the Internet, rarely responded to e-mails. She preferred the phone.

Some days later, she called.

"What was that link?" I asked.

"A synagogue. Waaall, Reform. But still."

"Still, what?"

"Where it *is*."

I called up the link again and scanned the impossible words, looking for an address. It was in small print:

Szim Salom Progresszív Zsidó Hitközség
1092 Budapest
Ráday u. 9.

I was astounded. A Reform synagogue had set up shop in a flat in my father's childhood home.

"Vaaary Reform," my father said. "Did you see? They have a lady rabbi." Indeed. Katalin Kelemen was the first female rabbi in Hungary.

"It must be small," my father ruminated, "to meet in an apartment."

"We should go see."

When I arrived in Budapest and walked into my father's kitchen,

I saw two things laid out on the counter. One was a set of tickets for Szim Salom's Rosh Hashanah dinner. My visit had coincided with the Jewish New Year. The other item was a palm-sized book with a fraying embossed cover.

"May I?" I asked. She nodded.

I picked up the tiny volume and leafed gingerly through frail yellowing pages of Hebrew type. It was the prayer book, gilt-edged and cloth-bound, that my father had pulled out of the box in the cellar to show her cousin Peter Gordon.

"My mother's," my father said. "When my mother died, the relatives in Israel sent this to me. . . . The relatives who wouldn't give me the deeds to my father's property. I had to get—"

"How old is this?" I interrupted. I turned to the front to look for a date, then remembered I was holding a Hebrew text. A bookplate had been pasted inside the back cover. Its Hebrew lettering and block-print illustration of a rabbi reading the Torah was accompanied by two handwritten inscriptions: first, in Hebrew, "Chaim David Ben Yitzhak Elimelech Sinai," then, in Hungarian, "Friedman István."

My father looked over my shoulder. I heard a sudden drawn-in breath.

"Oh my God," she said. "This is not my mother's."

The book belonged to her son. My father ran a finger over the letters at the bottom of the page. "This says that it was presented to me on the occasion of my bar mitzvah at the Jewish Gymnasium." Presented at the bar mitzvah that István's parents had failed to attend.

A few mornings later, my father and I climbed the wide steps of the Hungarian National Museum, which was participating in the Holocaust Rembrance Year. For two hours we navigated the vast maze of the museum's second floor, where the official history of Hungary unfolded in twenty marbled rooms. Eventually we arrived in the World War II room, a gallery devoted to the principle that wartime Hungary had no agency. The country was "practically defenseless," exhibit signage attested. Hungarians had to join the Axis because "there was no other power from which a revision of the Trianon treaty could be expected." In other words, they had to collaborate with the Nazis to get their property back. I cast a glance at my Fidesz father. The memorabilia relating to Jewish annihilation pointed largely to German culpability: a photo of Eichmann striking a Jewish man, SS regalia, a dummy of a Gestapo officer on a very real BMW motorbike. Two small plaques addressed the Hungarian deportations and the home-brewed brutality of the Arrow Cross with obscure indirection. ("Following the Nazi takeover on October 15, 1944, even those under protection were defenceless against the Nazi authorities and the different armed groups.") The signs were hung low; I had to crouch to read them.

My father insisted we skip the next round of rooms, devoted to the Communist period. "The Communists ruined Hungary. Why should I look at them?" We descended three flights to the basement level, where ancient history and the Roman ruins resided. In the corridor leading to the Bronze Age, a placard in a doorway caught my father's eye. It read, "Survivors." We stepped in and found a small windowless room, housing a temporary exhibit. On the walls were a series of portraits by Israeli photographer Aliza Auerbach. The subjects were Holocaust survivors and their descendants. This was the exhibit the museum had mounted for Holocaust Remembrance Year.

My father gazed around the room in confusion, Alice fallen down the rabbit hole. She walked over to the first portrait and, without my prompting, began to translate the accompanying text into English. It was an account from a Hungarian Jewish survivor

born a year later than my father. Her birth name was Dina Friedman. No relation, my father said. "As far as we know."

Dina and her family had been deported to Auschwitz at the end
of May 1944, along with the five thousand Jews who lived in the
northeastern county capital town of Nyíregyháza. "There we lost
our parents and our humanity was stolen from us," my father read,
and her voice echoed through the nearly empty room. "It never
occurred to us to return to Hungary." It was a long testimony. After a
few minutes, a museum guard came over and suggested that my
father buy the text in the gift shop instead of reading it out loud here.
My father gave her a cutting look and carried on with the translation. My mind was reeling back to our visit to the Jewish Museum
in 2004, ten years earlier, when the Holocaust Room exhibition had
only aroused her dismissal—"This is of no interest!"—and her irrita-
tion at a "braying" Israeli tour guide. Now her eyes were burning.

We made a slow circuit of the room. My father came to a halt
in front of a color photograph of the descendants of Dina Friedman Kol in Israel. Sixteen grandchildren and six great-grandchildren
were gathered around the aged couple in a clearing in the Jerusalem Forest.

"Let the people in Hungary look at them!" my father burst out.
"They turned their back. They said, 'Waaall, it's none of our business.' They never looked at who was taken. These people were just
like them. They spoke the same language. They were your neighbors. They were your friends. And you let them die! These were
the ones you allowed to die! Let them look, so they can go home
and not sleep in peace."

She said she'd seen enough.

I followed her up to the lobby and down the ceremonial steps.
By the time we reached the street, she was already second-guessing
her reaction, retreating from the most heartfelt passion for her
people's fate—and her own—that I'd ever heard her express.

"Waaall, there were a few who were righteous," she said. Christian Hungarians, she meant. "Like the doctor who gave my father his apartment," the Ráday 9 apartment where Jenő and István hid in the late spring and early summer of '44, while the physician and his family were vacationing at Lake Balaton. "And I could tell it from the other side," my father continued.

"What other side?"

"The point of view of the people in this country. From their point of view, the Germans did it. And the Jews brought it on themselves. Our family bought real estate in Hamburg when there was the economic crisis, and sold it when it got better, and that's how my father founded his wealth."

"So what?"

"So, I'm just giving their point of view."

We walked half a block before she spoke again.

"But to have that exhibit *in the National Museum*! Fantastic. It's very praiseworthy." After a few more paces, as if in response to another voice in her head, "Waaall, but it's in the cellar." My father gave a rueful snort. "If they had a visitors' book, I would write in it, 'Thank you! Thank you for putting the Jews in the cellar!' "

On the afternoon of September 24, my father and I took the bus into Pest. My father wore a tweed skirt and a dark pullover sweater that covered her arms; I wore a shawl over a long-sleeved dress and black tights. We both had on low pumps. We were on our way to ring in the Jewish New Year of 5775.

It was with an uneasy sense of déjà vu that I stood before the heavy double doors of Ráday 9 with my father and searched the address roster for the right bell to ring. When I hit the buzzer for the synagogue, it rang and rang.

"No one's there," my father said. "Let's go. I know a place we can get coffee, and their cakes are . . ." Here we go again, I thought. Another abortive trip to the natal home.

Just then, and as if in replay of our last visit, the door flew open and a resident breezed past. This time my father grabbed the handle. We slipped inside. The creaking and still patched elevator took us up a level. We turned left and followed the balcony that rings the inner courtyard to apartment #2.

"My God," my father said. She was staring in disbelief at the door. "This is the same apartment."

"Same as?"

"The doctor's." It was the apartment where my father and grandfather took cover in the late spring and early summer of 1944.

I heard footsteps and, to my great relief, the door opened. A cheerful and slightly frayed middle-aged woman stood on the other side. Edit Kovács introduced herself—she was the synagogue's shammes, as well as its cook, bookkeeper, librarian, and house-keeper. She apologized; she had been mopping the floor in the back of the apartment and hadn't heard the buzzer.

My father explained, in a rush of Hungarian, that her father used to own this building, that she'd grown up here, that she'd spent two months in hiding during the war in this very apartment. Edit spoke no English, but her moist eyes transcended language. She took my father's arm and drew us inside. My father and I gazed around. Two interior walls had been knocked down to make space for the main sanctuary. A lectern was set up at one end, a painting of the tree of life behind it. A wardrobe doubled as an ark. A cabinet held menorahs and seder plates. The back wall displayed photos of the old Jewish quarter in Budapest, taken by Szim Salom's youth group. At the other end of the apartment, a small room had been set up as a library, devoted to religious books and guides to Jewish sites in Hungary. The passage between the two had been converted to a social hall, with a folding table in the middle, walls adorned with children's drawings. An easel showcased Hebrew letters, drawn in finger paint.

That's what I saw. My father saw something else.

"This was the dining room," she said, poking her head into the library. "There was a grandfather clock right here. It had to be wound every night."

In the sanctuary, my father paced up and down the old parquet floor. "This is where I slept," she said, stopping by a row of folding chairs, "in the middle bedroom." Whose dividing walls had since been removed.

"How many people come to services?" I asked Edit.

"For the bigger holidays," she said, my father translating, "it can be forty or fifty. But usually it's no more than twenty-five. Sometimes only ten."

My father went to inspect the back corner. "This is where the radio was," she said. "This is where we'd listen to the BBC. With the sound turned down very low." This is where my father and grandfather heard that the Friedman family of Kassa had been deported.

I asked Edit how she'd come to join Szim Salom.

"I was Jewish but I didn't know it," she said.

"You weren't raised Jewish?"

"It was the Socialist era," she said. "Many people were hiding their Jewishness." She gave a sad smile. Her parents, she recalled, would light candles on Friday and Saturday nights, and have some sort of ceremony to which only their relatives would come. "But they didn't tell me what it was about. I thought it was just a family custom."

Edit was well into her thirties before she learned the truth. "My mother told me. She just said it, like, 'Oh, by the way, we're Jews.'" Edit received the news as revelation. "I always felt there was something different about me, but I didn't know what it was," she said. "I couldn't adapt to other people. I felt things differently."

She began to read up on Judaism, and a friend directed her to Bálint House, the one Jewish community center in Hungary. More recently, she discovered Szim Salom. It felt comfortable and welcoming, she said, and she liked its politics. From a stack of papers on the folding table, she extracted an English-language statement of Szim Salom's principles. They included: "We welcome everybody, regardless of his/her familiarity with Jewish liturgy and tradition"; "We reject any fundamentalist approach to Jewish tradition"; and "We affirm equal rights for women and men to participate in all aspects of religious life." I pointed to the last statement and gave her a thumbs-up. She returned my enthusiasm with a big smile.

Szim Salom had been established only two decades ago, the first Jewish Reform community in Hungary. Its organizers had applied for formal recognition from the state, a requirement for public funding. The request was denied. "They told us," Edit said, "'You can't be recognized because you don't have a cemetery, you don't have a school, you don't have this, you don't have that.' But we didn't have the *money* to make a school and a cemetery. If we got recognition, we could get support. We could buy a place to have a permanent synagogue." Instead, in the last twenty years, Szim Salom had moved from one apartment and storefront to another, wanderers at the whim of various landlords. Right now, they were renting from a man who owned two flats in Ráday 9. He lived in the other one, next door. How long he'd allow them to stay, no one knew.

"These people are thieves," my father put in. "They are trafficking in stolen goods." She switched to Hungarian and talked for a long time. I didn't ask for a translation. I could tell it was my father's diatribe about our family's lost real estate.

Edit listened patiently, nodding every once in a while. When my father paused to take a breath, Edit interjected that her grandmother had owned a store in Buda before World War II. It sold glass and dishware. "They took it away from our family, too," she said. She led us to the reception area and the folding table where a large leather-bound volume sat. It was their guest book. "Would you sign it?" she asked. My father sat down and deliberated, then wrote for a while in her old-fashioned Hungarian lettering.

"What did you say?" I asked.

"I was very surprised," she translated, "to see that at my father's house, there is now a synagogue. I found it on the Internet. I will keep the connection. *Toda raba*." She looked up at me. "That means 'Thank you very much' in Hebrew." She had signed it, the traditional Hungarian way, last name first: "Faludi Stefánie."

My father checked her watch. "Oh, it's already five o'clock," she said. We had to rush. Rosh Hashanah services and dinner to follow were being held across town at a hotel. Szim Salom was expecting a larger-than-usual turnout; the flat at Ráday 9 was too small.

The Hotel Benczúr was a generic modern conference center in the upper-crust embassy district that runs alongside Andrássy út, a few blocks from Heroes' Square. Shadows were lengthening as we came up from the subway's Millennium Underground line. The first thing I saw was the archangel Gabriel, perched on the thirty-six-meter-high pillar of Heroes' Square's Millennial Monument, the Holy Crown of Saint Stephen in one hand, the double-barred apostolic cross in the other. After two blocks we turned off Andrássy and walked the smaller silent streets girded by palatial consulates. Their formidable facades stared down at us from behind iron gates. My father grew nervous, then accusatory. "I thought you said you looked at a map," she said. "This can't be the right way. There's nothing here. We should go back."

I said I was sure. "Just two and a half more blocks."

"I told you, this isn't right. This is not a Jewish area."

We turned the corner, and I pointed to a string of twinkling lights: the entrance to the Hotel Benczúr. We headed toward the revolving door behind two teenage girls, dark-haired and in formal dress. My father eyed them. "Do they look Jewish?" she murmured to herself.

The services were in the Budapest Room, a conference room off a corridor lined with identical suites. The space was shoebox-shaped, antiseptic, and harshly lit. Two folding tables had been set up on the far end. Metal stacking chairs ran in rows down the middle. The ceremonies had just started. An usher handed us the text for the evening, a sheath of Xeroxed stapled pages. My father grimaced. "This is *not* a prayer book," she grumbled as we headed down the aisle.

We took seats toward the back. I noted with dismay the many available chairs. I counted about seventy attendees, including several children, two infants, and a dog. The services were informal. Rabbi Katalin Kelemen, a tolerant woman with a sensible bowl haircut and laughing eyes, smiled encouragingly at the speakers, no matter how badly they mauled their Hebrew recitations, and doled out hugs and kisses. Most of the assembled, as was evident even to my untutored ear, were new to Judaism. Like me, they picked their way awkwardly through the Shema and its blessings— the call to learning, the charge to remember the liberation from Egypt, the promise of prosperity. One congregant wasn't having trouble with the words: the one seated next to me.

The cantor rose to sing a haunting melody. The Torah scrolls were taken from the ark and placed on a lectern, and the rabbi invited some young people from the audience to help with the holiday's readings: Isaac's miraculous birth to Sarah, who at the age of ninety had given up hope of bearing a child, and Abraham's near sacrifice of their son, his hand stayed by an intervening angel. "This is a controversial story," Rabbi Kelemen said, my father whispering a translation in my ear. "We need to not just accept it. It's good to debate." Then a young woman was called up front to

conclude with the evening's haftarah passage: the prayer of the bar-
ren Hannah, despondent because she has no children, whose appeal
to God was answered on Rosh Hashanah. "And in due time Hannah conceived and bore a son, and she called his name Samuel, for
she said, 'I have asked for him from the Lord.'"

Rosh Hashanah is also known as Ha'rat Olam, the Pregnancy
of the World. The Jewish New Year celebrates the birth of the universe, but other births as well. So many of the prayers involve
pregnancy, motherhood, a yearning for children—Sarah's, Hannah's,
Rachel's. I looked over at my father, who was sitting very still.
And thought: What of your mother, Stefi, who grieved the loss of
two newborns before she had you, yet left her only child with
nannies and nursemaids and went out on the town every night?
And what of your father, who left you to fend for yourself on the
streets of wartime Budapest? Who didn't come to your bar mitzvah? Who wrote in his will, "To my son, István Faludi, one lira"?
And what of your daughter, who didn't have the grandchildren
you wished for, and who let you evict her from your life until, by
an act of extraordinary reinvention or reassertion, you invited her
back in?

I pulled out my notebook to scribble down some thoughts. A
hand flew down and pounced on my pen. "Stop writing!" she hissed
in my ear. "It's not allowed on Holy Days." Chagrined, I returned
my notebook to my purse. Even in this anything-goes Reform ceremony, I was getting the fundaments wrong.

The rabbi rose to give long-winded remarks. The audience
became restive. The children behind us began to whisper and
giggle. On the other side of the aisle, the dog let out a loud yap,
and everyone laughed. Everyone except my father. "It's not funny,"
she said. "This is a serious occasion, and they are mocking it."

When the Torah was carried down the aisle, my father nudged
me to touch my shawl to the scroll's sheathing and kiss it. An elderly

man was summoned to the front to blow the shofar. And then the services closed, per tradition, on the mourner's Kaddish.

The rabbi invited everyone to proceed to the banquet hall for dinner. My father picked up the photocopied "prayer book," then put it back down on the chair, then picked it up again.

"I think it's okay to take that," I said.

"I only want the last page," she replied. She carefully pulled the final sheet off the staple, folded it, and put it in her purse. "I want to say Kaddish," she told me. "For my parents."

We joined the others heading down the corridor. I found myself walking beside the rabbi's husband, an American. He asked what I was doing here. I said I was visiting.

"So, you are related?" he said, pointing to my father. I nodded. "But you don't speak Hungarian?" he said.

"Susan was born in the United States," my father interjected, in English. "When I used to live there."

"Ah, so you are"—the rabbi's husband looked at my father—"her grandmother?"

"No," my father said. "I am her . . ." She left it to me to finish the sentence.

I paused, not wanting to get into explications, yet also not wanting to cause any pain. One way or another, I thought, an identity would be denied.

". . . mother," I said.

A Kaddish for a parent, indeed.

25

Escape

In 2004 I set out to pursue the stranger who was my father. I didn't anticipate a laying down of arms, nor did I achieve one. In the years to come, our relationship would lurch from contention to détente to contention again. But by the fall of 2014, when we ushered in the imminent Jewish New Year in the room where my father had hidden as a teenage fugitive, we seemed to have arrived at an understanding, even a closeness. The accord came just in time. When I visited her that September, my father was as lucid and strong as I'd ever seen her. Less than half a year later, her constitution was in ruins.

They say that dementia is a disintegration of the self, a bleeding away of identity. Watching it take over my father's life that winter, I was tempted to think of it as the opposite: an onrush of all that she had been, all that she had experienced, suffered, fled. The paranoia and hallucinations afflicting her were rooted in the realities of her past, the histories she had walled off. Those histories now flooded into every synapse. My father's mind seemed to me like the limestone beneath Castle Hill; it was being hollowed out by what welled up from below. She thought that her mother was sleeping in the room next to hers. She thought that her ex-wife had come to see her in Budapest. She thought that she was living in the old summer villa down the block, that Nazis were battering down her front door. One late night in February 2015, my father's shouts that criminals were breaking into the house brought the police and then an ambulance, which escorted its unwilling passenger to a hospital. She spent an uncomfortable night in a chair in a corridor of the ER, with nurses and doctors asking "stupid things." Near dawn, she gave them the slip and hailed a cab.

"I cscaaaped!" my father gloated when I reached her on the phone later that day. She sounded her usual self, preening over her aptitude for evasion, filibustering without apology, recasting traumatic experience as escapade. "A to-do over nothing!" she said. "They put me in a horrible ambulance, very unusable. Everything squeaking and shaking all over the place, I thought the wheels were coming off. It took forever to get there, aaand . . ." Her monologue culminated with a report on an endless taxi ride home and a final feat of deception: not only had she skipped out on the hospital, she'd skipped out on the fare.

"Waaall," my father said when I pressed her on why she'd fled the hospital's care, "they pretended it was for my own good. But that's not the reason."

"So what is?"

"At the hospital, they kept asking, 'So, do you *believe* you're a woman?' They didn't seem to know that we are in the late twentieth century."

"Early twenty-first," I corrected.

"They have old ways of thinking. They don't like trans people."

Later that day, she settled on a new reason for her incarceration. "I got through this crisis, the other time—I always protected myself," she told me when we talked again. "I thought I was away from danger. I thought I had escaped them."

"Who?"

"These people who broke in, the police, the ambulance people, the people who called these people. I realize who they are: typical Arrow Cross. They think it's a crime, what I am. They see me and they are saying, 'You are a Jew.'"

If identity is the one thing you can't escape, my father's dementia presented her identity in concentrated form, relentless as a posse. "Did we fly to Israel this morning?" she asked me when I arrived in Budapest shortly after her "escape" from the hospital. "The plane was hipping and hopping, but when I looked out the window, it was the same view as here." The question at least displayed a remnant of self-skepticism. The more my father deteriorated, the more certain she became that her psychic landscape was real. A technician who arrived to repair her broadband Internet service was an undercover spy altering her online identity. Hordes of night intruders were storming through her house, rifling through kitchen cabinets and bureau drawers and her purse, painting the walls in invisible ink, and replicating all her books, Hans Christian Andersen volumes proliferating on every shelf.

My attempts to persuade her to accept assistance or come to the United States for treatment met with fury. "Get this circus out of here! Leave or I'll call the police!" she yelled when I arrived in February with her primary-care doctor and a home nursing service in tow; she chased me down the hall with a flurry of punches. The hallucinations were true because she believed them to be true. There was no use reasoning—she was adamant, impervious to logic. Sometime between her first breakdown in February and her final one in May, I learned not to argue. It seemed to relieve her when I entered into her mental road map, acknowledged her perceptions, no matter how fantastical.

One afternoon as we talked on the phone, my father brought up, apropos nothing, Tivadar Puskás, Thomas Edison's assistant.

"Waaall, a Hungarian came up with the telephone greeting."

Yes, I said, she'd mentioned Puskás before.

"'Hallo' means 'I'm listening.' "

Yes, I said, she'd told me.

"Hey listener!" my father said, laughing, and then her words turned earnest. "You are the one who listens to me."

And so I listened. Yes, I'd say, how awful to have strangers flocking through your house at night. Yes, how exasperating that your mother has installed herself in the guest room. Yes, the ambulance driver must be a card-carrying Arrow Cross officer. And yes, I said in early May, when I reached my father by phone in the psychiatric ward of St. János Hospital. Yes, it's terrible that someone sneaked into the basement and tried to burn the house down.

From the phone by her hospital bed, my father described to me the events of the previous night: She'd noticed a light on in the cellar and crept down the stairs to investigate. A man was standing by the gas tank, "blowing on the gas valve," attempting to start a fire. My father confronted him. "He wouldn't say anything," she recounted. "He wouldn't identify himself." She locked the arsonist in the cellar, ran back upstairs, and called the police. "But the police mixed everything up," she said. They took her away instead. "Which I violently opposed. I saved the house from burning down, and I am being punished for putting out the fire. It's aaabsolutely ridiculous. I save the lives of people and the least I ask for saving a life is don't throw me to the wolves. I'm the good guy. They totally miscast me. You need to talk to these doctors and get it all cleared up." Yes, I said, and bought a plane ticket.

From the taxi stand on Diósárok út, St. János Hospital looks like a Victorian asylum of the "moral architecture" variety, its Gothic brick-and-stone dormitories ranged sociably around landscaped grounds gone slightly to seed, gnarled vines crawling up the crumbling facades, a chapel to the patron saint of sick paupers stationed at the main entrance. I had stood outside these wrought-iron gates many times before, waiting to catch a ride up the hill to my father's house. The #59 tram terminates across the street from St. János, and when the connecting bus was late, I'd grab a cab at the hospital. But on the afternoon of May 13, I passed through the gates and hauled my luggage up four flights of dirty stairs—there was no elevator—and headed toward the internal-medicine ward.

From within, St. János appeared more Bedlam than beneficent. Years of draconian budget cuts had taken their toll. Many of the nurses were threatening to strike, protesting their paltry wages, which were one-tenth of their European counterparts. The bathrooms had no soap and no toilet paper. Patients were expected to bring their own. Likewise with dishes and utensils. I hurried down a long corridor and veered into a small overpacked room, its eight beds occupied by acutely ill women. It was unseasonably hot for May, and there was no air-conditioning. The late afternoon sun beat through a cranked-open window.

My father lay atop a thin mattress on what looked like an old army cot. She wore a frayed hospital gown and gave off the musky odor of someone who hadn't been bathed. She was half her size, or so she seemed to me. Her eyes were sealed shut, lips livid and cracked, her mouth frozen open in a grimace. She appeared to be comatose and breathed with a terrible rasp.

"I don't understand," I said, the hysteria rising in my voice. My father's neighbor and friend, Ágnes, who was accompanying me, did her best to translate my frantic rush of words into Hungarian. An orderly replied with a shrug, beads of sweat on his brow. "What's happened to her?" I asked. "Where's her doctor?" I stroked my father's thin arm, smoothed her hair, a wild unwashed tangle. On the night table, beside a canister of opened but untouched yogurt, sat a plastic sip cup with a name written shakily in Magic Marker, "Stefi."

The doctor, the orderly said, wouldn't be in until eight p.m. "Come back later," Ágnes translated.

"Stefi?" I whispered, laying aside the Lindt chocolates and P. Howard pulp novels I'd brought to cheer her up. "Stefi, can you hear me?" She gave no response. "Stefi, please wake up. It's Susan. Talk to me."

Four hours later, the doctor appeared. The room was dark now, a radio announcer chattering from a boom box on the other side of the ward. My father's breath came in guttering gasps. Her condition hadn't improved.

Dr. Anna Mária Molnárné advised me (though she spoke English) to relay my questions through Ágnes and answered them in streams of Hungarian, not meeting my eye.

"Maybe gallbladder inflammation," Ágnes summarized.

Another flood of words.

"Maybe an infection. Or it could be a little stroke." Ágnes hesitated. "The doctor says, 'You should prepare yourself for the worst.'"

I returned that night to my father's house. The doctor's words hadn't sunk in, or rather, I hadn't let them. I was thinking I needed some sleep to prepare for tomorrow's rounds: a morning appointment with a dementia-care specialist, a strategy phone session with a home nurse I'd hired, an afternoon consultation with a guardianship lawyer. I was plotting how to spring my father from St. János. I let myself in the front door—blessedly, in the haste of her forced departure, she hadn't armed the burglar alarm—and wandered through the silent rooms. I'd never been in the place alone. I'd so often felt confined here by my father's overweening presence. Now her absence overwhelmed me. I opened the fridge, considered the pizza that Ágnes had kindly left for me, closed the door again. I wasn't hungry. I climbed the dark wooden stairs to bed.

Toward morning, a nightmare gripped me, a terrible one. In the dream, I am lying in bed in my father's house. A noise startles me.

Someone has broken in. I arm myself with a serrated grapefruit knife and make my way into the hall. I see that my father's bedroom door is shut. I reach for the knob, but it's locked. I hear a sound behind me. I turn. My father is racing up the stairs, her raised arm brandishing a cleaver.

Terror woke me. The clock on the bedside table read 5:15 a.m. I lay awhile, quelling my panic. Was I still so afraid of her, even as she lay unconscious in a hospital room? Or was it her fear I was channeling? Maybe the meat cleaver wasn't aimed at me but intended for one of the many invaders of the many homes she'd spent her life defending, "saaaving." Or maybe, for all our recent intimacy, I remained among the invaders. I drifted in a troubled twilight until the phone rang. It was just past six a.m.

"Hallo," the voice in the receiver said. "This is Dr. Molnárné."

Yes, I said, unsure if I was awake or still in a dream.

"I'm sorry to inform you. Your father is dead."

"What? How could . . . this be?"

"Some time after five this morning."

"I see," I said, now alert—and accusatory. "What was the cause?"

"Nothing special," the doctor said. "She just died."

What was the cause? How could this be? The deeper questions weren't for the doctor. But the person I wanted to ask them of was gone. Days later, compelled by an inchoate urgency, I would search the recesses of the house for answers. *What was the cause? How could this be?* In the cellar, I found the key hanging from its string beneath the workbench pegboard, unlocked the steel cabinet, and yanked out the cardboard box that contained the "important" documents she'd allowed me only glimpses of. "*If anything happens to me, you should know where this is.*" What trove of illumination did it hold?

Here were the property deeds and the high school report card she'd shown me years before, the many lapsed passports and her U.S. naturalization papers. Here was my parents' divorce decree, my father's letter of application to repatriate in Hungary, my mother's handful of letters to my grandparents in the late 1950s, with the addendum from my father announcing my birth. Beneath them was a manila envelope with five aerogrammes from the early to mid-'90s, addressed in spidery handwriting in Hungarian, postmarked Tel Aviv: letters from my grandmother Rozi in the last decade of her life. Later I would have them translated. They were appeals for a response: "My health is very bad." . . . "I have been very weak and I am still weak." . . . "I have a horrible life." . . . "My Pistike, do not leave me!" The last letter, dated October 27, 1995, when Rozi was 95, ended this way: "Please write me, Pista. I suffer very much because you do not think of me. I am very alone, please let me know that you are alive, how you live, about your work. Please reply immediately. With many loving kisses, Mommy."

At the very bottom of the box, swathed in several layers of plastic, I discovered a six-inch stack of yellowing papers bearing stamps and seals and button-and-string closures, scores of sheets, individually folded. I sunk to the floor and pawed through them, looking for what, I couldn't say.

Születési anyakönyvi kivonat: Friedman Sámuel. 1867 Október 15. Férfi. (Certificate of Birth: Sámuel Friedman. October 15, 1867. Male.)

Halotti anyakönyveből kivonat: Friedman Jacob. 1886 Március 25. Férfi. Izraelita. (Certificate of Death: Jacob Friedman. March 25, 1886. Male. Jewish.)

Házassági anyakönyvi kivonat: Spišské Podhradie/Szepesváralja, Ezerkilencszázhuszonhárom, 1923 November 4, négy. Friedman Jenő—kereskedő—izr. Grünberger Rozália—izr. (Certificate of Marriage: Spišské Podhradie/Szepesváralja, November

4, 1923. Jenő Friedman—Dealer—Jewish. Rozália Grünberger—
Jewish.)

Certificate after certificate after certificate, some of them duplicates.
And duplicates of duplicates. In a quarter of an hour, I'd reached the
end of a cache of legal identities, opaque and unenlightening.

I couldn't get into the attic. My father had locked it, and when
she'd summoned the police that fateful night, they'd taken the interior keys. And then lost them. I called a locksmith to break into the
attic, and then into the attic's two inner rooms.

The reconstructed darkroom was just as it had been when my
father gave me the tour of the house in the fall of 2004. Dust covered every surface of every piece of equipment: wall-mounted
enlargers, developing sinks, processing trays, brown jugs for fixer
and developer fluid, printing tongs, timer, safelight. . . . A steel cabinet against one wall held a retinue of top-of-the-line cameras:
Hasselblads, a Rolleiflex, a Leica, Olympuses, a bellows camera
with mahogany frame. Another cabinet bulged with lenses, battery
packs, cables, filters, tripods, video cams, lightboxes, a sound-
recording console. On the floor, beside a furled projector screen
and tucked into carrying bags and leather cases, were a half-dozen
movie cameras of various generations, including the old Swiss
Bolex that a teenage István had purchased during World War II. I
thought: my father's house was already a mausoleum when she
was alive. She had locked up her history in every room: her boyhood in a cabinet in the basement, her profession behind an attic
door, her cross-dressing "flamboyance" in a wardrobe in the
upstairs hall. I closed the door and headed for the attic's neighboring inner sanctum.

This room was also part darkroom. The six-foot-high photo-
print drum dryer was strung with cobwebs. The cabinets behind it
were stuffed with studio lights, more tripods, and box after box of
contact sheets. The husks of several beetles and a wasp lay on the

floor. A large mound rose beside the drying machine, covered with a utility blanket. For a crazy moment, I thought the drape hid a body. I lifted a corner and peered beneath to find a mountain of discarded men's clothes: suits, coats, blazers, trousers, vests, button-down shirts, polos, dress shoes, hiking boots, mountain parkas, and a dozen or more large plastic bags into which male apparel had been sorted by category: pajamas, undershirts, briefs, belts, ties. One bag contained nothing but shoelaces. I stared at this midden heap of masculinity for a long time before letting the curtain fall. My presentiment had been right; a corpse was hidden here.

I called the locksmith again and asked him to replace the locks on the attic doors. For so long I had been determined to decode the riddle of my father. Now, it seemed important to honor her inscrutability.

On the morning of May 14, an hour after the doctor's phone call, I climbed the four flights of stairs in the internal-medicine building of St. János and traveled a long corridor to its terminus at the physician's station, where Dr. Molnárné was seated.

"Explain to me why she died," I insisted, but she insisted she didn't know. "Sepsis, heart problem, stroke. Could be anything."

She gestured toward a large transparent trash bag. "Here," she said. "Don't forget this." The sack contained my father's "effects": damp towels, her compression hose (for varicose veins), a set of unwashed eating utensils, her reading glasses, her terry cloth slippers, and the plastic sip cup with her name on it.

A maid making a desultory show of mopping the floor began prodding me out of the way with her mop handle.

"Stop it!" I snapped. She made a face and plowed past me.

"Do you want to view the body?" Dr. Molnárné asked.

My father lay on the far cot by the window in the overpopulated ward, the cot where I'd sat with her the day before. She'd died without privacy, but at least, I consoled myself, she hadn't died alone. Early morning shadow dimmed the room. A sheet covered the bed and her body, a white rose placed on top of it. I inched the sheet aside to find another shroud beneath, wound around her. I felt for the beginning of the winding and unspooled it slowly from her head and shoulders. Her face was turned toward the window. Her eyes, so resolutely shut during her last miserable days, were open. I began to shake, and then, control faltering, to sob. An elderly patient in the adjacent bed leaned over to pat my back. "Sorry, sorry, sorry," she said. I was grateful for her touch. And oddly comforted by the knowledge that my father had died here in the female wing, surrounded by women.

I studied my father's face, averted as it so often had been in life. All the years she was alive, she'd sought to settle the question of who she was. Jew or Christian? Hungarian or American? Woman or man? So many oppositions. But as I gazed upon her still body, I thought: there is in the universe only one true divide, one real binary, life and death. Either you are living or you are not. Everything else is molten, malleable.

As I tucked the sheet back around my father, a nurse came into the room. She presented me with a repurposed bandage envelope, containing two small items that hadn't made it into the trash bag of my father's loose effects. The nurse had collected them while preparing the body.

When I left for the United States a few days later, I would take the items with me, along with another token of remembrance, the cloth-bound prayer book my father had received on the occasion of her bar mitzvah, on the day a boy became a man. "For you," the nurse said, as she handed me the envelope. "Stefánie's." Inside it was a pair of pearl earrings.